from *psychotherapy* *to*

Sacretherapy®

Alternative Holistic Descriptions & Healing Processes for 170 Mental & Emotional Diagnoses Worldwide

Amelia Kemp, Ph.D., LMHC

Peggy
Be Well!

Mind Body Spirit Books
Tallahassee, Florida

Published in the United States by
Mind Body Spirit Books, a Florida Corporation.
Request forms are available at:
www.MindBodySpiritBooks.com

Sacretherapy® is available in other languages, please contact the publisher
and/or author to request translation for the print or audio versions.

Note: Sacretherapy® is not a substitute for direct psychotherapy. It should
be used as a companion to, or in conjunction with, any treatment that
readers of this book are currently engaged. The intent of this work is strictly
to add a holistic, spiritual component to the treatment of mental and
emotional issues and diagnoses.
Any personal decision to use any part of the Sacretherapy® process is an act
of your own freewill for which the author and/or publisher are not liable.

Publisher's Cataloging In Publication
Kemp, Amelia.
From Psychotherapy to Sacretherapy® / Amelia Kemp. – 1st ed.
Title on added t.p.: Alternative Holistic Descriptions & Healing Processes for
170 Mental & Emotional Diagnoses Worldwide.
Includes bibliographical references and index.
ISBN 978-0-9910284-0-5
Library of Congress Control Number 2013919703
1. Self Help   2. Psychology   3. Spirituality   4. New Age

Cover Design by © 2013 Yuliaglam/Inmagine
Manufactured in the United States of America
First Edition: January 2014
Second Printing: February 2014

This book is written in honor of every person who has ever felt disconnected, defective, depressed, anxious, humiliated or stigmatized due to a mental or emotional issue or diagnosis.

May this book ease your suffering and bring you peace!

CONTENTS

ACKNOWLEDGEMENTS

"One looks back with appreciation to the brilliant teachers."
—Carl Jung

I must begin by thanking my husband of 27 years for his tireless dedication and belief in this work! And to my wonderful son and friends who took their precious time to give me feedback and help proofread the manuscript. I love and appreciate you all! I must also thank my colleagues in both the mental health and metaphysical camps who were kind enough to do a peer review. Your input was tremendously validating and invaluable. I also thank my wonderful editor and attorneys whose attention to detail and professionalism was outstanding!

I would also like to acknowledge that this work has been extracted from a specific faculty of authors who were instrumental in my personal and professional evolution. They are philosophers, metaphysicians, mental health professionals, quantum physicists and spiritualists to whom I will be forever indebted and must take time to thank and acknowledge. Before I do that however, it must also be stated that in my conversations with research specialists at the United States Library of Congress it was deduced that *how knowledge is acquired* is in fact a philosophical issue and therefore, the ways and means that truths are gathered and expressed may in fact share similarities for truth is truth! As such, some of what is offered in this book also comes from sources I may have simply picked up during my journey of life and therefore am unable to pinpoint. I have however done my very best to recall and reference accordingly, even using plagiarism websites to check passages that resulted in no matches. Nevertheless, I am fully aware of the fact that there are many others, published and unpublished, not listed here who join this school of thought providing a stable paradigm over time. So, to all of you, physical or no longer physical, known and unknown, or forgotten, I honor your voices—understanding that many of you echo the sentiments in this book, in your like-minded quest for holism—for it is from all of your works that I have extracted universal principles and applied them to the field of *psychology and spirituality.*

The spiritual influences come from both traditional and non-traditional paradigms in western and eastern schools of thought, including metaphysical and esoteric theologies that extend into consciousness theories and quantum medicine. The psychological influences are a blend of modalities taken from Jungian, Transpersonal, Gestalt and Cognitive Behavioral therapies, and what is now termed Positive Psychology or the Psychology of Achievement.

These principles truly go back to antiquity, starting with the Egyptian and Greek philosophers from whom a great deal of spiritual and medicinal inquiry arose. As such, it is their contributions along with those of countless others that demonstrate that the *blending of spirituality, physics, quantum physics and psychology* is not "new" although it has often been labeled as a *New Age* or *New Thought*. This perception is obviously quite the contrary when we look at history and where these ideas are said to have begun. Yet, it is understood why those labels arose: Throughout history, any philosophy outside of the mainstream teachings "felt" *new* and was repressed and driven underground in societies that preferred and propagated sameness. Yet, today we are living in the most wonderful time in history where these ideas have been progressively *resurfacing* into what is being described as an "awakening." An *awakening* is where soulful contemplation takes place at the level of "thought" unimpeded by punitive measures, finally re-seeking to integrate the mind, body and *spirit* connection.

Thus, it is my privilege and honor to call the names of those who have come before me. The calling of one's name, however, is not simply the identifying of a specific person; instead it carries with it the *energy* essence of a soul that came forth. Further, it honors the part of the soul's *energy* that I/we embrace. As such, to call one's name is to honor the fullness of his or her being and the legacy the name evokes. Thus, in the tradition of *call and response* rituals, I will be calling on the *spirit* of these souls to summon their attention to these proceedings. Thereby, after each name will be the response: "I call your name." However, please feel free to skip the response and just read the names if the ritual does not move you to the same level of reverence that I hold for the specific souls. (Note: The years next to the names signify the years of contribution or of publication of a literary work that particularly influenced my life; or the years may represent the time the soul appeared in history and added to the expansion of holistic, spiritual or mental consciousness.)

Beginning with:

Imhotep – Egyptian Physician aka the true "Father of Medicine," Holistic Healer, Priest, Architect of the first pyramid and world's first recorded genius (around 2700 B.C.E. – 2950 B.C.E.) whose thinking influenced many Greek philosophers such as Hippocrates, Plato and Aristotle, all of whom were educated in the Egyptian Nile Valley, Kemet Temple-Universities Waset and Ipet Isut – I call your name.

Plato – Philosopher and Aristotle's mentor (428-340 BCE) – I call your name.

Aristotle – Philosopher, credited with the first "identifiable" work to bear the term "Metaphysics" (384-322BCE) – I call your name.

Helen Blavatsky – Co-founder of Theosophy Society (1875) – I call your name.

Charles and Myrtle Fillmore – New Thought Pioneers/Founders of Unity Church (1889) – I call your names.

Emily Cady – Unitarian/Author (1896) – I call your name.

Charles Leadbeater – Author/Clairvoyant (1903) – I call your name.

Thomas Troward – Philosopher/New Thought Pioneer (1904) – I call your name.

William Atkinson – Philosopher/Law of Attraction (1906) – I call your name.

Swami Panchadasi – Mystic/Clairvoyant/Author (1918) – I call your name.

Rudolph Steiner, Ph.D. – Philosopher/Anthroposophy (1918) – I call your name.

Pierre Teilhard de Chardin – Philosopher (1930) – I call your name.

Napoleon Hill – New Thought Author (1937) – I call your name.

Carl Jung, Ph.D. – Psychologist/Esoteric (1938) – I call your name.

Thomas Moore – Philosopher/Psychotherapist/Author (1940) – I call your name.

Robert Merton, Ph.D. – Sociologist (1948) – I call your name.

Albert Ellis, Ph.D. – Psychologist (1956) – I call your name.

Lawrence and Pheobe Bendit – Psychiatrists and Clairvoyant/Authors (1957) – I call your names.

Catherine Ponder, D.D. – New Thought Minister/Author (1966) – I call your name.

Shakti Gawain – Consciousness Teacher/Author (1978) – I call your name.

Thelma Moss – Parapsychologist/Author (1979) – I call your name.

David Burns, M.D. – Psychiatrist/Author (1980) – I call your name.

Louise Hay – Metaphysician /Author (1982) – I call your name. (See a Special Tribute to Hay in the Introduction.)

Marianne Williamson – New Thought Minister/Author (1985) – I call your name.

Esther and Jerry Hicks – Channels/Authors (1985) – I call your names.

Abraham – Group of Spiritual Entities/Law of Attraction (1985) – I call your names.

Bernie Siegal, M.D. – New Thought Oncologist/Author (1986) – I call your name.

Clarissa Pinkola Estes, Ph.D. – Jungian Analyst (1992) – I call your name.

Deepak Chopra, M.D. – Alternative Healing Guru/Author (1989) – I call your name.

John Bradshaw – Psychotherapist/Former Minister/Author (1992) – I call your name.

Neal Donald Walsh – Spiritual Teacher/Author (1995) – I call your name.

Valarie Hunt, Ed.D. – Psychologist/ Physiologist/Author (1996) – I call your name.

Carolyn Myss, Ph.D. – Medical Intuitive/Author (1997) – I call your name.

Leo Booth – Minister/Author (1998) – I call your name.

Iyanla Vanzant – Yoruba Priestess/Metaphysician (1998) – I call your name.

James Redfield – New Thought Author (2005) – I call your name.

Rhonda Burns – New Thought Author/Producer (2006) – I call your name.

Michael Beckwith, D.D. – New Thought Minister/Visionary (2006) – I call your name.

Amit Goswami, Ph.D. – Quantum Physicist (2008) – I call your name.
Wayne Dyer, Ph.D. – Psychotherapist/Author/Producer (2009) – I call your name.
James Cameron – New Thought Producer (2009) – I call your name.
Cyndi Dale – Medical Intuitive/Author (2009) – I call your name.
Bernard Haisch, Ph.D. – Astrophysicist/Former Seminarian/Author (2009) – I
    call your name.
Stephen Prothero – Professor of Religion (2010) – I call your name.
Tenzin Gyatso – 14th Dalai Lama/Nobel Peace Prize Winner (2011) – I call
    your name.

Let us give a moment of silence for any of those vessels that have transitioned back to pure positive *energy* with the God-source within the universe. Let us thank them for their courage and contribution to the foundations of spirituality, mental health, and/or holism, and let them know that their offerings did not go in vain. (PAUSE for silence). I offer this respect, for it is their synchronicity of thought that has magnified for me the "all is one" paradigm of consciousness. It is that constant thread amongst all of the above vessels from which Sacretherapy® is sewn. Therefore, I humbly join the ranks and files of those who came before me and those that are continuing to fortify the movement towards holism. The subtitle of my book is firmly rooted in this foundation of assurances as it proclaims: Any mental or emotional issue or *dis-ease* can be healed or aligned, if spirit is allowed to inform *these processes*. This has not been the case up to now in the majority of mental health care practices, despite this impressive outpouring of sources. So, let us move on to the *Introduction* that explains my call for holism in the field of mental health, which appears to be humanity's next frontier, where we move into a region beyond what has already been explored.

INTRODUCTION

Unlocking the Door to Holism – The Pathway to Sacretherapy®

Giving voice to this book caused me to tap into all that I am, and all that I've become and am becoming still. I felt truly anointed as I wrote each chapter, knowing this book can help you heal! It's been written for those of you who are seeking this type of holistic alternative information in your quest to realign with wellness. It is the first of its kind within the mental health field to offer a true alternative way to ***describe***, ***interpret*** and ***treat*** mental and emotional issues/ diagnoses, written by a mental health professional attempting to de-pathologize this diverse range of human experience. In fact, this book is designed to shift the paradigm toward alternative holistic mental health, by virtue of its intrinsic value and the empowerment it offers. For this book holds within it viable ***steps*** that can enhance your quality of life. It shows you how to realign your mind, body and spirit; relieve a great deal of guilt; reduce self-reproach; and help free yourself from any toxic conditioning, memes or programming you may have acquired during your physical journey, as it unlocks the door to the mental and emotional well-being that has always been yours by *divine right!*

Your unfoldment is the true masterpiece of this work; I stood on the shoulders of giants to carve it out. I paid tribute to many of these giants and pioneers in the field of psychology, metaphysics and alternative healing in the Acknowledgements section, with special honor to Louise Hay, whose work I will discuss later in this Introduction. As for now, however, when it comes to anything considered innovative or pioneering, there is much to say and not enough time to say it all. However, this Introduction will offer an explanation about the current state of affairs within mental health from my perspective and why I call for holism, which is what Sacretherapy® is all about. Thus, I ask that you indulge me as I introduce you to what resulted from my desire to offer this alternative perspective of viewing and treating mental and emotional manifestations.

I stated earlier that the *well-being* you seek is already yours by divine right. This premise is reflected in a statement on the World Health Organization's (WHO) website that reads: "… mental health is related to the promotion of *well-being*.…" However, the *divine part* of this *well-being* appears to be regularly left out of the treatment plan for the majority of the population in the world's western hemisphere. And this major void needs to be filled in order to honor the fullness of your being. Too many people show up to an initial therapy session and find that practitioners only offer the traditional *"rhythm and roll"* that focuses solely on the mind, body and social affairs. As a result, I've noticed during my 18 years of being a psychotherapist that most clients have only been treated with two things: traditional psychotherapy and medication. No wonder most initial intakes reveal that many people have seen multiple psychotherapists as they search for something more, even when they aren't sure what more is. People seem to know inherently that something is missing. So they courageously go from 'pillar to post' desperately searching for the key or keys to sustainable relief; for the elusive answer to their unformed question.

Many consumers oftentimes are encouraged to add medication; therefore, they have medicine cabinets full of prescriptions, having been told that the compound would be the key to the joy-filled life they've been seeking. And based on the current training of mental health professionals, a prescription was certainly the correct course of action; indeed, traditional "best practices" suggest that a combo of meds and psychotherapy is the ideal way to go. However, sometimes the "ideal" is anything but for the person taking not one, not two, but often three and four prescriptions simultaneously. And still these medicines don't produce the well-being in a bottle that the advertisers claim. They can't, because brain chemistry and the bio/psycho/social (which will be explained later in this section) are NOT the only factors that need to be addressed to achieve sustained mental health.

You would think that this would already have been understood, especially when we look at the statistics coming out of the Centers for Disease Control (CDC), showing that 2.4 billion psychotropic prescriptions have been prescribed annually since 2005. According to an article in the American Psychological Association's APA Monitor on "Inappropriate Prescribing" (2012), an estimated one in five Americans are now taking some form of psychotropic medication. That's a lot! In fact, according to statistics from the National Institute of Mental Health (NIMH) 57.7 million Americans have been diagnosed with a mental or emotional diagnosis, and the WHO reports 450 million people worldwide. So, clearly, many people are searching for relief. Yet, all that the mental health field seems to keep offering is the same old thing: another pill or another referral to another conventional clinician, instead of looking deeper into what may be missing in the treatment plan. So it becomes glaringly obvious that the search for sustained peace of mind must go beyond conventional interventions in order to truly unlock the door to optimum well-being.

Fortunately, the solution is not somewhere off in the distance; right here and now, other key components are available to achieve the peace of mind people seek. I think what's stopped us from employing these other components is that most psychotherapists, including me, were trained to treat mental and emotional issues with just the bio/psycho/social model of healing. Bio/psycho/social is short for doing a biological, psychological and sociological inventory of a client's history to gauge the factors contributing to the distress—with spirituality usually being left out of the equation. I believe, however, that the spirit is as much a part of the person's being as the bio/psycho/social, if not the most important component. Many philosophers believe the spirit is the eternal part that goes with us when we are released from the bio/psycho/social dimension. Therefore, I believe true mental and emotional well-being involves holism, which requires a deeper type of healing—which those of us in the metaphysical camp call an alignment that balances the mind, body, and spirit. This is what I have coined as *Sacretherapy®*. Simply stated, Sacretherapy® is a sacred form of therapy that honors the fullness of our being and is completely described in Chapter One.

Please note, however, that when I say "sacred" it doesn't simply mean holy but whole as in "holism"—mind, body and spirit. So I mean spirituality, NOT any specific religious dogma espoused by theology, but rather a soulful (sacred) experience that is transformative. Spirituality, then, is not synonymous with religion. Yet, to many in the field of psychology, spirituality is often seen as something pursued only by those interested in Pastoral Counseling. This thinking seems just as limiting as the bio/psycho/social model, if clients have to choose between psychology and theology. Theology without including the benefits of psychology falls short, as well. This is why I could never get my head fully wrapped around the idea of offering any intervention that was fragmented if I was supposed to be treating the WHOLE person.

Thus, it is this lack of holism, which treats the whole person, that I think contributes to the unsuccessful attainment of a more sustainable sense of relief. This also appears to contribute to why many have been torn between whether to seek professional help or just consult a pastor, versus both. People seem to intuitively know that there has to be more to getting help than just psychotherapy and prescriptions from trained professionals and likewise, they sense that there has to be more to seeking relief from trained clergy than just prayer and dogma. These concerns are legitimate and could be better addressed if people were offered integrative approaches like *Sacretherapy®*.

Without a step towards holistic approaches it appears that people can only continue to look forward to more of the same fragmentation, believing that there is nothing else mental health professionals can do to help. Yet, this is far from the truth, if the fullness of one's being were being addressed. As it stands now, most often the clinical hour is underutilized in either a therapeutic search for the historical incident or series of incidents attributed as the antecedent (cause) of one's suffering in hope of catharsis (resolution); or as a combination of what's already been stated and supportive counseling to help one accept his or her plight. When utilized this way, psychotherapy does not fully live up to the transformative and soul fulfilling resource it was meant to be.

The term "psychology" originates from two Greek words: psyche and logos, "psyche"—meaning the soul or mind, and "logos" (forming the suffix "ology") meaning to study or the study of. Therefore, the original meaning of psychology was "the study of the soul," which was seen as synonymous with universal mind or infinite intelligence. Thus, based on the historical origins we have certainly strayed from this holy intent.

Yet, the resistance towards holism also seems absurd when averaging the historical report card, as far back as the national deinstitutionalization of mental health patients that began in 1955. The past several decades have shown us that the traditional medical model could not cure what many call mental disorders but could only diagnose and describe these manifestations and/or manage symptoms. As such, I believe other approaches need to be pursued. And I imagine that those of you reading this book, and clients everywhere, also are seeking innovative ways to experience the relief everyone deserves. In fact, it has been said repeatedly within the metaphysical camp that "relief," whether it be mental, physical or spiritual, is the remedy that all medicine seeks.

Likewise, over the years, many clients have looked me dead in the eye, asking if a better quality of life was even possible, after having tried the conventional approach and been unable to report any sustained relief. Fortunately, for them, I have been genuinely able to offer hope and compelled to exclaim that a better way of life is available. I point out that there is a missing link in the treatment plan that may be the key to making a difference. I explain that the total well-being one desires may need to include integrating non-traditional holistic healing paradigms, in addition to the medical model. I emphasize "in addition to" as opposed to "instead of" because I honor the fact that all treatment modalities have their rightful place in the healing process. I am not an extremist sitting on either side of the argument. Therefore, even as I emphatically insist that a pill and psychotherapy may not be enough for "sustained" relief, I also acknowledge that they can certainly be powerful allies that help align brain chemistry when necessary. This is why best practices recommend the duality of medicine and psychotherapy, and why I am simply adding the spiritual component, calling for a triad.

However, in as much as traditional medicines are utilized in this pursuit, I must also submit to you that herbal remedies are being given their due respect within the Sacretherapy® process. For far too long, herbal remedies have been minimized by conventional behavioral medicine practices. I advocate that these non-traditional remedies can also be very helpful in aligning brain chemistry, depending on the degree of one's stressor, when used properly under the direction of an herbal doctor or practitioner. (Chapter Eight offers a section on utilizing medication as well as herbal remedies that may be explored within the Sacretherapy® process.)

So the question then, regardless of how we reconnect with the fullness of our mind, body and spirit, is "how" or "in what way" do we embrace holism in our attempt to optimize the trilogy of our beingness? First, I believe embracing holism requires an acknowledgment be made that there is another dimension to human beings beyond our physical apparatus. But getting the scientific community to acknowledge the nonphysical aspect is a daunting challenge. For that reason, holism is minimized and considered in America to be an alternative healing modality, offered only when the medical model has exhausted its physical interventions. In other words, it is offered as a last resort. Although, I do acknowledge that a very small number of psychiatrists and physicians are openly embracing what is now termed as Integrative Care, which is a blending of both western and eastern modalities (Eastern healthcare practices holism) and some are also beginning to embrace Quantum Medicine. Nevertheless, for the overall healthcare community and mass population to embrace this, a high level of advocacy will be needed along with a willingness to move beyond the conditioning, memes and old linguistic programming (discussed in Chapter Four) that most of us have internalized.

The definition and appearance of wholeness takes on an individual meaning and presentation depending on where one is on one's own soul-filled journey and what one's soul came into the physical realm to do. Therefore, no *matter* how distressing one's life may look, one could either be completely on track in a way that is just different from social norms and conditioning, or just out of alignment with one's mind, body and spirit, capable of coming back into alignment with well-being. (Chapter One fully describes the term alignment.)

Naturally, if you are unfamiliar with holism, just including spirituality may sound like positive thinking "hoopla," if you have not yet questioned the conditioning, memes and old linguistic programming (not to be confused with modern neuro-linguistic programming discussed in Chapter four) that those of us in the holistic paradigm have been releasing. Therefore, to take full advantage of the information in this book, it is hoped that you'll be open-minded to see if what is being offered here makes sense, and resonates with you.

The information presented here is a blending of my own original thoughts along with what has been extrapolated from some of the other sources that I mention in the Acknowledgements and in the Resources section in the back of the book. However, it was the work of Louise Hay that helped plunge me into my metaphysical journey 24 years ago, in 1989. Her work is what gave me the confidence and inspiration to move forward with this book. In Hay's book, You Can Heal Your Body (1984), her lists of probable causes for physical manifestations were right on target, 90 percent of the time! Therefore, I referred my clients to the book regularly, since one of my specialties, as a psychotherapist, has been addressing chronic physical illnesses. However, Hay's wonderful book covered fourteen mental diagnoses, out of the 170 described in most mental health dictionaries, medical encyclopedias, the Diagnostic and Statistical Manual of Mental Disorders (DSM), and the International Classification of Diseases (ICD); she lumped the remainder into the heading of insanity or psychiatric illness. This prompted me to come up with metaphysical symbolic meanings of my own to help clients seeking holistic alternatives. By drawing on all of my years in metaphysics since 1989, and having read more than two hundreds books on alternative healing, I found that the different nuances in types of emotional or mental distress were just as significant for the field of mental health as were Hay's breakdowns for the different types of physical diagnoses.

Therefore, for clients who were at the end of their rope and expressing a desire for holistic and alternative options, I would explore their experience by going "beyond symptomology to meaning" in order to get to the true basis of what was the *matter*. I would begin with the concept of symbolism, a term, psychiatrist— Carl Jung initially proposed as "unconscious archetypal symbolism" which was also later described as "symbolic sight" by Dr. Carolyn Myss (See Chapter Two). I would then share that a higher plane has been demonstrated to exist that can be seen as an electromagnetic field of *energy* that emanates through us and can be seen as light (See Chapter Two). I then shared that some believe that this light is the spirit; and, therefore, already within them is a source capable of transcending and realigning their mental and emotional manifestations. This type of information seemed to be really intriguing for my clients, and it instilled much-needed hope when it was obvious that pills and psychotherapy alone weren't working.

Motivated by their enthusiasm, I devised a holistic treatment plan that included the possible symbolic meaning of the issues they were facing mentally or emotionally. I also created personalized audio tapes to assist between sessions. My intuitive offerings on most of the diagnoses were openly received. Most said it "sounded right" and then began releasing the dysfunctional beliefs attached to their mental issues versus just managing their symptoms. In other words, the holistic metaphysical interventions were bringing relief that greatly fortified whatever treatment they were receiving from the traditional medical model.

As a result, I became inspired and was led to offer alternative holistic descriptions and healing interventions for all mental diagnoses listed in most medical dictionaries and psychiatric manuals, including the DSM and ICD, all of which are listed in this book. My list of mental and emotional diagnoses in Chapter Three can be used as a companion to Louise Hay's list of predominately physical diagnoses. As such, I feel a debt of gratitude for Louise Hay having left the mental health area open for an alternative treatment approach. It was a void worth filling; and once I committed to the process, my ability to get to the *energy* basis of the diagnosis via symbolism flowed like water, and it began to feel like I was born to write it. You see, in as much as I am a mental health professional, I also was once a client. Twenty-eight years ago, in 1985, I was hospitalized for a few weeks for major depression. I eventually emerged from that and later went on to obtain a master's degree in Mental Health Counseling; and for the past 18 years I have been a psychotherapist. My career includes having been a former Director of Mental Health Counseling within a school system; owning a private practice that I continue; serving as an Adjunct Psychology Instructor at two colleges; becoming a Certified Reiki/Energy Medicine Practitioner; earning a non-traditional doctorate in Metaphysical Theology and receiving a Ministerial Ordination; and becoming a Board Certified Alternative Medical Practitioner. The acquisition of this knowledge was not entirely expected, considering my challenging background, which I share in more detail in Chapter Eleven—Healing the Healer. And, although I did not consciously set out to encompass the quadrupling of these multiple disciplines, it appears that my journey that blends the traditional model with the holistic healing approach is what prepared me to offer this book; for surely it is the basis of what I call *Sacretherapy*®—the aligning of mind, body and spirit—that saved my life.

Sacretherapy® can be used without formal treatment, as well as with a therapeutic multidisciplinary approach, depending on your soul's preference and severity of symptoms. Therefore, if you plan to use it on your own, that's fine. Yet, if you become inspired to get additional help as a result of this book, or are already in therapy, I suggest that you share this book with your mental health professional to allow him or her to understand the intention guiding this work. However, if you are **SUICIDAL** and are not under the care of a psychotherapist, I urge you to **please get immediate help**. A holistic approach, like all other approaches, is not intended to heal instantaneously. (See Chapter Seven for a discussion of suicidal ideation, suicide attempts, suicidal manipulation and transitioning as an attempt to realign the mind, body and spirit.)

Finally, as a metaphysician, I humbly acknowledge that the alignment processes and healing information that I describe in this book are not mine alone to give. For I, like you, am simply a vessel, being poured through to offer my unique interpretation of this "ancient information" to those of you wanting to partake. Therefore, I only aspire to be a "stepping stone" on your eternal path of soulful discovery and aid you in the co-creative jubilation that coming into alignment brings.

A SPECIAL NOTE:

To Mental Health Professionals & Clergy who may also be reading this book: If you are interested in how to use this Alternative Treatment Modality within your respective places of service: Certified *Sacretherapy*® Practitioners Are Needed

(ALL AROUND THE WORLD)

For more information, see Resources or visit my website.

1
FROM PSYCHOTHERAPY TO SACRETHERAPY®

"If the head and body are to be well, you need to begin by curing the soul."
—Plato

In modern times, the term "psychotherapy" is short for psychological therapy and likewise, "*Sacretherapy*®" is short for sacred therapy. Sacre—(pronounced 'sacred' with a silent "d") is a verb derived from the French word *Sacrer*, *"to make sacred,"* and from the Latin word Sacrare, *"to set apart as holy."* Linguists have said that the term holy comes from the word "whole," suggesting that *holy* means to be whole or complete. Likewise, I coined the term Sacretherapy® because I believe it captures the essence of holistic healing. Sacretherapy® therefore, *is a holistic therapeutic modality created to treat mental and emotional issues that includes psychotherapy or counseling; but it is more comprehensive in that it involves a sacred process of aligning one's mind, body and spirit in order to allow the whole or holiness of one's being to inform and clarify the soul's sacred intention that it is divinely unfolding in this physical experience.*

The *Sacretherapy*® Process—You're Not Sick, You're Sacred!

The Sacretherapy® process as stated above includes psychotherapy or counseling while tapping into spirit. It does so, however, without promoting any specific path; for the soul is free from religious containment and flows in and out of divinity without walls. Still, in our attempt to describe and harness the soul's light, it appears that we have created nearly as many faiths and spiritual beliefs as there are people on the planet. Sacretherapy® supports this diversity, believing that each path is an attempt to remind mankind of our connection to spirit.

Yet, since the beginning of time, seekers have debated the question "what path professing 'truth' is the actual true path?" Sacretherapy® believes that a true path or true guidance always relieves you, makes you feel good, and reinforces your connection to your spiritual source. So any path that does all that would be considered a true path, complementary to your mental and emotional health. Therefore, to appreciate the spiritual aspects of Sacretherapy® may require embracing the idea that there is more than "one" right way to tap into spirit or the source of the universe that many of us call God. It means becoming cognizant that life is being lived beyond the borders of one's neighborhood of likeminded sociology and theology, and that there is diversity and contrast of universal proportions with equally valid scripture trumpeting the same God-source.

Appreciating Sacretherapy® may also require the willingness on your part to rethink and possibly amend the notion of a punishing God-source and instead embrace the idea that the Creator offers *total* **unconditional** love and utter relief. So here, you can release the fear of possibly having been punished with poor mental or emotional health for *having done* or for *not having done* some specific thing or list of things. Through *Sacretherapy®*, we learn that there is no specific list of things anyone has to do to receive the blessings of health and well-being because they are yours by divine right.

The Sacretherapy® process also embraces the belief that resuming mental and emotional *wellness is achievable,* and describes what it means to be a "well being." For the purposes of this book, a "well being" is in **alignment** with the fullness of his or her being: mind, body, and spirit. Alignment, as defined by most dictionaries, is "the process of adjusting parts so that they are in proper relative position with one another." This adjustment, then, is what I believe it takes to truly heal.

I first heard the term "alignment" in 1994 from Clarissa Pinkola Estes, Ph.D., a Jungian analyst and former executive director of the Carl Jung Center, who stated very briefly in one of her books that people do psychotherapy, analysis and meditation for *psychic alignment.* I appreciated her use of the term *psychic* and interpreted it as reverence to the *nonphysical* aspects of our being; but it was the term **alignment** that struck a nerve, and although she literally only used the term once, it caused me to think of the trilogy that makes up the mind, body and spirit.

As a psychotherapist, this aligning process fortified my belief that no *matter* how far from mental and emotional health one may be, healing only requires coming back into proper alignment with the fullness of your being. It also requires knowing the difference between the belief that "one *can't* change or re-align" with the belief that "one *won't* change or re-align", and instead come into an awareness that one can change and re-align. To re-align with wellness means to embrace the idea that one originally came forth into this physical realm as a "well being" **worthy** of the automatic wellness that comes with the **unconditional** love and acceptance that was afforded you as a testament of your birthright. Realigning, then, means understanding that this sacred contract you inherited by divine right is not altered by your behavior or any diagnosis; and, therefore, it does not change, no *matter* what you have experienced, good or bad, or felt you've done to yourself or others.

Thus, Sacretherapy® begins with the premise that **you're not sick, you're sacred,** and that the favor and well-being from the Source of the universe does **not** have to be earned. Sacretherapy® teaches that you are already good enough as an extension of that Source, regardless of what you choose to call that; for all is one. Therefore, there are no hoops to jump through, no comparisons to measure yourself against, no guilt to pardon, no shame to assuage, just the ever-ready-always-available-unconditional-pulsating-love that you inhale with every breath you take. Anything else you've learned that is counter to that is, in my opinion, from social conditioning that has been passed down by well-meaning people parroting the unhealthier aspects of our man-made religions that teach and serve us otherwise. They were only innocently passing down what they had been taught. And so your mental and emotional well-being is ready and waiting to be reclaimed. All it ever needed was for you to trust that it was there and a willingness to let it be. No *matter* what it may have taken to help you let go of the resistance to let it be—whether you used psychotherapy, medicine, natural herbs, or juju beads—if that helps to let it be, then let it be.

In retrospect, all this time, you may have thought that you were doing something wrong or that something was wrong with you. All this time, you may have thought that your prayers went unanswered; and you hoped that some day, in some way, something could redeem you. Well, today is "that day" because here you are—that soul-filled individual who has been searching and seeking, waiting and wanting to be that "well being" you came into this physical experience to be. So whatever your journey, I honor you and every tear that led you here. I am confident that what you are about to embark upon in this book is going to be one of the most worthwhile endeavors of your life. For in these pages you will find the steps that can lead to the missing pieces of mental and emotional well-being for which you have been searching. For you, this book was written.

Sacretherapy® has ***Eight Sacred Steps*** that include 170 aligning processes for all of the mental and emotional diagnoses or issues listed in most mental health reference resources including the DSM and ICD, along with 24 healing exercises— indicated by this therapy couch to bring you back into alignment with your mind, body and spirit; as well as a dozen additional aftercare practices and online support to maintain your alignment. We will briefly review each of the Sacretherapy® steps to give you an overview of what's to come. This process will be unique for each person, seeing as each soul is unfolding in different ways. You will be offered aspects of psychological therapeutic modalities coupled with spiritual principles, along with an understanding of how those interventions can expand the quality of your life. Some of you may be hoping for interventions that simply honor your *here and now* experiences and not take you through the mire and misery of yesteryear. Others of you may want to take stock of *the past* and review it all. Either way, the process can work.

I understand that some people do not feel completely understood without getting the chance to share the full details of why they think their lives are unhappy and out of alignment. And that's totally normal. Most clients couldn't believe that *I really understood* their dynamics unless they explained them several times in several ways. They often seemed to have been thinking that they would eventually say the one thing that would *stop me* from saying that they *could still* get back on track and be happy in spite of their previous experiences. Fortunately, nothing they shared could ever sway me, because I was convinced that any *mental or emotional* issue that is out of alignment could come back into alignment, if it is truly wanted. So, when the time comes, choose whichever way *you* want to embrace this work.

The steps are progressive, and so each builds upon the next. Therefore, it is recommended that you go diligently step by step. The steps, as stated before, are also not meant for you to stop therapy or your medication and/or herbal remedies if you are using any. Sacretherapy® honors a multidisciplinary approach. The difference is that in addition to psychotherapy it simply includes the spirit, which has been generally left out of the traditional treatment plan. As such, the journey from *Psychotherapy to* Sacretherapy® will be a mere hop, skip and jump for some, or a five-mile marathon for others, depending on where you are in your awareness of spiritual aspects that I usually call "*inner knowing.*" Either way, the journey will be empowering and life affirming.

I expect that by the time you have done the last step in this book, and usually much sooner than that, you will feel sheer and utter relief. You also will have come to trust your own "*inner knowing*" as guidance from spirit and will have begun to love yourself unconditionally. And that newly found self-love and trust in the *unconditional source within you* will reawaken the belief that your mental and emotional well-being is assured.

The only tools you will need for this journey are a journal, ink pen and a nice box or container for storing your Sacretherapy® work. You may also benefit from listening to soft, slow instrumental music or sounds that invoke spirit (music that aligns with wellness, not sadness) while you read this book and go through the steps. That, of course, is also optional. I just wanted to share that I wrote the entire book listening to one particular song titled *Devotion*, from the CD—*Beyond*, produced by New Earth Records (2010). (See Resources.) I just put it on "repeat," allowing it to gently whisper to me that "spirit was in the midst of this work," and it was very powerful. In any case, do what resonates with you. Let us now review the steps.

STEP ONE—Begins with offering you a better and more thorough understanding of the fullness of your *being* with a proposed sequence of events of your coming from the nonphysical into the physical being that you are. This step is filled with psycho-education that includes important terminology used in spiritual and metaphysical circles with regard to your mind, body and spirit. The terminology will define how we interpret the human experience. Next, a psycho-spiritual questionnaire will be offered that will explore **"What's the Matter"** and what the distressing issue or issues are that manifested in your specific physical experience. Two types of questionnaires are offered and incorporate the bio/psycho/social discussed in the Introduction, along with the pertinent spiritual information that is usually left out.

After the current and/or historical data portion of the questionnaire is completed, you can take an *optional energy* assessment to scan and note any areas in the surrounding *energy* field of your body temple, where *energy* may be blocked as a result of psychological distress. Once the combined psycho-spiritual-bio data sheets are completed, instructions will be given on where and how to store the file in your container or box that will be used as a symbolic vault labeled "The Past," which you will place in a location that you deem sacred.

STEP TWO—Lists the names of 170 mental and emotional diagnoses identified in most mental health books or resources worldwide so that you can select the diagnosis (s) that correlate with your particular *matter*. Using "symbolic meaning," we will hone in on the divinity inherent in what your symptoms represent. This is a beautiful transformative process I call *"Reframing the Matter."* After you have read the probable cause of the manifestation, you will be offered a sacred aligning process that is to be used as a daily exercise, which helps you remold the *matter* as you complete the other steps of bringing yourself back into alignment with the fullness of your being.

STEP THREE—Offers psycho-education with regards to understanding *"How the Matter Manifested"* in the first place, from a holistic metaphysical perspective. It includes a discussion of how your initiation into the physical realm was influenced by conditioning, memetics and old linguistic programming. It will show how all of that plays a role in how you arrived at your current perspective with regard to your mental and emotional issues. This step will show how the pleasant and unpleasant things that affect mental and emotional health can come into your experience from *self-fulfilling prophecies*. You will learn that such prophecies are basically predictions that manifest, due to one's beliefs that have roots in a universal principle called the "law of attraction." Through the use of several exercises, you will learn how to use those beliefs to your advantage, so that you can realign with what has been outlined in this section as your *true* human and spiritual rights, as a soul unfolding in this physical experience.

STEP FOUR—Suggests ways to release toxic *energy*. After having learned of how the *matter* manifested, some people experience a form of shock or grief for not having been told this information a long time ago. As a result, they may need a positive ventilation outlet to share what is temporarily perceived as a major loss. They may need to undertake a process I call *"Witnessing—The Heart of the Matter."* For when one perceives that his or her physical journey may have been accidentally thrown off balance, it can be therapeutic and cathartic to have a witness validate these feelings. To help transform the psychic injury, I have identified *four types of rage* that are described in this section with ***sacred rage*** being the most expedient.

Several exercises are offered to assist during the *witnessing* process, since many people have difficulty letting the *matter* go. Many get stuck in the *disbelief stage* where their anger is resistant to transforming into the sacred form of rage, and they prefer to blame those who assisted in their mis-creation, albeit unknowingly. And likewise, when the soul feels fully vindicated and ready for a new level of expansion, it also helps to have a witness join in rejoicing and validating that a broader and more meaningful *rite of passage* has taken place.

STEP FIVE—Helps you to continue clearing the old mental sets, while at the same time extract the good. By this point, you will have come to recognize that the past is really over, and want to honor your journey, but may still have difficulty finding the way. Therefore, we continue releasing the old pent up *energy* through processes I call *"Staying Clear of the Matter."* Unfortunately, those die-hard automatic responses don't like to curtsy and exit the stage without an encore. These patterns got set in motion and have become an automatic response. To facilitate this work, we will incorporate trusted rituals that are spirited exercises I call **Energy Disbursements** that get to the *energy* basis of the *matter* and help you fully release the dysfunctional pattern and any co-creators that took part in it. This work also entails learning how to forgive self and others, even when you don't feel that you or they deserve it.

Many people have difficulty with release work, which is why the Sacretherapy® exercises are designed to help you successfully release the perception of injury, whether it is self-inflicted and causing you self-reproach, or whether it is other-aided. Plus, to ensure that your desire to release the *matter* has extra support, I offer additional, personally guided, free and interactive clearing processes online.

STEP SIX—Shows you how to create the life you came forth to live. In this step, we begin embracing the possibilities of new life and new meaning. Here we will be using processes that I call **Pro-Creation.** The exercises consist of remolding the *matter* by *sculpting your sacred intentions* into a whole new shape and form that is pleasing to you. More creative divination systems are offered here, as well as traditional remedies that align. Most of these are soul fulfilling, life affirming and goal directed. At this stage, the *matter* you are dealing with that manifested as mental and emotional *dis-ease* can no longer abide at that level. The word *disease* is hyphenated because as metaphysicians, we view what is termed as *disease* as simply *dis-ease*, believing that *dis-ease* cannot remain in a body that is at ease. Therefore, where we create joy, there is no *dis-ease* because the emotions of joy and despair are too far apart on the alignment scale of human experience to interact.

STEP SEVEN—Prepares you for the ultimate embrace. Finally, you will be ready for the sacred process I call *"Entering the Sanctuary."* This step is all about perception, appreciation, gratitude and fully embracing your *inner knowing*. Here is where you give thanks for the fullness of your being and for all that you have become and will continue to become. You are given additional divination processes, exercises designed to remind you of how to see beyond your usual perceptive lenses and to invoke what I call *divine sight,* which will be developed in this step. Divine sight uses sacred lenses that acknowledge the nonphysical aspects of one's being, which at the core is an *energy* light that extends beyond one's skin. It has been called by many names, but what's more important than what it is called is what it represents. At this level you will have tasted the sweetness of your mental and emotional well-being, so much so that you will want to maintain your alignment for as long as you can, and as often as you can, for the duration of your physical life experience.

STEP EIGHT—Offers sacred suggestions for **AFTER-CARE** and *staying aligned*. Once you have elevated to this level, care must be taken to safeguard the ongoing alignment process due to the diversity of life experiences that you will encounter throughout the remainder of your physical life. It can be challenging to resist the insidiousness of the conditioning you uncovered, since the old ways of thinking were a more familiar way of being. Therefore, this step gives you a dozen additional sacred tools to preserve your holistic knowing. Those who have completed the Sacretherapy® steps are invited to attend a ***free*** optional online bi-weekly support group that I call ***The Soulful Living Exchange***™. These are 45-minute sessions with other like-minded souls that have reached this level. By collectively remaining steadfast to honoring your mind, body, and spirit, you will be fortified by the collective consciousness of the group where your spirit is consistently being rejuvenated and uplifted.

Finally, there are two other chapters that are ***not*** a part of the *Eight-Step Process* but are still important steps, in the sense that one path *"steps out"* of physical life and the other keeps "stepping on":

STEPPING OUT is the subtitle for the chapter that I call ***"Ending The Matter,"*** which is for those who may have come to the Sacretherapy® process very discouraged, so much so that they have been considering **stepping out** of the physical world in an attempt to realign with well-being. This chapter, then, is ***only*** for those experiencing suicidal ideation or who have threatened or attempted suicide before or are the survivors of someone that transitioned as a result of suicide. So please skip this chapter if issues with regard to suicide are not your *matter*, and move on to the next *Step*.

STEPPING ON is the last chapter that deals with what I call: ***"Another Matter—Healing the Healer."*** As the title suggests, this is where I take time to share with you how I came into alignment with the fullness of my being. I included my own personal journey because sometimes people feel more inspired to do their own work when they know that the *healer* has actually *healed* herself or himself. It seems to help close that gap between separate beingness and merges us together as one. It offers hope that a beacon of light does, in fact, exist that can guide us home. I am delighted to be that flashlight pointing the way, knowing that you may walk where I have walked, and you may feel what I have felt, and you will emerge as I emerged, out of the darkness into the light. For this is the wellness that alignment offers as these *steps* give you back to you. So let these *steps* be your tour guide on this sacred journey of holistic self-discovery and divine *inner knowing*. These are surely the steps that will inform and clarify your soul's sacred intention that it is divinely unfolding in this physical experience.

And so, let us begin. But first, if you are going to incorporate the music, now would be a good time to play your selection as we start. (Pause to select music.) Proceed to *Step One* in the next chapter.

2
WHAT'S THE MATTER?

Step One

*"We must no more ask if the soul and the body are one
than ask whether the wax and the figure impressed on it are one."*

—Aristotle

Since becoming a psychotherapist, I have continuously found myself asking clients, "What's the matter?" It's the same question that most people pose to one another when we detect that something is wrong. Yet, most of us don't know how profound and accurate of a question that really is, which is why I felt the question was the perfect name for this chapter. When I ask the question, as a psychotherapist, I'm assessing what in your physical experience has yanked you from your wellness. But as a metaphysician, I am in the process of determining what the *matter* is from a holistic perspective. This takes into consideration your nonphysical aspects, in order to get to the *energy* basis of the *matter*, which encompasses your mind, body and spirit.

To assist you in understanding what I truly mean by "What's the *matter*?" I am sharing with you a parable (below) or what I call a *stream of consciousness*—(which metaphysically is a divine block of thought intuited from a higher vibrational vantage point) to help you to fathom the 'fullness of your being' and how it relates to your mental and emotional well-being by starting with your transition from the nonphysical realm into the physical. You naturally don't recall becoming a zygote but the below parable should help you to understand the *energy* basis of what the *matter* is and how you and your thoughts were formed.

A Well Being – From Nonphysical to Physical
A Stream of Consciousness: The Matter of You

Welcome to your physical experience! You are just beginning to change form but will continue to be a wonderful well being. I know you must be a little disoriented. That will pass. You can't answer us verbally yet, but you can still communicate with us through telepathy as pure consciousness. You are still a subtle form of **energy**, in a different form that has just been expanded into a zygote, which came from the co-creative act of those you will come to call your earthly mother and father. For the next nine months, your energetic body will come to be surrounded by flesh, blood and bone, which will evolve into a larger form of solid **matter** that you will come to know as your physical body. Meanwhile, your subtle body, which you are accustomed to, and which is made up of light *energy*, will be busy working on different aspects of your physical body. Part of your *subtle being*, which we call your *subtle mental body*, will pave the way for your brain to remain plugged into universal intelligence; and the part that we call your *subtle emotional body* will pave the way for you to have continued access to subtle guidance from your energetic self.

Already within you is the *breath of life*, which you will breathe in and out, once your lungs are formed. This breath is what will allow you to stay formed as physical *matter*. Your physical body is strictly a temporary housing, more like a sacred temple or body suit. It will allow your *subtle energetic body* to experience the physical world through *five new senses* that will be added, since they were not needed in the nonphysical realm from which you were just deployed. These senses, which are sight, hearing, taste, touch, and smell, will allow you to interpret *energy* as **vibration** that will be formed into all types of *matter*. Those five senses, however, are not meant to override your *sixth sense*, which will keep you reminded of your true energetic self that you know as spirit. Thus, your *sixth sense* will allow you to reach the nonphysical parts of your *being* when you want. You will interact with other souls who are physically focused, some of whom choose to remain more cognizant of their *sixth sense* while on the earth plane. Therefore, they enjoy what earthlings call "clairvoyance," since they will be able to feel or see your energetic body as light. This is because, although your physical apparatus houses your energetic body, it is just too big to be contained in the body temple. And as such, light emanates from within you and shines around you as well. Nevertheless, whether or not you have selected *clairvoyance* along with your specific intentions, be assured that you won't need it to connect with the spirit within.

Prepare to enjoy your physical experience. It was designed for you to select and create anything you want, and for you to see your creations manifest. You already got to select the way you would look, the body you desired to experience the physical with, and the earthly parents that you felt resonated most with the divine intention you held when you decided to have this physical experience. They will be waiting and preparing to interact with you to the degree that you felt would most benefit your journey. So for now, just relax as your body develops, and get a lot of rest, because as soon as you are born you will be busy expanding your consciousness. Your advent in the physical world also will expand the consciousness of others who observe or interact with you. Your intention, however, is to expand and enjoy your own soul unfoldment. You may get a little distracted from time to time by all the other souls and their creations on the planet, but try not to forget that you are going forward with your own unique creative desires. So have a ball, and remember that 'the spirit that you are' is always with you. We will be watching and prepared to welcome you back into pure positive *energy* when you are ready to return.

⎯⎯ ⚭ ⎯⎯

The above *stream of consciousness,* describing the *matter* that is you, like other *creation* stories, is based on possibilities—this usually helps to bridge the gap between the nonphysical and physical aspects of you. As such, I hope this particular take on the possibilities of your reality with regard to your mental and emotional well-being will now help you understand the more straightforward explanations of your "being" that are forthcoming in this section.

I will explain *three terms* that were highlighted in the above *stream of consciousness* because they will be *constantly* used throughout this book: ***matter, energy, and vibration***; and I will demonstrate how they keep linking back to your mental and emotional wellness. I promise not to go off into a long and drawn out spiel on *physics 101,* but it is important that I briefly discuss the terms. So let's start with the word *matter* from a holistic and metaphysical point of view in order to demonstrate how it ties into the subtle *energy* basis of mental and emotional well-being.

The Subtle Energy Basis of Mental and Emotional Well-being

MATTER—We are constantly asking, "What's the matter," not recognizing how accurate a question that is; and so, let's break the *matter* all the way down, and then build it all the way back up to how it relates to what we are experiencing mentally or emotionally. You probably recall being told in grade school that *matter* can be solid, liquid or gas. However, you probably haven't thought about the fact that the *gas version of matter is invisible,* but you are aware that it is there because you can smell it. *Oxygen is also invisible,* but you are aware that it's there, because you are breathing it, even though you can't smell it. See illustration E-1, next page.

  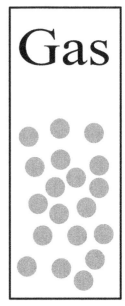

Illustration E-1

Well, your ***thoughts also are invisible***, like gas and oxygen, but you know that they are there because you are thinking them. Your *thoughts* then, like oxygen and gas, also are a form of *matter*, since *matter* can be invisible. This means then that even though you are 'thinking thoughts,' they *remain* in the nonphysical realm that was described in the *stream of consciousness* above. So within your physical body is your brain, which *downloads your invisible thoughts* through your mental and emotional processes. Those invisible thoughts are coming from the ***"subtle mental body"*** that was also discussed in the *stream of consciousness,* from the nonphysical realm; and they are, therefore, invisible to most people but can be seen as *energy* light by an electromagnetic field machine. These parts of ourselves that most people can't usually see, like gas and oxygen, are really just composed of *energy* that manifests into different types of *matter*, whether nonphysical or physical.

ENERGY—We've all said at one time or another that we "just don't have the energy" to do something. That sentiment is understandable since energy is generally defined by most dictionaries as the *capacity of a physical system to perform work.* That capacity is the amount of heat, light, radiation or power being released or absorbed as life force or vital essence. Therefore, the *energy* basis of anything as it relates to Sacretherapy® is its divine essence or life force. And we know, according to Einstein, that *"energy* cannot be created or destroyed, but only transferred." As such, we are always in the process of simply recharging our *energy* or disbursing and transferring it, since physicists have confirmed that *energy* is at the core of our physical bodies and emanates beyond it as the *subtle invisible matter* described earlier. See Illustration E-2.

This very same *energy* that is invisible to most people can be seen as light *energy* with certain instruments, but it is also visible to those with clairvoyance as shown in the illustration E2. This *energy* is what neuroscientists and quantum physicists also say that our invisible *thoughts are made* of, which again, is a lighter (subtle) *energy* and still a form of *matter* (like gas and oxygen which are also invisible) that you experience via the brain.

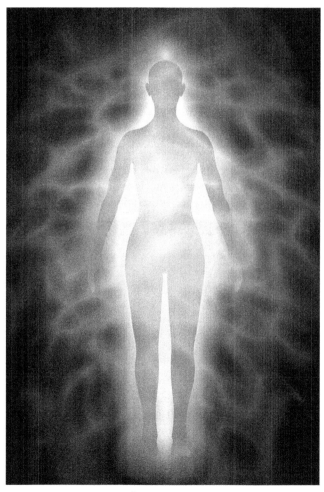

Illustration E-2

Your brain, which is downloading the thoughts, is like a conduit plugged into an *invisible universal intelligence* that you are interpreting via your brain, as illustrated below.

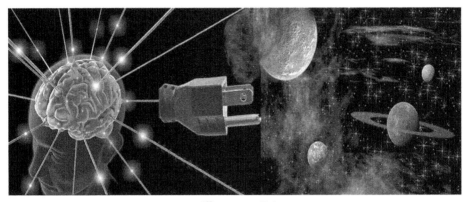

Illustration E-3

Note: *The brain, according to most medical dictionaries and other resources, is a highly complex network of about 80-100 billion nerve cells called neurons, interconnected by trillions of synapses through which thoughts are being produced.*

VIBRATION—The nerve cells or neurons mentioned above—vibrate. In other words, a vibration is *energy **or** matter* in motion, or a particle (neuron or photon) that continues to **move** its position. See Illustration E-4 below:

Illustration E-4

Your brain via your eyes is interpreting thousands of wave particles *as **light***, and at another frequency your ears will interpret ***sound***, because the frequency of the *energy*'s vibration determines how the *energy/matter* will manifest. For example, *energy/matter* can vibrate at one frequency and be experienced as gas; another frequency and be experienced as water; another frequency and be experienced as ice; another frequency and be experienced as a migraine headache; another frequency and be experienced as depression; and another frequency and be experienced as joy. Since every emotion from depression to joy is a derivative of thoughts, these emotions can be viewed as '*energy* or subtle *matter*' that is vibrating at a certain frequency, connected to your **subtle emotional body**. So where you are vibrating has everything to do with how you are going to feel. You may have heard the expressions that *"I'm picking up negative vibes"* or *"we were vibing."* Well those vibes are the same vibrations we are discussing here. The fact that vibrations keep changing positions, as was shown in the illustration E-4, lets you know that your *emotions can also keep changing* positions since both are simply *energy/matter* vibrating. Therefore, you are not stuck in one position or thought, since the core of you is *energy* that is vibrating. In other words, you *change how you feel* by shifting your *energy*, which is fully described in Steps Three–Five.

Many people find themselves feeling low and don't realize that they are simply thinking a thought that is causing them to vibrate at a lower frequency than they prefer. They also often state that they don't have the *energy* to do what is needed in order to raise their frequency to feel better. The reality, however, is that you have plenty of *energy* since it emanates from your core and beyond, although you may be expending it in ways that seem to deplete it. This is also what is meant by the statement, *"someone is losing his power or needs to take her power back,"* since it is *energy*. The question, then, is how am I using my *energy* and what do I need to do to re-energize (since it can't be created or destroyed) so that I can vibrate at a frequency that is in alignment with well-being? These are some of the questions that Sacretherapy® addresses throughout this book.

This is why Sacretherapy® honors the *fullness of your being*, which includes the subtle *matter/energy* that emanates beyond your skin, and adds it to the treatment plan. This is done because the nonphysical part of you, as described in the *stream of consciousness,* is ultimately the part of us that we call the *spirit*. Understanding this expanded version of who you are at the level of subtle *energy* can remind you of the tremendous power you have *within* to influence your own quality of life. It also can be a reminder that you get to point your thoughts in the direction/position that you want them to be, moment by moment, sort of like playing particle chess (since *energy* is made up of tiny particles), you play the game of life, knowing that not only does your *energy* position keep moving, but that it CAN move. An excellent demonstration of the quantum science behind a thought and emotions is depicted beautifully in the movie, *"What the Bleep Do We Know!"* 2004 (See Resources). The funny thing is that you have already been doing this unconsciously, even before your physical body was formed, as was described in the *stream of consciousness*.

The Etheric Body of Man—The Bridge of Consciousness, (1989) by Dr. Lawrence and Pheobe Bendit (a psychiatrist and clairvoyant) states: "In the older theosophical literature…the subtle mental body is where thought takes place, an astral body [aka emotional body] for feeling processes and an etheric or vital body is associated with the dense physical body." The authors submit that in later times, [later 1900's] when the differences between *energy* and *matter* began to fade, the aura was seen as a whole. Still, there are many who continue to advocate that the subtle layers need to be noted and honored. See illustration E-5 on the next page.

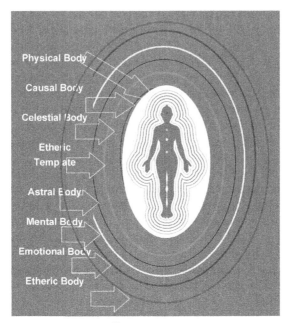

Illustration E-5

Thus, for the purposes of this book, we will concern ourselves with the interplay between the *subtle mental* and the *subtle emotional* bodies that interact with the brain. It is the *subtle emotional body* that interacts with the limbic system of the brain that handles our emotions. Therefore, the *subtle emotional body* is the nonphysical energetic part of you that sends out a signal to the limbic system regarding your dominant vibrational mood or feeling, and this is then felt by the physical body as depression, fear, joy, etc. The subtle layer of the body translates the *energy* data.

William Atkinson (mentioned in the Acknowledgements) wrote about this in his book, *Thought Vibration or The Law of Attraction In The Thought World* (1906). He stated: "When we *think* we send out vibrations of fine ethereal substance, which are as real as the vibrations manifesting light, heat, electricity…. [The fact that] these vibrations are not evident to our five senses is no proof that they do not exist…. Thought is a force—a manifestation of *energy*— having magnet like power of attraction…. We recognize the law that holds the circling worlds in their place, but we close our eyes to the mighty law that draws to us [like a magnet] the things we desire or fear…." This interaction he described is always going to be based on the thoughts you are thinking, which are noted to you via your brain that is vibrationally connected to the subtle mental body. And since these subtle energies are working together, you will naturally feel what you think, because first we think, then we feel, then we act or react.

This information is valuable for us to know, since these invisible processes are involved in determining our **degrees of alignment or misalignment** with our mind, body and spirit, which we will discuss later in this chapter, since *everything* begins with a thought. A thought cannot be seen, but the manifestations that one creates with thoughts can. We can see brain waves, which are shown as electromagnetic activity with brain imaging technology, but not the thoughts themselves, since they are invisible (again, like gas and oxygen).

Until a specific thought is pondered long enough to become a *thought form* and then manifest into the physical realm, we can't see it, according to Swami Panchadasi, author of *The Human Aura: Astral Colors and Thought Forms* (1916). However, there are people who can see into the nonphysical aspects of *matter* or *energy*, which is *translated at the frequency of light*. Some of those who can see it are identified as *clairvoyant*, a French word that means "clear seeing," while others who can see it prefer to describe themselves as just someone "who sees the light." I belong to the latter, as someone who sees the light. The ability to see subtle *energy* is truly a gift and what has helped me understand this dimension. Yet, I can truly empathize with how challenging it may be initially to understand or believe this without personal experience. Most of us have been taught that anything that can't be experienced beyond the five senses just doesn't exist. And unfortunately, from our human perspective versus a spiritual one, that meme (which is a unit of thought discussed in Chapter Four) got passed down without our consent and trained us away from appreciating the fullness of our being, especially at the level of thought.

It is also crucial that we understand the difference between the brain and the mind, which are often used synonymously. In fact, the brain is more like a remote control sending and receiving signals from our mind, which is a part of the nonphysical universal mind that our individual brains harness. It is okay to continue to use the terms interchangeably, as long as the user recognizes that our minds were operating before we inhabited our body temples, which the brain is simply a part of, as illustrated in the *stream of consciousness.*

If you can understand how your brain interacts with the thought world, and what your very essence is made of, and how everything that comes into being, including you, is some form of *matter* by way of thoughts, then you may begin to understand how powerful your thoughts really are. So what you think *matters*—pun intended, especially since the *thoughts you think determine how you are going to feel.* And how you feel greatly affects your quality of life. Most people feel somewhere between good and bad, but we all want to feel good. With that being the case, let's focus once again on the *stream of consciousness* that describes how we came from the nonphysical into the physical as souls unfolding, to see what went wrong.

A soul comes forth and is born into its physical housing, with a brain, senses, and the ability to think and feel, eager to create and bring its thoughts into manifestation, as some form of *matter*. Remembering its orientation during the zygote stage of its physical development described in the *stream of consciousness,* the *soul* has been oriented to expect a joyful physical life experience. It expects to be welcomed and set free to do that which it came forth to do. It expects to create unique creations and enjoy the originality of it all. It expects to co-exist with others who came forth with the same unique intention; but then something appears to go wrong, at least for those who have been *labeled* as having mental and emotional disorders.

The *labeled* soul gets 'labeled' because it had a *reaction* to being told that it must now squelch the *"innate knowing"* that it came here with divine individualized intentions. The souls who are labeled are told that they are *not* that which we call *"spirit."* They are told that only their observable 'physical *matter*' is what is real, and that only that which can be measured is measurable. They are told that what the majority group thinks overrides their individual ability to think. They are told that there is a hierarchy of other souls who dictate which souls get to have favor and which ones won't. They are told that the world is not a sacred place, providing equality and safety to all, and that anyone who thinks it is, is naïve. They are told that they cannot have or do what they want and to just deal with it. Thus, in essence, they are told that holding onto any notion of connection to that which is nonphysical may earn them a reputation of being "crazy" and outside of the normative curve.

As a result, the soul becomes confused upon hearing those things, because the soul could have sworn that it remembered hearing something totally different. In fact, this nudging from within doesn't feel like something they just remembered hearing, but more like something they know—an *inner knowingness* that was part of an assurance that was built into their DNA, which has been tampered with. So when these particular souls believe that they are forced to surrender their "freewill" to those types of admonishments, they often *react* strongly. As such, their **reactions** are misconstrued as symptoms with negative connotations and labeled as mental and emotional *dis-ease*. And lo and behold, a 'mental disorder' is created, born out of misunderstanding that a soulless initiation into the physical realm has occurred. In actuality, from a Sacretherapy® standpoint, people labeled "mentally ill" are simply attempting to remold the *matter* and honor the *energy* within their being, seeking a higher *frequency* that matches the *vibration* of well-being they were expecting. But during the search, the soul becomes restless, anxious, despondent, depressed, manic, enraged, lost, addicted, suicidal, homicidal, and/or develops a schizotypal personality, etc., in an attempt to realign with what one knows to be the core of one's being. The spirit is calling, so the soul longs for home, its true home, which resides in a psycho-spiritual space where a sense of freedom and sustainable well-being can be accessed.

Yet, despite the 'soulless initiation' that socialization often offers, some souls are able to buck the system, holding onto their *inner knowing*, able to emerge more connected, more enlightened, daring to live out the intention of their true creed, and find the joy they seek. But, many, many lose their way, as a result of the flawed (misaligned) initiation into the physical realm, losing sight of their *inner knowing,* and they begin to be conditioned to accept the lower vibrational mass consciousness. They begin to parrot beliefs that were passed down that they didn't even realize they had integrated, which is often toxic and counter to mental and emotional wellness. They do not realize that those they are parroting are often *equally or more unaligned* than those that have been labeled 'mentally disordered.' Perhaps worse, the labelers "don't know it" and may therefore be living "unconscious." But society doesn't call them out, for they are the 'majority holders' of the socialization and conditioning of the human experience and the gatekeepers of so-called agreed upon reality. (The flawed initiation and conditioning will be discussed in detail in Chapter Four.)

The Psycho-Spiritual Biographical Questionnaire™ (PSBQ)

As a result of the flawed and soulless initiation minimizing the nonphysical spiritual aspects of one's physical experience, Sacretherapy® allows one to explore one's sacred heritage through a probe that I call the Psycho-Spiritual-Biographical Questionnaire™ (PSBQ). The questionnaire probes one's awareness of the psycho-spiritual states of one's being, and extracts from that inventory what appears to be at the essence of the *matter*. It also offers one a chance to describe *"what's the matter"* and how the *matter* has manifested, along with one's feelings about its manifestations. Here one can either share current '*here and now'* feelings about the *matter* or offer a *full history*.

If you choose to inventory your *full history*, use the **Regular PSBQ** (Appendix A), and leave no stone unturned, because this will hopefully be the last time you feel the need to share the *matter* to this degree.

However, if you choose to start in the here and now, then use the **Radical PSBQ-R** (Appendix B) knowing that restating the past is not mandatory and often not necessary in order to heal and come back into alignment. In fact, restating the *matter* can sometimes send a person further out of alignment due to reactivating the negative *energy* associated with the thoughts.

Know that catharsis can come from empowering information that facilitates the elevation of your vibration, not only re-evaluation. Still, either approach will lead to the same destination, even though the Radical PSBQ-R appears to be the most progressive starting place in Sacretherapy® because to be present in the here and now without looking back is ultimately where both journeys take us. Having said that, please know that it requires keen discernment to be able to plant yourself solidly in the present moment, in order to begin with the Radical PSBQ-R. So please don't try to force yourself to be in a place that you may clearly not be. Just choose the questionnaire that feels like the best starting place for you, based on where you truly are in your soul's journey. I have no preference for you; I am just offering the options.

Either way, once you have done the questionnaire, you will have reflected on *yesterday's manifestations* and may have activated some negative *energy*. Therefore, within a week or so after that would be a good time to go get an *optional energy assessment* done to scan the *energy* field of your body temple, to determine if or how the psychological distress may be affecting your overall wellness. Although the scan is not mandatory, it is *highly* suggested since both the PSBQ and PSBQ-R can only collect from you information that you are consciously aware of.

The scan is done in the auric realm to assess the degree to which the subtle *energy* is flowing or to identify *energy* blockages that may have already begun to heal or may be beginning to be blocked. Adding the scan supports the Sacretherapy® goal of having done the full mind, body, spirit assessment. This is usually done by a Certified Reiki or Prana Practitioner, where one is fully clothed for the *energy* scan. Any *energy* blockages are then noted on an *Energy* Field Form (Appendix C), which is a biological-energetic chart. Each practitioner may use his or her own charting system, and so as long as it is comparable, any form is fine. Otherwise, feel free to take a copy of the one in this book with you. If *energy* blockages are noted, they will not be treated at the time of the scan, like going for an x-ray. However, you may request an *energy* treatment. (Note: Insurance companies in the United States do not yet reimburse for *Energy* Medicine/Reiki or Prana.) Clients who want the scan will have to pay out of pocket for this service until we as Holistic Healers are able to impress upon the traditional medical model that psycho-spiritual treatment modalities are valid sources of information, intervention and relief. Anyone unable to pay for this service may check out the books listed in the back, under Resources, which teach you how to scan your own *energy* field. The books, of course, do not prepare you to treat others but can definitely show you how to become acquainted with your own *energy* field.

If you choose to do the scan yourself, complete the *Energy* Field Form that will allow you to list your own findings. If you are choosing to do this work with a psychotherapist, more than likely he or she may not be trained in *Energy* Medicine/Reiki/Prana or even familiar with it. But if your therapist has agreed to support you in the Sacretherapy® work, then please share the results, but keep a copy of everything for yourself. Then, seal your copy of the PSBQ or PSBQ-R along with the *Energy* Scan in an envelope marked *"The Past"* and place it in that *symbolic vault* that was mentioned in the last chapter (your box or other type of container that will continue to be accessible for you to add your other Sacretherapy® work to, as you do the exercises throughout the book). Then store it in a place that you deem sacred. Proceed below with the PSBQ or PSBQ-R:

EXERCISE: Completing the Psycho-Spiritual Biographical Questionnaire™

1. Complete the **PSBQ** or Radical **PSBQ-R**. (See Appendix A or B).
2. Have or do an *energy* scan and then complete the *Energy* Field Form or have it completed by a Certified Reiki or Prana Practitioner. (See Appendix C).

Once you've completed and sealed the questionnaire, scan and forms, here is where we determine the lesson and blessing the findings reveal as it relates to your mental or emotional diagnosis, and to what degree the *matter* has affected your quality of life, using what is termed as "symbolic meaning."

Understanding Mental and Emotional Diagnoses via Symbolic Meaning

As we begin to come back into alignment with our spirit, we incorporate the use of *intuition*, which is in the spiritual realm of the unseen. Intuition asks us to discern what we intuitively extract from the *matter*, which points us in the direction of *symbolic meaning*. Here, we use *symbolic meaning* to know what the diagnosis **symbolizes** at a deeper level than just the description of symptoms. Understanding the symbolism of what our symptoms represent can help us gain insight as we are coming back into alignment. As such, the alternative descriptions that I offer encompass *symbolic meaning* as it relates to each diagnostic presentation of the *matter*. As stated before, I am not alone in my quest to capture *symbolic meaning;* many others also approach wellness from this paradigm, including some of the professionals who were introduced to you in the Acknowledgement section beginning with Carl Jung. You can, therefore, be assured that I am not a lone read. I am simply the first to apply it to all of the mental and emotional disorders that have been identified by mental health authorities worldwide.

Dr. Caroline Myss used *symbolic meaning* in her book, The Anatomy of Spirit (1997), a book that I highly recommend. She uses the term **symbolic sight** which she states, "lets you see into your spirit and your limitless potential for healing and wholeness." I also encourage you to embrace the other works listed in the back of the book that validate and fortify this perspective by other metaphysicians as well as Board Certified Oncologist Bernie Seigal, M.D., author of *Love, Medicine, & Miracles* (1990). Dr. Seigal's book also asks his patients to try to determine what the message is that the *dis-ease* is trying to convey to them. Likewise, as a result of authors like these over the past two decades, using *symbolic meaning* has emerged as a real energetic pathway to assist people in realigning with well-being.

I believe that, from a symbolic meaning point of view, the mental and emotional diagnoses listed in this book are only manifestations of interplay between psycho-spiritual states. This means that whatever the *matter* is, it may represent something else that may be going on spiritually—something that is being manifested mentally or emotionally. And therefore, upon discovering what the symbolic meaning is, one may use that expanded knowledge as an initial step in uncovering another piece of the psychic puzzle. This usually assists in bringing seekers back into alignment with the fullness of their being.

Reaction versus Disorder: How to Understand and Use the Alternative List

The alternative list of diagnoses describes "what's the *matter*?"—meaning what the *matter* actually manifested into and the name or label it was given by experts within the psychological community. However, as of 2013, the most recent and previous editions of the DSM, ICD and other medical references classifies these *manifestations* as disorders. And although I totally respect and understand that it is normative for the healthcare community to do so, I prefer **not** to think of the manifestations as "disorders" and prefer to classify them as "reactions."

According to most dictionaries, the term **disorder** is defined as "a derangement or abnormality of function; a morbid physical or mental state," which suggests that the manifestation did not *manifest* correctly. In my opinion, this is not completely accurate. All manifestations come into being in a prescribed manner based on universal principles surrounding the laws of creation, and that is the case whether we are experiencing the manifestation of *dis-ease* or the manifestations that are in alignment with wellness.

In any case, this is why I prefer the word "reaction." A *reaction*, according to most dictionaries, is "a *response* to some stimuli, situation or treatment." The operative word, then, was *response*, in that it is a reaction *to something*. This suggests that the *matter* may be a *temporary* manifestation and/or can be neutralized and realigned with the right antidote. I prefer that, because what we are actually dealing with here is *subtle matter* at the level of *energy*. Therefore, I offer alternative energetic antidotes for the 168 diagnoses (reactions) and worldwide syndromes that most medical sources have identified, including the DSM and ICD. I've also included three others: "*infidelity* and *obesity*, along with *religious addiction* within religious problems," since I believe these can also stem from emotional issues. Those additional ones bring the list to a complete total of 170 diagnoses since one is only added within a current clinical concern. I have listed them alphabetically for your ease of locating them, while including the alternative way to view the mental or emotional *matter*.

In addition to the names given the manifestations, most mental health sources, including the DSM and ICD, classify the severity of each as mild, moderate, marked or severe. I have done the same, believing that severity scales should be in conjunction with the different vibrational degrees of alignment; because I am always checking to see to what degree the specific "reaction" has penetrated one's imbalance with the fullness of being—mind, body and spirit, understanding that the vibrational frequency can move, as illustrated earlier in the definition of vibration. Therefore, if you have been diagnosed as having a mild case of some manifestation, change the terminology to *"mildly misaligned."* If you have been told you have a *moderate* case, change it to *"moderately misaligned,"* and so forth. The different degrees of alignment and the attached meaning are presented in the Alignment Severity Scale found on the next page of this book.

—◦◦◦—

ALIGNMENT SEVERITY SCALE

(From Misalignment to Realignment)

Mostly Aligned—means that one has an impeccable tendency toward thinking about the things that one prefers with positive expectation, and as a result can remain in a higher vibration most of the time and can shift one's *energy* to a higher frequency easier than most.

Mildly Misaligned—means that one *usually* has a tendency to think about things that validate one's well-being, but has begun to be disturbed by the diversity of stimuli in one's environment that isn't what one prefers. People in this category usually can find their bearing and shift their *energy* back to a higher vibrational countenance rather quickly.

Moderately Misaligned—means that *half the time* one's tendency is to think about things from the standpoint of "the cup being half empty instead of half full," which consumes a great deal of one's *energy*. As a result, it can be a bit difficult to shift one's *energy* to higher vibrational thoughts because of the tendency to point out anything that can reinforce one's belief that the cup is half empty.

Marked Misalignment—means that one has a *strong tendency* toward thinking about the things that one prefers not to be, and has a rigid allegiance to repeatedly reviewing that which is not preferred. As a result, it can be very hard sometimes to shift one's *energy* into a higher vibration because of such a pattern of obsessing.

Severely Misaligned—means that one has an *extremely practiced habit* of thinking about things that are unpleasant or destructive to self and/or others, with a high probability of acting on them. Therefore, one has an extremely difficult time trying to shift one's *energy* to a higher vibration, where true relief can be had. This is due to an extremely rigid interpretation or misunderstanding of some form of modeling or conditioning that was picked up and practiced during one's physical journey.

Please notice that the thread that was sewn between all of the severity states was based on the way and what a person was *thinking—in other words*, the intensity of the thoughts, frequency of the thoughts, and the direction of the thoughts. The good news here again is that with just the slightest *vibrational movement* toward well-being, as described in the section on vibration, the severity on this scale *can* change quickly, although incrementally, up the alignment scale. For example: one could be *severely misaligned* at 2 p.m., only be *markedly misaligned* by 2:30 p.m., *only moderately* misaligned by 2:45 p.m., and just mildly misaligned by 3:00 p.m. So just keep in mind here that alignment is a moment by moment individual thing. Literally!

Therefore, as we employ *symbolic meaning*, we will see that the cause of "*what's the matter*" can be due to what I am referring to as "*misaligned thoughts*" or "*divine intentions.*"

A *misaligned thought* is a thought that is not in sync with the fullness of your being. This means that your *inner knowing* is alerting you that there is some type of incongruency or clash between your mind, body and spirit. And oftentimes, it was stimulated by conditioning, memes and old linguistic programming, which we will elaborate on in Chapter Four. Also, as previously stated, *matter* can manifest as a "divine intention."

A *divine intention* is when a soul (person) came into the physical realm with the intention of living parts or all of its physical experience in a certain way, which is usually different from the norm, in order for its own soul expansion, despite how its specific life experience looks to others. This phenomenon has also been described as a "sacred contract" by Dr. Myss, on her Audio CD: Sacred Contracts (2002). So note that underneath every disorder, which I call reactions, I have the diagnosis classified as: **Misaligned Thought or Divine Intention;** and you will know which one it is by the classification being "italicized." To be crystal clear:

A. **Misaligned Thought** is a thought that is not in sync with the fullness of your being. The *matter* manifested this way due to an incongruent, unconscious and unintentional clash or inconsistency between your mind, body and spirit.

B. **Divine Intention** is an intention that the soul comes into the physical realm with; and, therefore, the *matter* is a manifestation that has been divinely molded the way it is. The soul may choose to live parts or all of its physical experience in this way for its own expansion. So here, my hope is to assist those with this type of *matter* in reclaiming and maintaining their intention, and/or how to come back into alignment with that intention.

Having offered this type of description of a *misaligned thought* and *divine intention,* it is certainly noted that most people are not used to seeing themselves from the vantage point of the nonphysical aspects of their being. They therefore most often do not recognize that their thoughts are a part of the nonphysical realm and are what points all of us in the direction of *dis-ease* or well-being. This is possibly because we are so used to mainly using our words to convey our feelings that we forget that our words are only an expression of our thoughts. Our words, then, being an 'expression of thought' also carry vibrations, and depending on the vibrational frequency we are attuned to in the given moment, the thoughts that the words convey can either attract the evidence of the well-being we seek or evidence of the *dis-ease* we are manifesting. Since we are used to using our words as conveyers of our emotional well-being, I felt that prescribing positively charged words that are set at the vibration of well-being would be the easiest way to bridge the gap between the physical aspect of you and the nonphysical (spiritual) part of you. And so, we'll begin to align the *matter* by extracting the *energy* of words in the form of affirmations.

An affirmation is a positive thought that affirms and reinforces your alignment with what's being desired. It's a ritualistic anchor that denotes to the universe that a shift in thinking has occurred, which is now emitting a positive vibration filled with expectation that the realignment with the spiritual source within you is taking place—mind, body, and spirit! Therefore, the alignment processes that follow the alternative descriptions of the mental and emotional *reactions* are going to be accompanied by the positively aligned statements or affirmations that you will be affirming. Know however, that affirmations alone cannot *undo the matter* you have already manifested; but they can stop the *matter* that has been *set in motion* from continuing to be created, and in turn, create new life that is aligned with the health and well-being you seek. I like to think of it this way: A *single sneeze* can travel the distance of 32 feet. And according to most encyclopedias, that single sneeze produces about 40,000 droplets of moisture and millions of germs with the average speed of 80 to 100 mph. Our thoughts produce similarly. For instance, you think a chronic thought that in turn produces feelings, actions, and reactions that you didn't particularly like. Well the reverberation of that energetic thought was sent out a certain distance. And like a sneeze, you will have to walk 32 feet, days, or further before you have passed through what you created or sent out. This is crucial to understand in order for you to remain patient with yourself as you journey through space and time. The good news is—according to most metaphysicians and Atkinson, author of *Thought Vibrations or The Law of Attraction in the Thought World* (1906)—"Positive thoughts are said to be infinitely more powerful than negative ones." And therefore, thinking a positive thought speeds up healing because the faster more powerful vibration attracts the positive vibrations of others resonating on the same wavelength. Likewise, a negative thought does the exact opposite, in that it moves slower and attracts other negative *energy*.

Think of it as giving your *energy* a positive charge to *boost* your "innate power" just like you would your car. For instance, you go to your car and it won't start. You realize the battery is down and you get out the jumper cables. You carefully attach the positive with positive. Hence, only something *positive* will spark *positive*. If you put the *negative* on the *positive*, it will kill the battery. Your *energy* works the same way: negative *energy* kills positive. Even when you use the cables correctly, sometimes it will still take time to recharge the battery enough to get it going. Therefore, just like your car battery, give yourself some time to penetrate the *old matter* that manifested as a result of all that will be discussed in greater detail in the next few chapters.

Learning theorists tell us that it takes a minimum of 24 times of doing something "successfully" for it to become a new habit. A habit becomes an automatic response that alerts your neurotransmitters to flow in a certain vibrational direction. Therefore, we are attempting to retrain the automatic thoughts to flow in a way that supports optimum well-being. And even in the case where the *matter* is of a *divine intention,* the process can still take a little while to override the old programming that caused one to believe otherwise.

Also, notice that I stated "positive affirmations," because an affirmation can be positive or negative. For instance, "I am not mentally ill" is a negative affirmation that keeps you focused on being ill and, therefore, will keep you manifesting *illness.* Whereas, "I am mentally and emotionally healthy" is a positive affirmation that keeps you focused on health and will keep you manifesting *well-being.* The point is to get into the new habit of focusing on mental health and to get out of the old habit of focusing on mental *dis-ease.* Most holistic healers agree that *"energy* flows where attention goes."

Thus, please keep in mind that the alternative descriptions and aligning processes that I offer have been intuited from the *symbolic meaning* I've extracted from my professional and educational training and from my personal and spiritual journey. Yet, there will ALWAYS be exceptions to any *matter* since *matter* is not fixed but subtle and pliable. Having offered that caveat, please note that these ideas may stimulate your own intuition with regards to the symbolic meaning, lessons and blessings that manifested in your experience. If that happens, by all means feel free to tweak the aligning process for your personal use, if needed, to fit your personal dynamic.

A *dynamic* is typically the interaction between motives, emotions and drives. In other words, your dynamics, as it relates to this book, are the particular ways in which your symptoms have presented in your life and the lesson and blessings that have sprung forth. The dynamics, then, may be what your soul needed to motivate and/or drive you back towards the "well being" that you came into the physical realm to be.

I've noticed, however, that regardless of the specific diagnoses, most people who are experiencing those reactions also experience some level of anxiety or depression during the course of their main diagnosis. Therefore, you may benefit from reading the aligning processes for anxiety and depression in addition to your diagnosis if you are experiencing either or both of those.

Finally, keep in mind that identifying the *matter* and using the aligning process will only be Step Two of an ***eight-step process***. For Sacretherapy® to assist you in completely aligning your mind, body and spirit, **be sure to follow through with**

all **the steps** and use the ***glossary*** in the back of the book as often as needed when terms used in this chapter need recalling. That way, you won't have to turn back to search for the meaning. Let us now turn to the Alternative Descriptive List of Diagnoses in the next chapter.

3
REFRAMING THE MATTER

Alternative Descriptions for 170 Diagnoses & Aligning Processes
(Including Worldwide Cultural Syndromes)

Step Two

"What we think about ourselves becomes the truth for us."
—Louise Hay

KEY: The alternative descriptions and aligning processes for each diagnosis or issue have three parts, broken down by three separate headings. **Part One**—"What's the Matter." **Part Two**—"Misaligned Thought or Divine Intention" and **Part Three**—"Alignment Process."

NOTE: The terminology used in this chapter to describe and align the *matter* is a blending of older and modern English, in that terms such as: "beingness," "come forth," "*energy* basis," and the use of the conjunction "for" at the beginning of sentences were often used by the early metaphysicians, theologians and channels mentioned in the Acknowledgments section. These writers, including William Atkinson, Charles Leadbeater, Charles and Myrtle Fillmore, and the contemporary teachings of Abraham via Esther Hicks, use language that articulates what I believe is a purer and clearer sense of what our spirit is trying to convey. Therefore, I honor the sacred terminology since it rings truest to the famous axiom quoted by philosopher Pierre Teilhard de Chardin that, "We are *spiritual beings having a physical experience.*" And as such, I have also integrated the older sacred terms into my understanding of spirit and offer them here, as well as sporadically elsewhere throughout the book. I offer them, trusting and believing that these older terms are more exacting, closer to spirit, and convey the restorative resonance I intend.

Part One   *What's the Matter*—Lists the specific name of the Reaction (disorder). Note: (If you jumped straight to this chapter to check out your diagnosis without reading the previous chapter, you may have difficulty understanding the alternative descriptions and rationale for depathologizing mental and emotional diagnoses and viewing them from a holistic perspective. So please go back and read the entire previous chapter before proceeding.)

Part Two   Classifies the Reaction as a ***Misaligned Thought or Divine Intention*** (the relevant one will be italicized.)

Remember: A ***Misaligned Thought*** is a thought that is not in sync or is incongruent with the fullness of your being, which includes your mind, body and spirit. Therefore, the *matter* manifested this way due to an unconscious and unintentional clash or inconsistency between the three.

Remember: A ***Divine Intention*** is an intention that the soul comes into the physical realm with and, therefore, the *matter* is a manifestation that has been divinely molded the way it is. A soul may chose to live part or all of its physical experience in this way for its own expansion. My hope is to assist those with this type of *matter* in reclaiming their intention and maintaining or coming back into alignment with it.

Part Three Is an ***Aligning Process,*** the first of many throughout the eight steps.

NOTE: The previous chapter began to explain why and how metaphysicians use *symbolic meaning* as an aligning tool, and this should help with any possible ***resistance*** that may come up as a result of one's natural inclination to resist something that is new. The alternative descriptions in this chapter may need to be slowly integrated. (*Step Three*, in the next chapter, will begin to fully explain *resistance* as it relates to conditioning, etc.; and *Step Four* will further elaborate on *resistance* and how to integrate new concepts.) Therefore, if the below alternative descriptions cause you to experience *resistance*, just breathe or take a break, and then read the next two chapters for more clarity and assistance. Although I have offered this caveat with regard to resistance, you may not need it because, for most people, the below alternative descriptions and aligning processes usually offer tremendous relief and immediately resonate with their spirit.

Instructions:

1. Find ***What's the Matter,*** which is *Part One* on the upcoming list below under "Alphabetical Listing of Diagnoses." It lists the name of the reaction/disorder (see Sample within these instructions). Beside the name, there will be a very brief definition of the reaction. However, for a complete description of how the diagnosis is viewed traditionally, I recommend that you look it up in any of the known medical resources, dictionaries, encyclopedias, or generally accepted sources. And for an even more thorough official description, which is often used by mental health professionals, there is also the *Diagnostic and Statistical Manual of Mental Disorders* (DSM), used within the United States, and the *International Classification of Diseases* (ICD), used internationally, both of which are highly technical and not really meant for lay persons – (See Resources).

2. *Part Two* lists the classification of the reaction as a ***Misaligned Thought or Divine Intention.*** Read how the reaction is classified (noting which one is italicized). Since this is a different perspective than what you may be used to, you may need to read it slowly, twice.

3. The final section, *Part Three,* is the ***Alignment Process.*** Review what's stated in the *alignment* process for your specific *matter* everyday at least ***three times*** a day: morning, afternoon and evening for at least two minutes each time. The reason I am asking you to do it three times a day is because we want to stimulate each of the three learning styles (visual, auditory and kinesthetic) to penetrate the previously conditioned ways you have interpreted the *matter*, and to re-encode this more positive perspective of the *matter* into your memory for easier recall. Also, the reason for only a minute or two, as opposed to a longer time-frame at this juncture, is because of what has come out of quantum physics with regards to the "creation process." This is described in *The Teachings of Abraham, Law of Allowing workshops* by Esther & Jerry Hicks (2006), as the *17-second combustion point,* which states that "17 seconds of *pure focused thought* is enough time to get the creation process activated."

Therefore, your job is to only send your desire out, affirmatively, with a clear enough thought to begin the creation process. Then you can fortify the aligning thought by consistently giving it more energy a couple more minutes each day, as I have prescribed in the forthcoming exercise; and the God-source of the universe will take the matter and eventually turn it into the physical manifestation you desire. Continue practicing this first process, with the positive expectation that your prayers and these affirmations are assisting in your attunement towards your highest good.

Continue doing the aligning process three times a day until it has become your *new* automatic thought. You will be able to tell that it has replaced the old thoughts when things come up and you automatically think this new thought versus the old one. Just keep in mind what was stated in the last chapter with regards to having the patience to walk through what your thoughts previously created and sent out. Keep in mind, the unleashing power of a positive thought over negative ones via affirmations. Below are instructions for how to do the aligning process exercise.

Sample Exercise: Aligning Process (three times per day)

Instructions: Read the ***Sample Process*** below, which uses *Seasonal Depression Reaction* to illustrate how the three parts of each diagnosis are broken down. Again, **Part One** describes *"What's the Matter"* and **Part Two** classifies the reaction as a *"Misaligned Thought or Divine Intention"* (whichever classification is italicized is applicable to the diagnosis). I then offer the alternative description of the diagnosis from the Sacretherapy® perspective. **Part Three** describes the *"Alignment Process."* **Part Three** is the **ONLY PART** of the three-times-per-day process that you will do everyday (see below).

Sample Alternative Description and Aligning Process:

Part I: ***What's the Matter:*** Seasonal Depression (SAD) Reactions—Seasonal periods of depression that usually begin in fall or winter and subside in spring.

Part II: ***Misaligned Thought or* Divine Intention:** The inherent understanding of the cycles of life. However, this awareness is muddled with the inaccurate belief that one's sunny disposition and mood are determined by an extra sensitivity toward solstices and equinox that are connected with the seasons. This comes about when one forgets that "for everything there is a season and a time," and as such, one's propensity towards the *light* is simply an outer representation of the call from the "inner light" that is brilliantly magnified day in and day out, all year long regardless of the outer season. Therefore, the only thing preventing one from a stable sense of well-being is a self-fulfilling prophecy that every fall or winter season one's *energy* will digress as one recalls the negative *matter.* Yet, if one would remember that alignment with one's mind, body and spirit is a year-round moment-by-moment process, then one could learn to move to a new *vibrational* set point where one is able to always shed "light" on the *matter*.

>*Part III: Alignment Process*—I am opening to the idea that the "full spectrum light" that I am seeking is within me. I am the one that determines whether the *matter* of life feels like a cold grey winter or a fresh spring beginning. As such, I feel brighter just knowing that as I align my mind, body and spirit, I can shift my *energy* to a place of greater peace of mind and joyful well-being. And for this "ray of hope" and healing light, I expect a sunshiny day!

Using the above example, the instructions on how to do *Part III* (the three times per day process) are outlined below:

First Time—In the morning ***read*** (visual) only Part Three, which is the section with the bolded heading titled **"Alignment Process,"** repeatedly for a minute or two silently. Some processes are longer than others and, therefore, may take up the allotted time, which is perfectly fine. If you came forth into the physical realm without sight, feel free to use the audio CD version of this book and/or contact the office to have your specific process translated into Braille for your personal use.

Second Time—In the afternoon, record the *Alignment Process* on a tape recorder or your phone, and **listen** (auditory) to yourself saying it over and over again for another minute or two. Note that after you have recorded it once you won't need to keep recording it; just listen to the same recording once daily for no more than the same minute or two. And if you don't have a recorder, read it out loud so you can hear it. However, if you came forth into the physical realm without the ability to speak, feel free to have someone else record it for you. And if you are without hearing and speech, still have it recorded, and hold the recorder in your hands tightly so that you can feel the vibrational offering coming through the speakers.

Third Time—In the evening, ***write*** it down (kinesthetic) one or two times, for no more than a couple minutes. Some aligning statements are longer than others and so writing it once will suffice. If you came forth without the ability to write, picture yourself writing the words on a piece of paper in your mind's eye.

The ***Diagnosis Directory,*** beginning on the next page, lists the name and page number of your single or dual diagnoses in alphabetical order. The **Worldwide Cultural Syndromes** follow the **American Diagnoses** and are alphabetized separately. After you have located your diagnoses, read them over, and then fold the page for easy access so that you can go back and read, record and write. Then go to Chapter Four—***Step Three,*** which will describe how your *matter* manifested in the first place.

Note: For your convenience a grey stripe was added onto all of the diagnoses pages for ease of flipping back and forth between diagnoses and Chapter Four which begins on page 123.

DIAGNOSIS DIRECTORY

WORLDWIDE CULTURAL SYNDROMES

Alphabetical Listing of Alternative Descriptions of Diagnoses
(To locate the page number of your diagnosis or issue, see the Directory Locator above.)

1. **Abuse** – **1A** – Recipient of Spouse or Partner Abuse/Neglect/Violence
     1B – Recipient of Physical/Sexual/Emotional Abuse not by a partner
     1C – Perpetrator of Abuse/Neglect/Violence of a child or adult
     (See Pedophilias – Pedophiles, for perpetrators of child sexual abuse)
     (See Antisocial Personality for perpetrators of rape of adults)

1-A. Recipient of Partner or Spousal Abuse/Neglect

What's the Matter: Spouse or Partner Abuse, Neglect, or Violence – **Recipient** of improper, severe emotional and psychological mistreatment; neglect; or acts of physical or sexual violence (that can range from restricting one's ability to leave the house, to pinching and shoving, all the way to attempted murder and rape) by an intimate partner, infringing on the human rights of personal safety, dignity, self worth, etc. (Also, for full listing of specific types of abuses look up domestic violence and intimate partner violence in commonly accepted sources. For acts of violence other than intimate partners, see Abuse and Post Traumatic Stress reactions.)

Misaligned Thought or **Divine Intention:** The unconscious inherent belief in resiliency. This, however, is mixed with a faulty belief that one is not worthy, is less valuable than one's partner, and may deserve punishment. This is due to toxic conditioning and one's practiced thoughts about the *matter*; which leads to the belief that one is stuck and without strength. One does not realize that one's agony is an indicator that spirit is calling to remind one that the spirit part of oneself is resourceful, resilient, and capable of showing one exactly how to release the toxic *matter* and create new life. For the spirit is strong, always gathering its *energy*, and finds a way to go on.

Thus, all one needs to be restored to the higher *vibration* of wholeness is a new thought, and the moment-by-moment realigning of one's mind and body with spirit (meaning one's inner spirit, not a religion that would suggest that she or he [men are recipients too] stay and just pray, but the guiding transformative spirit within). It is one's spiritual aspect that will restore one's resolve, with reminders of one's true value and worth, where one is able to imagine (visualize) healthier and happier outer circumstances and the safe haven one deserves. Then one gathers its courage, summons its *energy*, steps out on faith and acts! The spirit then connects with other souls that have come forth to assist one and/or one's children to a refuge that ultimately manifests into a real live place called: *a safe and happy home,* where one's dignity remains intact and body temple remains unharmed.

Alignment Process: I am coming to understand that I can change my circumstances; and that I am now and have always been a valuable and worthy soul, deserving of a peaceful, safe and loving home. Therefore, as I align my mind and body with spirit, I tap into my renewed strength; for now I know that I am capable of taking back my dignity and can live the life I prefer to live, one thought at a time and one moment at a time.

1-B Recipient of Physical/Sexual/Emotional Abuse not by a partner

What's the Matter: Abuse – Recipient of improper, excessive or severe emotional and psychological mistreatment; neglect; or acts of physical or sexual violence directed at a child, teen or adult that infringes on human rights of personal safety, dignity, self worth, etc.

Misaligned Thought or **Divine Intention:** The inherent understanding that one can be restored, as demonstrated by one's attempts to seek justice and/or be soothed. However, one forgets one's intrinsic knowing, resulting in split *energy* where one's vibration is mixed with the faulty belief that one is no longer as valuable, or is permanently altered and changed in some way due to the *matter*. One has forgotten that the spirit cannot be harmed and that one's value is eternal. Recipients of this reaction often believe that unyielding justice needs to be paid out of an angry desperation to be restored back to wholeness. Yet, somewhere within, one eventually comes to understand that the restoration one seeks is the whole or "holiness" that comes with realigning one's mind and body with spirit; for the spirit understands that only "hurting people" hurt others. It also nudges one to release such unaligned individuals. But until one advocates for one's own well-being, there is an *energy* block where one feels a furious need to be soothed by others and at the same time, feels full of resentment and inferiority due to the lack of self-worth.

Alignment Process: I am coming to understand the *matter* as I align my mind, body and spirit, recognizing that "only 'hurting people' hurt others." And I see now that no one really meant to hurt me, neglect me or desert me. I am a lovable and worthy soul capable of taking back my sacred power as I go forth with restored *energy* able to live the life I was meant to live; creating more loving, nurturing and gentle experiences.

1-C. Perpetrator of Abuse/Neglect/Violence

What's the Matter: Abuse – Perpetrator of improper, excessive or severe emotional and psychological mistreatment; neglect; or acts of physical or sexual violence directed at a child, teen, spouse, partner or other adult that infringes on the person's human rights of personal safety and dignity, self worth, etc. (See Pedophilia for perpetrators of child sexual abuse and see Anti-Social Personality for perpetrators of adult rape, and other acts of violence outside of self-defense.)

Misaligned Thought or **Divine Intention:** The inherent understanding that one can be soothed. Yet, it is without understanding that one can soothe oneself into a place of well-being without punitive acts that only recreate the *matter*. As such, one has a faulty belief that one can avenge oneself in the present for the painstaking *matter* of the past through revenge and or punishment by attempting to make another feel as vulnerable and powerless as one felt or feels. There is no realization that the reenactment of abuse is coming from the same misaligned place as the perpetrator that violated him or her came from, when enacting the horrible mistreatment in the first place. Thus, in order to realign with one's own mind, body and spirit, one needs to abstain from any further punitive outpouring, shift one's *energy* to elevate one's vibration to a place of peace, and do the release work that promotes self-love and forgiveness (all of which steps are inherent within the remainder of the Sacretherapy® process.)

Alignment Process: I am coming to understand that only "hurting people," like me, hurt others; and that no one really meant to hurt me, neglect me or desert me. I am coming to understand that the only justice to be served is through embracing the certainty of my own self-worth as I come into alignment with my own mind, body and spirit. I go forth with the knowledge that I avenge myself in the present for the past through self-love and acts of compassion. And I ask for forgiveness, as I forgive myself and others.

2. Academic Problem

What's the Matter: Academic Problem – Underachievement despite adequate intellectual functioning, among other symptoms. (Also, see Learning or Intellectual Disabilities.)

Misaligned Thought or **Divine Intention:** The inherent understanding that one came into the physical realm with one's own divine intentions. And as such, one is often unwilling to be forced to comply with standard learning practices, or experiences boredom with the status quo within traditional organized educational institutions. This comes from a lack of understanding that institutions offering socially agreed upon academic curriculum may still contribute to one's journey of molding the *matter*, even when one did not participate in the initial creation of it; for it is by the stimulation of other creations that one, in turn, expands and uniquely creates one's own original creations. Therefore, one only needs to come into alignment with one's mind, body and spirit in order to elevate one's vibration to a frequency where one can appreciate co-creative perspectives.

Alignment Process: I came into the physical realm with my own *inner knowing* that allows me to decipher for myself the type of information that I want to pursue, to increase my sacred knowledge. At the same time, I am coming to understand that in order to be the creator I want to be, I expand and grow from diversity; for there are many subjects and many ways "to know." And so, even as I prefer to focus on that which I came forth to learn, I allow others to share with me other divine information that opens my awareness to the vast *matter* and creative process of life.

3. Acculturation Problem

What's the Matter: Acculturation Problem – Problem adjusting to a new environment or different culture, among other symptoms.

Misaligned Thought or **Divine Intention:** The inherent understanding that one is meant to be comfortable. This however, is mixed with the faulty belief that one cannot tolerate even temporary discomfort as a result of the *matter* being different. One does not like to embrace different ways of thinking or going about things that are done differently. And as a result one determines that differences are wrong or bad, and that one cannot shift one's *energy* and change or adapt, often due to fear of leaving one's comfort zone. One does not realize that the core of the *matter* is primarily due to conditioning, etc., which is causing the difficulty. (Next chapter discusses conditioning.)

Alignment Process: I am opening to the idea that "all is one" and that wherever I am the Creator is, and all is truly well. I embrace differences, whether they involve cultures or environments, as part of the wonderful variety of *matter* the universe has to offer. Therefore, with flexibility and amazement, I move freely throughout the world, prepared to broaden my perspective of the *matter* and how much more alike we are than different, as individualized expressions of the universal Source.

4. Acute Stress

What's the Matter: Acute Stress—Exposure to a traumatic event that causes anxiety and dissociative symptoms that show up within a month following the event.

Misaligned Thought or **Divine Intention:** The inherent understanding that life experience includes positive and negative *matter*. However, this awareness is mixed with the limited belief that the soul cannot bear all the contrasting experiences of life with all its pain and glory, especially the horrendously negative and traumatic. One does not recognize that the spirit can withstand it all, given an adjustment period to realign with one's natural state of well-being. If one would give up one's core beliefs that "the world is not safe" and "life is not fair," and replace them with broader soothing perspectives, one could then incorporate universal principles that describe how to integrate the undesirable *matter*. In this manner, one's *energy* blockages surrounding the sacred sutra could be released and neutralized.

Alignment Process: I move forward understanding that I have everything I need within me to withstand the diversity of *matter* in the world and bring forth what I prefer to manifest. I release old beliefs with the new understanding that "life is fair" and "the world is a safe place" as I align my mind, body and spirit to attract the harmonious life experiences that echo those divine sentiments.

5. ADD/ADHD

What's the Matter: ADD/ADHD—A persistent pattern of inattention or hyperactivity, due to an inability to ignore extemporaneous stimuli and focus on one thing at a time, for long periods of time.

Misaligned Thought *or Divine Intention:* The divine objective to not take anything in one's environment for granted, scoping the *matter* out, or at least noticing that it is there, as a part of the landscape of life. If this reaction is mixed with hyperactive *energy*, there is the added impulse to go beyond noticing to experiencing everything in the moment it is sensed, honoring its divine presence. This appreciation can be cultivated as one expands one's ability to attend to one *matter* at a time longer. This is done by purposely grounding oneself in an environment with limited stimuli. In this manner, one practices transferring one's ability to hone in on the finer details of life to the immediate task at hand.

Alignment Process: I enjoy going with the flow and noticing the smallest details that life has to offer. I love that I know how to focus on seizing the moment. I love taking it all in with my panoramic sensing. And so now, as I align my mind, body and spirit, I transfer my skill of honing in and breaking the *matter* down to smaller pieces, in an environment with fewer stimuli that is equally worthy of my attention.

6. Addictions (Alcohol, Drugs, Food, Caffeine, Gambling, Internet, Porn, etc.)

What's the Matter: Addictions—A dependence and compulsive need for a substance, activity, or something that is psychologically or physically habit-forming; often utilized to escape the realities of what is or has gone on in one's life during normal (wakeful) consciousness.

Misaligned Thought or **Divine Intention:** The sacred understanding that relief is, in fact, achievable. This awareness, however, is mixed with the limited belief that the *matter* cannot be soothed and remolded during normal consciousness. Therefore, the desire to align with one's mind, body and spirit is sought in an altered state, from something outside of oneself. This reflects a lack of understanding that one does not need to seek an altered state to regain connection with one's Source. All one has to do is be willing to shine a sacred light on the *matter* and not focus on the undesirable aspects of it; for it is one's fear of misalignment that makes the *matter* worse and postpones the *energy* shift needed to experience the relief one seeks.

Alignment Process: I am opening to the idea that my *inner knowing* has always been informing me that the relief I seek is available. I was right to reach for soothing, since life is supposed to feel good. And I now extract the same relaxation and gratification from an unaltered state; for it feels so good to know that I can achieve this sense of well-being and have what I want. By simply aligning my mind and body with spirit, I go forward, open to consciously connecting with my source, one day at a time, one moment at a time, until my heart's desires manifest.
(Note: Specifics on how to create the new *matter* is discussed in chapters 6 & 8.)

7. Adjustment (With Anxiety, Depressed mood or Conduct disturbance)

What's the Matter: Adjustment Problem – An expected or unexpected severe or excessive reaction to a stressor that is considered maladaptive and usually develops within three months of the onset of the stressor.

Misaligned Thought or **Divine Intention:** The inherent understanding that life is always calling one to a new vantage point. This however, is mixed with one's preference that the *matter* of life remain static and be void of unexpected changes. One's reaction, however, is the natural consequence of being creatures of habit, resistant to change. The adjustment one needs to make is therefore being offered as a reminder that the core of life really is an ever-expanding energetic phenomenon where one's outer circumstances are always changing. Therefore, all one need is to come into alignment with one's mind, body and spirit and one will gather the courage one needs to answer the call of life.

Alignment Process: I accept that I came forth for the ebb and flow of life. And gratefully embrace this sacred reminder that realigns me with the core of my being every time I inhale and exhale the breath of life. For I am, an adaptable creature, capable of shifting my *energy* in any direction the *matter* takes me as I align my mind, body and spirit. Therefore, I go forward, knowing that my well-being is sustained through motion, not stasis.

8. Adolescent Antisocial Behavior – (See Antisocial Personality.)

9. Agoraphobia (with or without panic)

What's the Matter: Agoraphobia—Anxiety about being in places or situations where escape or help may be difficult, and as a result may only feel safe at home; can occur with or without panic symptoms.

Misaligned Thought or **Divine Intention:** The inherent understanding that one should feel safe in the universe. However, this is mixed with the faulty belief that one is devoid of one's own emotional self-sufficiency; and that one's own inner knowing cannot be trusted to soothe oneself back into alignment when confronted with *matter* that reeks of uncertainty. One intrinsically senses that the security and certainty one seeks is at home; but one does not realize that true "refuge" comes from an assurance that the comfort of "home" is always with us, divinely located within. As such, one need only align one's mind, body and spirit to the vibration of well-being in order to experience the security one seeks.

Alignment Process: I am opening to the idea that the assurance I seek is within me, which comes from the certainty that there is a God-source within the universe to which I am connected. It is available to me at all times by elevating my vibration to a frequency where safe positive thoughts exist. Thus, I can trust this Source to inform and guide me "home" wherever I am; for wherever I am, the GOD-source is, and all is truly well.

10. Alcoholism—(See Addictions.)

11. Alzheimer's

What's the Matter: Alzheimer's—Degenerative memory loss that usually leads to dementia, confusion, mood swings, gradual loss of multiple body functions, and withdrawal from family; attributed to multiple etiologies.

Misaligned Thought *or Divine Intention:* The inherent desire to release the past and arrive at a new vantage point where one may begin again; trusting and relying on others to guide and protect as one seeks the new plateau; attempting to start fresh each day unencumbered with yesterday, or this morning, or even a minute ago. One is truly beginning to value and underline the precious present moment by commanding that attention be paid only to the here and now. Slowly withdrawing from loved ones with whom one shares sacred contracts while systematically forgetting and releasing everything. One demonstrates that the strength of one's relationships is not necessarily cumulative, but based on a moment by moment discovery of a new and sacred *matter* that connects us all.

Also, if one's presentation is mixed with moments of agitation, one's unconscious divine intent may be mixed with split *energy* to both stay and advance forward which causes an exacerbation in disorientation between two realms which triggers pain mediating hormones to be released that cause irritability and anger. One may be soothed by affirming that it is okay to continue re-acclimating oneself to subtler energies that balance the physical and nonphysical.

Alignment Process: I value how sensing my connection with the Source of the universe is a moment by moment endeavor. I came forth to remind myself and others to slow down and enjoy the wonder of life and grace in each moment. As such, I go forward with the yearning and expansion that comes from seeking a new horizon where I continue on as a "well being." I see my life as a magnification that I am more than my body and brain as I re-acclimate myself to subtler *energy* as a spiritual being connected to the God-source within.

Note: To loved ones with a family member with this reaction: You may read and ask the loved one to repeat the aligning process in their minds if they have reached the latter stages, for even at the last stages of this reaction their soul can still hear you. Also, for your comfort, there is a poem that is apropos if your loved one is no longer lucid that you can imagine them saying to you: "For I only have this minute, 60 seconds in it; how shall I spend it, for eternity is in it." (Author Unknown)

12. Amnesia

What's the Matter: Amnesia—Partial or full loss of memory to recall past experiences, events, and/or information; can be temporary or permanent.

Misaligned Thought *or Divine Intention:* The inherent understanding that one can begin again. Whether the condition is temporary or permanent, the *matter* can stem from a belief that a fresh start will wipe the slate clean. One's condition is fueled by a desire to start over, without transitioning, wanting to get it right. One gives oneself the luxury of forgetting one's mistakes and avoiding any feelings of self-reproach, while gracefully getting out of undesired experiences without the ridicule of others. However, one does not realize that at any moment one can consciously begin again and remold the *matter* by aligning one's mind, body and spirit, one moment at a time.

Alignment Process: I have everything I need within me to face any and everything that I have created in my life. I will remember whatever there is worth remembering and forget whatever need be forgotten. I recognize that I am divinely guided and with this knowledge, I embrace self-love and compassion for the life I have lived. Understanding that as I align my mind, body and spirit, I am always in the process of becoming.

13. Anorexia Nervosa—(See Eating Disorders/Reactions.)

14. Antisocial Personality (or Adolescent Antisocial Behavior)

What's the Matter: Antisocial Personality—A pervasive disregard for and violation of the rights, feelings, and safety of others, which in the most extreme form can also include crimes of violence and sexual assault, coupled with a lack of remorse. (Also, see Perpetrators of Abuse and/or Pedophiles for acts towards children.)

Misaligned Thought or **Divine Intention:**—The inherent understanding that the *matter* can be soothed. This awareness, however, is mixed with the faulty belief that vengeful acts are what will soothe the *matter* that caused one to feel disempowered, empty and disconnected from the source of one's being. One does not recognize that the vengeful act only offers relief in the fleeting moment, which is why repeated acts are often sought for continued relief that never can be sustaining. One does not understand that nothing outside of oneself can fill one's emptiness or fix what one's feels is broken other than the Creator of all the justice there will ever be. As such, when one's disconnection feels so far from the God-source within, it can seem difficult to realign.

When this is the case, medicinal remedies can often assist with soothing one back into alignment with one's mind, body and spirit. One can be enabled to take responsibility for these unaligned criminal acts in whatever way universal laws and civil laws deem necessary for the betterment of all concerned. This will be coupled with one's own thoughts that attract what the consequences will be with regard to redirection and rehabilitation (realignment). Then, regardless of where one does the realignment work (prison, institution or community), once realigned with one's own inner spirit, the relief one sought can be fully experienced. True justice is then served, and redemption will have been achieved.

Alignment Process: It feels good to now know that within me is the "well being" I seek. I am capable of compassion and the self-love that I thought was absent; for I, like all soul-filled beings, am connected to the Source of the universe and can realign with it, even if medicinal remedies are needed to facilitate this conscious reunion. I was right to seek relief, which means I inherently knew that I could be soothed and just needed a positive outlet. So I forgive myself for past unaligned acts and ask for forgiveness. Recognizing that there is no punishing Source in the universe, I go forward humbled and thankful for the grace that comes with the redemption of unconditional love.

15. Anxiety (Generalized Anxiety)

What's the Matter: Anxiety—The anticipation and intense worry, uneasiness, and apprehension of a future event that is being perceived as stressful. (Also, see Panic Disorder.)

Misaligned Thought or **Divine Intention:** The inherent understanding that well-being is available as demonstrated by one's constant search for assurance. However, this intrinsic understanding comes with split *energy*—mixed with the overwhelming discomfort with uncertainty. Thus, the *energy*-split is due to not understanding that the very assurance one seeks cannot be based on the insecurity that comes with "blind faith," where one just hopes that the *matter* will turn out well. Rather, the assurance must be based on universal principles that demonstrate that all truly is well when one comes into alignment with the fullness of one's being. When one does not understand how self-fulfilling prophecies and universal laws can shape one's life, apprehension of the "what ifs" surrounding the feared stimuli can keep one from moving on and creating the joyful life experiences one seeks. As such, the fearful trepidation is simply an indicator that what one is focusing on or obsessing about is incongruent with (doesn't match) what one truly prefers; and that what one prefers is actually achievable.

Alignment Process: I am coming to understand that the certainty that I am reaching for can only be accessed with my *inner knowing.* Therefore, I embrace this sacred passageway recognizing that it is the path that will deliver unto me the assurance I seek; that all is truly well. I now go forth creating my life, one courageous and purpose-filled moment at a time. Shifting my attention to that which is soothing and in sync with what I prefer, I recognize that within me is a divine and confident "well being."

16. Asperger's Syndrome

What's the Matter: Asperger's Syndrome—A developmental reaction characterized by limited social interaction, repetitive patterns of behavior and restricted interests. The Asperger's diagnosis was removed from some mental health manuals in 2013 and was added to the autism spectrum. I add it here to honor those previously diagnosed.

Note: In a society where many people dislike being alone and don't even enjoy their own company, most people are eager to socialize and share likenesses. Therefore, it may seem strange to people to observe others who actually like themselves and prefer their own company and find contentment in exclusive activities. Thus, what is being viewed as social impairment could also be viewed as emotional self-sufficiency.

Misaligned Thought *or Divine Intention:* The inherent understanding that one is an individualized expression of spirit. As such, souls who are born with this reaction are not conformist. Therefore, one chooses not to adapt to social cues or norms and may be attracted to restrictive or unorthodox stimuli. These souls may come forth to just relish in having manifested their spirit into physical *matter* and are simply satisfied with the idea of temporarily being human. Therefore, one's intention is to remain emotionally self sufficient. Preoccupied with one's own interest, one is not absorbed in worrying about what other people think of him or her; that is, unless society convinces one that honoring one's own divine intentions is maladaptive. Then, one may begin to dishonor one's differences. Thus, it is the error of putting people in the so-called "normative curve box" of comparison that can trigger any negative emotion surrounding this *matter*.

Alignment Process: I came in the physical world as an individualized expression of the God-source. As such, I enjoy the fact that I am content and can self-soothe easily with very few external interests. I magnify that I came to be a human being versus a human doing. I love that I do not have to conform to the typical social cues and expectations to be understood, be loved and be accepted. I can just be. In this manner, I am inadvertently teaching the world that there is more to the fullness of our beingness than conformity.

17. Autism

What's the Matter: Autism—A developmental reaction that is characterized by what is considered by some as impaired social interaction, repetitive patterns of behavior and restricted interests, usually viewed as the other end of the spectrum when compared to Asperger's (above).

Misaligned Thought *or Divine Intention:* The inherent understanding that one is an individualized expression of God. As such, souls who are born with this reaction are also not conformist. Therefore, one chooses not to adapt to social cues or norms and are often attracted to restrictive stimuli. Preoccupied with one's own interests, one is not usually absorbed in worrying about the *matter* of others or what other people think of one; that is unless society convinces one that honoring one's own divine intentions is maladaptive. Then, one may begin to dishonor one's differences.

Note: In a society where many people dislike being alone or don't even enjoy their own company, it may seem strange to observe others who actually like themselves and prefer their own company and find contentment in exclusive activities. Therefore, what is being viewed as social impairment could also be viewed as emotional self-sufficiency. As such, what we may be talking about here are simply degrees of how one chooses to embrace one's alignment.

Alignment Process: I like the "me" that I've come forth to be. I am uniquely divine and content with very few external interests. As such, I conform to my own internal cues expecting to be understood, be loved and be accepted.

Note: If one's reaction is regarded as severe, simply affirm: I like the "me" that I've come forth to be; for I am uniquely divine.

18. Avoidant Personality

What's the Matter: Avoidant Personality—Hypersensitivity to potential or actual rejection and criticism, which causes marked social inhibition.

***Misaligned Thought or* Divine Intention:** The inherent desire to do what is right. This is mixed however, with the faulty belief in a rigid "standard" upon which the rightness or wrongness of one's *matter* and worthiness is measured. This is usually based on rigid social norms that minimize positive differences and promote stereotypes that one rejects and feels one should not, or does not, live up to. Not understanding that while one wages a silent protest of non-participation through avoidance, one joins the establishment by looking outside of oneself for the very same validation and acceptance one fears and appalls. As such, one does not recognize that if one comes into alignment with one's mind, body and spirit, one will realize that the only standard one need measure oneself against is oneself; and the only acceptance one need seek is self-acceptance, which will come through elevating one's vibration to the frequency of self-love.

Alignment Process: I am coming to realize that I must first love myself, and then I will attract others that will love me the same. I do possess beauty, talents and gifts that I want to share with the world. I also recognize that I, like all others, am a unique being, with the humanity to offer compassion to myself, and others. And so, as I lighten up and reveal my individual differences, I realize that others will be doing the same.

19. Bereavement

What's the Matter: Bereavement—Temporary or mutated state of grief due to the transition (death) of a loved one: family, friend, or pet.

Misaligned Thought or **Divine Intention:** The inherent understanding that sacred agreements between two souls are eternal, as demonstrated by the ongoing love one feels for the transitioned soul. This however, is mixed with the faulty belief that one cannot go on with life happily without the comfort of the other soul that has been a significant part of one's physical journey. One does not recognize that all sacred connectedness exists on borrowed time in the physical realm and is otherwise multi-dimensional. As such, when one experiences a loved one's transitioning back to the God-source (without this understanding) one mistakenly resists mastering self-sufficiency—whether it be facing the fear of being alone, having to make decisions on one's own, financial acuity, how to create new meaning, or embrace and cultivate new life. As a result, one temporarily lacks the motivation to independently summon one's energies to create new *matter*. Grief, then, is elongated when one refuses to adapt and embrace the growth such major change offers. And as such, one need only align one's mind and body with spirit in order to elevate one's vibration to the frequency of the comfort and well-being one seeks.

Alignment Process: I am capable, competent and unafraid to go forward and do what I came forth to do as an individualized expression of God. I see now that only part of my physical experience was to be shared with my loved one who has fulfilled his or her sacred contract, and now I must fulfill mine. And so, I will carry with me the joy and strength that I gained from our sacred connection as I embrace the *matter* of this new and glorious day.

20. Bipolar I & II

What's the Matter: Bipolar I & II—Mood instability that can vacillate between periods of extremes from depression to hypomania to mania.

Misaligned Thought or **Divine Intention:** The inherent understanding that life is supposed to be joyous and that when it isn't life can be depressing. As such, one desires to demonstrate that life can be stretched to its edges beyond the confines of the mundane. However, one has mixed this intrinsic understanding that life is supposed to be happy, full of *energy* and joyful without regard for the middle way. And as such, "all or nothing" extremes create splits in *energy*. Because one is not appreciating that being "balanced" is where a more sustainable vibration of peace and joyful contentment is achieved. Thus, one need only embrace the understanding that peak experiences certainly fortify our existence but can burn up our energies if the burner is always left on high. (See: *Degrees of Alignment Scale*–Chapter Two.)

Alignment Process: I love my capacity to feel the ultimate exhilaration of the moment, as well as my ability to feel the opposite when pondering what a joyless life can bring. Yet, I am coming to understand that within my range of emotion is the middle way, which balances my *energy* with the yin and yang of life. And so, now I feel empowered to know that there are simply degrees of alignment with well-being; and that I am the one that gets to choose where I set my vibe which is an *energy*-based set point. As such, I gratefully integrate this awareness as I come back into alignment with my mind, body and spirit, one sacred and balanced moment at a time.

21. Body Dysmorphic

What's the Matter: Body Dysmorphic—Preoccupation with an imagined or minor physical defect that often causes people to see themselves as unattractive.

Misaligned Thought or **Divine Intention:** The inherent understanding that one's body temple was not meant to be used as one's focal point to "focus on" but rather to "focus through." However, one's focus is reversed and one has a faulty belief that one's value is based on one's physical aspect. This leads to an unrealistic desire for perfectionism and discomfort with the smaller foibles of human beingness. Not understanding that the *matter* of beauty in one's life includes imperfections; hence the expression, "beauty is skin deep." This means that the physical is such a thin layer of the deeper tissue of soulful beingness that it is almost irrelevant in comparison to the depth of one's inner beauty. Here, one looks at one's reflection but does not fully see. And as such, the *energy* split affecting one's perception of self-worth and value is as thin as the skin one is in. However, one only need come into alignment with one's mind, body and spirit in order to replace the shallow lens and reach the vibration where one is able to find the true beauty that exists in all things.

Alignment Process: I am coming to understand that I am more than my body temple, and that the beauty I seek that will bring me true contentment is within. I see that I have been looking with my physical eyes and need to expand my vision with my eye of the soul where the beauty in all things is magnified. As I deliberately look for the good, I continuously discover more and more aspects about the fullness of my being that I am coming to adore. Beginning with this new moment I can truly say that I do like my _____ (fill in the blank with something soulful), and my _____ (fill in the blank with something about your personality), and my _____ (fill in the blank with something with regard to your intelligence, skill, talent), and my_____ (fill in the blank with something physical). I am so grateful for this new awareness. (Note: you may change what you fill in the blanks as often as you like.)

22. Borderline Intellectual Functioning

What's the Matter: Borderline Intellectual Functioning—Intellectual functioning that is lower than average but not as low as what would be considered in the range of an intellectual disability.

Misaligned Thought or Divine Intention: The intrinsic understanding that one came into the physical realm already with a base of knowledge from one's *inner knowing.* One came forth challenging the *matter* on what it means "to know" and to communicate that "knowing." Understanding that life is full of differing degrees of aligning with "universal intelligence. As such, as one continues to align with one's mind, body and spirit, one is able to recognize that remaining connected to one's Source is the most important subject one needs to master.

Alignment Process: I came into the physical realm knowing that everything I need to know is within me. I trust that the "universal mind" to which I am connected will guide and nudge me to any other insights that I may need as I expand and evolve.

23. Borderline Personality

What's the Matter: Borderline Personality—A pattern of instability in interpersonal relationships, self-image and emotions marked by frantic efforts to avoid real or imagined abandonment, coupled with other symptoms that include extremes ranging from idolizing to devaluing others to inappropriate intense anger when wishes are thwarted, etc.

Misaligned Thought or Divine Intention: The inherent understanding that how one feels about oneself *matters.* However, this awareness is mixed with the faulty belief that one does not really *matter.* One therefore devalues one's own self-worth, and often feels invisible—thinking that one's value can't be seen. As a result, one looks outside of oneself for validation of one's existence. Not realizing that as one projects the deep insecurity, the desperate acts to connect with loved ones is what prevents the solid connection that one is seeking. This causes strong splits in *energy* from the superficial connection based on idolizing others when one's needs are being met, which shifts to despising rage (drama) when needs are not met. Consequently, one needs to understand that the security one seeks is not outside of oneself, but lies within. Thus, by coming into alignment one can elevate one's vibration to the frequency where one's relationship with the God-source in the universe offers the reliable connection one seeks, which is stable, never abandons and reflects one's true value.

Alignment Process: I am coming to recognize that the security and connection I seek can only come from the God-source within me. I find comfort in knowing that my self-concept rests on the fact that I am connected to the source of my being, and therefore I am already worthy. As I accept and embrace my worthiness more and more, I will also attract unto me the love, peace and fulfillment I seek, which mirrors my own. As such, my connection to others comes easily and effortlessly, drama-free, as I love and value myself.

24. Breathing Related Sleep Disorder (Reaction)—(See Sleep Reactions.)

25. Bulimia—(See Eating Reactions.)

26. Childhood Disintegrative Disorder (Reaction)

What's the Matter: Childhood Disintegrative Disorder—Condition in which children develop normally up to ages 2 through 4, and then experience significant loss of previously considered normal functioning in at least two areas: language, social skills, release control, play, motor skills or adaptive behavior.

Misaligned Thought *or Divine Intention:* The divine desire to demonstrate that one can maintain its connection with one's spiritual core without the need to continue fully developing all aspects of its body temple. Therefore, it is one's intention to deliberately experience how the true *energy* basis of connection with oneself, the Source of the universe, and others can commence without the typical body functions, social or adaptive behaviors. As such, one emphasizes that the core of one's being is more than the workings of one's physical apparatus. Therefore, one is not regressing but re-acclimating oneself to the purer positive *energy* from which it came.

Alignment Process: I love that I recognize that the typical developmental milestones expected for one's body temple were not necessary for my advent in the world. It was beginning to become too cumbersome, and so I have simply elected to stay closer to the vibration of spirit, which is my core. I have simply released that which I believe assists me in offering my greatest contribution to human beingness, which is to inform the world that I, along with others, consist mostly of *energy*; and I am quite pleased with who I am and what I came forward to do.

27. Chronic Motor or Vocal Tics

What's the Matter: Chronic Motor or Vocal Tics—The presence of either motor tics or vocal tics (not both) that are much less severe than Tourette's.

Misaligned Thought *or Divine Intention:* The divine objective to bring heightened awareness to the variety of ways the soul can communicate its beingness, with nonverbal self expression and nontraditional verbal offerings being used to emphasize the *matter* that the *energy* basis of our connection to one another is beyond traditional communication patterns. In so doing, one's soul is calling for broader acceptance of everyone's unique idiosyncrasies to be embraced without the need to label them as pathology.

Alignment Process: I am coming to realize how acceptable I really am. And this self-acceptance allows me to accept others who, like me, came forth with differences. I offer my magnified example of the fact that the connection with the God-source within is varied and expansive. I am proud of my willingness to overtly display my individual uniqueness, because it demonstrates the tremendous range of human beingness that there is and thereby can bring much relief to others in a sacred yet idiosyncratic world.

28. Circadian Rhythm Sleep Disorder (Reaction)—(See Sleep Reactions.)

29. Communication Disorders (Reactions)

What's the Matter: Communication (Reactions include Expressive Language, Stuttering, Phonological, Mixed Receptive-Expression, & Communication Not Otherwise Specified)—The presentation of an impairment in communication that is substantially below what is considered normative communication skills.

Misaligned Thought *or Divine Intention:* The sacred objective here is to communicate that our connection and ability to co-create with one another is not based on language; nor is it based on how fast or slow we express our sentiments, how we pronounce our words, or whether or not we can find the words at all. It is based, instead, on how we send and transfer our positive *energy* back and forth to one another. Thus, one is attempting to expose society's conditioned reliance on linguistics by calling attention to one's more subtle and refined non-verbal ability to speak telepathically to others without words and still accurately convey the *matter*.

Alignment Process: I am coming to appreciate the idea that I came forth with the divine intention to remind the world through my example that I can communicate with or without words. Whether I speak fast or slowly, I still get the sacred point across that I, like others, am an *energy* being. I am simply housed in this body temple for my spirit to enjoy the physical dimension, regardless of how I articulate my individual experience. And with this certainty, I share my truth.

30. Conduct Disorder (Reaction)

What's the Matter: Conduct Reaction—A persistent and repetitive pattern in which the social rules, rights or property of others are violated by adolescents and children.

Misaligned Thought or **Divine Intention:** The inherent understanding that one's true authority is within. However, this understanding is overly generalized by the faulty belief that one may enforce one's will and authority on others. As such, one acts without respect to another's person or property, due to one's belief that one's own freewill has been violated. The *matter* manifests as one's "acting out" of revenge that comes out of the belief that one is being squelched. One believes that one is not allowed to honor one's own internal desires, usually by well-meaning parents or other authorities. Not understanding that the confiscated power one temporarily finds in the "unruly" and unaligned moment of protest further exasperates one's disconnection to that inner voice that is calling from within. The freedom one seeks can still be acquired without mocking parental or social guidance, even if the adult figure that has authority over one is unaligned. This is done by demonstrating one's self-sufficiency and responsibility; and fostering the win/win negotiations, which facilitate positive co-creative decision making with one's authority figures.

The vibration of self-sufficiency and responsibility begins with trusting that if "something" within says you shouldn't do this or that, that you will interpret that guidance as *inner knowing* from your spirit. And then when you align with that inner source, you may begin practicing obtaining your desires through visualizing the *matter* within your imagination (a virtual reality). For within your mind, you are able to live out your freedoms in the simulated environment, where your thoughts and preferences are then manifested as mutual respect, summoning parental cooperation. All of this comes about as a result of honoring your own internal permissions, until you are economically able to live on your own.

Alignment Process: I now know that it is natural to want freedom and trust my own *inner knowing.* Yet, I am coming to understand that the freedom I seek comes with demonstrating responsibility and self-sufficiency. Until I am grown, I look forward to co-creative decision-making and negotiating with the well-meaning authority figures in my life. Even when the adults are unaligned at times, I realize that I can still enjoy the full extent of my freedoms in my virtual reality, since the realization of my desires begins with my positive thoughts.

31. Conversion (Reaction)

What's the Matter: Conversion (Reaction)—A condition in which psychological stressors are manifested or converted into physical/neurological symptoms with no apparent physical cause.

Misaligned Thought or **Divine Intention:** The inherent understanding of the mind and body connection. However, this *matter* is mixed with the belief that stressful events are too difficult to manage with ease. In the extreme, this belief can cause one to loose one's sensory perception or experience a reduction in movement. One does not understand that the mental stressor becomes converted into physical symptoms as a magnification of the idea that one has lost one's senses; and therefore movement has become stuck due to one's rigid inability to get beyond the undesired *matter.* The fact that no biological explanation can account for the cause of the *matter* further emphasizes that the greater conflict is intertwined with the psyche and needs to be resolved at the level of thought, since all creation begins with a thought.

Alignment Process: I am coming to realize that my thoughts are powerful creators, and that everything I need to handle any *matter* is within me. I am willing to develop sacred muscles that strengthen my desire to come back into alignment with my mind, body and spirit. I now remember that I came into this physical dimension intending to remain a joyous "well being," and I now reclaim, with full sensory perception, that sacred birthright.

32 Corprophilia—(See Paraphilias C.)

33. Culture Bound Syndromes aka Cultural Concepts of Distress—(See Below for the *Worldwide Culture Syndromes* starting at the end of the *North American Diagnoses* and begin with diagnosis #143. Note: worldwide cultural syndromes are also listed alphabetically.)

34. Cyclothymic (Reaction)

What's the Matter: Cyclothymic (Reaction)—A recurrent mood instability where moods alternate between a milder version of hypomania and mild depression.

Misaligned Thought or **Divine Intention:** The divine awareness that one came into the physical realm for the joy of living. This understanding however, is mixed with an unconscious belief that a contented life cannot be maintained and is, therefore, a *matter* filled with perpetual ups and downs. But, one need only understand that alignment with one's mind, body and spirit is a sacred moment by moment process. Without that understanding, the split in *energy* causes one to fluctuate in the resolve to find a balance. Likened to the more intensified extreme poles, one finds it agonizing when life is supposed to be joyful but becomes uninspiring and listless. One, therefore, need only realize that a more sustainable peace and contentment is achievable by finding the divinity contained within the middle way. (Balance is discussed in chapters six and nine.)

Alignment Process: I love my capacity to feel the exhilaration of happy moments as well as the agony the thought of a joyless life can bring. Yet, I am now coming to understand that within my range of emotion is the middle way. I feel empowered to know that there are simply degrees of alignment with well-being, and that I am the one that gets to choose my vibe, which is a sacred *energy*-based set point. I gratefully integrate this awareness as I align my mind, body and spirit, one balanced moment at a time.

35. Delirium

What's the Matter: Delirium—Disturbance of consciousness, disoriented, with reduced ability to communicate logically, focus, and sustain or shift attention.

Misaligned Thought or **Divine Intention:** The inherent understanding that there is a continuum of consciousness. However, this awareness is mixed with a contradicting belief that there is separation between physical and nonphysical consciousness. As such, when one's *matter* is unaligned, there is a temporary withdrawal of conscious awareness with regard to one's in-the-moment physical reality as one seeks to interact with the spiritual realm. As a result, one does not understand that by remaining ever conscious of one's alignment with mind, body and spirit, there would always be a sense of ease with regards to the *matter* when navigating between the multi-dimensional layers of consciousness.

Alignment Process: I appreciate the fact that I am both physically and spiritually focused. I am beginning to learn how to embrace the duality, which is apparent when I am attempting to orient the physical part of me by using my physical senses in the spiritual realm. I now know that it is a temporary adaptation, and so I can trust my sixth sense to bring me back into alignment with all that I am.

36. Delusional

What's the Matter: Delusional (Reaction)—The presentation of one or more non-bizarre delusions (probable real life situations) that persist for at least one month in a person that has never been diagnosed with a psychotic illness, and/or not the result of a substance, medication or medical condition.

Misaligned Thought or **Divine Intention:** The inherent understanding that there are many probable realities being conjured at the level of thought. And so, one is hoping that by a "retreat to" or "escape from" the *matter* of one's current reality, that one can be soothed by the creation of another. One does not understand that wanting things in one's life to cease, change or evolve to a new level of status or prominence is a natural desire that can be realized without it remaining at the level of thought (in one's imagination). Therefore, all one needs to do to resolve the split *energy* and view or mold the *matter* from a new vantage point is to come into alignment with the fullness of one's being—where all possibilities can manifest based on the law of creation.

Alignment Process: I love knowing that a different reality that is more to my liking can be had. I also love knowing that I have already been perfecting the skills of how to create new life within my imagination, which can be viewed as a "virtual reality" since every creation begins with a thought and strong desire. And so, I go forward ready to begin creating for myself the life I believe I deserve, as I patiently mold my "thoughts" into the manifestations I desire. (Step Six covers how to create new life.)

37. Dementia

What's the Matter: Dementia—Loss of intellectual capacity including memory impairment that can lead to withdrawal from family; often due to physiological effects, a general medical condition, and/or multiple etiologies.

Misaligned Thought *or Divine Intention:* The inherent desire to release the past and arrive at a new vantage point where one may begin again; trusting and relying on others to guide and protect as one seeks the new plateau; attempting to start fresh each day unencumbered with yesterday, or this morning, or even a minute ago. One truly values and underlines the precious present moment by commanding that attention be paid only to the here and now. Slowly withdrawing from loved ones with whom one shares sacred contracts while systematically forgetting and releasing everything.

One demonstrates that the strength of one's relationships is not necessarily cumulative, but based on a moment by moment discovery of a new and sacred *matter* that connects us all. Also, note that if one's presentation is mixed with moments of agitation, one's unconscious divine intent may be mixed with split *energy* to both stay and advance forward. This causes an exacerbation in disorientation between two realms, which triggers pain mediating hormones to be released that cause irritability and anger. One may be soothed by affirming that it is okay to continue re-acclimating oneself to subtler energies that balance the physical and nonphysical.

Alignment Process: I value how sensing my connection with the Source of the universe is a moment by moment endeavor. I came forth to remind myself and others to slow down and enjoy the wonder of life and grace in each moment. As such, I go forward with the yearning and expansion that comes from seeking a new horizon where I continue on as a "well being." I see my life as a magnification that I am more than my body and brain as I re-acclimate myself to subtler *energy* as a spiritual being connected to the God-source within.

38. Dependent Personality

What's the Matter: Dependent Personality—A pervasive and excessive need to be taken care of or depend upon others that leads to fears of separation and other symptoms.

Misaligned Thought or **Divine Intention:** The inherent understanding that all of the needs one has will be met. However, this awareness is mistakenly generalized to the God-source within others as opposed to the God-source within oneself. As such, one believes that others are more competent to handle one's *matter* and provide for one's needs. This is coupled with the unaligned fear that tapping into one's own inner power may lead to independence, which is falsely equated with aloneness. As a result, one does not understand that coming into alignment with one's own mind, body and spirit is what the proverbial "call and response" of self-sufficiency commands. Likewise, one only need to be fortified in order to answer the call, by understanding that one is never truly alone because the security one seeks comes from the God-source within.

Alignment Process: I now understand that I have the same inner resources that I have been leaning on in others. I now look forward to coming into alignment with my own self-sufficiency, which commands that many choices with regards to my well-being be made by me for my self-sake. For I now recognize that these internal nudges are sacred indicators of my awareness and desire to trust my own *inner knowing.* A knowing that I have come to realize is the God-source within that informs all decisions. Therefore, I go forward taking small steps each day that honor and demonstrate this divine understanding.

39. Depersonalization

What's the Matter: Depersonalization (reaction)—The persistent or recurrent experience of feeling detached from or outside of oneself, observing one's body or mental processes, but one's ability to distinguish what is physical reality from nonphysical reality remains in tact.

Misaligned Thought *or Divine Intention:* The awareness and unconscious desire to know that one is more than just one's body-temple. This is sometimes magnified when major distress is such that the spirit shifts its focus from the physical *matter* temporarily, offering one a broader subtle perspective. This can cause one to question the experience and probe whether one is merely an "observer" using one's body to fulfill divine intentions, or more. This is evidenced by one translating the experience as multidimensional—to the degree that one's understanding of consciousness is expanded, causing one to be dually aware of both physical and nonphysical realities that they know cannot be explained away as pathology.

Alignment Process: I now recognize and honor the fullness of my being, having deliberately experienced depersonalizing the personality part of me. I accept and appreciate that I came into the physical with the intention to remain aware of the nonphysical aspects of my beingness. I now see this capacity as a gift in that I no longer need wonder about the mind, body and spirit connection. I return my attention back to the joy of living, now that I am more certain that I am a spiritual being having a physical experience. And for this, I am so grateful.

40-A. Depression—(See 40-B Depression with only Seasonal Patterns; for Dysthymia, Post Partum Depression, or Depressive Personality, see below.)

What's the Matter: Depression—A period of extreme unhappiness, despair, hopelessness, lack of interest, lack of *energy*, fatigue, disturbance with sleep, and other symptoms.

***Misaligned Thought* or Divine Intention:** The inherent understanding that one came into the physical realm for the joy of living. However, due to the *matter* in one's life not reflecting one's *inner knowing*, one mistakenly believes that one is unable to live the life that one was meant to live. As such, life does feel sad or gloomy, since one understands that life is supposed to feel good and be filled with one's heart's desires most of the time. But, one does not understand that what keeps one from feeling better and achieving what one wants is the persistent recall of the negative *matter*. As one refuses to release the pain, and instead uses it to rationalize one's unhappiness, it becomes a self-fulfilling prophecy to which universal laws respond. Yet, all one need do is accept that alignment with one's mind, body and spirit is a moment-by-moment process and understand that there are degrees of alignment connecting one to the well-being one seeks. Once this is understood, one can then begin to move to a new vibrational set-point where the joyous matter one seeks can manifest. (See: Degrees of alignment on Alignment Scale in previous chapter.)

Alignment Process.—I am opening to the idea that where I choose to focus my attention is my choice, even when it doesn't feel like it is. I get to choose whether "the cup is half empty or half full." I feel empowered to know that I can incrementally shift my *energy* to greater peace of mind, since there are degrees of alignment with my mind, body and spirit. I am so grateful for this awareness.

40-B. Depression with Seasonal Patterns (formerly known as Seasonal Affective Disorder (SAD reactions)

What's the Matter: Depression with Seasonal Patterns—Seasonal periods of depression that usually beginning in fall or winter, subsiding in spring. (This reaction was used in the instructions as the sample for this chapter but restated here as an official part of the alphabetical listings of mental and emotional reactions.)

***Misaligned Thought* or Divine Intention:** The inherent understanding of the cycles of life. However, this awareness is muddled with the inaccurate belief that one's sunny disposition and mood are determined by an extra sensitivity toward solstices and equinox that are connected with the seasons. This comes about when one forgets that "for everything there is a season and a time," and as such, one's propensity towards the light is simply an outer representation of the call from the "inner light" that is brilliantly magnified day in and day out, all year long regardless of the outer season. Therefore, the only thing preventing one from a stable sense of well-being is a self-fulfilling prophecy that every fall or winter season one's *energy* will digress as one recalls the negative *matter*. Yet, if one would remember that alignment with one's mind, body and spirit is a year-round moment-by-moment process, then one could learn to move to a new vibrational set point where one is able to always shed "light" on the *matter*.

Alignment Process: I am opening to the idea that the "full spectrum light" that I am seeking is within me. I am the one that determines whether the *matter* of life feels like a cold grey winter or a fresh spring beginning. As such, I feel brighter just knowing that as I align my mind, body and spirit, I can shift my *energy* to a place of greater peace of mind and joyful well-being. And for this "ray of hope" and healing light, I expect a sunshiny day!

41. Depressive Personality

What's the Matter: Depressive Personality—A pervasive pattern of having a gloomy, pessimistic, critical outlook towards self and others, along with other symptoms. Carrying a similar *energy* basis as Dysthymia, except duration of Dysthymia is shorter.

Misaligned Thought or **Divine Intention:** The inherent understanding that one came into the physical for a joy-filled life. This understanding is altered or misaligned when the *matter* in one's life doesn't reflect that knowing and one develops the unaligned belief that life is no longer worth getting excited about— as a defense to protect oneself from any further emotional let-downs. At that point, one adopts a pessimistic lackluster persona filled with low self-esteem due to having attached a negative interpretation to aspects of one's physical journey thus far. One thereby generalizes the experience to the future. As such, it is the entrapment of one's interpretation that prevents one from pursuing new joy, since one's negative take on the *matter* is what reinforces a deeper allegiance to negativism. One does not understand that the joyous life one once thought was possible is still achievable if one would come into alignment with one's own mind, body and spirit. Realignment would restore one's enthusiasm in knowing that the more satisfying existence one seeks is found by having faith in the God-source within; not by putting one's faith outside of oneself and in others that sometimes disappoint. Others are simply attempting to come into alignment with their own desires, as well. The path to fulfillment is the more optimistic mood adjuster found within.

Alignment Process: I am opening up to the idea that I was right when I once believed that a more satisfying life experience was possible. I see now that I must look inside myself for the fulfillment I seek and not look to others that are reaching for the same. I like knowing that by aligning with my own mind, body and spirit, the enthusiasm that I once had will return and yield me positive outcomes. I now go forward with confidence to hope, dream and create the joyful life experiences that I came forth to live.

42. Developmental Coordination (Reaction)

What's the Matter: Developmental Coordination (Reaction)—A marked impairment in development of motor coordination that interferes with academic achievement or activities of daily living, i.e., sports, shoe-tying, handwriting, holding onto things, along with other symptoms.

Misaligned Thought *or Divine Intention:* The divine understanding that one is more than one's body temple and that everything that one attempts to do or achieve from the simple to the complex is done through universal coordination. And as such, one comes forth with the divine objective of demonstrating this premise to oneself and the world. Through the magnification of motor coordination, one models that it is okay to take our time and evolve slowly through life—and discover that we are still worthy to be loved, enjoy life and make our mark, even when we leave some knots untied, fumble, and end up dropping things that only seem important at the moment. One demonstrates that it is also okay to draw outside the lines and not have to put everything in writing, but rather communicate and connect with other souls through simplicity. One models that we can't get it wrong with the Source of the universe in the midst of all coordination.

Alignment Process: I honor the fact that like everyone else, I came into the physical realm with specific desires. I love trusting that the coordination that I seek is handled by the God-source in the universe. And with that knowledge, I fully intend to accomplish whatever else it is that I came forth to do with divine orchestration.

43. Dissociative Amnesia

What's the Matter: Dissociative Amnesia—Inability to recall important personal information of a stressful or traumatic nature that is too extensive to be explained by ordinary forgetfulness.

Misaligned Thought or **Divine Intention:** The belief and divine understanding of resiliency. This awareness is mixed with a contradicting belief that intense unwanted experiences cannot be integrated consciously and must therefore be integrated unconsciously. However, one's contrasting understanding of the *matter* still does not diminish the fact that holding onto yesterday's unpleasantries interferes with today's energetic potential to experience joy in the precious present moment. One is attempting to come back into alignment with one's well-being by choosing to forget the *matter* so that one can make a fresh start and choose again. Yet, one need only align one's mind and body with spirit in order to look at the *matter* from a higher vibrational perspective where one is always free to begin again.

Alignment Process: I love knowing that I can remember whatever is worth remembering and forget whatever I choose to forget by consciously focusing my attention on the desired *matter*. I also love knowing that I have expanded beyond the parts of my life that have already been lived; and I am finding new joyous contentment in the precious "now" and sacred possibility of tomorrow.

44. Dissociative Fugue

What's the Matter: Dissociative Fugue—An unexpected altering of consciousness, where sudden travel away from home or work is accompanied by an inability to recall one's past. This may be coupled with confusion about one's personal identity or suddenly assuming a new identity, usually triggered by a major stressor.

Misaligned Thought *or Divine Intention:* The unconscious understanding that in order to create new life, one must release the *matter* of the past. This is fortified with the inherent knowing that wherever one goes, one is safe within the universe. Therefore, one expects to attract only those souls on the planet that will honor one's highest good, and lead one back to a safe harbor with loved ones. In the meantime, the soul may temporarily carry on under a new identity, free to embrace and mold new *matter*.

Alignment Process: I am free to choose the life I want to live and change course midway, at any given point in my life, and to do so with all of my physical faculties. I understand that I can change the entire circumstances in my life by simply focusing on only that which I desire and leave the past behind. I love knowing that the world is safe, and that I am free to roam the universe and recreate how I see myself gradually or in a holy instant.

45. Dissociative Identity Disorder (Reaction)

What's the Matter: Dissociative Identity (Reaction – formerly Multiple Personality Disorder) – The presence of two or more distinct identities or personality states; identity fragmentation rather than separate personalities.

Misaligned Thought *or Divine Intention:* The divine understanding that there are many aspects to one's soul that come forth striving to make themselves known. One's sacred objective is to cast a light on the faulty belief that there is only one way of "being" that is classified as normal. One knows that the diversity of life experience clearly illustrates that the *matter* of life expands beyond the normative curve. Thus, one asks of oneself and the world that the idea of "acceptable or unacceptable beingness" be re-examined as one realigns with one's mind, body and spirit seeking to fully integrate one's multifaceted, multidimensional, "blended being."

Alignment Process: I am a blended being with both dominant and passive aspects that emerge as a result of the fluctuation I experience based on my alignment with my mind, body and spirit. As such, I applaud my courage to allow aspects of all that I am to come forth at different times. I am free to embrace the parts that I like and dislike without self-reproach or denial, and I choose to love and accept the fullness of my being with unconditional love.

46. Domestic Violence—(See Intimate Partner Abuse 1b above.)

47. Dysthymia

What's the Matter: Dysthymia—A less severe form of depression, with low, dark moods that occur nearly every day for two years or more. Carries a similar *energy* basis as Depressive Personality reaction, except duration of Depressive Personality is longer.

Misaligned Thought or **Divine Intention:** The sacred understanding that one came into the physical realm to live a joy-filled life. As such, when one's *matter* does not reflect one's *inner knowing*, one develops the belief that life is no longer worth getting excited about. This is mainly a defense mechanism to protect oneself from any further emotional let-downs; and, therefore, an *energy* block is created and manifests as a low-grade depression. This lackluster persona is mainly due to having attached a negative interpretation to previous aspects of one's physical journey and generalizing the past to the future. It is the entrapment of one's interpretation that prevents one from pursuing new joy, since one's negative take on the *matter* is what reinforces a deeper allegiance to negativism. One does not understand that the joyous life one once thought was possible is still achievable if one would come into alignment with one's own mind, body and spirit. Realignment, then, would restore one's enthusiasm as one accepts that the more satisfying existence one seeks is found by having faith in the God-source within, not by putting one's faith outside of oneself and in others who sometimes disappoint. As such, one understands that the others are simply attempting to come into alignment with their own desires as well. Therefore, the true path to sustained fulfillment is the more optimistic mood adjuster found within.

Alignment Process: I am opening up to the idea that a more satisfying life experience is possible. I see now that I must look inside myself for the fulfillment I seek versus looking to others that are reaching for the same. I like knowing that by aligning with my own mind, body and spirit, the enthusiasm that I once had will return and yield me positive outcomes. I now go forward with confidence, to hope, dream and create the joyful life experiences that I came forth to live.

48. Eating Reactions (Anorexia, Bulimia, Binge Eating, Obesity, Avoidant/ Restrictive Food Intake)

What's the Matter: Eating Reaction—Disturbances in weight and eating behavior from refusal to maintain normal body weight to binge eating, to forced vomiting, to overeating.

NOTE: Obesity has not traditionally been included amongst the eating disorders, but rather viewed as a medical condition. However, I have added it because I believe that in addition to being medically induced, it can also be a reaction where one attempts to self-medicate with food. As noted, I distinguish a reaction from the term "disorder" and, therefore, also do not see obesity as a mental disorder but rather an emotional reaction for only those using food to self-medicate. Those who are not using food to self-medicate may very well have come forth into the physical realm choosing their larger body type as it relates to the diversity of body-temples, just as those who may have selected to be naturally thin. Otherwise, when food is being used to self-soothe, I believe that obesity, like all eating reactions are the result of interplay between spiritual, individual, environmental and sociological factors including familial modeling. It's a *matter* of being in alignment with health.

Misaligned Thought or **Divine Intention:** The inherent understanding that one is supposed to be fulfilled. However, when one uses food to fill or self-medicate, one's *energy* is split due to an unconscious belief in strain that competes with the desire for relief and fulfillment. Straining the physical apparatus to its limits by 'over-filling, emptying or starving' the body temple in an attempt to relieve and assuage one's fear of being weighted down with the responsibility to manage one's own emotional well-being and ask for what one truly hungers for (desires). One distracts oneself by overly nourishing others, which adds to the strain. One does not understand that a "well being" finds relief through ease, not strain or the ability to restrain from eating or "swallowing junk" from others. One needs to understand that the true fulfillment one seeks is not a physical *matter* but spiritual; and, therefore, fulfillment is achieved "ease-z-est" when one aligns one's mind, body and spirit with the God-source within, where true nourishment and gratification is "digested" holy (wholly or fully).

Alignment Process: I go forward with the new understanding that I am more than my body temple; for it is only the temporary housing of my spirit, which is weightless. I can therefore relax now, as I embrace the reflection of my flesh with self-acceptance, trusting that the skin I'm in is divine, wonderful and holy. I also understand that I am an emotionally self-sufficient being, capable of soothing myself with the "ease" that true fulfillment brings as I align my mind and body with spirit. Therefore, I prepare to whet my appetite for a spirit-filled sustenance that assures me that I can have whatever my heart hungers for.

49. Elimination Disorders (Reactions)

What's the Matter: Elimination (Reactions); (Encopresis and Enuresis)—Repeated voiding of urine during day or night in bed or clothes, or repeated passage of feces in inappropriate places whether involuntary or intentional for at least three consecutive months.

Misaligned Thought or **Divine Intention:** The inherent understanding of the soul's sacred ability to digest and release. This awareness, however, is often mixed with the conflicting belief that some *matter* in life is too overpowering to contain. As such, the feeling of being overwhelmed, overly controlled or frightened is often demonstrated in one or two ways:

1. Sometimes, when the reaction is a child's fright, the misaligned thought may be connected to the 'fear of the dark' due to his or her sensitivity to the duality of the physical and nonphysical realms where one may be able to see or sense harmless *energy* that he or she may mistake as the boogey-man. If this is the case, the elimination issue is to eliminate the dark (fearful vibe) and to be brought back into the light (a higher vibration). This can be achieved by placing numerous night lights that light the path to the bathroom which helps to ground the child, as are temporary receptacles that can be placed within the child's room, until the child is reassured that the light of God surrounds them and is within them, and therefore they are safe.

2. Sometimes, however, if one believes that it is a person that is the cause of his or her fear or overwhelment, then the elimination issues may symbolize one's desire to eliminate stress via an unconscious wish for the object of one's fear or overwhelment to "piss off" (enuresis) or "cut the crap" (encopresis). Likewise, inadvertently one demonstrates that there is never an opportune time or place to "waste" one's power. As such, all one needs is to understand that by aligning one's *energy*: mind, body and spirit that one can be taught how to be less affected by other souls outside of oneself, without making a mess.

Alignment Process: I am happy to know that my inner-light gives me the power to contain and soothe myself. I selectively choose the perfect place and time to eliminate all undesirable waste. And so, I hold onto what makes me feel good about myself and let go of other people's stuff (mess).

Note: If under age 6, affirm: My inner-light gives me the power to love and contain myself and eliminate others opinions.

50. Emotional/Verbal Abuse—(See Abuse.)

51. Exhibitionism—(See Paraphilias A.)

52. Feeding (Reactions) of Infancy or Childhood

What's the Matter: Feeding Reactions (Pica and Rumination)—Persistent feeding and eating reactions: a) Pica—involves eating non-nutritional substances on a persistent basis such as paint, plaster, string, hair, cloth, sand, etc., often associated with cognitive impairment and pervasive developmental disorder; b) Rumination—involves regurgitating, re-chewing and re-swallowing food.

Misaligned Thought or **Divine Intention:** The inherent understanding that one's true sustenance and nurture comes from within. However, due to one's environment, one develops the belief that others cannot be trusted to provide the nurture one needs. And as such, one's *inner knowing* is taken out of context where the emotional nurturing one seeks is mixed with the literal sustenance one needs, and is therefore minimized. One then believes that both nurture and sustenance must come from within; and, therefore, one begins to reject nourishment that can be extracted from food. Thereby, anything goes.

However, the method chosen to obtain one's sustenance can damage the body temple, which counters the initial sustenance or nurture found in it. This is the same case with the *matter* of digesting food, or the symbolism of regurgitating and re-chewing the slices of life that have already been lived. Both are counter to nurture and ultimately life-sapping. All one need do to benefit from both the internal and external forms of nurture and sustenance is to realign with the fullness of one's being, mind, body and spirit. Then one will be truly fulfilled.

Alignment Process: I am coming into alignment with the idea that the sustenance and nurture that I was reaching for are both literal and spiritual. And so, I love knowing that I can trust other souls to assist me in fulfilling my basic human needs. Therefore, I go forward fully digesting the "bread of life" that is meant to sustain my body temple. I allow my spiritual aspects to reinforce that I am loved and loveable and worthy of nurture.

If under age 6, affirm: I love knowing I can trust others to assist me with my needs.

Note: Caregivers may read the fuller aligning process to infants and children. They may also tape the process to soft music and place it on "repeat" at night for them to hear while sleeping. The child may pick up the message subliminally.

53. Fetishism—(See Paraphilias C.)

54. Fictitious Disorder (Reaction)

What's the Matter: Fictitious Reaction—Deliberate fabrication of mental or physical symptoms for the sheer psychological purpose of wanting to assume a sick role with no environmental incentives.

Misaligned Thought or **Divine Intention:** The inherent understanding that the universe provides. However, this awareness of the *matter* is mixed with the faulty belief that this assurance only applies to those in peril. As such, one believes that one's needs, will be met better if one is sick or blatantly needs support. This is further complicated by the fear that when one demonstrates healthy well-being, there will be no one to lean on because self-sufficiency is the logical expectation. But as one comes into alignment with one's mind, body and spirit one would understand that taking total responsibility for one's own needs does not come without support from others or the ability to lean on the God-source within.

Alignment Process: I am coming to appreciate the fact that I came into the physical realm as a well being, competent and capable of standing in my own power. I also love knowing that the divinity within me isn't feigned but is a genuine and authentic wellness, tied into the majesty and strength of the Creator. I go forth eager to demonstrate my well-being and vigor for life.

55. Frotteurism—(See Paraphilias A.)

56. Gender Dysphoria—(See Gender Identity.)

57. Gender Identity Issue (GID or GD)

What's the Matter: GID or GD—Reactions in which a person feels that either the genitalia of their bodies feels wrong and different from how they see themselves or they feel uncomfortable with the aspects of gender that society assigns them. However, both cases share the same *energy* basis of feeling there's a mismatch.

Misaligned Thought *or Divine Intention:* The innate understanding that at the core of one's being is spirit. One knows that neither gender nor genitalia determines one's connection, value or prescribed journey. As such, even when one comes forth in a specific gender, one can choose to embrace and experience the *energy* of the other. What a master demonstration of faith and constancy it is to allow oneself and others to witness the un-impenetrable core of the *matter*, which is our *energy* being! One is showing that even if one transforms the outer physical layer, one does so without affecting the nonphysical layer. One stands firm to behold that "I Am that I Am," even when one of the most socially misunderstood life choices puts it to the test.

Alignment Process: I came into the physical realm knowing that "I am that I am of I AM!" I love the fact that this is so, whether others can or cannot embrace and join me in this certainty. It is clear to me that the God-source in the universe loves me unconditionally and is the granter of all desires; for this Source tells me to: *Knock and the door shall open.* As such, I honor my desire to knock open barriers and demonstrate that the core of our being is unaffected by the physical apparatus. I am a divine, moldable and transformative being; and for this sacred awareness, I am grateful.

58. Generalized Anxiety – See Anxiety.)

59. Histrionic Personality

What's the Matter: Histrionic Personality—Pervasive and excessive attention-seeking behavior, often provocative or seductive, along with other symptoms.

Misaligned Thought or **Divine Intention:** The inherent understanding that one came into the physical realm with divine importance. However, one misinterprets the *matter*; and, therefore, a faulty belief emerges where one thinks one must be the center of attention in order to convey one's worth. This causes one to implement an ineffective strategy to feel one's value, and receive the admiration and loving support one seeks. One does not understand that validation of one's attractiveness and worth from others is not how one receives what one desires. As such, one only needs to come into alignment with the fullness of one's being where a broader perspective of the *matter* and understanding of universal principles exists. Then one would appreciate that it is our "thoughts" that are *attractive*, in that they attract and bring to us those things that match our inner beauty where the cosmetic layers of personality are removed and the authentic self that is *spirit*, is fully exposed.

Alignment Process: I am thrilled to know that within my body temple is a beautiful and divine magnetic sensor that attracts to me a mirroring image of the self-worth and inner beauty I feel. As I align my mind, body and spirit, I see now that I can genuinely summon from the universe the love and admiration I prefer; for it is simply a reflection of my connection to the God-source within. As such, this sacred alignment is now the *center* of my attention.

60. Hoarding – Also See Obsessive Compulsive Reactions.)

What's the Matter: Hoarding—A compulsive and excessive gathering or collection of items along with the extreme difficulty or unwillingness to discard them. Often leads to significant emotional distress, the reduction of living space and may create an unsafe environment.

Misaligned Thought or **Divine Intention:** The inherent understanding that abundance is achievable. However, this is mixed with the faulty belief that well-being is a fleeting thing. This causes tremendous discomfort with uncertainty. As a result, one gathers as much as one can, not realizing that the *energy* of hoarding blocks the very well-being one seeks. One does not understand that it is the obsessive thought or *compulsion to acquire* and *fear of letting go* that keeps one out of alignment; for the *matter* manifests because of the *energy* one is investing in it. Therefore, by coming back into alignment with one's mind, body and spirit, one would recognize the abundance and security one seeks is assured. One would know that one always has a choice of where to focus one's thought, even when it doesn't feel like it. One simply need be willing to shift one's attention gradually to the more comforting thoughts that affirm well-being.

Alignment Process: I am opening to the idea that I came into the physical realm with unlimited resources. I see now that the assurance and security I seek is within, which tells me that I can now choose thoughts that affirm that "well-being" abounds. I joyfully let go and release the *matter* back into the universe. I understand that abundance is meant to flow in and out of my experience. As I align my mind, body and spirit, I go forward with complete trust that all of my needs and desires have been gathered for me by the God-source in the universe.

61. Hypochondrias

What's the Matter: Hypochondrias—Preoccupation with fears of having a serious illness, despite medical evaluation and reassurance that nothing is wrong.

Misaligned Thought or **Divine Intention:** The inherent understanding that one came into the physical to fulfill one's desires and that those desires can, in fact, be filled. However, one's awareness is mixed with the faulty belief that there is a time limit or an expiration date on the *matter.* Therefore, one is fearful that time will run out before one has achieved the goals one became physically focused to experience. One does not understand that it's the wasted time spent on worrying about one's physical apparatus that is the only thing stopping or squelching one from living the wellness that has already been achieved and is continually being sought. All one need do is to come back into alignment with the fullness of one's being in order to experience the true source of one's well-being.

Alignment Process: I have all the time that I need to get done what must be done by me. As I continue to align my mind, body and spirit, I trust that as long as I remain at ease, I will continue to manifest the "well being" that I came into the physical to be.

62. Identity Problem – (See GID—if identity issue is due to sexual orientation.)

What's the Matter: Identity Problem—Uncertainty about who one is—one's beliefs, values, goals, etc.; usually begins in late adolescence.

Misaligned Thought or **Divine Intention:** The inherent understanding that one came forth with one's own sacred intentions. However, this divine awareness is mixed with the faulty belief that one must conform or be given permission to embrace certain aspects of oneself. This, thereby, creates an inner conflict between what is sanctioned by the physical world society and what is truly being sought at a deeper level of soulful beingness. One, therefore, need understand that only by embracing one's true heart's desires will the *matter* of alignment with one's full identity be achieved: mind, body and spirit. Then the peace and contentment one seeks will be realized.

Alignment Process: I now give myself permission to enjoy all that I came forth to be as I lovingly embrace all aspects of my identity. I am relieved to now understand that my only goal in this physical realm is to live a joy-filled life, however that plays out. With or without the validation of others, I get to choose how I want to create my life, and where and with whom I want to co-create it. And for this sacred awareness, I am so grateful.

63. Infidelity

What's the Matter: Infidelity—A breach of trust breaking one's religious vows or agreement of sexual or emotional fidelity; sharing physical or emotional intimacy with someone outside of the marital union or relationship; a disloyal act.

Misaligned Thought or **Divine Intention:** The inherent understanding that the soul came into the physical realm to have what one wants and to be free. However, when one perceives that one's freedoms are being squelched, one thinks one has to sneak one's freedom as a result of conflicting messages that one cannot truly have what one wants. That is, if what one wants is believed to be socially or morally taboo. This causes a split in one's *energies* that can be triggered by a desire to relate and connect with a *variety of souls*; and/or by a desire for revenge for not getting what one wants from *one soul*. In both cases, this appears to be a *matter* of unmet needs that are being sought outside of oneself at the expense of personal integrity and honor. One does not understand that the freedom one seeks to have and do what one wants is always available if one is willing to come into alignment with one's own mind, body and spirit, first. One need only seek from within what one desires and then honor one's *inner knowing* by summoning the courage to ask for what one truly wants. Then if one's request is not granted, one would be wise to either release what one does not prefer and/or hold out for what one truly wants, in order to live a life of integrity. One need only understand that enjoying a variety of souls is wonderful if that is what one prefers, as long as one enters into these sacred contracts with other souls wanting the same. And when two souls are ***not*** likeminded on this issue, "truth" regarding the different preferences is honored from the outset. One needs to trust that whenever one honors "truth," fulfillment comes and brings with it the joyful connection one seeks.

Alignment Process: I go forward with the understanding that the fulfillment I seek must be summoned from within me, first. As I align my mind, body and spirit, I will manifest what it is that I want with honor; for sexual and emotional intimacy is a sacred co-creative act that I long to fully experience. I have the courage and integrity to ask for what I desire, trusting that the God-source within provides me with all that I need to fulfill this sacred desire. (See Relational Problem).

64. Insomnia – (See Sleep Reactions.)

65. Intellectual Disability aka Intellectual Developmental Disorder – (formerly known as Mental Retardation)

What's the Matter: ID or IDD—Deficits in cognitive functioning (IQ) that impact academic abilities, social interaction and a range of activities of daily living, ranging from mild to profound.

Misaligned Thought *or Divine Intention:* The divine objective to demonstrate that one's beingness is beyond the body temple and intellectual functioning. As such, one came forth choosing not to go beyond an elementary embrace of the physical realm, where one can continue to experience the *matter* of life with a fresh and simpler look at things. One chooses to appreciate the *matter* at face value versus the mind boggling seriousness of adult-imposed conditions, where one is expected to read between the lines. One chooses the freedom to enjoy one's physical experience accepting little-to-no rigid expectations from others. This way, one's soul is unburdened by having to earn, prove, or do something specific to receive the unconditional love and acceptance it came forth to enjoy.

Alignment Process: I came into the physical realm as a divine student of the universe and with only one subject to master—which is to love myself, as a unique and acceptable expression of the God-source within. My physical brain taps into universal intelligence as I go forward creating the life I came forth to live.

66. Intermittent Explosive (Reaction) or Disruptive Mood Dysregulation (Reaction) DMD

What's the Matter: Intermittent Explosive Reaction—Distinct episodes of a failure to resist aggressive impulses that result in serious verbal or physical assaultive acts or destruction of property lasting about three months; or **DMD** (reaction), which has similar aggressive symptoms but duration lasts for at least 12 months or longer.

Misaligned Thought or **Divine Intention:** The unconscious understanding that one is supposed to have one's hearts desires. However, this is mixed with the belief that not having what one wants causes such a disturbing *energy*-in-motion that it cannot be contained. As a result, the externalization of one's discontent is experienced as raging *energy* attempting to remold or destroy the *matter*. One does not understand that one actually *can* have what one wants, if one is willing to align the mind, body and spirit. By beginning to use the vibrational tools that soothe the *matter*, one will achieve the joyful emotional release and contentment one seeks.

Alignment Process: I now go forward, understanding the *matter*. I recognize that I came into the physical realm to create and have what I want. Therefore, when that which is opposing or confining is presented to me, I now realize that I can manage my *energies* and maintain my composure. As I align my mind, body and spirit, nothing can overthrow or override my ability to create the life I want to live. For this reminder of my connection to the Source, I am truly grateful.

67. Kleptomania

What's the Matter: Kleptomania—Recurrent impulse to steal items even though the items are not needed for personal or monetary use.

Misaligned Thought or **Divine Intention:** The inherent understanding that the abundance of life is for the *taking*. However, this awareness is mixed with the unaligned belief that something outside of oneself is more valuable and needed to add meaning and to soothe the *matter*. One does not understand that since one **can** actually have what one wants *legitimately*, true contentment cannot be *lifted* from others. One need only understand that inner and outer manifestations are not embezzled from the universe but given; and not taken, but free, when one comes into alignment with one's mind, body and spirit. Thus, acquiring what one desires requires one to patiently embrace a delay of gratification, where one is granted desires by universal laws versus breaking man's judicial laws. As such, one utilizes the principles of the law of creation and creative visualization to assist in the gradualness of bringing one's hearts desires into manifestation. And likewise, know that what one creates and receives from the Source of one's being can never be repossessed or confiscated.

Alignment Process: I now understand that I have all that I need within me to acquire that which I desire internally and materially. I see now that what is truly valuable and worth acquiring is my alignment with *spirit*, since it is through universal laws that my heart's desires materialize. As I align my mind, body and spirit, I do so with patience and appreciation for the creation process, understanding that the divine fulfillment I seek is truly free. (See Chapter on Pro-creation.)

68. Klismaphilia – See Paraphilias C.)

69. Learning Disabilities

What's the Matter: Learning Disabilities—Issue with the ability to receive, process, analyze, or store information in the areas of reading, writing, math, listening, speaking and/or reasoning.

Misaligned Thought *or Divine Intention:* The inherent understanding that one came forth with one's own divine instruction. One has chosen to demonstrate that there is a mismatch in the rigid expectations of traditional academia as it relates to the *matter*. One is demonstrating and underlining (with chalk) that the diversity of learning styles and quest for specific knowledge could be better matched with more flexible teaching styles, outside the box. As such, a conflict ensues over what it means to acquire a base of knowledge in order "to know" anything. As a result, one recognizes that education authorities often minimize the fact that each soul is an individualized expression of God. And as such, comes forth into the physical realm with a unique base of knowledge that is purposeful and divine. The education system could benefit, likewise, from developing "individualized soul plans" (ISP) versus the traditional "individualized education plans" (IEP) that currently continues to command that learners do the adapting versus adapting the lesson.

Alignment Process: (for 13yrs and up): I am well aware that I came into being with a dynamic ability "to know" and focus on only the aspects of "being" that are important to me. I am coming to understand that I am here in part to magnify the diverse ways that knowledge can be imparted. I, therefore, freely release the expected adherence to the standardization of what knowledge "is or isn't." As such, I love knowing that I am one of the ones divinely guided to gift the world with this sacred example of how to accept and honor different forms of intelligence.

Alignment Process (for kids): I am filled with divine knowledge and came forth to focus on only the aspects of "being" that are important to me. I am proud to be an example of how to accept and honor sacred learning styles as I uniquely look into the additional information that is of value to me.

70. Malingering

What's the Matter: Malingering – A manipulative intentional decision to fake mental or physical symptoms to avoid responsibilities or consequences.

Misaligned Thought or **Divine Intention:** The divine understanding that one came forth with the assurance of freedom and grace. This awareness however, is mixed with an unaligned belief that one can exploit the *matter.* One misrepresents one's full capacity, hoping that grace will exempt one from taking responsibility for one's actions, and that one can avoid a reduction in one's freedom. One does not understand that the way to leave one's freedom intact is through demonstrating genuine honesty and well-being versus portraying *dis-ease.* If one would only shift one's *energy* with integrity, one could come into alignment with one's authentic mind, body and spirit. Then one would be sending a clear and genuine signal out to the universe of what one prefers; and one would resolve needing to negotiate one's gracious freedoms.

Alignment Process: I now understand that as I align my mind, body and spirit, I can go forward in life without pretense. I am able to attract the circumstances and experiences that I most desire with integrity. And by doing so, I hold on to my freedoms. I take responsibility at the level of thought by tapping into an inner knowing. And connect with a source within that helps me summon from the universe all that I need to enjoy the grace that truth and divine accountability brings.

71. Marriage Problems/Partner—(See Relational Problems & See Infidelity.)

72. Masochism—(See Paraphilias A.)

73. Mental Retardation—(See Intellectual Developmental Reactions)

74. Motor Reactions—(See Developmental Coordination, Stereotypic or Tic Reactions.)

75. Multiple Personality—(See Dissociative Identity Reaction.)

76. Narcissistic Personality

What's the Matter: Narcissistic Personality—Characterized by various symptoms including an exaggerated sense of self-importance, persistent need for admiration, devaluing and lacking empathy for others, with a strong sense of entitlement, expecting to be catered to and furious when it doesn't happen.

Misaligned Thought or **Divine Intention:** The divine and inherent understanding of "how great thou art." However, this awareness is mixed with the skewed belief that one's gifts and needs are greater than those of other souls. One does not understand that the fact of the *matter* is every soul comes forth with equal glory and excellence in a multitude of areas, worthy of admiration and honor; for "all is one." One need only undertake the aligning work with one's mind, body and spirit to elevate one's *vibration* to the level where one recognizes other souls' gifts in order to have a joyous co-creative experience.

Alignment Process: I love that I already knew that deep within me is incredible value. I am happy to expand that knowing to include the fact that others also came forth with the same. Having clarified that, I go forward assured that it is the universe, not other souls, that validates for me, "how great *'we'* art." I embrace the fact that only the universe is set up to *cater* to my *desires* and bring them forth into manifestation. For this insight, I am truly humbled.

77. Narcolepsy—(See Sleep Reactions.)

78. Necrophilia—(See Paraphilias A.)

79. Nightmare Disorder (Reaction) aka Dream Anxiety Disorder (Reaction)

What's the Matter: Nightmare Reaction—Repeated frightening dreams that cause intense fear and may also cause difficulty in the daytime with concentration along with anxiety, depression, and/or irritability.

Misaligned Thought or **Divine Intention:** The inherent understanding that the *matter* of life manifests the good, bad and ugly. And as such, one inadvertently chooses to focus on one aspect versus the balanced view. Thereby, one adopts the skewed belief that the *world is not safe.* This vibration, then, is being magnified during one's dream state. One does not understand that when one focuses most of one's *energy* on observing the "undesirable" *matter* of this world, one can feel like one is in a *nightmare*; and this can interfere with restorative sleep, putting into motion the sentiment "no rest for the weary." But if one could just embrace the *diversity of life*, then the perspective of *contrast* could soften one's angst into a relaxing slumber. One, thereby, could attract more experiences when one is awake that validate the dominance of well-being in the world.

Alignment Process: The world *is* safe and I am safe within it. I appreciate the fact I am opening to the idea that I can rest in the knowledge that universal laws are at the core of all self-fulfilling prophecies. Therefore, the fact of the *matter* is nothing can come into my experience without active attention to it, since I have vibrational influence over what comes. I can now relax and begin practicing the new habit of focusing on thoughts of well-being by day-dreaming about what I want, which will be reflected back to me in my *slumber*.

80. Obesity – (See Eating Reactions.)

81. Obsessive Compulsive Disorders (Reaction) & OCD Personality
(If **Hoarding**, See Above for Hoarding Reaction.)

What's the Matter: OCD & OCD Personality – **a)** OCD: Unwanted recurrent intrusive obsessions and/or compulsions that are recognized as unreasonable and are severe enough to cause marked anxiety or distress, which interferes with one's daily functioning; **b)** OCD Personality: Preoccupation with rigid morals, ethics, and values, with an excessive need for perfectionism and control.

Misaligned Thought or **Divine Intention:** The inherent understanding that one's well-being is supposed to be assured. However, this awareness is mixed with split *energy*, where one also believes that well-being can be a fleeting thing, which causes tremendous discomfort with uncertainty. As a result, one blocks the very well-being that the obsessive thought or compulsion is trying to align with, by the constant attention to the feared *matter*. One does not understand that the *matter* manifests because of the *energy* one is investing in it. However, one may take solace in the fact that the constant focusing of one's attention to that which is undesired is only because it has become a habituated thought. As a result, one submits to the *automatic thought* without recognizing that one always has a choice of where to focus one's thoughts, even when it doesn't seem like it. To break the habit, one must offer a new vibration and practice thinking new thoughts, which may initially require more focus; but in time, one will successfully shift one's attention to the comforting thoughts of well-being that one prefers.

Alignment Process: I am opening to the idea that I came into the physical realm as a "well being" with the power to focus my attention positively. As such, I can gradually re-train or un-train my automatic responses back into alignment by being much more aware of where I am focusing my attention. I see now that the assurance I seek is within, which tells me that I can now choose thoughts that affirm that well-being abounds. I will practice "obsessing" about only that which I desire and be "compulsive" about honoring my divine power to choose.

82. Occupational Problem

What's the Matter: Occupational Problem—Career or job dissatisfaction, underachievement, uncertainty, career transitions, etc.

Misaligned Thought or **Divine Intention:** The inherent understanding that one came into the physical realm with multiple divine intentions. However, this awareness is mixed with an unaligned belief in "shoulds" and thinking that one *should* have reached a certain milestone by now. One does not understand that the rigid adherence to the *matter* on a certain timetable is what's often interfering with the next level of creativity that one prefers to experience. Sometimes one also believes that "someone or something" outside of oneself is what's preventing the opportunity for expansion or recognition. And, therefore, one does not realize that when one aligns the mind, body and spirit, one summons one's increase from the universe. Increase does not come from an employer or by networking but through "universal orchestration" where one's requests are divinely employed. As such, one also need not try to please others who desire one to take a different path than what one's inner knowing has divinely intended. One is free to follow one's own heart's desires and contribute to the world what one uniquely came forth to create, which is truly the only job.

Alignment Process: I came into this physical experience to share my vocation, talent and gifts with the world. I recognize that it is my connection with the fullness of my being that determines my increase, placement and expansion. Therefore, as I align my mind, body and spirit, I acquire the patience and confidence to pursue my heart's desires sufficiently, one at a time. I give myself permission to express all that I am, and all that I came forth to be, as my life's work and financial prosperity unfolds "bit by bit" in this physical experience.

83. Oppositional Defiance Disorder (Reaction)

What's the Matter: ODD—A recurrent pattern of negativity, defiant, disobedient and hostile behaviors of a child or adolescent toward authority figures that persists at least six months.

Misaligned Thought or **Divine Intention:** The inherent understanding that one can trust one's own inner knowing and oftentimes override external information and guidance. However, one does not understand that we are also co-creators and come into families and sociological networks for the benefit of allowing diverse viewpoints. We need only know that others, young and old, help us to clarify the matter and not stunt what it is that we want to create. Therefore, one need not protest that contrasting perspectives exist amongst those who come before us as guides. Instead, one can honor the balance that comes out of the opposite "yin and yang" forces of life.

Alignment Process: I love that I already trust that I know what is good for me. And now, I also like knowing that any direction or advice being offered by adults is simply information that I can agree with or not. I am coming to realize that I am expanded by the interaction each time I patiently listen to someone's unique and well-meaning request or viewpoint. And so, until I am grown, I look forward to the mutually respectful, co-creative diversity inherent within my relationships with the well-meaning authority figures in my life; for they are truly my sacred guides.

84. Pain Disorder (Reaction)

What's the Matter: Pain Reaction—Pain, mostly attributed to psychological factors, that causes significant distress or impairment in social, occupational or other important areas of functioning, causing a need for pain medication. (See Somatoform.)

Misaligned Thought or **Divine Intention:** The inherent understanding that one came forth into the physical realm to comfortably evolve, learn and grow. However, this awareness of expansion is mixed with the conflicting belief that life's lessons are learned painstakingly or through punishment. In this case, pain is manifested whether aimed at others or from self-reproach due to a lack of compassion and forgiveness for oneself or others. One does not understand that there is no punitive Source in the universe that is judging the *matter*; rather, there is only an unconditional loving Source that offers ease and comfort as one grows into alignment with one's mind, body and spirit.

Alignment Process: I honor the fact that the *matter* does not have to be made *painfully* clear for me can learn my lessons more gently. I am opening myself to the possibility that "love" teaches, too; and so does compassion, when I take time to align my mind, body and spirit. Therefore, I release and forgive the past, going forward with softened eyes of flexibility where a more joyful version of myself is always tied to divine relief.

85. Panic Disorder Reaction—With or Without Agoraphobia

What's the Matter: Panic Reaction—Recurrent unexpected anxiety-induced panic attacks (at least two) followed by a sustained period where one fears having another one. Often co-occurring with Agoraphobia where there is the additional fear of being away from home due to fear of help not being available. (See Anxiety and Agoraphobia.)

Misaligned Thought or **Divine Intention:** The inherent understanding that one is safe in the universe. However this awareness is only partially embraced as one develops a limited belief that one cannot handle the *matter* of life in its full spectrum of universal proportion. Likewise, one may not feel safe outside of one's comfort zone and seeks to discover the optimum level of emotional tension the soul can mediate; out of a fearful ambivalence to engage. Relegating oneself to confinement, which is perceived as a safe space, one tries to drown out the call of life. But one does not understand that one cannot hide from the diversity of life. And as such, one need only recognize that the safety and ease one seeks is a *matter* that can only be found in the unlimited boundaries discovered when one aligns one's mind and body with spirit.

Alignment Process: I am opening to the idea that I came into the physical realm expecting there to be a diverse environment from which I pick and observe both desirable and undesirable things. I am now recognizing that the ease and security that I seek as I navigate through the world is within me. As I come into alignment with my spirit, I am more and more confident in the fact that wherever I go, the God-source within me is; and I am truly safe.

86. Paranoid Personality

What's the Matter: Paranoid Personality—A pattern of pervasive distrust and suspiciousness of others to the degree that one fears others will exploit, harm, or deceive, despite there being no evidence to support this expectation.

Misaligned Thought or **Divine Intention:** The inherent and unconscious understanding that trusting the universe requires faith. However, this understanding of the *matter* is mixed with a simultaneous distrust in the universe and the inhabitants in it. This is coupled with one's faulty belief that one is not worthy of loyalty and respect from fellow soul-travelers. One does not understand that the distrust is due to one's low self-esteem and strong attention to the negative aspects within the world; and that one lacks faith in self and others. This, then, brings the *matter* one fears into sharper focus, due to the universal principle, "like attracts like." As such, others *vibrating* with the same issues are brought to one's attention. However, the trustworthy relationships one seeks do not come from "being on the lookout" or "standing guard." Rather, when one aligns one's mind and body with spirit, one ceases to merely *hope* that mankind will behave the way one prefers; instead, one develops faith, trusting that all is truly well.

Alignment Process: I am opening to the idea that I am a worthy being and can trust that nothing and no one can alter my experience without my subtle invitation. I now realize that the only villain I seek to contain is within me. I understand that the fellow souls with whom I interact are merely mirror reflections of where I am vibrating. As I align my mind, body and spirit, the evidence of loyalty and unwavering support that I desire will appear more evident. With this clarity, I go forward in faith.

87. Paraphilias

What's the Matter: Paraphilias—Recurrent, intense sexually-arousing fantasies, sexual urges, or behaviors generally involving one of the below that are listed here in three separate subcategories:

A. Suffering and Humiliation of Self or Others; Exhibitionism (exposing private parts); Voyeurism (peeping Tom); Partialism (aroused by parts); Frotteurism (rubbing against nonconsenting/unsuspecting people); Telephone Scatologia (obscene phone calls); Sexual Sadism and Masochism (pain/humiliation); Necrophilia (corpse); Zoophilia (animals).

B. Pedophilia—Suffering and Humiliation of Children.

C. Fetishism of Non-living Objects and Items; Paraphilias NOS; Corprophilia (feces); Klismaphilia (enemas); Urophilia (urine).

D. Transvestic Fetishism.

(NOTE: The Misaligned Thought and Aligning Processes for each category of Paraphilias are discussed separately on the pages that follow.)

87-A. Paraphilias A—Suffering/Humiliation of Others, Exhibitionism, Voyeurism, Partialism, Telephone Scatologia, Necrophilia, Zoophilia

Misaligned Thought or **Divine Intention:** The inherent understanding that fear can be relieved regardless of the *matter*. However, this understanding is mixed with the faulty belief that by controlling others, one's own fear of vulnerability will be shed. One thereby seeks relief by projecting one's own feelings of humiliation and vulnerability on others through exploitive acts. One does not understand that true relief comes from an unarmored place and not from punitive acts or violence. One need only understand that the vibration of "well-being" and the vibration of "violence and exploitation" are far apart on the scale of alignment with one's God-source within. One needs to appreciate that when one is forcing one's will on a non-consensual soul or corpse, whether a person or animal, one is violating the freedom of others. One needs to know that misalignment in *energy* can cause an injury to one's psyche that further exacerbates the disconnection one has from the Source within. (See Severe Misalignment on the Alignment Scale in previous chapter.)

Alignment Process: I came into the physical realm to honor and co-create with other souls. I forgive myself and ask to be forgiven by any soul that I harmed and exploited on my journey. I now understand that sexual activity is meant to be consensual, between people with the ability to give informed consent, with the parties attempting to co-create at the blended level of physical and spiritual. I now choose to "live and let live" by deliberately aligning my mind, body and spirit to a vibration that allows me to appreciate the fullness of my being, which includes my capacity to respect and dignify others sexually.

87-B. Paraphilias B—Pedophiles: Suffering, Exploitation, Humiliation of Children

Misaligned Thought or **Divine Intervention:** The inherent understanding that emotional pain can be soothed. However, this understanding is mixed with the faulty belief that soothing can be had through revenge. As such, one seeks revenge for having one's own innocence tampered with as a child; and/or "acts out" one's fear of engaging in age-appropriate adult sexuality. In both cases, one's natural sexual *energy*, which stimulates desire for sexual intimacy and joyful release, has mutated into an unaligned desire with an inappropriate outlet. As a result, one goes forth with *split energy*: mixing up the vibration of *relief and healing* with the vibration of *humiliation and abuse* of children. One does not understand that there is no true relief or redemption in revenge that's been stolen from innocence. Innocence and purity do not absolve one's misalignment, since the vibration of well-being and the vibration of abuse are far apart on the scale of alignment with spirit. Thus, the true justice and relief one seeks and deserves can only be obtained by aligning with one's own mind, body and spirit, where the restoration of one's purity, innocence and *kundalini energy* are divinely transformed.

Alignment Process: I came into the physical realm with my innocence and purity intact. I recall my creed to honor every soul that came forth with the same. I release the desire to act upon any further revenge or unhealthy desires and move toward seeking consensual sexual unions with age-appropriate adults capable of offering such. I now forgive myself, and ask to be forgiven, for any child I once harmed, as I was harmed. I also want to forgive others who harmed me. Having re-clarified this, I now choose to deliberately align my mind, body and spirit so that I may experience the true relief and justice that inner redemption brings.

87-C. Paraphilias C – Fetishism of Non-living Objects and Items

Misaligned Thought or **Divine Intention:** The inherent understanding that sensuality is a diverse *matter*. However, one believes that sexual fulfillment may be stimulated by *items* or objects versus people. At the same time, some unconsciously fear intimacy with another person out of concern of being the one "objectified." One does not understand that the security one seeks (in order to be sexually uninhibited and treated with the unconditional acceptance one craves) doesn't come from items or objects outside of oneself but from the security found within. Thus, by aligning one's mind, body and spirit, one may choose to allow the sacred seduction and connection that is achievable with other souls.

This may still include items to be used as an enhancement of the *matter* versus a complete substitute for pleasure. That way the "object" of one's desire no longer need be personified. However, it must be noted that whether or not one chooses to come into alignment with the co-creative splendor of others, it is understood that as long as one is not hurting anyone or exploiting the items of others, all desires may be pursued and fulfilled in the privacy of solitary indulgence.

Alignment Process: I came into the physical realm for solitary and co-creative jubilation. As such, I am opening to the idea that I also have the ability to be vulnerable and intimate with other souls that came forth for the same. I appreciate being reminded that I have the divine choice of how to embrace my sacred sensuality. For this divine offering, I embrace my joyful release.

87-D. Paraphilias D – Transvestic Fetishism

What's the Matter: Transvestic Fetishism—Cross-gender dressing and affinity for the opposite gender apparel that can also stimulate arousal. (See Paraphilias C—for Items and Objects.)

Misaligned Thought *or Divine Intention:* The belief and inherent understanding that the core of all human beings is *spirit* that possesses both masculine and feminine characteristics. Therefore, in addition, to what has been offered above in Paraphilias C with regard to items/objects, in this *matter* there is also a refusal to be limited to or by gender in self-expression or sexual expression. Out of this profound and unique appreciation for both genders comes the desire to experience both energies without feeling the need to line up with either one on a permanent basis. And so, in addition to the above aligning process, I suggest the below process be added, if needed.

Alignment Process: I came into the physical realm to embrace both the feminine and masculine aspects of my being. As such, I am free to fully embrace the persona of the opposite gender. Understanding that I am a spiritual being, I know that I am genderless at my core. As I align my mind, body and spirit, I go forth with the divine clarity that *"all is one."*

88. Parasomnias – (See Nightmares, Sleep Terror, or Sleepwalking.)

89. Partner Relationship Problems – (See Relational Problems & Infidelity.)

90. Parent/Child Relationship Problems – (See Relational Problems.)

91. Passive Aggressive Personality

What's the Matter: Passive Aggressive Personality—A pattern of indirectly expressing true feelings through actions versus clear and direct communication, via procrastination, forgetfulness, stubbornness and intentional inefficiency; or failing to do fair share, often due to feeling unappreciated and/or misunderstood.

Misaligned Thought or **Divine Intention:** The inherent understanding that harmony is essential for co-creation. However, this understanding is mixed with the faulty belief that one must fake the *matter*. As a result, one lacks the courage to express one's disdain directly, due to the fear of being exposed for not being the perfectly-poised and well-adjusted person one prefers to be *seen as*. This, then, adds to the *energy* split where one attempts to disguise harboring negative feelings and inadequacies. One does not understand that summoning the courage to offer straight-forward assertive communication to express one's feelings is a more effective way to clarify the *matter* and shift one's negative *energy*; for honesty facilitates harmony. Therefore, all one needs is to come back into alignment with one's mind, body and spirit in order to elevate one's perspective to a *frequency* where one will be able to deal more genuinely with others. Then one is able to experience the mutually rewarding co-creative relationships one desires with others who are also perfectly imperfect and accepting of the same.

Alignment Process: I am opening to the idea that it's okay for me to be imperfect and honest about the *matter*, even when I fear the outcome. I now understand that I get my needs met through the integrity of straightforward communication and taking responsibility to clean up my own *energy* first. Once I am aligned with the Source of my being, I will attract the same as a result of my willingness to live a genuine and authentic existence.

92. Pathological Gambling

What's the Matter: Pathological Gambling—Persistent inability to control gambling impulse that disrupts personal, family or vocational pursuits, often accompanied by feelings of helplessness, guilt, anxiety or depression.

Misaligned Thought or **Divine Intention:** The inherent understanding that life is filled with abundance. However, this understanding is mixed with the faulty belief that tapping into the *matter* of prosperity and well-being is a *gamble* and cannot be attained with ease. It's the idea that "I must put my britches on the line and risk everything" in order to tap into the abundance of life. One does not understand that the only *"sure bet"* to place in the *game of life* is played within, as one comes into alignment with one's mind, body and spirit. This is where one's well-being and prosperity is then summoned by self-fulfilling prophecies or universal laws; and as such, one's life consistently reflects how well one masters the *energy basis* of the game.

Alignment Process: I am opening to the possibility that my well-being is assured and comes risk-free with the ease that trusting in the God-source within me brings. As I come to understand universal principles, I can now bet on the fact that I can use my imagination to visualize the many ways that prosperity can come into my experience. I will be led to take "right action" out of that divine nudging that will come from within and manifest as abundance. (See Chapter on Pro-Creation after completing the other Steps.)

93. Pedophilia – (See Paraphilias B—above.)

94. Peer Relationship Problems – (See Relational Problems.)

95. Phase of Life Problem

What's the Matter: Phase of Life Problem—Having to do with difficulty in adjusting to major life changes.

Misaligned Thought or **Divine Intention:** The inherent understanding that change is a crucial *matter*. This understanding, however, is mixed with the faulty belief that changing the *matter* in one's life is extremely difficult or not doable at all, due to habituated patterns and routines to which one has become accustomed. This is often coupled with some trepidation with regards to the lack of certainty that the new life choice brings. One does not understand that the greater, most secure part of one's *matter* that is always stable is the spirit within. As one aligns with the fullness of one's being, the spirit is always available at every new horizon. With this assurance, one can embrace life changes with much more ease and actually know it's possible to adapt, in a holy instant. Still, having said that, the call of life is not about "the swiftness of change" but about having the courage and willingness *to change*. This way, regardless of *how long* one takes to realign one's *energy* with the new platform in life, the act, itself, will be divinely indicative of soulful transformation.

Alignment Process: I am opening to the idea that change can come with ease; and that the greater part of me that is my spirit is with me wherever I am. As such, I am coming to realize that my sacred intention when I became physical was to allow the ebb and flow of life to expand me. I go forward relieved and invigorated knowing that the secure well-being I seek in all of my life experiences is assured.

96. Phobias—(Situations, Places, Animals, Objects or Things, etc.)

What's the Matter: Phobias—Marked and persistent fear of a situation, place, animal, thing or object that provokes an immediate anxiety response and can take the form of a panic attack and/or cause avoidance behavior.

Misaligned Thought or **Divine Intention:** The divine understanding that life is filled with a variety of *matter*. However, this understanding is mixed with a faulty belief that something can separate and disconnect one from the Source of one's well-being. One does not understand that everything is connected to the same *energy* Source within the universe. One forgets that one came to experience the spectrum of life and allow all of its variations. Therefore, anytime some undesired *matter* appears in one's experience, one would do well to remember that inherent within it is also divinity, because "all is one." One need only remember that *all things can be assimilated* as one comes into alignment with one's own mind, body and spirit. This way, one is able to hold onto one's comfortable sense of well-being without being yanked by the thing that is not preferred, by simply finding the value within it.

Alignment Process: I came into the physical realm knowing I would encounter both desirable and undesirable things. I came knowing that the spirit in me has endowed me with *enormous appreciation* for diversity. And I have *sufficient courage* to embrace the diverse ways that *matter* manifests as humans, other living organisms, objects and things. I want to embrace this (fill in the blank) with my innate *inner knowing* that all is well; and my knowing and trusting that *everything* in the universe is made of and connected to the same loving *energy* we call God. I want to feel my connection to the divinity that created this (fill in the blank), understanding that it has value and a sacred purpose, just as I do. With this assurance, I just expanded my capacity for the diversity life offers.

97. Physical Abuse—(See Abuse.)

98. Pica—(See Feeding Reactions.)

99. Postpartum or Peripartum Depression

What's the Matter: **a)** Peripartum or **b)** Postpartum Depression—Peripartum is when the depressive or anxiety symptoms begin during pregnancy; and **b)** Postpartum is when symptoms continue after the normal two-week baby blues and manifest as a lingering depression, mania, mixed or brief psychotic episode, often coupled with severe anxiety and panic attacks. These are associated with preoccupation with the infant's well-being, ranging from over-concern to disinterest to delusions with increased risk to infant.

Misaligned Thought or **Divine Intention:** The inherent understanding that the passageway of souls into the physical is a sacred *matter*. However, this understanding is mixed with the unconscious and unaligned belief by the mother that she should be more emotionally prepared for this humongous honor and responsibility. Therefore, she feels unworthy when faced with the acute awareness that *the well-being of the body-temple of another soul* is temporarily in the hands of the mother-soul who still has unmet needs. Thus, a crisis emerges for the ever-still-evolving-mother who temporarily panicked is testing to see what support she can elicit from loved ones. She is trying to ensure that what seems like an overwhelming life sentence is not hers to carry alone. She does not understand that she is simply the vessel through which this soul enters the physical realm and not the destination. Meanwhile, she decompensates, with the unconscious hope that *if she regresses, it won't be expected of her to be this perfectly-wise-selfless-mother-figure* that she cannot relate to (in this unaligned moment). She does not realize that the soul that has come forth already knows the parents the soul has vibrationally selected through a sacred contract; and the soul is *expecting* the union to be a *co-creative mutual evolution* based on *unconditional love.* This is a lesson the baby-soul's advent is already teaching the mother-soul; and the mother must learn to love herself *without conditions* in order to offer the newly-arrived baby-soul the same.

Alignment Process: I am opening to the idea that I really do not have to be perfect to be this baby soul's earthly mother. Besides, he/she picked me; and so I have already done something right by being a vessel for this soul to come into the physical realm. All I need to do is be a compassionate guide and provide the same patience and caring that I, too, deserve. I offer the best of me, with my strengths and weaknesses, as I look forward to the co-creative moments ahead of us, where we will teach each other the true meaning of unconditional, perfectly imperfect love.

100. Post Traumatic Stress Disorder (Reaction) (PTSD)

What's the Matter: PTSD Reaction—Intense reaction of fear, helplessness or horror symptoms following the exposure to or witnessing of an extreme traumatic stressor.

Misaligned Thought or **Divine Intention:** The unconscious understanding that relief is achievable. However, this understanding is mixed with the faulty belief that seeing or experiencing the human condition at its worst cannot be integrated into the psyche without extreme discomfort. One does not remember that any *matter* and agonizing emotion can be soothed and released. One need only understand that one can realign one's mind, body and spirit with universal principles (such as that anything that has gone out of alignment can come back with ease) simply by refocusing attention and *energy* on the joy of living. One can blend that knowledge with the understanding that we came into the physical world knowing we would be exposed to a variety of both negative and positive manifestations. Therefore, we don't have to allow the extremes of that diversity to separate us from our alignment.

Alignment Process: I am opening to the idea that I have the power within me to realign with well-being anytime I am ready to withdraw my attention from any unwanted *matter*, present or past. The discomfort can actually be over if I allow it to be. I now understand that by coming back into alignment with my mind, body and spirit, I can refocus my attention on the joy of living. I give myself permission to go forward, investing my time and *energy* only on the *matter* that makes me feel good.

101. Psychotic Reactions / Brief Psychotic Reactions or Attenuated Psychosis Syndrome
(Or See Schizophrenias for a Longer Duration of Psychotic Reactions.)

What's the Matter: Psychotic Reaction—A brief short-term experience either involving delusions, hallucinations, disorganized speech, or gross or catatonic behaviors that last at least one day but less than one month, with a full return to a previous level of functioning.

Misaligned Thought *or Divine Intention:* The inherent understanding that life experience includes the physical and nonphysical, thereby ensuring that nonphysical levels of consciousness be duly noted. As such, one temporarily withdraws or releases expected rigid ways of perceiving what is real from what is unreal to fully experience the range of human experience. Therefore, the fullness of one's being is not confined to the "agreed upon" parameters of human thought, which is abstract and beyond the current understanding of brain chemistry.

Thus, one's ability to perceive beyond the conventional constructs of consciousness that connect the physical with the nonphysical can become blurred. And, due to its fuzziness, one can become panicked without the familiar anchors of beingness. But one need not fear its ascent to expanded consciousness and obscure reality, and instead take comfort in the fact that there are simply subtle degrees of alignment connecting the physical and nonphysical realities. Therefore, the true basis of one's reality—whether one is physically focused, nonphysically focused or somewhere in between—is based on the unchanging reality that one's spirit is the part that is always stable.

One may take solace in the fact that *all thought is invisible* and exists within the nonphysical realm. Therefore, it could be argued that most people are first seeing things in their *mind's eye* that aren't really there (physically) until they manifest, and/or hearing things that aren't really being said, to some degree, both literally and figuratively. The experience of what constitutes reality is relative to each person's ability to fully perceive the moment-by-moment alignment with one's mind, body and spirit. The grasp of reality, then, lies within the consensus of the participants that agree that this particular thing or experience is or isn't reality, which is then, and only then, labeled the normative curve. As such, each person gets to determine what reality is, based on his or her own perceptions. (See Chapter Four that describes more about how disorders are determined.)

Alignment Process: I am grounded in the fact that the God-source part of me is that which is stable. I honor the fact that these other realities that I have experienced have expanded my understanding that life is no longer a question of what is "real or unreal" but rather what is "physical and nonphysical." For this sacred delineation and clarification, I am relieved, as I find the perfect blended balance for me. (See Using Psychotherapy, Medication, & Herbal Remedies in the Sacretherapy® process in Chapter Eight.)

102. Pyromania

What's the Matter: Pyromania—Episodes of deliberate and purposeful fire-setting as a result of fascination or affective arousal with fire, versus any monetary or other gain.

***Misaligned Thought* or Divine Intention:** The inherent understanding that one can be soothed. However, this understanding is mixed with the faulty belief that soothing is an external *matter*. One has trouble getting a grasp of what the *matter* is, especially in an impulsive moment where one's *energy* appears "too hot to handle." This is underlined by the origins of the word pyromania meaning "fire" and "loss of reason," which put together means a "fiery loss of reason." As such, the essence of the *matter* is captured in the "loss of self control," where one seeks relief or gratification in seeing one's mistakes *burned* to a cinder; or seeing what may be a "boring life" go up in *smoke*, causing one to *burn* with rage or unexpressed passion. This is where one would like to "fire up" one's life in ways that can soothe and calm the *blazing energy*. This differs from arsenal in that pyromania *burns* within with the need to externalize one's discontent by projecting or transferring one's *energy* onto a real fire for confirmation of the *inferno* within; which, thereby, offers temporary relief. But for sustained relief, one needs to understand that containment and positive expression of one's energies can only be achieved when one aligns the mind, body and spirit.

Alignment Process: I see now that there are many things in life that can set my soul on *fire* and replace disappointment and the boredom of humdrum living when I take time to align my mind, body and spirit. The only "*matches*" I need to *strike* are those that line me up with what I truly desire, which is the thrill of a totally *hot*, exciting, joy-filled life. Now that I am aware of what my *fiery* behavior was seeking, I recognize that my *burning* passion was not meant to *destruct* but was sizzling to *construct* creations that can be easily contained.

103. Reactive Attachment Disorder (Reaction) of Infancy or Early Childhood

What's the Matter: RAD Reaction—Pattern of marked developmentally maladaptive social relatedness causing excessive inhibition, ambivalence and hypervigilant behaviors, etc., associated with child abuse and extreme neglect.

Misaligned Thought or **Divine Intention:** The inherent understanding that one has everything one needs within them, and therefore is able to self-soothe. However, this understanding is interrupted by the belief that one's basic needs *cannot* be met by others because of what has been gathered from one's caregivers so far. One has been let down by the adults that one shared *sacred contracts* with to be guides; the ones who inadvertently appear to have lost their own higher *vibrational* connection with the Source of their being. As such, due to one's early imprinting, one becomes conditioned away from one's own natural inclination for well-being. One mistakenly focuses one's *energy* on the perceived *disconnection* versus *connection* with love and affection from others.

As a result, one does not understand that all humans do not disappoint and that some can offer nurture; for anything that has gone out of alignment can come back. As such, the split in *energy* can be restored as one attunes oneself back to the core imprinting of one's being, which is spirit, the only true caretaker of one's mental and emotional needs. Likewise, as one shifts one's *energy* back to the frequency of positive expectation, one will be fostered by healthier caregivers who are able to offer the nurturing that one needs; and one can then gradually demonstrate mutual attachment. (Also see Abuse.)

Alignment Process: **For Ages—8 years old to teens:** I came forth as a loving *energy*, seeking joyful relationships with others. I am worthy of affection and enjoy creating more loving and nurturing experiences.

Alignment Process: **For Ages—1 year old to 7:** I am loving, lovable and worthy!

104. Relational Problems (Couples, Parent/Child, Siblings)

What's the Matter: Relational Problems—Significant stress-inducing chaotic relatedness among one or more members of a relational unit, where depending on severity, toxic behaviors and symptoms can cause members of the unit to experience an assortment of mental and emotional reactions ranging from enmeshment to emotional cut-off and disengagement.

Misaligned Thought or **Divine Intention:** The inherent understanding that one came forth into the physical realm for a co-creative union with other souls. However, this *matter* is mixed with the faulty belief and fear that differing preferences and points of view will cause a disconnection with other souls. One does not understand that one's most sacred intention, in addition to co-creating with others, was to honor one's relationship with oneself. As such, the *energy* tear between one another is triggered by one's misaligned attempt to demand total in-sync likemindedness, which can never be. No one can give up the core parts of the self to accommodate another's preferences or insecurities (at least not for long).

The human condition reeks of conflicts where one attempts to control the *energy* of others; this is futile since every soul showed up in different body temples with different divine intentions. Therefore, the work with all relationships is to come into alignment with one's own connection to one's mind, body and spirit, and allow others to do the same—preferably without being threatened by others honoring their own *inner knowing*. When one allows another those freedoms, the harmony one seeks can be restored and the *energy* connection between the two is further fortified, not dispersed; for "loving" and "controlling" are vibrational antonyms.

Alignment Process: I am opening to the idea that loving my loved ones includes freeing them to be the persons they came forth to be. In so doing, I free my own spirit to be the person I intended. The beauty of co-creation is the art of negotiation that comes without domination; but with confirmation that I can still love and be loved while honoring my own sacred intentions and divine points of view, as I offer the same.

105. Religious or Spiritual Problems (Including Religious Addiction)

What's the Matter: Religious/Spiritual Problems—Questioning of faith, spiritual beliefs, values, religious path, and/or religious addiction.

Misaligned Thought or **Divine Intention:** The inherent understanding that the God-source within the universe is loving and diverse. However, an inner conflict occurs when one is told information that does not jibe with universal truths. Thus, one begins to question religious dogma that insists that there should be just one rigid way to tap into this Source—especially since one's observation of life demonstrates that this Source appears to be connected to all and known in boundless ways. As such, an *energy split* appears in one's spiritual convictions when one's religious path contradicts one's higher *inner knowing.* One then finds that due to one's ever evolving expansion, one can no longer *"pour old wine into new wine skins"* and meet the usual demands of compliance and conformity. As a result, one is called to go on his or her own search for spiritual truths that are more expansive, loving and void of rigid punitive religious confinement. Or sometimes if one is too fearful of what one suspects, one may choose to flood oneself with a particular path and become addicted, in an attempt to block out the contrasting information that points to diversity, balance, and an unconditional God that loves all, supports all and rejects none.

Alignment Process: I am opening to understand that I was taught to believe someone else's beliefs. I now recognize that I have my own *inner knowing* that is calling me to expanded spiritual knowingness as it relates to who I am and who and what the God-source is within me. I am coming to recognize that there is a multitude of ways that one can tap into this universal Source. I see that all of these ways offer some form of relief and spiritual awakening, which adds confirmation to my eternal life. Yet, most importantly, I am beginning to understand that this God-source is a loving *energy,* larger than any one doctrine, and it loves me unconditionally; period, no "buts."

106. Rett Syndrome—

(**Note**: This diagnosis is being included here for those who have been previously diagnosed with this reaction. However, it must be noted that the diagnosis has been removed from official mental health manuals and instead appears to have been absorbed within the Autism Spectrum.)

What's the Matter: Rett Syndrome—Multiple neuro-developmental deficiencies to include loss of language and loss of motor skills, following a period of normal functioning after birth; typically affecting girls.

Misaligned Thought *or Divine Intention:* The divine understanding that one maintains one's spiritual core despite one's body temple. One has come forth with the intention to deliberately experience how true connection with oneself, the Source of the universe, and others can commence without the typical body functions, social or adaptive behaviors. As such, one emphasizes that the core of one's being is more than the *matter* of one's physical apparatus. Therefore, one is not regressing but re-acclimating oneself to the purer positive *energy* of spirit.

Alignment Process: I love that I recognize that the typical developmental milestone's expected for one's body temple was not necessary for my advent in the world. It was beginning to become too cumbersome, and so I have simply elected to stay closer to the vibration of spirit, which is my core. I am simply releasing that which I believe will assist me in offering my greatest contribution to human beingness, which is to inform the world that I and others, too, consist "mostly" of *energy*; and am quite pleased with who I am and what I came forth to do.

107. Rumination—(See Feeding Reactions.)

108. Sadism—(See Paraphilias A.)

109. Schizoaffective Reaction

What's the Matter: Schizoaffective Reaction—An episode where a mixture of bipolar symptoms (manic or depressive) manifest along with certain schizophrenic symptoms.

***Misaligned Thought or* Divine Intention:** The inherent understanding that the thoughts one thinks are a blending of nonphysical and physical, and they come from an awareness that one came forth into the physical for exhilarating joy. However, when one's *matter* does not manifest that *inner knowing*; one then prefers to disconnect from one's physical aspects and plug into the nonphysical, where one connects with a layer of consciousness where one's joyful wishes are played out. As such, one does not understand that what is preventing one from experiencing the sustained well-being one seeks in the physical is merely one's rigid insistence on "all joy or nothing." But if one would understand that there are simply degrees of alignment, one could always shift one's *energy* to a higher vibration and ultimately enjoy an existence blended with joyful peak experiences. Then, one will remain grounded in the reality that as long as one is aligning with the God-source within, one will achieve the divine balance. (See Alignment Scale in Chapter Two.)

Alignment Process: I am grounded in the fact that the stable God-source part of me is what keeps me balanced. As I continue to align my mind and body with *spirit*, I am assured of experiencing the joy of living that I came into the physical realm to enjoy. It is no longer a question of "all or nothing," for me; but, rather, I determine "how and to what degree" I embrace my blended beingness. With this sacred understanding, I am relieved. (See Using Psychotherapy, Medication, & Herbal Remedies in the Sacretherapy® process in Chapter Eight.)

110. Schizoid Personality

What's the Matter: Schizoid Personality—A consistent pattern of *aloof* detachment from social relationships and a restrictive range of expression of emotion, preferring solitary activities and to be by oneself.

Misaligned Thought *or Divine Intention:* The inherent understanding that the most important and fulfilling connection a human being can have is with oneself; that being one's *inner self,* which is the Source of one's being. As such, the *matter* of this personality manifests because one has no need to display a range of emotion to remain connected with one's inner Source. At the same time, one recognizes that the *energy* basis of any connection that one were to have with others is only meant to enhance one's experience; but it is not necessary for alignment with one's own mind, body and spirit.

Alignment Process: I love that I have come forth with the divine intention to show how one can be fulfilled and align with the God-source of the universe without the conventional forms of social interaction. How wonderful it is for me to offer this demonstration to the world, knowing it can assist those who are perhaps alone or lonely, and missing their loved ones, to know that it is more than possible to find contentment and inner joy with just oneself and God.

111A. Schizophrenias—Type A and Type B

Type A – (Schizophrenia, Schizophreniform, Shared Psychotic Disorder/ Reaction)

Type B – (Catatonic Type—See Schizophrenias B—below or see Schizoaffective above and/or see Psychotic above for Brief Psychotic Disorder/Reaction.)

What's the Matter: Schizophrenias A—A reaction in which a person cannot tell what is reality, which interferes with the capacity to meet ordinary demands of life; may include prominent hallucinations, delusions, disorganized speech or disorganized behavior. (Note: If Schizophreniform, symptoms are temporary and last less than six months.)

Misaligned Thought *or Divine Intention*—The inherent understanding that the fullness of one's being is not confined to the "agreed upon" parameters of human thought, which is abstract and beyond brain chemistry. One's ability to perceive beyond the conventional constructs of consciousness that connect the physical with the nonphysical can become blurred; and due to its fuzziness one can become panicked without the familiar anchors of beingness. But one need not fear its ascent to expanded consciousness and obscure reality; instead, one can take comfort in the fact that there are simply subtle degrees of alignment connecting the physical and nonphysical realities. Therefore, the true basis of one's reality— whether one is focused on the physical or nonphysical or something in between— is the unchanging fact that one's spirit is the part that's stable.

One may take solace in the fact that all *thought is invisible* and exists within the nonphysical realm. Therefore, it could be argued that most everyone is first seeing things in the mind's eye that aren't really there (physically) until they manifest, and or hearing things that aren't really being said, sometimes both literally and figuratively. The experience of what constitutes reality is relative to each person's ability to fully perceive one's moment-by- moment alignment with mind, body and spirit. The grasp of reality, then, lies within the consensus of the participants that agree that this particular *matter* or experience is or isn't reality; and reality is then, and only then, labeled the normative curve. As such, each person gets to determine his or her own reality, based on his or her own perceptions. So the schizophrenias can be viewed as a magnification of this perceptually diverse vantage point. (See Chapter Four that describes more about how disorders are determined.)

Alignment Process: I am grounded in the fact that the God-source part of me is that which is stable. I honor the fact that these other realities that I have experienced have expanded my understanding that life is no longer a question of what is "real or unreal" but, rather, what is "physical and nonphysical." For this sacred delineation and clarification, I am relieved as I find the perfect blended balance for me. (See Using Psychotherapy, Medication, & Herbal Remedies in the Sacretherapy® process in Chapter Eight.)

111B. Schizophrenias B—(Catatonic Type)

What's the Matter: Catatonic Type—A temporary form of Schizophrenia, most popularly known for marked psychomotor disturbance, ability to maintain body postures against gravity, an unresponsive stupor, daze, mutism, etc.

Misaligned Thought *or Divine Intention:* The inherent understanding that consciousness extends beyond one's body temple. And as such, one can appear to get frozen between states of consciousness, depending on one's degree of alignment with one's mind, body and spirit. Likewise, with regards to this *matter*, one appears to be temporarily lost in the "center of thought" contemplating how and where to begin again. Having experienced the blending of the physical and nonphysical realms, both of which are alluring, one demonstrates for all concerned that undivided attention be paid to the focusing of thought in order to realign with the fullness of one's being.

Alignment Process: I go forward with the understanding that I am a blended being that is physical and nonphysical. I love having found the junction point in consciousness where I get to suspend time, still the body, and realign with my connection to the God-source of the universe. I have discovered that it is the worthwhile time spent contemplating thought before I act that has the greatest chance of manifesting my idea of a joy-filled life worth being responsive to.

Note: Caregivers may read the process to the loved ones, for they can hear you.

112. Schizophreniform—(See Schizophrenias—A.)

113. Schizotypal Personality

What's the Matter: Schizotypal Personality—A pervasive pattern of perceptual distortions and eccentricities where one makes incorrect interpretations of casual incidents and external events as having a particular and unusual meaning specifically for them; thereby causing a reduced capacity for close, social and interpersonal relationships.

Misaligned Thought *or Divine Intention:* The inherent understanding that we each create our own reality. That being the case, one finds that it is easier to remain aligned with the fullness of one's being when alone versus when interacting with others. This is due to the frustration experienced when trying to figure out the equally self-imposed realities and intentions of others. This *matter* is coupled with the recognition that others don't usually share one's interest in the nonphysical aspects of being. As such, one recognizes that the "normal" interpretation of the mundane aspects of life is not one's focus; but, rather, one is oriented towards the "paranormal" possibilities. This is mostly due to one's own divine intention, having observed how so many misinterpret the vastness of life experience. One's soul, therefore, magnifies the premise that even if one draws the incorrect or alternative conclusions about one's life experience, it does not separate or disconnect one from the God-source within.

Alignment Process: I came into the physical realm intending to remain consciously aware of the nonphysical aspects of my being. In so doing, I enjoy demonstrating that I get to determine my perception of reality. Therefore, I carry on with my ability to conjure alternative possibilities. I enjoy the broader meaning I attach to life, trusting the reality that my God-source within is the only validation I truly need.

114. Seasonal Affective (Reactions)—(See Depression with Seasonal Patterns.)

115. Selective Mutism

What's the Matter: Selective Mutism—A persistent failure to speak in specific situations where speaking is expected, which interferes with social communication, education or occupation; lasting at least one month.

Misaligned Thought or **Divine Intention:** The inherent understanding that at the level of *energy*, communication is not dependent on words but is further clarified by them. However, this awareness is mixed with the belief that one's words will not change the *matter*. Having had one's words minimized or overlooked, one goes into the silence. However, regardless of others' reactions, one need not retreat from conveying one's rightful sentiments with words; for there is much to say with regards to keeping oneself and relationships in alignment. Therefore, when one comes forth with the added gift of spoken language, one need only offer and honor the *energy* transmitted with one's own words; vowing to remain in alignment with one's own sacred intentions. Then, once alignment with one's own mind, body and spirit has been achieved, there is plenty of time for purposeful exploration of who one is without one's voice.

Alignment Process: I came into the physical with the divine ability to speak myself into alignment even when things are being said or done that I do not like. I am coming to understand that I always have the power to communicate with the ever-flowing God-source within me. Therefore, I convey my sentiments freely understanding that no one's voice need drown out my own.

116. Separation Anxiety

What's the Matter: Separation Anxiety—Recurrent excessive distress a child may experience when separation from home or primary caregivers occurs beyond that which is expected. (For Adults, See Dependent Personality.)

Misaligned Thought or **Divine Intention:** The unconscious and inherent understanding that one is supposed to feel safe and that safety, in fact, exists. However, this *matter* is mixed with the belief that there is a person or place outside of oneself that makes one feel safe in the world. And as such, one believes that one cannot survive and/or thrive without one's loved ones being near. But one does not understand that the safe place one seeks is found within. Therefore, to feel safe only requires one's awareness that the God-source within the universe connects one to a sustaining sense of well-being. As such, looking outside of oneself for constant comfort is a distraction from the deeper work that lies within, since maturation from childhood to adolescence is a *matter* that requires ever increasing emotional self-sufficiency.

Alignment Process: I now realize that I am safe because I am not "by myself" and, instead, I am "with the spirit part of my being" that is attached to everyone; and so there is no separation. I now understand that my loved ones can certainly enhance my feeling of connectedness, but they are not the source of my sustaining comfort; for my peace cometh from within.

Note: Ages 7 and younger affirm: My spirit within me connects me to my loved ones and all is well.

117. Sexual Problems (Reactions)

What's the Matter: Sexual Problems (Reactions)—Various disturbances that affect the processes that characterize the sexual response cycle (excitement, plateau, orgasm, resolution), including pain for women or erectile dysfunction for men, amongst others.

Misaligned Thought or **Divine Intention:** The inherent understanding that the connection between two souls is sacred and commands vulnerability. However, this *matter* is mixed with a conscious or unconscious fear of being "screwed" by someone psychologically and/or financially; and fear of the emotional pain it could cause after having been so vulnerable and gritty. The perception of being dominated can translate into believing one is either being emasculated or objectified, causing one to seek rigid control (which is rigid with an f = frigid). One has forgotten one's inherent understanding that pure sexual union requires two equally vulnerable partners. As a result, one has the faulty belief that sex can be embarrassingly invasive and/or result in an over-exposure of one's private parts (inner and outer) if another sees one unleashing sensuality that is expressed as tender, raw passion. As such, a disallowance and confusion between one's "hormones" and a "whore moans" (female or male) may ensue due to social taboos and restrictions on permission to enjoy sexual expression. One forgets that the co-creative *energy* exchanged in the sensual act is "spirit to spirit" as much as it is physical. Therefore, one's reluctance to allow oneself to fully surrender to sexual gratification of the body temple can interfere with experiencing the divinity inherent within the fullness of one's being that the soul came into the physical to glorify.

Alignment Process: I now reclaim my sexual prowess knowing that it has been embedded within me from the divine. I am free to release my hormones and joyously explore the fullness of my being, mind, body and spirit, understanding that the sexual co-creative act between two souls is also holy.

118. Sexual Abuse/Assault/Rape – (See Abuse A – Recipients; See Abuse B – Perpetrators.)

119. Shared Psychotic Disorder (Reaction)—(See Schizophrenias A.)

120. Sibling Relationship Problem—(See Relational Problems.)

121. Sleep Problems / Reactions (Insomnia, Breathing related, Circadian, etc.)

What's the Matter: Sleep Problems / Reactions—A variety of factors (mental, emotional, physical, etc.) that disrupt the body's natural cycle of slumber.

***Misaligned Thought or* Divine Intention:** The inherent understanding and appreciation for restoration. However, this *matter* is mixed with the faulty belief in "no rest for the weary," which causes one to resist restorative sleep and awaken tired. And as such, when the *energy* blockage is due to weariness, one only need align the mind and body with spirit, then one would understand that one can still rest with or without active slumber. Employing relaxation and meditative techniques that elevate one to the vibration of peace and tranquility, the body temple acquiesces and extracts from it the beneficial rejuvenation needed.

There are also instances, however, when slumber does not come when society's clock claims it should, and one may feel unconsciously pressured to conform to the dictates of culture when one is simply not in need of rest—not having used up its *energy* reserves. Therefore, one may unconsciously feel the need to resist conforming to specific norms with regard to being scheduled and regulated; for surely one's own internal clock will have one honor one's own need for sleep and restoration.

Alignment Process: I am opening to the divine idea that I am rejuvenated when my body temple signals me, as opposed to a society-based standard of when and where or how much sleep I need to function effectively. As such, I honor my body temple with relaxation and meditative rituals that replenish and align me with peace. I trust and honor my own "*inner knowing*" to cue my body temple when I should lie down in the comforting bed of restoration. For this divine awakening, I rest in peace.

122. Sleep Terrors—(See Sleep Reactions.)

123. Sleep Walking—(See Sleep Reactions.)

124. Social Anxiety/Phobia

What's the Matter: Social Anxiety—Excessive self-consciousness that brings on anticipatory anxiety and avoidance behavior in social situations, due to fear of being judged, criticized, embarrassed or humiliated by other people.

Misaligned Thought or **Divine Intention:** The inherent understanding that interaction with other souls on the planet was meant to be a more soulful exchange versus the emphasis on the body temple. Therefore, one feels that a quick or elongated social interaction does not fully represent the fullness of one's being. As a result, this incomplete interaction causes one undue anxiety. This is due to an unconscious faulty belief that validation of one's value comes from outside of oneself. As such, the *matter* turns into an issue of one's attention being externally focused versus internally focused and, therefore, superficial. One does not understand that despite anyone's foibles or gift of gab, others can see one's inner light. Therefore, one need only come into alignment with the fullness of one's being—mind, body and spirit—in order to maintain and exude one's true worth. (See Anxiety & see Phobias.)

Alignment Process: I am opening to the idea that there is more to social interactions than the superficial. I now understand that I am a "soul-filled being" with much more depth to realize. As I align my mind, body and spirit, I trust that I am always aiming to represent the best of me, which is my inner light. I look forward to connecting with others on a much deeper basis; for they, like me, are individualized expressions of the God-source in the universe. And they are seeking equally meaningful interactions that awaken our humanity. With this divine awareness, I am socially free.

125. Somatoform (aka Hysteria or Briquet's Syndrome)

What's the Matter: Somatoform—Physical complaints of symptoms where no physiological explanation can be found, which appears to indicate that the distress is psychological in nature.

Misaligned Thought or **Divine Intention:** The inherent understanding of the mind and body connection. However, this understanding is mixed with the belief that life's *matter* cannot be dealt with on a straightforward basis. One unconsciously transmutes the *matter* into psychosomatic manifestations that are void of a physical and medical explanation. As such, the absence of explanation emphasizes that *dis-ease* is predominately an outer manifestation of "thought" within the nonphysical realm. Having forgotten one's profound *inner knowing*, one does not appreciate the fact that since the cause is at the level of thought the cure is also at the level of thought. Therefore, as one gets to the core of the *energy*-based reaction, one will return to the wellness that is most dominant within one's energetic body by simply aligning one's body and mind with spirit.

Alignment Process: I am opening to the understanding that I came into the physical realm as a "well being" and that at the core of my being is *energy*. This is a subtle *energy* that connects me to the universal *energy* of spirit, which offers me the "free will" to amass all of the wellness that I am willing to allow, in any given moment. In this precious moment of now, I choose to realign my body temple with the *energy* that exudes wellness. I allow myself the right to bask in the sacred relief that allowing well-being offers.

126. Specific Phobia—(See Phobias.)

127. Spiritual Problem—(See Religious/Spiritual Problem.)

128. Stereotypic Movement (Reaction)

What's The Matter: Stereotypic Movement (Reaction)—A variety of motor behaviors that are repetitive, causing self-inflicted physical harm enough to require medical treatment (if protective measures were/are not used), i.e., head banging, self-biting, hand waving, hitting parts of own body, etc., and/or using objects with those behaviors.

Misaligned Thought *or Divine Intention:* The inherent understanding that the body temple is not the basis of one's being. As such, the soul understands that the inner spirit is what's most important and cannot be harmed. As a result, this reaction appears to convey one's attempt to realign with the vibrational resonance of one's nonphysical energetic body (often facilitated by music). The soul has made its point that no physical *"matter" matters*—not even the body temple when compared to the larger part of one's being, which is a subtle inner-knowing that well-being must commence from within. If one feels one must symbolically "bang my head against the wall," etc., to prove it's just a "housing" (in order to make this point clear and fulfill one's own divine intention), one will do so until realignment with the spirit is honored. (See Mental Retardation or See Anxiety, if present.)

Alignment Process: I came into this physical apparatus to clarify and magnify repetitively that I am more than my body temple. I am the spirit within.

Note: If severe or profound mental retardation is also present then caretakers can read the affirmation to their loved ones.

129. Substance Abuse or Dependence—(See Addictions.)

130. Substance Induced Psychotic Disorder (Reaction)—(See Addictions Psychotic Reactions (Brief.)

131. Telephone Scatologia—(See Paraphilias A.)

132. Tic Reactions

What's the Matter: Tic Reactions—Sudden and recurrent, painless, non-rhythmic stereotyped motor movements or vocalizations that may be simple or complex.

Misaligned Thought *or Divine Intention:* The inherent understanding that there are a variety of ways the soul can communicate its beingness. One uses nonverbal and nontraditional verbal offerings to emphasize that the *"energy basis"* of our connection to one another is beyond traditional communication patterns. As such, this *matter* acknowledges that everyone comes forth with unique idiosyncrasies that can be embraced and integrated without labels.

Alignment Process: I am coming to realize how acceptable I really am in what appears to be a sacred, yet, idiosyncratic world. This self-acceptance allows me to accept others who, like me, came forth with differences. I offer my magnified example of the fact that the connection with the God-source within is varied and expansive. I am proud of my willingness to overtly display my individual uniqueness, because it demonstrates the tremendous range of human beingness that there is. For this divine awareness, I am so grateful.

133. Tourette's Syndrome

What's the Matter: Tourette's Syndrome—Most commonly known for sudden inappropriate expression of socially unacceptable words or phrases and obscenities with no filtering process, along with vocal and facial tics.

Misaligned Thought or Divine Intention: The belief and inherent understanding that the soul came forth to say and do what one wants. Therefore, one chooses to ignore social customs and norms. The *matter* can be a misaligned thought or divine intention depending on one's alignment. If the *matter* manifests without obscenities, one has divine intent; but if it includes obscenities, the *matter* is based on an unaligned thought. In the case of the latter, one is allowing oneself to go ahead and do and say what one pleases, with a built-in reaction as a "hall pass" to do it. And in so doing, one is demonstrating how foul "language" can be when not expressed authentically. One does not understand that the vibration of "authentic beingness" is much higher than the vibe of being offensive and inappropriate. Actions and words that heckle and offend carry the *energy* of one's "insecurity" versus "security." Therefore, one needs to understand that one cannot be at the vibration of the insecurity one abhors and the vibration of the freedom one seeks simultaneously.

The Alignment Process: I love the freedom to express myself in genuine and creative ways outside of what is considered socially acceptable. It's liberating to say only what I truly think and do only what I want to do. And so, as I align my mind, body and spirit, I go forward, understanding that I can speak my truth and still be respectful of other souls' differences. For this revelation, I am humbled.

134. Transgender—(See Gender Dysphoria.)

135. Transvestic Fetishism—(See Paraphilias C & D—Transvestic Fetishism & Objects/Items.)

136. Trichotillomania

What's the Matter: Trichotillomania—The recurrent urge to pull out one's own hair, among other symptoms, which results in noticeable hair loss in any region of the body where hair may be expected to grow.

Misaligned Thought or **Divine Intention:** An inherent understanding that hair is symbolic of protection and warmth. In this matter, one further understands that true protection and warmth comes from a place that hair can't cover, which is within. However, this insight is mixed with a conflicting symbolism where one reaches for an unyielding warmth and protection from outside of oneself via people, things and/or achievement. One does not understand that dependence on external gratification is a hairy thing. As such, this energy block can only be truly relieved when one takes time to comb through one's deeper roots and align one's mind and body with spirit. One needs to recall the inner knowing that spirit is the only matter that can provide the warmth and protection one truly seeks.

Alignment Process: I am coming to understand that my *inner knowing* will always provide me with the warmth and protection I seek. I have learned that as I pull from my spiritual roots, I discover that well-being is my lock. As I align my mind, body and spirit, I release the need for external certainty and embrace the warm feeling of security that comes from a much deeper shaft within.

137. Urophilia – (See Paraphilias C.)

138. Vascular Dementia – (See Dementia.)

139. Vocal Tics – (See Chronic Motor or Tic Reactions.)

140. Voyeurism – (See Paraphilias A.)

141. Written Expression Disorder (Reaction) – (See Learning Disabilities.)

142. Zoophilia – (See Paraphilias A.)

WORLDWIDE CULTURAL SYNDROMES
MENTAL AND EMOTIONAL REACTIONS

Beyond Western Cultural Classifications to Worldwide Cultural Reactions

Note: In keeping with the above alternative descriptions and aligning processes, the following reactions, which are presentations within a cultural context, do not supersede the premise that the basis of mental health can be described with *symbolic meaning* that is at the level of thought. This is because the same *energy* permeates all of mankind's physical and nonphysical experience and supports the "all is one" premise that we are much more alike than we will ever be different. The cultural syndromes below are provided to honor the specific social microcosm's view of how reactions manifest, depending on ethnography. As such, the following names of reactions and traditional descriptions serve as the idioms that reflect the language of a people. (For complete medical descriptions of cultural syndromes, see commonly accepted medical dictionaries, encyclopedias, manuals and/or the latest edition of the official *International Classification of Diseases*—ICD.)

143. Amok (aka amuk or amuck)

What's the Matter: Amok – Indigenous to Malaysia; involves a sudden aggressive or violent episode by a male with no previous history of violence "running amuck (amok)." This is viewed by some as the person having been possessed; and is viewed by others as a dissociative episode, possibly triggered by the perception of having been slighted or insulted, followed by amnesia, with a return to a normal state.

Misaligned Thought or **Divine Intention:** The inherent understanding that anything that has gone out of alignment can come back. However, this understanding is mixed with the faulty belief that someone or something outside of oneself holds the power to one's happiness or despair. As such one seeks revenge, hoping to resolve the *matter* and regain one's ability to align with the joy-filled life one originally intended. One does not recognize that the vengeful act only offers relief in the disconnected moment, which is why one feels the need to forget the unaligned act. As such, the fulfillment one seeks can only be had as one learns to self soothe. For some with this reaction, disconnection can feel so far from the God-source within that medicinal remedies are often needed to assist with soothing one back into alignment. One needs to understand that when one realigns with one's mind, body and spirit, one need not disassociate to escape from the realities of the physical. Instead, one can ground oneself in the knowledge that no *matter* is too great to prevent well-being.

Alignment Process—It feels good to now know that I was right to seek relief, which meant I inherently knew that I could be soothed. I see now that all that I ever need to feel better about myself is already within me. I go forward prepared to align my own mind, body and spirit, forgiving myself for any past unaligned acts. I am coming to understand that there is no punishing Source in the universe; and since I am connected to that Source, within me is also a loving gentle being.

144. Ataque de nervios

What's the Matter: Ataque de nervios – Indigenous to certain groups of Caribbean, Latin America and Latin Mediterranean people; attributed to an acutely stressful or traumatic event, involving panic-like symptoms along with dissociative experiences, and returning to one's previous level of normative functioning.

Misaligned Thought or **Divine Intention:** The inherent understanding that well-being is achievable. However, this understanding is mixed with the belief that seeing or experiencing the human condition at its worst cannot be integrated into the psyche without extreme discomfort before realignment with well-being can take place. One does not understand that any agonizing emotion can be soothed and released relatively quickly if one is ready to release the *matter*. This reaction is likened to PTSD in North American culture. One needs to understand that if one realigns one's mind, body and spirit with universal principles, any *matter* that has gone out of alignment can come back, by the refocusing of attention on the joy of living. One needs to blend that knowledge with the understanding that we came into the physical knowing we would be exposed to both desirable and undesirable manifestations; yet these do not have to separate us from our alignment with the very well-being we seek.

Alignment Process: I am opening to the idea that I have the power within me to realign with well-being anytime I am ready to release the past, even if it were yesterday. The unpleasant *matter* can actually be over, if I allow it to be. I now understand that by coming back into alignment with my mind, body and spirit, I can refocus my attention on the joy of living. I give myself permission to go forward, investing my time and *energy* on the *matter* that makes me feel good.

145. Bilis and colera

What's the Matter: Bilis and Colera (aka **muina**) – Indigenous to Latin American and Latin Mediterranean groups; involves the emotions of anger and rage that directly affect the nervous system, gastro, etc.

Misaligned Thought or **Divine Intention:** An inherent understanding of the delicate balance between the mind, body and spirit connection and how our emotions translate and permeate the body temple as ease or *dis-ease* within our gut (gastro). When misaligned, any time one's emotions are not joyful, one *can* feel sad; and the sadness can lead to toxic anger and resentment. One does not understand that one has the power within to change the *matter* by trusting one's internal guidance, which is felt within the gut. One needs to bring oneself back into conscious alignment by focusing one's attention on well-being, where the *vibrational* shift in *energy* releases the toxic emotion.

Alignment Process: I came into the physical realm expecting to be a joy-filled being, capable of stomaching both the undesirable and desirable. I am opening to the idea that my alignment with my mind, body and spirit is a moment-by-moment quest, as I embrace the divinity of *flexibility* that promotes wellness. I go forward declaring to trust my gut more, understanding that it is the God-source within calling me to the joyous life experience I passionately seek.

146. Boufee delirante

What's the Matter: Boufee delirante—Indigenous to West Africa and Haiti; considered to be a brief period of psychosis involving sudden outburst of agitated and aggressive behavior, marked confusion, and psychomotor excitement; (Likened to Brief Psychotic Disorder in North American Culture.)

Misaligned Thought *or Divine Intention:* The inherent understanding that life includes both the physical and nonphysical. In manifesting this *matter*, one temporarily withdraws or releases expected rigid ways of perceiving what is real from what is unreal within the human experience; one understands the perception is abstract and beyond the current knowledge of brain chemistry. When one's ability to perceive the *matter* beyond the conventional constructs of consciousness (that connect the physical with the nonphysical) become blurred, one can become panicked without the familiar anchors of beingness. One need not fear one's ascent to expanded consciousness and obscure reality; instead, one may take comfort in the fact that there are simply subtle degrees of alignment connecting the physical and nonphysical realities. The true basis of one's reality—whether one's focus is physical, nonphysical or somewhere in between—is the unchanging fact that one's spirit is the part that's stable. (See Chapter Four, which describes more about how disorders are determined.)

Alignment Process: I am grounded in the fact that the God-source part of me is that which is stable. I now see that my attention to the nonphysical was never about me "falling apart" but, rather, my attempt to "reconnect" with the fullness of my being. I honor the fact that these other realities that I have experienced have expanded my understanding that life is no longer a question of what is "real or unreal" but, rather, what is "physical and nonphysical." For this sacred delineation and clarification, I am relieved as I find the perfect blended balance for me. (See Using Psychotherapy, Medication, & Herbal Remedies in the Sacretherapy® process in Chapter Eight.)

147. Brain fag

What's the Matter: Brain fag – Indigenous to West Africa, (similar to "studiation madness" in Trinidad); affects students in high school and college with concentration and recall problems; fatigue and burn-out; and somatic complaints about the head and neck.

Misaligned Thought or **Divine Intention:** The inherent understanding that one came into the physical realm to reach one's human potential that is a broad and expansive *matter*. However, when this knowing becomes imbalanced and rigid—misaligned—to the degree that one is basing one's "beingness" on performance as a human "doing" versus a human "being," one's *energies* wane. One does not understand that the psychology of achievement is based on a myriad of intentions that stimulate the mind, body and spirit. As such, if one recognizes that one's creative genius comes with ease and inspiration versus pressure or shame, one will honor one's intellectual capacity by reaching the divine potential one came into the physical to express.

Alignment Process: I came into this physical experience with divine intelligence. I love that my brain is tied into infinite knowing. As such, I can enjoy the creation process with ease, as my thoughts create the *matter* that I prefer to manifest. I will now go forward with the understanding that there is a balanced approach to pursuing that which is important to me, which includes soothing relaxation and joyful inspiration.

148. Dhat

What's the Matter: Dhat – Indigenous to India, similar to jiryan (India), sukra prameha (Sri Lanka), and shen-k'uei (China); involves severe anxiety and hypochondriacal concerns associated with the loss of semen via intercourse, nocturnal emissions, masturbation, or in urine resulting in feelings of weakness and exhaustion and loss of vital *energy* or chi.

***Misaligned Thought or* Divine Intention:** The inherent understanding that one possesses the vital *energy* of life. However, this *inner knowing* is mixed with a belief that one's *energy* and value is strictly tied to one's masculinity, which is tied to one's virility. As such, one fears that one's vital *energy* will be compromised if any unnecessary semen is expelled. This concern, paired with an already deteriorated self-worth, causes undue shame. This is especially associated with a perceived lack of power to sustain one's masculine ability to measure up to the task of implanting one's vital *energies* into the larger womb of cultural expectations and socialization. One does not understand that the predominant *energy* that gives one his life force, value and self-worth is the *subtle energy* of spirit that is inherent within one's entire being, not in a select organ. One needs to understand that the *energy* exchanged in the sexual act is as much spirit to spirit as it is physical. There is no punitive reduction of energies associated with sensual release, since it is a gift from the ever *potent* God-source within.

Alignment Process: I am opening to the idea that I came forth into the physical realm as a pulsating *energy* and individualized expression of the God-source within the universe. As such, the same loving *energy* I possess is the same ever-flowing life force that permeates my entire being. Therefore, my ability to tap into the fullness of my being is simply based on my alignment with my mind, body and spirit; for I am a potent "well being" with endless value and worth. (Also See Koro, Anxiety and Sexual Dysfunction.)

149. Falling-out (aka Blacking Out)

What's the Matter: Falling Out/Blacking Out—Indigenous to Southern United States and Caribbean groups; characterized by dizziness or light-headedness followed by a sudden collapse, where one is able to hear what's going on but feels powerless to move.

***Misaligned Thought or* Divine Intention:** The inherent understanding that there are some things in life we simply *don't stand for,* as the worthy divine beings we are. However, this understanding is mixed with the faulty belief that one cannot "stand" what one sees; thus, one thinks that the stressful *matter* in life is too difficult to withstand. As such, one believes that he or she is unable to flexibly adapt to life circumstances that are ever changing. One does not understand that one is a co-creator with the *matter* life presents; and, therefore, when the *matter* is displeasing, one has ample life force or prana to *pick oneself up*, get back in the game (of life) and remold the *energy*. One only needs to *fall* into alignment with one's mind, body and spirit to integrate the diversity of life experience.

Alignment Process: I am coming to realize that I am an adaptable and powerful creator. When I "stand" on universal principles, everything "falls" in line with my heart's desires. The God-source in the universe assures me that everything I need to create or handle any *matter* is within me. I go forward acknowledging the strength of this life force and behold its loving energy as I align with my mind, body and spirit.

150. Ghost Sickness

What's the Matter: Ghost Sickness – Indigenous to some American Indian tribes. Reaction is said to be caused by the ghost/spirit (aka Chindi—evil spirit) of someone dying and/or deceased, where one feels a variety of frightening symptoms consistent with anxiety and panic.

Misaligned Thought or **Divine Intention:** A belief and reverent understanding of the continuum of eternal life, where ancestors who transition join the collective *energy*. As such, "ghost sickness" is the ability to delve into the nonphysical realm and commune with the spirit of loved ones in person or in dreams. However, one misinterprets the interaction as an *intrusive external force* with negative intentions due to unresolved grief issues. As a result, one embraces this subtle *energy* with a severe anxious reaction. One does not understand that when a loved one transitions, the loved one's spirit is *not malevolent but benevolent* and can only visit in love and peace. Thus, any dream or perceived interaction to the contrary is one's own projection of the *matter*. And as such, one's own feelings of disconnection from the source of their being are realized. Thus, by focusing on reconnecting with one's own mind, body and spirit versus the spirit of the soul that has already transitioned, the split in *energy* would be healed.

Alignment Process: I am coming to understand with greater clarity the eternal connection between the physical and spirit world. I love knowing that the God-source in the universe is only a loving *energy*. And with that truth, I can now relax having clarified that the best way I can preserve my well-being, please my loved ones, or honor my ancestral lineage is to acknowledge that they have returned to pure *positive energy* as loving benevolent beings. So all I need to do now is come into alignment with my own mind, body and *spirit* to perceive and benefit from that same loving energy, which I am reminded also exists within me. (See Bereavement.)

151. Hwa-byung

What's the Matter: Hwa-byung (aka Wool-hwa-byung) – Indigenous to Korea. Reaction involves the suppression of angry feelings being experienced as a hot or heated sensation in the chest and/or upper and middle abdomen, along with various other symptoms associated with anxiety or depression. (See Adjustment and Somatoform reactions above.)

Misaligned Thought or **Divine Intention:** The inherent understanding of the oneness of mind and body. However, one has not extended that awareness to how the mind controls the body and one's overall well-being. As such one holds a faulty belief that one's well-being is granted by someone or some power apart from oneself. And when what one seeks is not granted by others, one feels that one cannot express discontent outwardly for fear of further disallowance. As a result, one outwardly suppresses the inward feelings of angry *matter*. But one does not recognize that the angry emotion or fire (hwa-byung) that burns within is 'creative fire' that *energizes* one to cook up new ideas and strategies to live the life one prefers to live. Therefore, all one need do is understand that the angry emotions can be released and soothed by aligning one's mind and body with spirit. Then one's passionate desires can be expressed openly and brought into joyful fulfillment (See Alignment Scale in previous chapter.)

Alignment Process: I am opening to the idea that the freedom and well-being I seek are simmering within me. I have equal access to the God-source within the universe. I go forward with the burning passion to come into alignment with my own mind, body and spirit. I give voice to my authentic desires and I allow myself the full range of emotion that ignites my creative fire.

152. Jikoshu-kyofu – (See Taijin kyofusho below.)

153. Khyol (aka Khyāl cap)

What's the Matter: Khyol – Indigenous to Southeast Asia and Vietnam), Reaction is often known as "wind illness", that is sometimes accompanied by fever (*krun*) and dizziness (*vilmuk*) in addition to other somatic disturbances associated with cold or flu-like symptoms (that are not climate related but brought on by internal stressors) with differing degrees of severity from mild to life threatening. (Also see Somatization and Anxiety.)

Misaligned Thought or **Divine Intention:** The inherent understanding of the mind, body and spirit connection. Whereas the *energy* basis of the "wind" often symbolizes one's *breath of life* (air which carries prana-life force) connected to one's spirit. However, this intrinsic understanding is mixed with *split energy* due to imbalances between mind, body and spirit where one's *energy* becomes stifled in one area and presents as physical manifestations, i.e. *dis-ease.* As such, one need only realign the body temple with one's mind and spirit by seeking the middle way (balance) in order to allow the well-being that belongs to one by divine right.

Alignment Process: I am opening to the understanding that I came into the physical realm as a "well being" with the *breath of life*—filling me with life-force (prana) that ultimately becomes "the wind beneath my wings" that carries me to a place of higher consciousness for renewal. Therefore, I gladly tap into this *subtle energy* that connects me to the universal *energy* of spirit, as I bring myself and life circumstances back into balance with wellness principles that realign my mind, body and spirit.

154. Koro

What's the Matter: Koro – Indigenous to Malaysians in South and East Asia; aka *shuk yang, shook yong,* and *suo yang* (Chinese); *jinjinia bemar* (Assam); or *rok-joo* (Thailand). Reaction includes a sudden fear that the penis, vulva, and/or nipples will recede into the body and possibly cause death.

Misaligned Thought or **Divine Intention:** The inherent understanding that sexual release or connection is an *energy* exchange. However, this awareness is mixed with the faulty belief that enjoying one's body temple in ways that bring sensual gratification is *"to die for."* But one misunderstands that only the ego must *die* for the spirited *energy* of sexual orgasm to come alive. One's confusion is understandable, however when sexual repression is socially enforced, it causes one's natural psycho-sexual desire for penetration and tantalization to recede into the body of social intolerance. As a result, one does not recognize that the vital *energy* that flows throughout one's body temple that creates the climatic release is a *divine* source, not a diminishing force. As such, one may embrace one's inclinations knowing that the spirit within came into the physical to glory in the *energies* released in sensual expression. Therefore, one only need to align one's mind and body with spirit to maintain one's natural well-being, which is forever perky and well-endowed.

Alignment Process: I am opening to the idea that my natural desire for joyous sensual gratification is a life-giving *energy* and embedded within me by the God-source in the universe. Therefore, every part of my body temple is permanently endowed by this holy vital *energy.* So I am free to embrace the fullness of my being and joy found within sensuality as often as I choose, whether by myself or with another consenting adult. I now understand that my permissions come from a higher power and authority within; and for this awareness, I am divinely relieved. (See Anxiety and Sexual Reactions.)

155. Latah

What's the Matter: Latah – Indigenous to people of Malaysian or Indonesian origin and found in other parts of the world: aka amurakh, irkunii, ikota, olan, myriachit, and menkeiti (Siberian groups); bah tschi, bah-tsi, and baah-ji (Thailand); imu (Ainu, Sakhalin, Japan); and mali-mali and silok (Philippines). Reaction can involve temporary dissociative or trancelike behaviors as a result of a sudden startle or fright where one exhibits echolalia *(imitation of words or phrases)* or echopraxia *(imitation of movements).*

Misaligned Thought or **Divine Intention:** The inherent understanding that relief is achievable. However, one may not recognize that regardless of how *startling* and *frightening* one's own life experiences may appear to be, one demonstrates that one's relief cannot be sustained by simply mimicking another's life, persona, words or actions. One is therefore invited to embrace self acceptance and understand that instead of attempting to flee or "snap out of" one's life in the unaligned moment, it is far better to go within and re-acclimate oneself with one's own *inner knowing.* This knowing guides one with "what to say" and "what moves to make" that can handle the *matter.* In this manner, one tunes into the true source that keeps one grounded and safe as one continues to confront life experiences that are not preferred. One will then come to know that the fearful shock one experiences is simply an indicator that one may need to *speak* and *move* in the direction of one's own preferences and align with the security found within one's own mind, body and spirit.

Alignment Process: I am coming to understand that the *outer direction* I am seeking during times of *startling uncertainty* can only be attained with my *inner knowing.* I embrace this sacred guide, recognizing that any frightening *matter* is simply my indicator that the path to security and well-being is within. Therefore, as I align my mind and body with spirit, I go forward with the confidence that the spirit within me is fearless.

156. Locura – (aka *loco*) – Indigenous to Latin American and Latin Americans in the United States.) (See Schizophrenias.)

157. Mal de ojo

What's the Matter: Mal de ojo (meaning "evil eye")—Indigenous in Mediterranean cultures. Reaction is attributed to an adult giving an envious or admiring look to children (mainly), which is said to give off negative *energy* from the eyes and cause the person receiving the gaze to experience various distressing physical or somatic symptoms.

Misaligned Thought or **Divine Intention:** The belief and intrinsic understanding that as *energy* beings we transmit *energy* from one person to another. However, one does not understand that the *energy* light of others, especially children, is so brilliant that it attracts attention from others who are benefiting from that gaze. The gaze that comes from others is *not* with negative intent per se but with the desire to connect with the light within themselves. As such, the ones that are believed to be affected need understand that it is not how others *look* at them but how they look at themselves that will *matter*—while also, understanding that *too much* of any particular *energy* can still create imbalances, even when the *energy* is positive. Therefore, the affected one need simply come back into alignment with one's energies by aligning the mind, body and spirit, trusting that nothing outside of oneself can penetrate one's spirit.

Alignment Process: I came into the physical realm understanding that I am an "energy being" capable of giving and receiving *energy*. As such, the core of my being is worthy of admiration, as is the core of light in others. I magnify for the world that the light of God is not just in the most innocent, talented or beautiful amongst us but exists brilliantly in everyone who aligns mind, body and spirit. I am simply a ray of *energy* reflecting that truth. (See Adjustment Reaction.)

158. Nervios

What's the Matter: Nervios – Indigenous to Latin American groups and amongst Latinos in the United States; and also as *nervra* among Greeks in North America. Reaction is brought on by stressful and difficult life experiences, causing emotional distress, and various physical and somatic disturbances, resulting in a temporary inability to function.

Misaligned Thought or **Divine Intention:** The inherent understanding of the mind and body connection. However, this understanding is mixed with the faulty belief that the mind cannot assimilate life changes with ease. This is due to an unconscious discomfort with uncertainty and an unwillingness to accept one's need for flexibility. As such, one's rigidity can cause a variety of somatic reactions depending on the level of one's resistance. One does not understand that the split in *energy* is due to a psycho-spiritual conflict that is deeper than the outward appearance of the *matter*. Therefore, if one would align the mind and body with spirit, then one could soothe one's nerves, disperse the *energy* blockage and appreciate the broader outlook of the *matter*.

Alignment Process:—I am coming to understand that open-mindedness and a flexible embrace is all I need to ease my need for certainty. I am opening to the idea that the certainty of *how to handle life* is attained through my *inner knowing*. As I align my mind and body with "spirit," I go forward, trusting, that any and all *matter* can be integrated with divine perspective. For this awareness, I am relieved. (See Anxiety and Somatoform.)

159. Pibloktoq

What's the Matter: Pibloktoq – Indigenous to the Arctic and Subarctic Eskimo regions. Reaction involves an abrupt dissociative episode accompanied by various physical, manic and somatic symptoms lasting up to 12 hours and ending with complete amnesia with regards to the episode. (See Dissociative and Amnesia.)

***Misaligned Thought* or Divine Intention:** The unconscious belief and understanding that one can always remove one's attention away from the *matter*. However, this understanding is mixed with the faulty belief that intense unwanted experiences cannot be integrated "consciously" and with ease. As such, one decides to rid oneself of the cumulative *matter* in one massive display of discontent, so powerful that it causes one to temporarily lose consciousness. However, the longing to release the pent-up *energy* is also mixed with one's rigid hold onto yesterday's unpleasantries which interferes with today's potential to experience joy in the present moment. And, therefore, all one need do in order to come back into alignment with one's well-being is to align one's mind and body with spirit. Here, one can "consciously choose" to release the *matter* with ease versus "unconsciously forgetting," and thereby seek a new reference point where one can begin again.

Alignment Process: I have everything I need within me to face any and everything that I have created in my life. As such, I allow myself the full range of emotion: the good, the bad and the ugly, for each have enlightened aspects. I can choose to remember what I want to remember and forget what I want to forget. With this divine knowledge, I embrace self-love and compassion for the life I have lived, understanding that I am always in the process of becoming.

160. Qi-gong Psychotic Reaction

What's the Matter: Qi-gong Psychotic Reaction—Indigenous to China. Reaction affects those who may practice this health enhancing exercise of vital *energy* "inappropriately or obsessively," which may in turn act as a stressor that triggers or precipitates various dissociative or psychosomatic symptoms.

***Misaligned Thought* or Divine Intention:** The belief and understanding that the core of one's being is *energy*. As such, one finds oneself most aligned when consciously interfacing with the *energy*-spirited beingness within one's core. Therefore, one forgets that the life force of qi (chi) is about balance; and, as such, one can extract equal value and joyful contentment in one's physical apparatus when one comes into alignment with one's mind, body and spirit. Then one may understand that there is plenty of time to appreciate one's nonphysical energies when one transitions back into pure positive *energy*. One can then embrace the fact that until that time, one is in the physical realm to enjoy the fullness of one's being and also to give attention to the *matter* that is physical.

Alignment Process: I am opening to the understanding that the duality of my being commands a balanced embrace. As such, I go forward consciously aligning my mind, body and spirit so that I can enjoy those things that are physical and those things nonphysical. I recognize and appreciate that the life force (qi) within me is ever present, regardless of where I choose to focus my *energy.*

161. Rootwork

What's the Matter: Rootwork (aka *hoodoo)* – Originated in West Africa (aka *Ggbo*) and is found throughout the African diaspora to include the Caribbean and Southern United States within African American, African Caribbean and European populations; and is found in Latino societies as *mal puesto* or *brujeria.* Reaction may cause panic and anxiety, along with various other symptoms, due to one's fear or belief in being harmed (via *hoodoo*).

Misaligned Thought or **Divine Intention:** The belief and intrinsic understanding that the *root* of the universe is subtle *matter* that can be molded and shifted. However, one does not understand that the *energy* Source within the universe is not punitive but is a loving *energy* that brings relief and not *dis-ease.* Therefore, to alleviate the *matter,* one only need come back into alignment with the fullness of one's being which is *rooted* in the spirit of well-being.

Alignment Process: I am opening to the idea that the fullness of my being is *rooted* in well-being. Therefore, nothing and no one outside of me can shift or mold my *energy* but me and the God-source within me. As such, I align my mind and body with spirit which elevates my vibration to the frequency where I am confident of my well-being. For I trust that I am connected to a loving and benevolent Source in the universe and all is well in my life.

162. Sangue dormido – Indigenous to Portuguese Cape Verde Islanders)
(See Somatoform and Conversion Reactions above.)

163. Shenjing shuairuo – Indigenous to China);
(See Depression and Anxiety Reactions above.)

164. Shen-k'uei

What's the Matter: Shen-k'uei – Indigenous to Taiwan; aka *Shenkui* in China. Reaction involves marked anxiety or panic symptoms attributed to excessive semen loss from frequent intercourse or masturbation, feared because of belief that a loss of semen is a loss of one's vital essence and thereby life threatening. (Similar to Dhat and Koro.)

***Misaligned Thought or* Divine Intention:** The inherent understanding that one possesses the vital *energy* of life. However, this awareness is mixed with the faulty belief that one's masculinity is threatened or diminished via sexual expression, coupled with the fear that enjoying one's body temple in ways that bring sensual gratification is detrimental to one's life. As such, when sexual repression is socially enforced, one's natural psycho-sexual desire for penetration and release is shamed; it, therefore, mutates into unhealthy restraint. One does not understand that the vital *energy* that flows throughout one's body temple that creates the climatic release is a *divine* source, not a diminishing force. The spirit within came into the physical to glory in the energies released in sensual expression. Therefore, one only needs to balance and align one's mind, body and spirit to maintain one's life force, which is filled with sacred virility.

Alignment Process: I am opening to the idea that my natural desire for joyous sensual gratification is a life-giving *energy* and embedded within me by the God-source in the universe. Every part of my body temple is permanently endowed by this holy vital *energy*. I am free to embrace the fullness of my being and joy found within sensuality as often as I choose, whether by myself or with another consenting adult. My permissions come from the authority within. For this awareness, I am divinely relieved. (See Dhat, Koro, Sexual Reactions, and Anxiety above.)

165. Shin-byung

What's the Matter: Shin-byung—Indigenous to Korea. Reaction involves anxiety due to what has been described as ancestral spirits possessing a loved one, causing various other symptoms.

***Misaligned Thought or* Divine Intention:** The belief and inherent understanding that there is a continuum between the nonphysical and physical world; and as blended beings, one may interact on many levels with the spirit world fulfilling sacred contracts. However, one does not recognize that once a soul transitions, it returns only to "pure positive *energy*"' incapable of malevolent intentions. Therefore, one may channel the *energy* of another soul as a co-creative act, but not be overtaken by it. As such, one need not experience any decline in one's own well-being but instead come into greater alignment with one's own mind, body and spirit within that one already *possesses.*

Alignment Process: I came into the physical realm understanding that I am a blended being with access to higher spiritual knowing—an *inner knowing* that allows me access to multiple dimensions. These are dimensions where loving *energy* flows through the physical and nonphysical realm. This loving *energy* is accessible to me when I am in alignment with my own mind, body and spirit. Therefore, I embrace this loving *energy* with the understanding that the *God-source within* me is the same "positive spirit" that *possesses* the body temple of every living being.

166. Shubo-kyofu – Indigenous to Japan); (See Body Dysmorphic.)

167. Spell

What's the Matter: Spell – Indigenous to European and African Americans in the Southern regions of the United States. Reaction is described as a trance-like state where one communicates with deceased relatives or spirits; could be misconstrued as psychosis in clinical settings.

Misaligned Thought *or Divine Intention:* The belief and inherent understanding that at the core of the universe is *energy*; and that at different levels of consciousness, one is able to interact anywhere on the continuum of physical to nonphysical by aligning one's mind and body with spirit. One's *vibration* is able to reach a frequency where one's clairvoyant abilities are sensitive enough to connect with loved ones and other souls that have crossed over to the other side of the continuum of life (where loved ones realign with pure positive *energy*).

Alignment Process: I love knowing that I have within me the capacity to elevate my vibration to a level that can bridge consciousness. I am a multidimensional soul that honors the fullness of my being. For this validation, I am so grateful.

168. Susto

What's the Matter: Susto (aka *espanto, chibih, pasmo, 'perdida de alma',* or *tripaida*)—Indigenous to Mexico, Central America, South America and some Latinos in the United States. Reaction involves a frightening event that causes the soul to leave the body, which then results in a combination of various uncomfortable physical symptoms.

Misaligned Thought or **Divine Intention:** The belief and intrinsic understanding that the body temple is simply the housing of the eternal soul. The soul, then, has unlimited access to the spirit world, where the soul leaving the body (aka astroplaning) to interface with that dimension is considered a natural phenomena. However,, this *matter* is mixed with the belief that the soul cannot *remain* in the body to realign with the source, and that the body temple experiences *dis-ease* as a result of seeking its realignment. This is not the case, since one's body temple remains connected to one's soul as long as one is breathing, taking in oxygen, which is the prana of life. One can, therefore, realign in the physical or nonphysical realms. As such, reorienting or grounding oneself back into the physical, after experiencing the duality of dimensions, need not be a disruption in ease. This experience, instead, could be a joyful reconnection that honors the realigning of one's mind, body and spirit.

Alignment Process: I came into the physical realm with the awareness that I would have unlimited access to the fullness of my being. I now recognize that anytime I seek comfort, it is natural to focus my attention on the spiritual plane in order to align my mind and body with spirit. I realize that as a blended being, I am simply allowing my soul its freedom to interface with multi-dimensions. For this confirmation, I am relieved.

169. Taijin kyofusho (or Jikoshu-kyofu – a subset of Taijin kyofusho)

What's the Matter: Taijin kyofusho—Indigenous to Japan. Reaction involves a social phobia where the person has intense fear of public embarrassment or scrutiny, where one's body or specific body parts may be viewed as being offensive to others; (Jikoshu-kyofu—fear of offensive body odor).

Misaligned Thought or **Divine Intention:** The inherent understanding that one's body temple does not fully represent the fullness of one's being. However, one forgets that the *"matter* of the body temple" was created simply to allow the spirit access to experience the physical world. It was not meant to be used as one's focal point to "focus on" but rather to "focus through." As a result, when one's focus is reversed, one has a faulty belief that the validation of one's value is based on the physical aspect. Therefore, one seeks confirmation from outside of oneself versus the inside. One's attention to one's beingness is externally focused and superficial when one does not understand that one's value and beauty comes from within. One's interaction with others is meant to be a much more soulful exchange. One only needs to come back into alignment with the fullness of one's being in order to see and feel one's true worth.

Alignment Process: I am opening to the idea that there is more to social interactions than the superficial. I finally understand that I am a soulful being with much more depth to realize. As I align my mind, body and spirit, I trust that I will continuously discover more about my inner beauty, divine intelligence and profound potential to connect with others on a much deeper basis. I see that they, like me, are individualized expressions of the God-source in the universe, seeking meaningful interactions that awaken our humanity. With this divine awareness, I am socially free. (See Body Dysmorphic, and See Social Anxiety.)

170. Zar

What's the Matter: Zar – Indigenous to Ethiopia, Somalia, Egypt, Sudan, Iran and other North African and Middle Eastern societies. Reaction includes dissociative symptoms where one describes having been possessed by unkind spirits that inflict *dis-ease,* and then participates in a ritual to clear it.

Misaligned Thought or **Divine Intention:** The belief and inherent understanding that there is a continuum between the matter of the nonphysical and physical world; and as blended beings, we may interact on many levels with the spirit world. However, one does not recognize that once a soul transitions, it returns only to "pure positive energy" incapable of malevolent intentions. Therefore, one only need come into alignment with the positive aspects of one's own mind, body and spirit within that one already possesses to achieve a more sustainable sense of well-being.

Alignment Process: I am coming to understand the eternal connection between the physical and spirit world. I understand that when our spirit transitions, it returns to pure positive *energy* as only a loving, benevolent being. As such, as I come into alignment with my own mind, body and spirit, I understand that the God-source within the universe is the same positive spirit that possesses the body temple of every living being. For this divine confirmation, I trust that all is truly well! (See Bereavement.)

4
HOW DID THE MATTER MANIFEST?

The Flawed (Misaligned) Initiation—Understanding Conditioning, Memes and Old versus New Linguistic Programming

Step Three

"We stand bewildered before the mystery of our own making and the riddles of life that we will not solve, and then accuse the great Sphinx of devouring us."
—Helen Blavatsky

As stated in the *stream of consciousness*—the *matter* of you (Chapter Two), an "aligned" soul comes forth expecting to live out its sacred intentions, free to do what it feels would assist in the manifestation of that desire. Then something happens that confuses the soul and causes it to try to adapt to its new environment and the other soul-filled people within it, but often at great cost. Yet, the ability to adapt is a necessary survival tool for all life. However, there is a difference between "adapting" versus "assimilating" to the degree that other people's preferences and voices drown out your own voice. This happens when people begin to worry about fitting in and wanting to comply with other people's wishes, especially if it is their parents, spouse, peers or others that they are attached to and respect or love. They worry about what would happen if they exercised an independent thought and didn't follow the status quo of what they were told they should do or be. They then sometimes become fear-based and tentative about their own *inner knowing*. No longer at ease, and now open to mental and emotional *dis-ease* where living with an element of fear becomes a way of being, they begin to do what Jungian analyst Dr. Estes author of *Women Who Run With the Wolves* (1992) calls "normalizing the abnormal." They start to propagate the same information and admonishments that held them in captivity, yanking them from their own well-being, causing therapists everywhere to ask "What's the *matter*?"

Some fake it, though, by pretending to go along with the crowd in order to not lose affection and acceptance. And others just plain old "sell out," *consciously* knowing full well that they are giving up their power (*energy*), while others choose to go numb and live their lives unconscious to the fact that they have become ***"conditioned."*** The untrained eye can be oblivious to this. It's an insidious thing that creeps up on you, and before you know it, the soulful initiation from the *stream of consciousness* is almost null and void, but fortunately, not quite.

Let's explore the concept of *conditioning* along with *memes* and old *linguistic programming,* since they greatly help to explain "how the *matter* manifested" in the first place. Let's explore them one by one:

I: Conditioning—has to do with how we come to learn what is considered the preferred or expected response to something, and under what conditions that learning takes place, which can be to one's benefit or detriment. Naturally, when it benefits one's soul, negative *matter* does not manifest. Therefore, it's only when it's to one's detriment that we concern ourselves. Conditioning has been around for as long as man has been around with a desire to enforce individual 'preferences or will' upon one another. But the term "conditioning" was made popular by two scientists: Dr. Ivan Pavlov, who brought us *classical conditioning*, and Dr. B.F. Skinner, who taught us about *operant conditioning.* The two types have distinctive features; but in order to spare you the psychobabble, I will move ahead in laymen's terms. In layman's terms, conditioning is sometimes referred to as *associative learning,* since it is based on how a behavior can be associated with consequences, i.e. rewards and punishment. Therefore, in order to become conditioned, something must become dependent upon something else (conditional).

Here's a well-known example: A baby elephant in a circus is taught to give up its natural desire for freedom and stay in its cage by having a chain around its ankle. It tries to get it off, but is whipped with a strap every time it tries, until it gives up and eventually stops even trying. Once the elephant is fully grown, the same little chain is used to keep the elephant in its place. However, the full-grown elephant could easily yank the chain off with its adult strength and size, and even destroy the whip and whip holder; but due to early conditioning, the elephant surrendered its power a long time ago and may not even recall that it was the one that surrendered. It is still afraid that if it did try, it would be whipped again, not realizing that it has the ability to now be free. This is also known as ***learned helplessness***—when animals or people become conditioned to believe that a situation is unchangeable or inescapable—invoking powerlessness.

Here's another example using humans this time: Let's say someone or let's just say it could be you, may have been taught as a child to give up your natural desire for freedom by being forced (similar to chained) to believe that there was only one way to be *considered good*. You didn't really agree with that, and you tried to assert your different opinion but were whipped with a belt (similar to the strap elephants were whipped with, literally or with words) every time you did, until you gave up and eventually stopped even trying. And then, once you became an adult, the same admonishment (words or whips) that was used when you were a child was still being used to keep you in your place. But you, like the elephant, surrendered your power a long time ago. In fact, you, like the elephant, may not even recall having ever surrendered and/or are still afraid of being whipped if you tried to free yourself, due to the conditioning of *learned helplessness*. And as a result, you don't realize that you have the ability now to truly be free. Note: Giving up on trying to assert one's freewill as a child or baby elephant is certainly about survival, but not asserting one's freewill as an adult is usually about *conditioning*.

II. Memes—The term "meme" was coined by evolutionary biologist Richard Dawkins in his book, *The Selfish Gene* (1976), which is described as a "unit of culture" (an idea, belief, pattern of behavior, etc.) that is "hosted" in one or more individual minds and which can reproduce itself, thereby jumping from mind to mind. This conclusion was also confirmed by sociologist Douglas Hofstadter, author of *The Meme Machine* (1985), in his study of memes. "A meme spreads like a virus and can penetrate any mind, downloading the information seamlessly as it also issues instructions on how to spread itself more," according to the book: Virus of the Mind, by Richard Brodie, whose book expands on the groundwork of the before-mentioned scientists. Brodie, however, builds on how memes can affect a person's "freewill" in many areas of human experience, likened to a computer virus, infecting people without their ever being the wiser. Memes can implant information in you that you didn't even realize you were operating your life with (other people's beliefs).

Meme evolution, based on the three above sources, is not designed to benefit the individual, but is solely invested in just spreading more memes. All three books are worth reading and describe several kinds of memes, but the one that we mostly need concern ourselves with as it relates to Sacretherapy® is from Brodie's book called the *strategy-meme,* where you can *consciously* program yourself with memes versus having them unconsciously implanted. That's really important to know because that means that the *strategy-meme* allows you to consciously choose the memes that can benefit your well-being. The strategy-meme, he says, takes into consideration that anything claiming to be *dogmatic truth* is in actuality more like a half-truth that may be useful only in certain contexts. It's sort of the "meme of memes" that can override the other memes like an anti-virus protection for your computer that searches and debugs.

The implications of how memes impact mental and emotional well-being are pretty clear. A "*meme,*" which is basically an *inherited belief,* can be spread without any regard for your individual needs, which can obviously have detrimental consequences. For example, mental illness is something most people fear because, due to *memes*, it has been labeled to be outside of the normative curve. It does not seem to *matter* that this curve was created and decided on by a dreadfully small number of people. There are billions of us on the planet, and yet, less than a thousand committee members per country, if that many, are the final decision makers of what's normal for the rest.

And since memes can affect any mind, memes can also be spread into the well-meaning mental health profession, too. The professionals, in turn, unknowingly, spread the memes to others, and so forth. Thus, if someone's way of thinking or behaving is different from what the majority meme-holders have decided to classify as normal, then that person may be described as "mentally ill" instead of just "different." Being seen as "different" won't serve the self-perpetuating meme, and therefore, doesn't spread as fast as something taboo like mental illness. (Meme theories explain this concept in detail.)

The same thing goes for well-being. If it were a popular meme to believe that "Well-being is already yours by divine right," that would call into question a lot of other beliefs with regard to "sickness." It would mean that the Universal Source of all there is created you as a "well being." And if that's the case, then a great deal of self-reproach and needless suffering wouldn't be an issue. And therefore, that type of meme could put a lot of our well-meaning religions out of business, unless they were being utilized strictly for praise, because there would be no punishment, no damnation, and no need to be saved, since there wouldn't be anything to be saved from. It could put the mental health profession, and some other healers, out of business as well, because no one would be in need of our assistance with their healing. People would simply know that they were "well beings." They would *know* to go within and take counsel from their own *inner knowing*, their own inner guidance that comes from the source of their well-being. What a glorious meme that would be. Oops, I guess I just spread it.

Thus, it is the strategy-meme that I desire for you to underline and remember from this section on memes, because the strategy-meme is the meme that can stop other memes in their track. To facilitate this, I offer seven questions that you will be asked towards the end of this chapter that can greatly assist you with how to counteract memes.

III. Neuro-linguistic programming (NLP)—is a term that was coined by Richard Bandler and John Grinder. According to Barbara Gibson, author of *The Complete Guide To Understanding & Using NLP*: NLP has three components: "neuro" relates to the brain and the neurological processes involved with sending and receiving information; "linguistic" concerns the verbal and nonverbal information the brain processes; and "programming" relates to how the verbal and nonverbal information sent and received by the brain is interpreted or assigned *meaning*.

NLP isn't as popular as it was in the 1970s, but I still appreciate the value I found inherent within its essence. The Founders' intention for NLP was based on their desire to describe for people how to use models of language and communication to get the results they want in their future. This I totally support, since how we express the diversity of life experience is crucial, for much is in a *word*. As such, right alongside the founders of NLP, I also want to assist people in getting what they desire using language and a communication style that is in the best interest of preserving well-being. The ***old linguistic programming*** that I've been pointing to throughout this book did just the opposite, since it used emotionally charged language to control people. NLP came onto the scene in an attempt to use language in positive ways to assist people instead of controlling them. Prior to NLP, many used the old models of language and communication to get the results they wanted—but that ended up being toxic. Old linguistic programming was negative and the updated version coined by NLP founders is quite positive.

In fact, the Association for Neuro-linguistic Programming says on its website that "phenomenological research is free from hypotheses, pre-conceptions and assumptions, and seeks to *describe* rather than explain." Therefore, how we *describe* something like mental and emotional issues is crucial. Describing them negatively can be detrimental, which is why the Sacretherapy® approach offers an alternative description of mental and emotional diagnoses in an attempt to de-pathologize the *matter* of one's human experience.

Let's fast forward beyond the *neuro* and *programming* aspects of NLP, since I believe that by now you already have a good idea with regards to how information can be taken in through the senses, based on what has already been stated under conditioning and memes. So we needn't approach it from a third angle. But what I do want to *describe* from the NLP model is how the language part of NLP affects mental and emotional well-being; for surely the way ***language and words are*** imparted can trigger blind obedience, compliance or conformity to the conditioning at hand.

Let's try demonstrating this using a few terms from the field of mental health. What do you think of when you hear the words "ADHD?" Do you picture someone enjoying and appreciating all the stimuli one observes in his or her environment or someone bouncing off the walls? If you chose the latter, the media-charged *word* may be what helped you to give it that interpretation, as well as perhaps your personal conditioning. What about the words "mental disorder"? Do you picture someone who speaks and behaves in a way that is different from you, or someone that you feel is crazy or unstable? If you chose the latter, the emotionally-charged *words* may have gotten you, again, as well as your conditioning.

Let's do one more. What about the words "religious problem." Do you picture someone whose spiritual beliefs are just different from yours or someone you believe is going to hell for not complying with a supposedly sanctioned path? Again, if you chose the latter, the *words* more than likely triggered an interpretation based on social upbringing (conditioning) and media propaganda; a meme that went unchecked, and there you went with the easier automatic thought, *unconsciously* surrendering your own ability to give the issue a more thoughtful consideration.

Here's where the expression "choose your *words* carefully," really means to choose your *thoughts* carefully, too. Words *matter.* Seeing "words and matter" side-by-side is interesting since *words* are expressed thought, which forms *matter.* Therefore, words are also transmitters of *energy.*

Your choice of words, the language you use, and how you describe your experiences will greatly influence your ability to come into alignment. As such, a willingness to begin listening to your own *inner knowing* is crucial versus swallowing "whole" someone else's *words* about what they told you is right or wrong. For instance, if what is being shared in this book resonates with your spirit, and you decide to share it with someone else that you respect and they hate it, will you allow their energetic *words*, or voice, to drown out your own, or will you trust your own *inner knowing* (spirit) that feels that this may be good for you? Some people let others rob them of their joy by telling them that their willingness to embrace a new outlook is a bunch of positive-thinking hoopla. This is because it contains ideas that the admonishers don't understand and are too stuck in their own conditioning to allow themselves to check it out. So please, check it all out for yourself. Every book listed in the resources and bibliography in the back of this book is valuable, and you are also encouraged to find others on your own, then draw your conclusions. That way, you will immediately recognize that the sentiment of others is coming from their own conditioning, memes, and old linguistic programming; and it has nothing whatsoever to do with you and your desire to expand and increase your knowledge to have a better quality of life.

Still, many times if the others in our lives have a convincing enough rationale as to why we should abandon our own instincts and trust theirs instead, many of us abandon our own *inner knowing* without giving it *another thought.* And isn't it amazing how that expression "give it another thought" is something we say all the time, not realizing how we must have already instinctively known that our "thoughts" are what everything else rests on. Yet, having not paid enough attention to our words and language, we tend to rationalize like this: "So-in-so is my parent, or my best friend, or my pastor, or my professor, and he or she seems to be older or wiser, so I abandoned my own *inner knowing* without researching it or doing any further investigation. Not even thinking that I should be asking more questions of myself, I just gave up on what I thought was right for me, because I don't think I really know anything, and/or the last time I trusted myself I got it wrong."

Now naturally there are times when listening to someone else's suggestions can be extremely helpful to us. But usually that's only temporary, when we are truly stuck in some type of crisis or chronic negative emotional pattern that doesn't allow our well-being to inform our own higher knowing. When we are benefiting from listening to our own *inner knowing* and already feel good about what we are doing, we should not listen to someone else. We should, instead, recognize the divine intention of what psychotherapists call "individuation work," meaning an individual journey into what I call soulful self-sufficiency.

Self-sufficiency, however, does not mean to be without the support of family, friends or one's culture, but it does mean to be capable of going it alone and without the validation of all of them, if need be. In other words, we don't always have to have an "amen choir" to sustain that which we already know so well. It is just so easy to get caught up and bombarded with communication and language that tells you that what you think is not as valid, or equal to, every other soul on the planet. And hopefully, by now, you are coming to realize that what "you" think *matters*.

Now that you have a clearer understanding of conditioning, memes and old linguistic programming versus new NLP, let's pull them all together and review the main points that will be important for you to keep in mind as you move into the next chapters:

Point One: Many of your automatic thoughts, reactions and beliefs may not even be your beliefs. They may instead be something that was ingrained in you, without you having ever taken the time to even question what it is that you have subscribed to, with regards to your mind, body and spirit. And these automatic, unexamined thoughts may be interfering with your ability to realign with the fullness of your being.

Point Two: You may be parroting and protecting viral thoughts that you didn't mean to download and integrate or pass on.

Point Three: The words you choose to express your experiences can make the difference between feeling content or distressed, happy or depressed, and hopeful or anxious, discombobulated or connected to the Source of your being.

It's crucial that you understand this before you can effectively employ Sacretherapy® because it is the 'fullness of your being' that we are tapping into to align your mind, body and spirit, not just your brain chemistry. And the spirit aspect of you only knows well-being. The other aspects that we have reviewed in this section have been offered only to inform you of some of the hindrances that may have prevented you from allowing your natural well-being. You should understand, however, that releasing the conditioning, memes, and old neuro-linguistic programming cannot be done in a quantum leap, but will be slowly integrated into your life because the old ways of thinking have become automatic thoughts or longstanding habits. This chapter can serve you if you get stuck anywhere along the Sacretherapy® processes. I suggest you return to this section if that happens and identify the challenge you may be experiencing "in the moment" by asking yourself the questions below that I call your ***insight inventory.***

EXERCISE: INSIGHT INVENTORY

1. What specific conditioning, and from whom, is preventing me from believing that my well-being is assured, and thereby preventing me from allowing my well-being in this moment?

2. Is there an unconscious meme that I am loyal to and protecting that I need to rid myself of by employing the strategy-meme to search for and debug, in order to honor what feels closer to my own truth?

3. Or am I taking issue with the choice of words being used in one of the processes in this book, since I am used to wording things from "the way they have been or used to be," versus "the way I prefer them to be," not understanding that an affirmation must be worded from a new vantage point? In order to begin to affirm your well-being in the "here and now," not "someday," you need the new vantage point of changing your *present* moment that you are aiming to relieve, which is why the aligning process in the previous chapter is about what we want *right now.*

Inherent within the title: *The Power of Now* (1997), the author—Eckhart Tolle' does a beautiful job reinforcing the fact that the past need not affect your now. (See Resources.) Likewise, I believe that there is no conditioning strong enough, or no meme imbedded deeply enough, and no old linguistic programming influential enough to **completely** drown out your ever-calling *inner knowing*, which is available, right now. That may seem impossible, given all that's been shared. But, it's a "meme" if you believe that a traumatic event or some other diagnosis or life altering experience must leave you with long-term consequences or negative effects. None of these things have to hold any power.

Your True Genetic Predisposition—The Metaphysics of Physics

Just like a traumatic event or childhood reaction doesn't have to affect your "here and now" or leave you with lifelong negative effects, nor does the bloodline of the family you choose to co-create with in your physical experience. And this is the case, even if you believe your *matter* is because of a genetic predisposition. Philosopher Kahlil Gibran—author of *The Prophet* (1923)—reminds us of the metaphysics of physics in his famous poem, *"On Children."* He states: "You simply came through your parents, but you are not from them." I also tried to convey this point in the *stream of consciousness* from Chapter Two that depicts our advent from nonphysical to physical. Metaphysics helps us to get to the *energy* basis of the *matter*, which is the true pre-disposition of our being. And so, with all due respect to genetics, I think that it is used too often as the easy scapegoat or validation of why you have a particular condition and/or are doomed to have it.

The typical conversation goes like this: "Mental illness runs in my family. My mom had it, and two great aunts, and I think my father's cousin's niece also had it. So it finally got me." But if you could adopt Gibran's infinite wisdom that you came from the God-source in the universe, then that would be the only genetic down-line that you need to consider.

Therefore, having similar genetic makeup only suggests that you and your family process stress similarly; and if you lived with them, you may have undoubtedly also witnessed modeling of unhealthy ways stress can be expressed. That's all. After all, if you did get to pick your parents, you may have chosen them for a variety of reasons, and their *dis-ease* doesn't have to be one of them. And if you did develop something similar, you don't have to keep it. You can change your vibrational pattern. You are not doomed to hold on to *dis-ease*. I understand that many believe in the power of genetics because of the famous "twin studies" that showed that some twins who were raised in different environments ended up with the same or similar outcomes. But how about all the twins who were not in the research who didn't have the same outcomes? Generalizing from the specific to the general doesn't always work. Therefore, it would serve us to use research to its logical conclusions but be mindful of its limitations.

Your *matter* was not necessarily predestined, unless it was a divine intention— which takes us back to what Dr. Carolyn Myss stated in her book, *Sacred Contracts*. Dr. Myss agrees with the premise that you may very well have contracted for a specific set of circumstances before you incarnated into this physical experience, and naturally you don't recall doing so.

Still, you may be saying, "But I was born with it," or "I was tormented," or "I was bullied," or "I was beaten," or "I was raped," or "I was robbed," or "I was addicted," or "I was kidnapped," or "I was shamed," or "I was blamed," or "I was blank, blank, blank, so how dare you say that none of that has anything to do with my "here and now?" Well, please know that my intention is not to minimize the life experiences you have had so far. I am only trying to offer you the relief of not having to believe you are doomed, by describing your circumstances and experiences from another perspective. Therefore, I still must say that even those horrendous experiences don't have to have any influence over how you choose to live your life "today or tomorrow", unless you choose to keep believing that they do. It is your choice to keep thinking about the negatives, and by thinking about them, you keep re-activating those memories. By doing so, you keep your finger on the rewind button of a tape recorder playing in your mind. And that would still be the case even if the *matter* happened a second ago. If you keep saying it, or were to play the tape again, it's redundant living. We just haven't been taught to recognize this.

Self-Fulfilling Prophecies—Don't Escape Universal Law

Here is where an understanding of self-fulfilling prophecies can serve you. A self-fulfilling prophecy is a term coined by sociologist Robert Merton. In a nutshell, it is a prediction that comes true due to one's beliefs, based on the universal "law of attraction." The law of attraction (LOA) states that our beliefs are attractive like magnets drawing to us what we strongly or chronically think about. (The law of attraction is a term no one seems to know who coined, but as I noted in the Acknowledgements section, it was used in 1906 by William Atkinson in his book, *Thought Vibration or The Law of Attraction in the Thought World* (1906). It also was described by Thomas Troward in his Edinburg Lectures on Mental Science in 1904. But Troward did not use the exact coined phrase. Other research suggests that the concept of the *law of attraction* dates back to Esoteric traditions as far back as antiquity.

Self-fulfilling prophecies and the *law of attraction* are basically synonymous, energetically speaking. What you have been conditioned "to believe" is crucial to your quality of life; and anything you are currently living or have experienced before need not have an influence on the rest of your life unless you keep pushing the rewind button described earlier. If you could just think about any moment in the past as *life that's already been lived*, you could begin to tap into the peace of mind that each "new moment" offers.

Honoring the "newness" inherent within any given moment, despite the pain of the past, was illustrated beautifully in the movie, *The Lion King* (1994), where the wise monkey who serves as a Shaman hits the *exiled lion* with his stick. And the lion yells, "Ouch, what did you do that for?" And the monkey Shaman says, "It doesn't *matter*, it's in the past." Then the Shaman proceeds to hit him again, but this time the lion jumps out of the way to avoid the pain, having instantly received the lesson and the blessing.

Thus, if the past (up to a second ago) is causing you depression or anxiety or whatever else, then why would you want to keep re-experiencing it, or manifesting it, in your *now* when **you don't have to**? Like the lion, you can extract the lesson and the blessing from the painful experience and move on. The lion did not try to argue with the Shaman, demanding to know "why?" He understood the essence of the Shaman's lesson within the painful experience, which was to remind him that painful things happen; but once they have happened, it's over, in the past. And any further attention to it can waste valuable 'here and now" time that can be used to create new life, which is formative.

Therefore, if you want a better tomorrow, you may have to be willing to do something different and embrace your *matter* with a new perspective. I've offered you Sacretherapy® that shows you the way to go forth with the fullness of your being, unencumbered by yesterday. So, how then, do we become and remain cognizant of how the distortions of yesterday's beliefs and conditioning interfere with our well-being, and begin releasing them? First, we start by taking time for *thoughtful* reflection and paying attention to our own outcomes that our own life is teaching us, versus continuing to embrace the automatic inherited thoughts from others. Whether it be from your parents, your spouse, your mentors, your pastors, or your best friends, begin to take *five extra minutes* to ponder what is being said or offered before swallowing it whole. Then ask yourself:

EXERCISE: WORKSHEET SELF ASSESSMENT

1. Does that statement resonate with me?
2. Does that statement make sense to me?
3. Do I even know where this type of thought first came from?
4. Does that statement limit me in any way?
5. Does that statement require that I give up my viewpoint or does it expand it?
6. Does it make me feel small, ashamed, silly, awkward, stupid, or bad in any way?
7. Does it make me feel better, honored, empowered, happy, free or good in any way?

The answer to a particular question will determine if it is worth taking in the thought that was shared by the other person. If the answer is "Yes, it makes me feel good," and if you do choose to take it in, it would be with *your own* unique spin on it. If your answer affirms that another's offering made you feel bad or reduced you in some way, then you may need to let that person's thought pass you by. However, if you felt bad because what was offered brought to your attention that you were out of alignment, you can use that feedback as the motivator to realign. Otherwise, simply say to yourself, "I'll pass on that thought." You'll never have to be rude or feel insulted by anyone, just *don't* take it in. They don't even have to know that you are choosing to not receive the message. It's not about correcting, re-directing or getting into a debate with them; it's about your own mental health, and learning to live your own truth by honoring your own *inner knowing.*

The Unspoken Rite of Passage—Your Real Human/Spiritual Rights

As a psychotherapist, it has become apparent to me during my career that due to conditioning, memes and old linguistic programming, a lot of people don't seem to know what their ***innate rights*** are. Some really don't know that as long as they are ***not* hurting or infringing on anyone else's rights,** they have the right to live the life they want to live! Some don't seem to realize that the rights one has chosen to grant oneself are deeply ingrained within the historical debate over what's 'right or wrong,' which was created by man and comes out of a constellation of moral perspectives. These perspectives are based on theories of moral dogma that most philosophy camps agree range from: **moral absolutism**—where morals are rigidly black or white (recall *conditioning*); to **moral relativism**—which acknowledges a grey area where morals are viewed as subjective based on one's culture (recall *memes*); to **moral nihilism**—where nothing is judged as inherently right or wrong and acknowledges that what's right or wrong is based on a diversity of human constructs (recall *independent thought*).

As such, most people's moral code of what's "right or wrong" was created by other people attempting to guide or control another person's ability to decide what's appropriate. This is an attempt to reduce their *own* fears of which "rights" another may choose to exercise in this physical experience that might contrast with theirs.

I have also noticed that some people, due to misunderstanding their individual right to choose what is right or wrong for them, have actually thought that they **"have to"** do what the others in their lives want them to do. Or else! And some actually think that they only acquired *any rights* at all when the forefathers, who were the authors of *The Constitution of the United States* (1787), wrote out the rights. They do not realize that the *Constitution* was simply "acknowledging" their rights, which the authors emphasized should be **"self-evident."** They state that **"amongst these"** rights are life, liberty and the pursuit of happiness, which meant that your rights are "in addition to" the other rights that should also be *self-evident* or obvious. Therefore, "amongst these" implies that for the sake of brevity, they could not take time to list all the rights in their entirety; for the list of one's rights is exhaustive.

Inherent within "life, liberty and pursuit of happiness" was the understanding that "life" means that one is free to *"live and let live!"* But letting others "live" the life they came forth to live seems to be quite difficult and frightening for many people. In fact, as a psychotherapist, out of **all the things** that I have observed that can frighten mankind, I've noticed that what we *fear most* is each other! We don't trust each other. We don't trust the goodness of the God-source within one another to prevail.

We have seen such devastating *matter* manifest out of *unaligned thoughts* that we forget that those things only manifested as a result of **unaligned moments**, where individuals were briefly diverted away from the awareness of their **sacred rights,** which come from the God-source within the universe and not from moral dogma. Therefore, if we could begin to embrace that premise, then we can begin to trust that we can 'live and let live" on the basis that our fellow soul travelers are filled with the goodness and well-being of the God-source within them.

We could offer one another the respect and "liberty" we deserve; the same "liberty" that is amongst the "rights" that the forefathers also acknowledged. And this same "liberation" is what I honor and am calling for, based on the premise that for one to partake in one's right to *pursue happiness,* one must be liberated to do so. Liberation, therefore, means to be set free from bondage, the bondage of fear that prevents us from allowing each other our liberties; for, it is this very fear that binds us.

Thus, in the spirit of "liberation" and the "live and let live" premise, let me be clear about what I believe your true God-given spiritual rights are, within the context of all that's been discussed in this chapter. These rights are naturally amongst an exhaustive unspoken list that does not infringe upon the rights of others, as already discussed. And, if these rights, which are listed below, resonate with you, please feel free to copy this page and hang it in your bathroom or home office as a reminder, or go onto my website and download the one-page scroll. I call this outpouring the *Sacretherapy Preamble of Your Unspoken Human and Spiritual Bill of Rights*, as I step out on faith to make the following declaration:

EXERCISE: Reclaiming Your Unspoken Human and Spiritual Bill of Rights

Instructions: Stand in front of a mirror and recite the following rights to yourself, stating your first name before each and every right:

The *Sacretherapy®* Preamble of
YOUR UNSPOKEN HUMAN AND SPIRITUAL BILL OF RIGHTS

You have the right to release the conditioning.
You have the right to let go of the memes.
You have the right to not allow stereotyped emotionally-charged words to
squelch you, and instead use language that promotes connection
and brings out your new linguistic programming, at its best.
You have the right to create and honor your own moral code that
honors and acknowledges the rights of others.

You have the right to say "I don't agree," and still be respected.
You have the right to say "Back off."
You have the right to say "No."
You have the right to say "That hurt."
You have the right to all of your feelings.
You have the right to be right, when you're right.
You have the right to make mistakes—BIG ones and small.
You have the right to ask for forgiveness and the right to want to be forgiven.

You have the right to love yourself unconditionally, no *matter* how
many mistakes you think you've made.
You have the right to see yourself differently from

how ANYONE else sees you.
You have the right to see others differently from the way
others may see them.

You have the right to even see GOD differently than
ANYONE else sees God.
You have a right to your own beliefs.
You have the right to embrace any and all spiritual paths.
You also have a right to not embrace any particular path and ignore
the disapproving eye, for that which we call
God is omnipresent and within you.
Wherever you are, God is, not in any one specific religion or building.

You have the right to walk away from ANYTHING or ANYONE
that you feel threatens your rights or well-being, even if it's your mother,
your father, your spouse, children, siblings, best friend, career, etc.
You have the right to be happy and pursue your own goals!
You have the right to love anything and everything that someone
else hates or thinks is wrong, so long as it does not
infringe on anyone else's rights.

You have the right to remain single your entire life and
not marry *just* to have sex.
And you have the right, as a *single* adult who does not marry, to
not sneak around and determine your own guidelines on how
to embrace your natural healthy desire to enjoy "safe" sex with
another *single* consenting adult.

You also have the right to marry, and keep all your rights;
and to marry for love, and marry someone within or outside your race.
You also have the right to marry within or outside your
faith, and/or marry within or outside your
gender. For love is love and God *is* love.

You also have the right to not like my right, to list the
above as rights, and not like me honoring the "live and let live" right.
And therefore, **you have the right**
to disagree with everything listed as your rights.
You have the right, dear souls. You have the right!

And so, in accordance with the *spirit* of the below words of the Constitution:
"We hold these truths to be *self-evident*, that all
men [women and children] are created equal,
endowed by their Creator, with certain inalienable rights,
amongst these to be,
life, liberty and the pursuit of happiness."

You Have The Right!

Amelia Kemp, Ph.D., LMHC   *Your Own Inner Knowing*

_____   _____
Signature of a Fellow Vessel   Signature of the God-source within

5
WITNESSING: THE HEART OF THE MATTER

Step Four

"Everything undesirable passes away,
if we refuse to give it recognition by word, deed, or thought as a reality."
—Emily Cady

As we begin to restore our sacred freedoms, we recognize that *blind obedience* is a descent into a cellar of unconscious winery where one can become drunk with regret and rage. This is like an altered state of intoxication where "liquid self-acceptance" is sought but never found, calling into question what it means to be whole or holy. When someone perceives that his or her identity has been injured or anesthetized, even accidently by well-meaning people, he or she often go through a sacred detox while releasing the conditioning, memes and other toxic norms. When this happens, it helps to have someone who can validate the perception that a soulful injury has occurred. I call this process "***witnessing***" because it is a tender 'soul to soul' ritual that honors how the specific *matter* manifested. This is a divine time where healing balm is being administered to get to the *heart of the matter*. During this period, one often feels a sense of longing for what one believes could have been, had one known or had the courage to trust one's *inner knowing* sooner.

Had one known one's rights and had all of this information, one believes one would have aligned quicker. Oftentimes, I hear people say, *"I sure wish someone had told me all of this a long time ago!"* They frequently confess that they had been baptized or christened as babies or kids, but were told it was done to ensure that their soul returns to the Creator when they transition (die), but nothing was said about their connection to the Creator here in the physical. Instead, they were given the list of admonishments of *what they had to do* or could *not do* if they wanted to ever return to the Creator, versus the freedom of what it is like to be aligned with this God-source in the here and now.

And so, they get a bit distraught because now they believe that their lives may have gone differently had they been "initiated" properly. They want someone to own up to the atrocity! They need someone to blame. A lot of time has been lost; time spent complying, sneaking around, covering up and trying to do what others said was right. But all that time, one was searching for one's authentic self that continued to be elusive. They recognize that "something inside was telling them to do or say something" but wasn't sure what would happen if they did. And as any clinician can testify, they have diligently sought guidance by often having gone to the wisest in the family, to the most sanctified in the church, to many other sources both typical and nonconventional, to finally seeking out psychotherapists and psychiatrists, but still something was missing. Something kept on nudging. But they couldn't quite identify it—until now, having it finally spelled out (no longer whispered) that their freedoms were, in fact, God-given freely. So there is angst of massive proportions covering up grief.

Likewise, when the soul is finally freed, and has come into a new level of expansion, it also helps to have a witness validate that a new rite of passage has occurred. Yet, until one can embrace both the glory and temporary isolation that come with the *freedom of freedom*, one's anger and grief often becomes rage. And that rage can be manifested as one or more of the four types: *sacred rage, screaming rage, raging rage, and mutant rage.* I will now describe the nature and role of each type of rage that must be brought into alignment.

Sacred Rage (Processing) versus *Screaming Rage* (Denying)

Sacred rage is just what it sounds like—rage that is sacred, worthy of respect, holy, in that it makes one whole. The fragmented soul is gathering itself, processing its historical data and picking up the scattered pieces of *matter* that lead back to that crucial *quantum moment* in time where one was intentionally busying oneself—trying to repress the disdain of one's conformity and compliant existence. Blotting out the unconscious abyss of troubling reality, too painful to acknowledge with 20/20 vision, *sacred rage* chooses to become temporarily nearsighted, not wanting to see from an expanded view. It believes that if what one sees at a distance remains fussy and far enough away it will not look as bad; or it decides to just go blind and refuse lessons in Braille.

Sacred rage is trying to get the sandman out of one's eyes having been jolted from a "toss and turning" slumber only to discover that the distracting dream was in fact a nightmare, except no one was screaming; but there was definitely fright. And rightly so—for it isn't every day that one awakens to find that *"the life he or she wanted to live could have in fact been lived"* had the small print been read. Forced now to accept or reject the invitation to remove the psychological cataracts, one is faced with a magnifying glass that enlarges the *matter*, where undeniable evidence leads to *soulful sightedness*; and with this clearer vision comes the sorrow. *Sacred rage* is processing, trying to decide "was it surrender or theft"; or "was it sacrifice or barter" or "was it naïveté or survival?" All one knows for sure is that there is a "bereft-ness" to the *matter* that makes one's heart skip a beat or palpitate out of rhythm. ***Sacred rage*** is haunted by memories of the times when the *energy* in one's belly didn't jibe with the powers that be. It is where one knew the "*matter mattere*d" but lacked the courage to stand up for what one believed. Left now with what ***sacred rage*** believes are permanent losses and scars, one is filled with both longing and self reproach for having abandoned oneself.

And so now ***sacred rage*** is trying to "right a wrong," hoping to integrate the new information within one's being, like a *tattoo-sleeve* imbedded within the skin broadcasting one's new understanding. This should not be mistaken as rebellion, for it is not; this is the joyous exuberance of relief—that celebrates no longer needing to seek approval to be one's authentic self. One is now freed to trust the confirmation from within and is high on natural endorphins. One experiencing ***sacred rage*** has, therefore, successfully but painstakingly connected the dots, understanding now where the misalignment began and is eager for the misalignment to end. That is, if it can only soothe the toxic *energy* still spewing from its inner child—***screaming rage***.

Screaming rage is hurting and hurting bad, furious, longing to aright a desecration. One who feels ***screaming rage*** has suffered dismemberment from the body-temple, which has sent the soul hovering outside one's skin searching for reconnection. A severing, therefore, has occurred from one's "*self*" and one's "*inner knowing.*" But ***screaming rage*** keeps one in denial, unaware that he or she is temporarily behaving as if one is devoid of spirit and therefore too numb to summon a redeeming tear. Continuing to look outside of one's self—one calls on the "weeping women" to gather collective *energy* to decompose and sanctify the *matter*; but for one experiencing ***screaming rage***, comfort cannot come from ordinary rituals or from those who perpetuate the flawed initiation—for they only deepen the pangs of disconnection.

Therefore, ***screaming rage*** must face itself and the God within, one on one; no intermediary will do, nor is one needed. *Inner knowing* is used to transmuting *energy* from those who present the *matter* enraged, ravaged and ferocious. *Inner knowing* understands that they are attempting to realign, even while they are too blinded by their own fury to see the light—the healing light that patiently calls, despite the belligerent snub. ***Screaming rage*** is in the wilderness, in desperate need of manna. Hungry and tired, on borrowed *energy*, and desolate, ***screaming rage*** looks but does not see; unequipped, at least it thinks so but is not really. For within ***screaming rage*** is the same *inner knowing* that instructs everyone on how to put things back together again. It is the theologian within offering communion to all—proclaiming "he or she that is weary come home."

Thus, both ***screaming rage*** and ***sacred rage*** experience excruciating pain, as it relates to the *matter*. But ultimately, ***sacred rage*** is what shifts the *energy* and prevails—for it is release work. Release work sanctifies tears; it makes "*consciousness* conscious." It is like the melting wax from a burning candle running down the altar—able to be neatened-up later. It is a séance awakening the "living-dead." It is therefore, a true energetic pathway for healing grief.

Release work is greatly facilitated by what I call "ritualistic recycle bins" that remold the toxic *energy*, since *energy*, as we learned earlier, cannot be created or destroyed and can only be transferred. As such, the letter-writing technique is an excellent way of releasing or transferring the toxic pent up *energy* from one's *thoughts*, which are nonphysical, to the physical realm onto a piece of paper. The paper absorbs and neutralizes the toxic *energy*, since paper is a living organism with *energy* at its core, having been extracted from a tree. Trees are accustomed to the recycling process, since each season, they are in the process of bringing forth new life depending on the climate.

As we move forward toward our ultimate goal of releasing and bringing forth new life via the letter-writing technique, we take time now to honor those wanting to take stock of the past in order to fully embrace the here and now. For this, I often have my clients do '**pre- and post-letters**', not just regurgitations but letters that get to the atomic essence of the *matter* and shift *energy*. The ***pre-letter*** honors the lost life that one imagines could have been but never was. Here, we honor *perception*, not judge it. As such, here you share your perception of exactly what happened and why you felt what happened was wrong. This may require a series of letters if you perceive that there have been multiple injurious acts. Then, later, at the end of the next chapter, *Step Five*, the ***post-letter*** is written for the *reframing of life* that has already been lived, from a broader perspective and higher vibration. With the additional tools you will have gained, that letter will be written with a more soul-filled insight, compassion, and ability to forgive any and all co-creators, including yourself.

At this juncture, however, you will begin by exploring any ***sacred rage*** or ***screaming rage*** you may be feeling, and have your outpouring *witnessed*. So only do the ***pre-letter*** for now. If you are doing this work with a psychotherapist, share the letter with that person. If you are doing this work on your own, share the letter with someone you really, truly trust. However, if the person is not a therapist or clergy, be sure to emphasize that he or she is there ONLY to listen and witness, not to try to process it with you. The energetic transference of a hug is sufficient! So please be clear that since your witness is not a therapist, the witness will not be expected to act in such a role. And if any friend or family member attempts to process with you, please select a different witness. Please follow the instructions on the next page for the pre-letter exercise:

EXERCISE: Pre-letter

Do only the pre-letter now. (Go to Appendix D in the back of the book to find the suggested templates to form the pre- and post-letters.) Take a few days to work on the letter. Then, once you have shared the pre-letter and had it witnessed, seal it in a letter-sized envelope and add it to that symbolic vault you created in Step One that you labeled "The Past." The *post letter will be done later,* after you have completed the clearing processes in the next chapter. Once you've stored the pre-letter, take a few days to rest, and then you will be ready to proceed with *Raging Rage* and *Mutant Rage.* **PAUSE HERE TO COMPLETE THE EXERCISE.**

Welcome back. At this point, you should have completed your pre-letter regarding your feelings about the flawed (misaligned) initiation. I trust that the letter was a positive ventilation outlet for you. Still, some of you may be experiencing anger and discontentment provoked by the pre-letter that brought up the old *matter.* This is why revisiting the past can be tricky, since on one hand it attempts to anesthetize the expired and contaminated *matter*; but on the other hand, once the venting is over, the remaining particles tend to get inflamed and can become very sore. If that is the case, there is yet another *energy* block that needs to be addressed. I once heard somewhere that a contaminant to the *"soul's ego"* may come back into what we call alignment with just strong medication and righteous ventilation, but an infection that festers and mutates the *"soul's soul"* needs surgery. When that happens one may be unconsciously experiencing what I refer to as *Raging Rage,* which will be described next.

Raging Rage: Resistance—Refusal to Let the Matter Go

When people don't easily progress through the Sacretherapy® *Steps, they often are encountering* deeper levels of **resistance** in addition to conditioning, memes and old linguistic programming. Steps Two through Five seem to summon the most resistance due to **cognitive dissonance.** *Cognitive dissonance* happens as a result of something new being offered that just doesn't jibe with one's current beliefs, as I explained in Step Two. For some, the Sacretherapy® information is completely new, but yet it *feels right* in one's gut, and, therefore, can be so transforming that it can set off what has been described as a "chemicalization." *Chemicalization* is a term coined by Dr. Catherine Ponder, author of *The Dynamic Laws of Healing* (1985). Ponder states that "a literal chemical reaction in the spiritual and physical system is occurring." I totally agree, in that new neurotransmitters are being formed and the subtle mental and subtle emotional bodies are equally involved. Therefore, with all of the new changes, some do not feel secure enough within themselves to *trust it* and fully embrace the make-over. This type of cognitive dissonance is what causes the *raging rage.*

Resistance occurs because people have been holding onto the *matter* and continuing a pattern for so long that sticking with what they know feels more comfortable, even if what they are holding onto enrages and restricts them. People could be fuming inside but refuse to let it go because the resistance is often tied to *pride.* Some people don't ever want it to admit that they were wrong. They *want* to be right or to at least appear right. So they could care less about conditioning, memes or old linguistic programming, for as far as they are concerned, all of that stuff was fine and for their own good. Switching gears to expand one's knowingness to a point where softening embraces flexibility this far into the game seems too scary, and may even seem reckless. Better to bet on what they thought they knew, and keep 'hitting the ceiling' with unresolved *raging rage* than to risk trusting their *inner knowing,* and reaching for the well-being they sense could be near and certainly deserve.

If what I just described is happening to you, then before we proceed any further into conquering *raging rage,* let's take a moment so you can gather yourself. To figure out what it is specifically that is stopping you from allowing your well-being will require going into the silence and listening to that still soft voice. To facilitate this, I offer the forthcoming relaxation exercise that aims to help you elevate your frequency to the highest vibration possible where your natural healing endorphins are easily released, offering you the optimum sense of well-being that can broaden your perspective of the *matter* of what's causing the raging rage. As stated previously, metaphysicians believe that *dis-ease* cannot remain in a body that is at *ease.* And so, *discontentment* cannot remain in a body that is *content.* As such, we will proceed with relaxing you and then once a higher vibration has been achieved we will begin to *"probe"*—which basically means you will be asked to answer some poignant questions that help to get to the heart of the *matter.* Please commence with the relaxation exercise below:

EXERCISE—Relaxation Technique

Instructions: Follow this easy relaxation technique, which is pretty standard in that all relaxation scripts are designed to slow your breathing down and allow you to take in more oxygen to regain your sense of well-being. There are literally hundreds, if not thousands of versions of guided relaxation imagery that you may use, but I call mine: ***Breathe the Breath of Life***™. (Also, if you feel overwhelmed or upset at any time during the Sacretherapy® steps, please feel free to go to my website and download a *free* online guided audio relaxation CD for your comfort.)

My ***Breathe the Breath of Life*™ *Relaxation Series*** includes several from which you can choose. (See Resources in back of book.)

> **First Step: *Breathe the Breath of Life***—you will take three deep breaths with a 3-second break between each—slowly breathing in and out to the count of five–one-thousands. So *inhale* to the count of one-one-thousand, two-one-thousand, and then exhale slowly to the count of three-one-thousand, four-one-thousand, five-one-thousand. Do the sequence three times. (The purpose of the deep breaths is to allow the life force that is attached to the oxygen molecules to stop the "fight or flight" anxiety response that was activated by the pre-letter. The intentional intake of deep breaths also will tell the brain to stop the production of a hormone that is secreted when we are in psychological or physical pain.)

> **Second Step: *Self Soothe***—The most standard way that I was taught in graduate school to self-soothe was to trigger the natural healing endorphins in the brain by rubbing one's skin. There are several ways to do this but the most popular is to cross your arms and place your hands onto your shoulders and repeatedly rub your arms *slowly* down to your elbows; however, I also found that rubbing your knees up to your mid-inner thighs in a circular back and forth motion *slowly*, works very well. So do whichever feels more comfortable.

> Now, begin to do this up and down or back and forth 10 times slowly. This should feel really nice, warm and soothing. (This type of soothing touch is likened to rubbing your skin after you accidently bumped it—seeing as we automatically know to rub our skin when we are in physical pain. Thus, we can offer this same nurturance to ourselves when we are in emotional pain to cause the brain to secret serotonin, which then triggers the natural healing endorphins to be released, restoring our sense of well-being.)

> **Third Step: *Shift Your Energy***—while rubbing your upper arms or mid to lower thighs you will begin speaking to yourself using soothing sentiments in the form of positive statements that will help to shift your *energy*. Say to yourself the following script: *"It's okay to be a little overwhelmed. This is new stuff and so it's normal for it to take a while to get used to. I'm probably doing better than I think. I want to be the well being that I became physical to be. I want so much to trust my inner knowing. And so, right now in this moment, I recommit to letting the past go, so that I can enjoy much more of my here and now."*

Your *vibration* should have been elevated by the relaxation exercise. So now, please get your journal or a pen and paper and prepare to journal your answers to the questions listed in the next exercise titled: Raging Rage. The answers usually get to the heart of the *matter*. However, the swiftness of uncovering the answers to those questions depends on your willingness to be transparent. Insight can come slowly or in a holy instant if you are willing to tell the truth. If you do, the time it takes to align with the Source of your being seems to be measured in quantum leaps and bounds.

EXERCISE: WORKSHEET—Raging Rage

1. What's causing you to hold onto the negative manifestation?
2. What enrages you the most about it?
3. Is any self-reproach possibly present?
4. Who do you want to blame, and if it's you, why must you keep blaming yourself?
5. Do you understand that only people who are hurting hurt others?
6. Can you imagine the conditioning, memes, and old linguistic programming that person (or people) got hooked into that may have caused him or her to unleash those beliefs or behaviors onto you? Or given those same parameters, can you muster up any compassion for yourself and why you did it?
7. How is the negative manifestation, self-reproach or resentment helping you in this present moment?
8. How is the negative manifestation, self-reproach or resentment hurting you in this present moment?
9. When do you plan to let it go?
10. What would your life look like without the resentment or self-reproach?
11. What could be restored without it?
12. Is holding onto these things a cover up for you not coming into alignment with your own life?
13. Is there something you can't face or accept that's causing the raging rage you feel?
14. Is there someone you are trying to impress by holding onto it?
15. Is there someone that you are worried about who might think less of you if you let it go? Perhaps some secret pact between you and another person who is hurting?
16. Does coming into alignment frighten you because you would then have no excuse for not taking full responsibility for your own happiness?

Allow your responses to marinade a minute. Don't judge them, don't change the answers, just let them be. The answers may seem a bit embarrassing to admit, but that's okay. This is what we psychotherapists call "inner child" woundedness, and so it's all right if some of the responses seem childish. Often, childhood is when the original injury occurred. All adults have an inner-child who didn't get some needs met when they were a child. Many adult interactions become re-enactments of that childhood wound. Therefore, by no means does it mean that you are immature to have an inner-child. It simply means that you are human, carrying an unresolved disappointment from your childhood.

So, just let it out. Cry if you need to. Anger usually makes us cry because anger and pain are heads and tails of the same coin. Plus, we are mourning the fact that we are not feeling connected to the fullness of our being. So please don't hold back the tears. You, too, fellows; men need to cry, too. The Creator didn't accidently give you tear ducks for you to not use them. Tears relieve pressure. And emotional pain is built-up pressure—it's *"energy"* in motion. So if you let it flow, you can let it go. But if you keep swallowing it, then it will continue to decay and ultimately mutate.

Review your answers and then just sleep on them before you continue. Take a warm bath and just chill out for the rest of the evening and return to this spot in the book in a day or so. If you are working with a therapist, share your answers with that professional. **PAUSE**.

Welcome back. Hopefully, you took my suggestion and took a few days or a week away from this work. If you did, I hope you gained some necessary insight into what's stopped you from letting go of the past. And if you did, that's fantastic and, therefore, the below exercise will fortify that which you have already come to know. However, if you **still** feel some *Raging Rage* and believe you answered the previous questions honestly, what you may actually be experiencing is what I call: *Mutant Rage*. This is the final form of rage that usually needs to be expressed during the Sacretherapy® process; and, therefore, doing the Mutant Rage exercise should aid you tremendously in your need for witnessing.

Mutant Rage—A Petition for Justice

For something to become mutant it must be the result of some form of mutation. Likewise, according to the dictionary, mutation is the result of something being damaged or changed from its natural state or evolution. As such, when one's natural state or desire to evolve has been damaged (temporarily), the anger one feels naturally evolves into rage. That very rage, if unchecked for a long period of time, can mutate into mutant rage. When this happens, there is often a need for prolonged witnessing, where one's suffering needs to be appreciated to an even greater extent. And if this is the case, the resistance is interpreted as a sort of petition for more "outcry," in which case, the matter needs to be duly acknowledged and honored.

Mutant rage, which began with anger and the natural desire for revenge, are normal human emotions along the path that many must take as they move more and more into alignment. Thus, for some, here is where getting the facts straight is crucial as the case is presented. As such, the chronicles and files of the *rage* must be looked at with the microscopic lens of a "Quantum Physicist" in order to break the *matter* down to its smallest particle to find the *energy* basis of it, and a "Genealogist" will assist to validate its multigenerational lineage. Both of these consultants are employed by your *sixth sense* which of course is your *inner knowing*. Your "Quantum Physicist" will point out the finer, almost invisible details that have eluded you about your rage that have interfered with your ability to move on. Your "Genealogist" will enable you to trace the laceration back as far back as it can possibly go, even until the rocks cry out hallelujah. For this is an exercise in giving voice. Voice can stimulate advocacy. Advocacy feels like justice. And justice can bring relief.

With the assistance of your *Quantum Physicist and Genealogist* you will use the following exercise to release the pent up mutated *energy* that was discovered. *Energy* that has been holding you captive in your thoughts (which are invisible) and bring them into physical manifestation by sharing your findings in a speech and/or letter of petition where you get to lobby to a particular audience. It doesn't *matter* if the audience that you are addressing is physical or gone back to nonphysical, since the speech or letter of petition will not actually be mailed. This is a *vibrational* exercise to shift your *energy*, not another's. Therefore, in these speeches or letters of petition, feel free to be real and express the tiniest iota of *energy* that can be extracted from it. It's about releasing that raw emotion and being unscrupulously transparent. So tell everybody off, if need be. No time for being politically correct or worrying about the gentlemanly or lady-like finishing school manners. So have at it!

EXERCISE—For Mutant Rage:

1. Using the skills you honed from your *Quantum Physicist*, you will write about your research and how it identified the *energy* basis of the *matter* exposing where the toxic *energy began its momentum*. You will then tell your audience how you would have preferred it to have been, how you wished it was, and how you know it could have been to have prevented the laceration. Lay it out for them. You instruct. You inform. You notify these so-in-so (s) how it's done! Pour your heart into it.

2. At the same time, employ the skills you acquired from your *Genealogist* to validate where in your lineage that you felt it all started, whether it be your great grandmothers or great-great grandfathers. Since you now know that "only people in pain hurt others and then pass it down," you may address

anyone from the country's forefathers to the Creator of the universe, if that's where you feel it all started. Feel free to also lobby any advocacy organizations or policy-makers that you feel would support your cause. The letter or speech is to whomever you feel conspired with it, created the environment for it, and keeps it going.

3. In other words, you can write your speech or letter of petition to whomever you feel is the source of your misery and how this situation would not have been, had they done this, that or the other. So this is your chance to outline how you **prefer it to be**. Whatever, "it" is.

4. You will find that the vibrational benefit of this exercise is enormous because you are finally getting to describe exactly what you desired all along! It can shift and clean up your *energy* in ways both expected and unexpected. You already wrote about ***what you didn't want*** in the *pre-letter* and that still left you wanting. And so, this time, let's tell 'em, by writing ***what you did want*** and do want ***now***, to avenge yourself in the present for the past. And nothing is more gratifying than conjuring a successful outcome as sweet revenge. Some say "revenge is best served cold;" but as metaphysicians we say it is best served *vibrationally*, without them even realizing what hit 'em.

5. Thus, this exercise lets them know that they messed with the wrong soul! How could they dare! They had *no idea* the range and soulfulness within your body temple and what you came forth to do! But it's okay; you'll get it straight and show them the "well being" that you really are. Oh yeah, you'll get 'em now!

6. After the letters and/or speeches have been written, read them out loud to your trusted witness or therapist. Then have that person read the words out loud back to you. This will allow you to *hear* how the offenders would hear it. Then "outcry" will have been achieved, and "advocacy" will have been established. The universe is on notice and all finally feels well within your soul. **PAUSE HERE** and begin the exercise.

You will undoubtedly like your speeches and letters, after they've been witnessed, and so feel free to have a few people over to your house to read what you wrote to them. Your invitation could simply say:

> "I've written a letter or speech on how I would like **the world to be better** if (blank) was this way, (whatever "blank" is) and was told it may be worth sharing with a few of my closest *like-minded* friends. I'll be serving refreshments. Please come. The reading is at 5 p.m. sharp. The occasion is simply a *"Wouldn't the world be even better if…"* get-together. If you choose to attend, there is only one rule: You can only give feedback about how *you also want "it" to be,* not how "it" is or how you don't want "it" to be, because I want to keep the vibe in a direction that feels good.

Naturally, having a get-together is certainly not mandatory or a necessity; but it could be powerful and create an even stronger sense of victory. And if it is done, it can also add to a sense of empowerment and relief. But at the very least, it can be the final culmination of advocacy that helps to shift your *energy* back to the level of **sacred rage**, which is worthy of attention. Regardless of whether or not you host a communion, the celebration of the soulful work done in this chapter has already been honored; for it has forced most people that partake to take nothing for granted.

It has caused many to look deeper than their usual glance at what life was teaching. It has wiped away glare and brought clarity into focus, making just about everyone get their stories straight. It has forced them to stop expecting others to do their thinking for them, and made them show up, take notice and be fully present. But mostly, it has helped many confront the real culprit who caused their lives to be less than happy, which most found was an inner antagonist that repeatedly ignored the sacred call. And so, although many may have begun this chapter with a sense of loss, drunken rage, contempt, and needing a witness, they usually end it filled with a sobering calm and self respect.

They now have respect for having called back the fragmented pieces of the soul, where the letters, worksheets, speeches and petitions become testaments of moments of life that's been lived, documented, and preparing to be archived. Like an art form, seeing one's life in ink, after having been transformed from nonphysical *energy* into the written word, it is a *matter* to behold. Yet, once beheld, you are free to extract every bit of healing *energy* from it, ensuring that it is a worthy, authenticated piece of work that allowed you to feel heard, understood and validated. And once that is so, the realignment work may continue and you will be ready for the next step which is: How to Stay Clear of the Matter, discussed in the next chapter. However, before you move on to the next step, the suggestion in the below sub-section regarding an "optional energy treatment" may further facilitate your alignment.

Exercise: Optional Energy Treatment

Please note that since you have released a great deal of pent-up *energy*, you could more than likely benefit from an *energy* boost and cleansing to realign your energetic body—such as a Reiki or Prana treatment, if you feel depleted or drained by the work so far. Both treatments, as stated in Chapter Two, usually work only within the auric or *energy* field and are basically the same, with just different names that will boost your *energy*, some use light touch but all clear blockages and also focus a little on breath-work. I recommend a treatment because in addition to feeling fatigued, sometimes at this point within the Sacretherapy® process, some people begin to have corresponding physical symptoms due to long-term *energy* blockages. Louise Hay, the metaphysician I honored in the Introduction and salute as my personal honorary metaphysical mentor, describes this beautifully in her book, *You Can Heal Your Body* (1982). She explains that pain in the joints, back, legs and feet are often indicators of rigid thinking patterns, lack of flexibility or refusal to move forward with life. Therefore, if this is happening, I highly recommend you use her healing remedies as a complement to this book.

If you decide to get the *energy* treatment, know that some Reiki or Prana practitioners enjoy focusing mainly on the chakras, which are described as seven-to-twelve *energy* portals. The number depends on the chakra paradigm being used. However, as a Certified Reiki practitioner myself, I believe that in addition to the chakras, all the living cells within the body temple are life forms and directly receiving prana (life force) through the subtle bodies; and, therefore, are also *energy* portals. For, where there is life, there is *energy* at its core. If my knee is aching from me being inflexible and unwilling to bend (as Hay teaches), I can send *energy* directly to the knee and it can clean up the *energy* blockage, as well. Therefore, I recommend that the *energy* treatment be **equally** spread over your entire body temple, not just the chakras.

Most people benefit from the treatments and are glowing when the treatment is over. Check your local area for a certified practitioner of either *energy* form. To learn more about chakras, I recommend the book, *The Anatomy of Spirit*, by Dr. Carolyn Myss, and *The Subtle Body—An Encyclopedia of Your Energetic Anatomy*, by Cyndi Dale (See Resources).

6
STAYING CLEAR OF THE MATTER

Step Five

"Seek not to change the world, but choose to change your mind about the world."
—A Course in Miracles

We stay clear of the *matter* by paying attention, clearing everything through our *inner knowing* and learning how to trust and respect its counsel; not ducking and hiding out, or avoiding the luminosity and diversity of life, but by honing in on our divine sensing and willingness to hear the sacred call. Learning how to see through the lens of symbolic meaning, we come to know what "this, that and the other" represents. And by doing so, we can finally come from an unarmored place of grace and sanity, keeping our diagnostic reactions to a bare minimum. Then, just finding ourselves mildly misaligned on the alignment scale in Chapter Two would be cause for pause, and an *energy* audit from our *inner knowing* would ensue.

We stay clear of the *matter* by being aware of where we are with regard to any given *matter* and where we are going, versus where we've been or what we have been through. We then look for signs on how to get from underneath, around and on top of the *matter*. We trust the clues that we are heading in the right direction as we prepare to be guided back into alignment. We surrender the protest that we are being guided by the nonphysical unseen reality and accept there is more to our physical beingness than what meets the eye. We allow that inner nudging to prompt us into investigating the layers of what it means to be a soul-filled being. Thus, we begin trusting that this *inner knowing* is like an oracle with prophetic sight, revealing the way, offering life-changing, dead-on guidance.

Guidance reminds me of mile markers. Surely we have all driven on a highway where we have seen mile markers. Mile markers let you know where you are at all times. They are truly guides. Our *inner knowing* serves the same purpose, for it let's us know how close we are to where we are going and alerts us when we have arrived. So mile markers tell us how far we are from our exit. And if we get lost on our way, the marker helps us identify exactly where we need to turn in relation to the *matter*. If we completely break down, we can pinpoint from where it is that we need to be towed, to be lifted and carried to another vibrational vantage point where we are able to regain our composure and get back on the interstate of life as soon as possible.

Once in tow we refuse to allow our allegiance to cultural mores to sever us from that which nurtures the soul; instead we actively find the exit and "haul tail" to the nearest rest stops available along the way. Then once we have arrived at the hypothetical rest stop (repair shop) we refuse to let pride shame us into not exposing that once again, another "defective part" of the *matter* has broken us down. We courageously expose life's scars and scabs proudly, as we allow humility and intrigue to prompt us into investigating the many *layers* of what it means to be a resilient, ever-expanding threefold being—mind, body and spirit. We get back into our restored vehicles, and move on.

Clearing Layers: It's an Onion

Sacretherapy® reminds us that there are many layers to the *matter*—like an onion. And like an onion, it is difficult to get to its core without tears welling up if the fumes are not contained. Thus, *clearing layers* is likened to staying clear of the stench that made us cry when we got anywhere near a whiff of the *matter*. The goal, then, is how to get to the *core of a thing* without it interfering with your ability to be the "well being" you came forth to be. We also want to determine how to maintain your well-being *more often* so that you can enjoy devouring the hypothetical onion layers that are analogous to your ever-evolving alignment; and at the same time, learn how to handle the unpleasant odor of other people's onions that may still bother you, too.

Having begun to take back your power and release your victimization in the last chapter, we want to maintain your victor-hood in this one. Likewise, there may be negative reactions from your friends and loved ones, as they can no longer sniff out the layers of your onion, since much has already been peeled.

Before we proceed with getting to the *core* of your onion, I would first like to offer a caveat because this is the step in the Sacretherapy® process where some people begin to experience ***double resistance*** due to either their own difficulty to cut their onions under water or the difficulty of others containing their fumes. Therefore, please keep this following caveat in mind throughout the remaining steps:

Caveat: You may not necessarily be the only one feeling the resistance. It may often be your loved ones, too. In fact, most of my clients were excited and feeling pretty good about coming back into alignment and wanted to share this information with family and friends. Yet, their loved ones weren't always as supportive as they had expected or hoped. If this happens, know that in order to stay clear of the *matter*, you would be wise to recall all that you learned in the earlier chapters about conditioning, memes and old linguistic programming. Remember to keep in mind that you were raised in a world environment where it is almost in vogue to complain and share horror stories, so embracing a more positive stance may seem a little weird at first. This is only because it is just easier to join the club and point out the stinky layers of other people's onions and commiserate about our own. This is why during this step, I often tell my clients about what I call the ***crab pot synergy:***

When crabs are put into a pot to be steamed, the ones on the top try to crawl out of the pot. But the ones beneath them pull them back down, even if it means pulling their legs off. I see this with some of my clients' families and friends when the clients are trying to empower themselves or start to pull away and tap back into their well-being. Their family and friends appear to do everything they can to pull them back down in the steaming pot. It's the old "misery loves company" type of thinking that is actually just an attempt to soothe themselves. So, please know that this is not uncommon when people start to grow or embrace something different.

Family and friends, due to their own misalignment and insecurities, may often belittle your efforts instead of supporting them. And likewise, they may mimic and echo the larger society that says *"be like us or else!"* This is only because some family and friends don't realize that they also have the power to move beyond the conditioning, etc., and so they become a little intimidated and alarmed that their loved one is doing the work that they haven't had the courage or desire to do for themselves. They may begin to make little comments trying to prevent you from shedding more layers such as:

"What are you trying to prove?"

"You know you're not that strong."

"Come on now, isn't this good enough?"

"I'm just worried about you and don't want to see you fall on your face."

"Why can't you just be satisfied with the way things are?"

"If having what you want was really doable,
don't you think I would have it by now?"

"Life is hard, so the sooner you get your head out
of the clouds, the better."

"You're being naive and gullible; life isn't fair, and
that's all there is to it."

Yet, all those statements are just code for "stay put and unfulfilled like us." And if it works to discourage you from evolving to your highest potential, it simply reassures them in their limited belief that there isn't a better way. So it soothes them back into a comforting lull of having never tried or having given up. Therefore, if you are starting to experience any of that, just try to understand it and send them some positive *energy* by visualizing thoughts of them being happy, and keep on keeping on.

On the other hand, negative feedback from them can also be an indicator of a "self-fulfilling prophecy" if you are having mixed feelings yourself about embracing a different school of thought and reaching for a higher quality of life. And if this is the case, then undoubtedly your loved ones are only mirroring your own ambivalence. It's what we call the *law of attraction in action*. Thus, as soon as you begin to release your own resistance, they will either eventually ask you to share what you are doing with them, as you become a beacon of light, (which is discussed in Chapter Nine) or they will leave you alone and you will be free to be. But in the meantime, if you are having *extreme* difficulty maintaining your wellness due to the meaning you have attached to their comments or behavior, then you may need to decide if they are one of the co-creators of the old *matter* that also needs to be released, until you are aligned enough to not be yanked by what others are saying or doing. Remember, it is always an inside job. We can't change them, but we *can* change our response to them; it's just gradual and takes more practice.

Energy Disbursement Processes—Let Go What Goes

As a psychotherapist, I recognize that anything new to our system can set up cognitive dissonance in us because it goes against our conditioning. Cognitive dissonance is the distress caused by two conflicting beliefs. But I believe that even when something is completely foreign, the "core of our being" knows when something sounds right or feels right. That being said, things are going to come up in life that will make you question this information; things beyond family and friends that could possibly remove you from the newfound well-being you are beginning to experience. So, as these things come up, you can use one of the energy disbursement processes in this chapter and online relaxation exercises to realign.

One of the most consistent things that comes up and pulls people away from their alignment is something I totally agree with, that was said by Iyanla Vanzant on *The Oprah Winfrey Show* (1998) that I can only paraphrase: *we don't like to allow things to enter and exit through our physical experience. We like to hold on, instead of letting go. We become energetically constipated, instead of allowing toxic people and things to be released.* So don't let that *energy blockage* in the pit of your stomach prevent you from releasing the *matter*. You will survive it although it will undoubtedly hurt—chemicalization usually does. So brace yourself and let the toxic *energy* go, then watch it disperse into the larger dark *matter* of the universe.

Despite the toxic stuff that comes out of us and others that looks like resistance, I sincerely believe that every person wants to feel good; of course they do. It's just hard for some people to move away from that which is a habitual dysfunctional pattern. Some may prefer to *"stay clear of the matter"* by continuing to comply and put up with other people's preferences and repress the *matter* until it builds up. So they often end up with the proverbial constipation. They're afraid to take life's antacids because there just doesn't seem to be enough deodorizer around strong enough to clear the air. And then there are others who just aren't sure if they are ready "yet" to do the alignment work necessary to feel better and remove all the painful layers of that hypothetical onion. As a result, instead of a stomach ache, they end up needing gastric bypass surgery. But fortunately, the steps in this book can penetrate the more resistant cases too, if well-being is truly wanted. So whether you are moving smoothly through the Sacretherapy® steps or are experiencing great resistance, be patient because your evolution and alignment is assured, if you keep at it.

Still, many people wonder how long will it *really* take to fully clear and release the *matter*, given all the *conditioning* that they are trying to release. Well, it is certainly a process, the "sure but steady" type, which is moment by moment, day by day, week by week, and month by month. Yet, to my delight, Sacretherapy® seems to be able to penetrate symptoms fairly quickly, and I think it's because it is holistic and involves your mind, body and spirit. I have even seen it *significantly* increase client's quality of life in as little as four months when they were already believers in the spiritual realm and not rigid about any specific path. They were, however, **the exceptions**, uncharacteristically motivated and doing sort of an escalated version of this, which was about two steps per month.

But most people need a minimum of eight months, doing one *step* per month, which is **highly recommended**, and includes aftercare. And since there are two or three exercises on the average in each *step*, that's about one exercise per week in addition to your daily *three times a day aligning processes*. That's doable and realistic. Plus, even if you went a little slower, just about anyone could successfully do it in a year. That's still only 12 months, compared to the many years most people have been dealing with the *matter*. So one year of coming back into alignment is a soulful *energy* investment worth making. Sacred work cannot be rushed, nor should it be. **However, those timeframes are for those with a belief in a spiritual base.** Those who don't have one may obviously take a little longer but will benefit equally from the process.

People who don't believe in a higher power usually need more time spent in Steps One and Two dealing with the psycho-education portions of this paradigm. Fortunately, people eventually recognize that they do not have to embrace any religious path or adopt any specific terminology. And reading other perspectives of holistic work from the other resources in the back of the book also helps. So regardless of where you are and how long it takes, know that it's okay, and that realigning with your wellness is an ever-evolving unfoldment. Remember, it's an onion. So please don't beat yourself up, if thoughts pertaining to *the old matter* come up from time to time during this process.

Remember, *Learning Theorists* say it takes 24 times before something can become a new habit. So just trust the process and remember that *you are not sick, you're sacred.* And it's not that you're undisciplined, it's conditioning. Therefore, the following disbursement process is being offered to assist you.

Disbursement Process: Traditional Psychology Blended With Ancient Chinese Secret

Since our thoughts are what create the *matter* in the first place, it makes sense that *staying clear of the matter* would naturally include an intervention that focuses specifically on the thinking process, with the following caveat: our brains don't need to be told what to do to realign with wellness. However, it can still be beneficial to join our cellular intelligence in its intrinsic knowing by doing cognitive (thinking) exercises that magnify and *flow with the positive energy* that is already being summoned by our thoughts. In this section we will attempt to fortify your ability to reconnect with the well-being that is already within your vibrational and spiritual DNA by offering a technique that may help to release resistance.

EXERCISE: The exercise is broken down into **two parts:**

Part I—Reframing

Throughout the steps, we have already been doing processes to free your thoughts of the *matter* at the level of mind. And so, Part I of this process is simply fortifying your ability to realign. The term "reframing" comes out of traditional **cognitive behavioral therapy** and is a pretty standard and effective tool that I, along with most psychotherapists, have used for many decades. It is known in the psychotherapy world as a technique called "reframing thoughts." It is based on the same premise used in Chapter Three, which I called *"reframing the matter"* or *"reframing the diagnoses."*

Reframing is typically described by psychotherapists by using the analogy of visiting a framing shop where you have a picture *framed.* The shop usually has you choose several frames and shows you how the picture will look in each frame. It's pretty amazing how an inexpensive print can look like a fine art piece inside the right frame. And even more astonishing is how a very expensive limited edition masterpiece can look like a five-and-dime store poster in the wrong frame. Our thoughts are very similar, depending on the "frame of reference" through which we chose to view the thought. This aligns with the parable "the cup is half empty or half full." We obviously want to *reframe* our thoughts in a way that will be more advantageous to our sense of well-being by picking the frame that feels better. In other words, we use *reframing* to change the "meaning" or interpretation of the *matter*, to realign.

Some psychotherapists and other healers would have you state your current thought about the situation, and then offer a soothing *reframe* which many have found to be effective. Yet, from a Sacretherapy® perspective, I prefer that you do the reframing portion from the vibrational frequency that aligns with the wellness you are seeking, instead of you also stating how you are actually feeling while unaligned. Both approaches work and so it is simply a *matter* of preference. However, I see more value in focusing **only** on how you *want to feel* as opposed to stating both. You already know how you currently feel, so we don't need to give the unwanted *matter* any more energy. And it's not that I want you to pretend to feel something that you are not feeling; I just want you to view it as **creating the feeling** of something that you really want to feel, since every creation begins with a thought.

Remember, we metaphysicians say *energy* flows where attention goes. Therefore, when the reframing example comes up know that you will ultimately skip the current statement of "how I feel now" to avoid the split in *energy*. We want to avoid encoding both thoughts, since they are vibrationally at different frequencies, and instead send a clear signal aligning with spirit of what you are reaching for. Encoding, as you learned earlier (Chapter Three) is how thoughts are stored in our memory, and so, if desires are paired with opposing thoughts, they can *energetically* cancel out one another, offering us no real vibrational movement.

Please read the example reframes below. The *actual thought* is only provided so that you can quickly select the *reframed thought* that you need in that unaligned moment.

ACTUAL THOUGHT	REFRAMED THOUGHT
I feel really depressed.	≈ I really want to feel better.
That bad thing should not have happened.	≈ I want so much for good things to happen
It's taking too long to get better.	≈ It's an onion, I am getting better, just another layer
One more pill and I'll scream!	≈ This one more pill may stop me from wanting to scream
I hate my life, it sucks.	≈ I want to like my life and find ways to suck on what's sweet
Why did I have to be born this way?	≈ I came into this physical realm with divine intentions.

I'm crazy and everybody knows it.	≈	I'm unique, like others, and want to be crazy about myself.
People don't like me being different.	≈	I look forward to accepting myself.
My <u>blank</u> really hurts.	≈	It's going to feel so good when my <u>blank</u> feels better.
My *dis-ease* is progressing.	≈	My desire to feel my well-being is really increasing
I'll never be good enough.	≈	I want to know my value and feel my worth.
I wish I was dead to stop the pain.	≈	I want to begin again, in this moment, and create new joy.
Why can't I just be normal?	≈	I look forward to my *peace of mind* being normal for me.

Those scripts above are only examples. So feel free to write a list of your own reframes and write them in advance of the pending difficult moment. Anticipate the thoughts that you know you regularly obsess about, and make a reframe of those in advance (while in a good mood, sort of like buying hurricane supplies before the storm), before the thought comes up again. Writing the reframe from this vantage point of *prevention* versus *intervention* shouldn't take you out of alignment if you think of it as acquiring tools to maintain your good mood. This way, the list is ready when it happens, so that you are only focusing on what you prefer. Then when it comes up, read the *reframe*.

Part II—Tap into Alignment: Mixing Reframing with Tapping

Now, Part II is optional but highly recommended. The process is called *tapping*, which has been somewhat controversial due to western medicine not appreciating or understanding the foundations of *energy* medicine. In any case, like anything else, there are those who have benefited and those who have not. I will allow you to draw your own conclusions as to its efficacy. *Tapping* borrows and incorporates the above intervention of *reframing thoughts* from **traditional psychotherapy,** and also borrows *acupressure* from the ancient **Chinese energy meridian system**. The term "tapping," however, is said to have been coined by Roger Callahan, Ph.D. Dr. Callahan—a psychologist devised *Thought Field Therapy* (1980), which was later adapted and promoted by Reverend Gary Craig, an ordained minister and engineer who coined his version as *Emotional Freedom Technique* (EFT) in 1993. There are several websites promoting tapping, and many offer a free "how to manual." The bio-*energy* portion of the process involves tapping on nine acupressure points of the meridian system located on your hands and head. It **takes no more than 5 minutes to start doing it** and is quite simple. The process also borrows from relaxation techniques and state of the art information coming out of neuro-science with regards to reducing arousal in the **amygdala**, which is the stress detection part of the brain, thereby assisting with reducing resistance.

Thus, due to its potential to reduce resistance and bring relief, I invite you to check out this quick and very simple "physiological intervention" to possibly accompany the traditional cognitive behavioral process of *reframing your thoughts* as illustrated in Part I. You may visit the founders' websites to see it being illustrated (live), by going to either: Reverend Craig's site is at **emofree.com** and/ or Dr. Callahan's site is at **rogercallahan.com.** If either of those websites ever changes, just Google: Tapping, Emotional Freedom Technique or Thought Field Therapy. (See Resources.) There are also other diagrams of tapping that may also be found on over a dozen tapping websites since Reverend Craig released the name *Emotional Freedom Technique* to the public domain. The actual *tapping* on all the websites that I visited is done the same. So feel free to explore them all. Once you have checked *tapping* out, try doing it in your mirror first, so that you can see that you are touching the correct points. You may want to try tapping a few times to see if it resonates with you. Then, if after a few attempts you prefer not to use it, just continue to *reframe your thoughts* as illustrated in Part I.

The above processes, along with others offered in this book, are only fortifying something that is *already beginning to move in a positive direction* because of the new thoughts that you have begun to offer vibrationally since *Step One.* So remember: it's a mind game predominately—*mind over matter.* And never has the power of our thoughts been made clearer than when the power of visualization was demonstrated by Dr. Dennis Waitley—a psychologist, through a program that he called *"Behavior Motor Rehearsal"* which is described in his book: The Psychology of Winning (1986).

Waitley used this program on athletes and determined that the same firings registered on the machines when the athletes ran the drill in their minds as they did when the athletes physically did the drills. And *prisoners of war* have also validated the power of a *thought* by stating that visualizing doing certain exercises is what kept their bodies in shape, and visualizing being home along with doing other positive things kept them emotionally soothed, which makes sense since first we *think* and then we *feel.* (To learn more about how to visualize effectively, see the book: *Creative Visualization,* by Shakti Gawain, Rev. 2002), (See Resources.)

Our thoughts, then, are powerful indeed; so much so, that we must understand that once we have created and manifested a thought there is no way to take it back. In other words "we can't deactivate a thought, but we can activate another one," which is what the *Teachings of Abraham—Law of Allowing workshops*, by Esther & Jerry Hicks (2006), reminds us. Therefore, the goal is not to try to *undo the thought* or *stop thinking the thought* that has you feeling bad, but rather, to *replace the thought* with a different thought that you would prefer to think. That is, a thought that will summon different emotions and a different quality of life. This has been an enduring theme in psychology since the 1960s, led by noted cognitive behavioral psychologist Albert Ellis, author of *Rational Emotive Behavior Therapy (REBT)—Living with a Neurotic* (1957). Ellis wrote more than 75 books on REBT and stated, *"Realize you control your own destiny."* He emphasized this further by his statement that *"You largely constructed your depression. It wasn't given to you. Therefore, you can deconstruct it…"*

Ellis is joined in this philosophy by equally notable psychiatrist William Glasser, M.D., author of *Reality Therapy* (1965). Glasser stated that *"…revisiting the painful past can contribute little-to-nothing to what we need to do now."* And as such, what we need to do "now" is reframe your thoughts to the best possible perspective you can think of without going to extremes, such as: *I really feel terrible* to *I feel fantastic.* That obviously won't soothe you because the jump between the two emotions is too extreme. And metaphysically, the *frequencies* of the two emotions are too far away from one another in the vibrational world of thought. So just reach for something realistic, such as moving from: *I really feel terrible* to *I really want to feel better;* and then bit by bit, frequency by frequency, your mood will be elevated as you come back into alignment.

Another tool you can employ to clear the *matter*, when it comes up, is to just let the subject go completely. This is helpful when you have decided that the *matter* at hand is too acute or painful in the moment. When this is the case, you can do what Atkinson (mentioned previously) suggests, which is to follow the advice within the expression: *"Don't give it another thought"*, literally. You can think of something else completely unrelated to replace the bothersome thought. This works, too, since we can't think two thoughts at the same time. The only problem with this technique is that the bothersome thought can keep coming back, right after you finish thinking the nonrelated thought. Therefore, for this technique to work, you usually need a small list of unrelated positive things to think about (which we will be developing in the forthcoming exercise). For instance, instead of focusing on the upsetting topic, you could think about the ice cream you like or your favorite comedy. Anything that you know makes you feel good can be used, as opposed to trying to reframe the negative thought, if it's too difficult in that unaligned moment. And that pleasant unrelated thought will raise your mood and vibration as well.

However, please know that sometimes, in a difficult moment, it's also quite okay to just "cry it out." Tears release pressure and pent up *energy* as well; so, sometimes a good hearty cry about the *matter* is the immediate release we need, and then, afterwards, we are better able to employ these other techniques to realign.

Either way, regardless of what technique you use, it's sort of like having your fingers on the volume button of your remote control, where you just keep increasing the sound register one decibel at a time, one new thought at a time, to get to the higher vibration. There is a metaphysical book that describes this concept beautifully with regard to shifting emotions titled: *Ask & It Is Given,* by Esther & Jerry Hicks (2004). (See Resources.) And one final resource is a book by David Burns, M.D., titled *Feeling Good* (1980). I truly love the title: *"feeling good"* because changing our thoughts to thoughts that feel better, is always the aim of the work. And since how we feel is what determines our quality of life, it is truly helpful to have as many positive resources available when those challenging moments are upon us. Therefore, the remaining sections that comprise this step on *how to stay clear of the matter* are intended to assist you in broadening your toolbox of interventions that feel good.

Honoring Your Journey—Extracting the Good

Staying clear of the matter is not only about having strategies on how to avoid or get rid of the bad, but it is also about how to recognize and keep the good. As such, in our *release work*, we do not want to release that which was dear—especially since we are coming to recognize from the *stream of consciousness* described in Step One that we came into this physical realm to experience the joy of living, not only its sorrow. Thus, by all means, as we are learning to release the bad, "We don't want to throw out the baby with the bath water." Knowing that our life journey has also included the good and neutral, as well as the bad, allows us to have a more realistic balanced view of the *matter*. Many people have a lopsided view of the life they've lived mainly because of where they're focusing their attention and putting the emphasis. They inadvertently let the bad experiences outweigh the other moments that were often equally impactful, or at least could have been if they had not continued to put their *energy* into recalling the negative *matter*. So let us take time to shift our *energy* in order to recall and extract what was good.

I recognize that if you are in the habit of focusing on the bad things, the idea of recalling the good may seem much easier said than done. I often have clients insist that there was nothing good in their past. Yet, they eventually, although begrudgingly, are able to cough it up. They do so begrudgingly because they sense that detaching from the loyal commitment they've had to the negative *matter* will expose that a greater quality of life, could have, in fact, been had.

Therefore, be compassionate with yourself as we begin to extract the positive *matter*. And know that it's okay, due to resistance, that you may not be able to think of anything in this particular moment. You will, however, eventually be able to, because it is impossible not to, since you have lived a lot of life! Remember in *Step One* when you completed the PSBQ or PSBQ-R and crunched the numbers of how many quantum moments you have lived so far in this lifetime? Well, let's recalculate those totals again to demonstrate what I mean. There are 365 days a year, and if you multiply that number by your age, it will give you a total of how many quantum moments (seconds) you have lived and an idea of how many experiences you have had. And as a reminder, there are 3,600 quantum moments in every hour. So even if you've had three dozen horrible things happen in your life, and the emotional or physical pain of each lasted for many months, there would still be much of your life left to savor.

No one cries or frowns 24 hours a day, seven days a week, 365 days a year, every year. No one! So the only reason it seems hard to conjure the "good" is because you've gotten used to concentrating on the negative things and trained yourself into *framing* your experiences as "the cup being half empty instead of half full." Thus, be assured that if you start with when your physical journey began the day you were born, you would recognize that you have experienced many moments of joy that got minimized, along with many valuable life experiences worth preserving.

To preserve something, according to most dictionaries, means to keep it alive, intact, or free from decay, and maintained. As such, you will find that there are both dormant and obvious morsels of your life that are worth jarring. Those morsels are already stored in your long-term memory, but we want to take a moment to underline them for easy future access, as described in *Step Two*. **Memory has three parts: encoding, storage and retrieval.** We already discussed a little about *encoding* early on and in the material on reframing thoughts. Thus, you may remember that if things are encoded *improperly*, they are not as easy to recall. Plus, if they were paired with something unpleasant or traumatic, then the one that was more vibrationally dominant is the one that is easier to remember. And if that's the case, that is how the other got minimized and placed in a storage file that is difficult to retrieve. So we want to take this time to *re-encode* the pleasant aspects of your "life that's already been lived" for the sheer purpose of allowing those things worth remembering to trigger positive feelings, which will greatly facilitate bringing you back into alignment.

Positive feelings trigger the natural healing endorphins in your brain. Endorphins give you a sense of well-being. However, you must release serotonin and adrenaline to trigger the endorphins. This is why most antidepressants involve some sort of interplay with serotonin so that your natural endorphins can serve you. Yet, what gets in the way of experiencing your natural positive feelings is, of course, negative emotion. Emotional pain often causes you to activate the *fight or flight* response that was mentioned briefly involving the amygdala. As such, when you are feeling negative emotion and anxiety, you are secreting cortisol combined with other pain mediating hormones that can make you feel awful in the process of attempting to resolve the pain. Therefore, when you are feeling mentally and emotionally upset, you are secreting a lot of the above mentioned hormones, and deactivating the brain chemistry that releases endorphins. This is why you feel extra awful. And now that you know what's adding to you feeling bad, you can stop the unwanted secretions by remembering to *think a different thought*—one that will release the brain chemistry that triggers endorphins. This is where retrieving all of those good memories that lay dormant can be used for "medicinal" purposes at just the right moments to help you feel better and realign.

So let's get started ***re-encoding*** **the positive memories** and put them in the vibrational medicine cabinet that you can reach for any time. Try the below exercise.

EXERCISE: Extracting Positive Memories

Please go get your journal and a pen. I am going to help you to come up with 10 or 15 good things that will be enough for now, but the more the merrier. You will usually only need a half dozen or fewer in that uncomfortable unaligned moment to bring you back into alignment. Still, the more you have, the more you get to choose from. So let me help you summon some positive memories. There are 20 triggers below to choose from, so it's okay if you have to skip a few if they don't trigger a positive memory. Just be sure to write down anything positive that comes up for you in response to each. Now, think of the following:

1. Something that makes you crack a smile every time you think it.
2. Something that was just so stupid you had to laugh.
3. Something you did that was darn near genius or at least you thought so.
4. Something you'll never forget that someone who loves you said.
5. Something great that happened when you were in elementary school.
6. Something you consider the most prized possession you own and how you felt the day you got it.
7. Something you did at your favorite birthday party (it could have been yours or someone else's party.)
8. Something that was unexpectedly fun that you initially did not want to do.
9. Something really good that happened when you were in middle school.
10. Something that tastes so good that you could eat it every week.

11. Something so silly you're debating whether to even add it to this list.

12. Something you thought after your very first wonderful kiss.

13. Something you won or found that made your day.

14. Something your mama did that you really liked and will never forget.

15. Something your daddy said that was really great.

16. Something a teacher said that instilled hope.

17. Something a sibling or cousin or friend did that was unexpectedly kind.

18. Something good that happened when you were in high school.

19. Something you did that was fantastic on one of your vacations.

20. Something that reminds you that there is something good in all of us that balances out the bad.

That should have gotten your juices flowing. Go ahead now, if you are on a roll, and add to the list other memories that you want to preserve. PAUSE.

───── ⚬⚬⚬ ─────

Once you have completed the exercise and have your list, tape it inside the door of your medicine cabinet. That way, you will have both your physical medicine and your emotional medicine in the same place for easy access when needed. It doesn't hurt to put a copy in your glove compartment, too, just in case something comes up when you are away from home or at work. Knowing you are always prepared with your tools nearby can help you to shift your *energy* quicker. Think of it as your positive trigger sheet to your inner retreat.

Part of the reason for gathering the positive memories that you will preserve is to activate within you a balanced view that there are also good parts of the unaligned people in your life, as well as strangers. Think about it: If the people that you feel have interfered with your well-being got the same list, they would also be able to come up with pleasant answers. So, this is why developing a balanced view of your past *matter* and the past *matter* of others is important. Everyone has had life worth preserving. In any case, I hope those memories will also facilitate the work you are about to do in the next section on forgiveness. But first, I hope you share my pride in you for taking time to retrieve all those pleasant memories. You had only forgotten or perhaps intentionally locked them away, thinking that the bad things outweighed the good, and they didn't. And now they are ready to be employed for duty any time you need them. Plus, the same joy you got out of thinking about them today will be the same joy you will feel the next time you activate them. And remember that since you can't think two thoughts at the same time, using these thoughts to replace the negative ones will serve you well in bringing yourself back into alignment.

Savor the fruits of having completed this exercise before moving on to the next. In fact, stop here for today and pick back up tomorrow, because I want you to relish the fact that you have had **more** good moments than you realized. And by just acknowledging that, you enter a vibrational stance where **if** you keep looking for the good, more good will be summoned because *like attracts like.*

How to Forgive Self & Others: When They Don't Deserve It But You Do

Beginning to extract the good, as you did in the previous exercise, is an excellent entrée into forgiveness work. You have been reminded that the bad aspects of life cannot drown out the good—unless somehow we let it! But now, having worked so diligently on lining our *energy* back up with wellness, we have no intention to allow the bad to outweigh the good again. You didn't do all that work for nothing. Doing those aligning processes three times a day, the worksheets, the pre-letters, rage letters, speeches, tapping, reframing thoughts, and preserving the good wasn't easy, but they have been preparing you for this next step.

Until now, you have not been asked to forgive. And so, in your mind, it may have been one thing to release and a whole other thing to forgive. I understand. Forgiveness is a sacred thing of moving from the vibration of a victim to the vibration of a victor. Forgiveness involves *understanding and compassion.* And compassion is not always easy to summon. So you will not be asked to forgive all at once. Like everything else we have done, it's a process. I've told psychotherapists that I've trained that it isn't reasonable to demand someone to instantly be able to forgive and move on. Everyone isn't ready to do it in a holy instant. Hurt and anger are heads and tails of the same coin, and are very different vibrations from forgiveness.

Forgiveness, however, is certainly and ultimately the goal, no *matter* how awful the offense. Iyanla Vanzant, mentioned earlier, is the author of *One Day My Soul Just Opened Up* (1998), and she says that even *poison can be ingested with the right antibodies.* I believe this wholeheartedly. And so, let the positive memories that you have extracted and all of the release work you've done now be the *spoon full of sugar* that lets this *medicine go down*, as we make the next vibrational move towards forgiveness.

The word "forgive" means to give. And so, as the cliche' goes, "something's got to give and that something means you." But you are not forgiving *them* for *them*. You are doing it for *you*. It's about emotional self-sufficiency and the ability to self soothe. It is also about taking back your *power*, which is the same as taking back your *energy* as we discussed in Chapter Two. This is *energy* that got drained due to your focus on *them* and what *they* did that you swore you would never forgive. But ask yourself this question: "Is taking it to your grave worth keeping you from your well-being?" I mean is it worth dying for? Well is it? I ask because resentment is the fastest way to accidently "release the body temple" and return to the nonphysical.

Even though it may not be considered flat out suicide, it does kill the body. It turns into *dis-ease* and breaks down the immune system. So you may have decided that *they* don't deserve to live with your forgiveness, but don't you? The interesting thing about this is that you are probably *not even hurting them* with your refusal to forgive. You are ONLY hurting *you*, because *they* may have forgiven themselves a long time ago and have gone on about their business. *They* may already be experiencing the joy of living that you are depriving yourself of because of them.

Let me put it this way: I once heard somewhere that "We have **ALL been wounded** and we have **ALL wounded others**, too!" So that means that **NOT ONE OF US is completely innocent**. And we don't have to be. We and they can just be sufficiently divine. The *alignment* chart in Chapter Two may be worth reviewing here, in that there are degrees of alignment where we are closer to optimum well-being at some moments and closer to misalignment at others. But the good news is that it is a moment by moment thing. That horrible act or thing that was said or done to you, by them, happened in one of their unaligned *moments*. And since *like attracts like*, then it must have also happened in one of your unaligned *moments*, too. Ouch! I know no one wants to hear that. I don't particularly like it either, but universal laws are like gravity; they just are. As is said, "It is—what it is." So let's review this concept using the following example to demonstrate how *like attracts like*:

If I don't like myself and I'm thinking thoughts that are self-deprecating while I'm out and about in the world, running around doing my thing, then I am a magnet for others who also don't like themselves very well, either. And then, bam, the co-creative blending of like energies is mixed. In other words, I think the thought that "I don't like my life," and at that point it is just a thought that is invisible. But as I keep thinking the same thought a lot, it becomes a chronic thought and turns into a *thought form*— which in laymen's terms can be thought of as a thought that has now begun to take shape and form. But in actuality, it is a little more than just the manifesting of a thought. (For more on *thought forms,* see the book, *The Human Aura: Astral Colors and Thought Forms* by Swami Panchadasi, in the Resources section.)

If I keep thinking that thought about how I don't like my life, I attract others who don't like their lives either, through a self-fulfilling prophecy or the law of attraction. I am then matched up with someone vibrating at the same frequency that I am. We meet and have a co-creative experience that isn't pleasant, since we both dislike our lives. We have nothing positive to offer one another in the unaligned moment. So something bad is said or done because we are vibrating at a frequency that attracts more bad things. But we, in turn, blame the other person for saying or doing this bad thing, because we don't realize the creation power of our thoughts and feelings about ourselves or our lives, and now we want it to go away. But it hasn't gone away because we're the one that won't let it go away, because we keep thinking the same self-deprecating thoughts.

It's like pushing the rewind button on life experiences that were unpleasant as evidence of why you don't like your life. And so, again, if I think the thought that "I don't like my life," I will keep attracting others who don't like theirs. And each time I meet someone else where something bad or sad is done, I keep adding the negative experience to my collection of evidence of why I don't like my life. I rationalize that I don't need to forgive anybody for anything since *they* keep saying and doing bad things to *me*. (All the while, I am not realizing the role my chronic thoughts play in all that is manifesting in my life.) STOP. End of example.

⸙

When that type of script plays out, it is often used as justification for not forgiving, since most people have collected a lot of evidence over the years that definitely backs up why they feel someone is unforgivable. Yet, the unforgiven need not be in a permanent place of exile. There is always room for redemption—if you could just begin to recognize that YOU, not they, have the power to influence the quality of your life. Wasting time and *energy* focusing your attention on the negative things they did is non-productive. But focusing on the positive things you did is a better use of *energy*.

Plus, what about when you are the one who wants to be forgiven, and the other soul won't forgive you? Many people have difficulty when they are not given the chance to make things right. One can feel quite tormented by what feels like unfinished business. But, if you have tried to make it right and the other soul is unable to allow it, release that person. It doesn't necessarily mean that they have not forgiven you; they may have, at the *energy* level of spirit, and for whatever reason have already released you and just prefer to not re-engage. Even if they have not forgiven you, for whatever reason, be assured that nothing more needs to be done except the sacred work of forgiving yourself. This is crucial to understand because more often than not, forgiveness cannot come from others until you understand that you are worthy of forgiveness and have forgiven yourself! This is because 'like attracts like' so if you are not at the vibrational resonance of compassion and redemption, you cannot summon it. But if you have forgiven yourself and the others still haven't shifted their *energy*, then take heed and trust that those sacred contracts have been fulfilled.

Remember my earlier offering: we have **all** injured others; and so, that means they've hurt someone too, maybe it was even you. Therefore, you are not some awful soul needing to be eternally punished. You are partially human and just made what most people refer to as a mistake. No *matter* how terrible or large it was, even if at the time it was deliberate, it's still just a mistake, caused by an unaligned thought. And you are so much more than your mistakes. We all are. So are they.

As I stated before, during my years as a psychotherapist, I found that out of all of the things that we fear as a people, ***we are most afraid of each other***. And if I were to expand on that, I would have to submit that we are fearful because we have not been taught about the innate divinity within each and every soul. Thus, we fear another's condemnation, judgment and lack of tolerance for the raw aspects of our humanity. With that in mind, let's first focus your attention on ***forgiving yourself*** for anything and everything you feel you've said or done that harmed yourself or another person. Then you can work on forgiving others.

There's a sacred process to forgiveness that many authors have taken time to describe. Most describe it as actual stages that a person ultimately goes through in order to forgive. And from what I've noticed over the years, most are correct in their observations. Likewise, my description of the stages of forgiveness below echo the collective therapeutic opinions of how forgiveness unfolds, however, mine offer a metaphysical spin, beginning with: 1) ***revenge,*** where *energy* is blocked, to 2) ***detachment***, where *energy* is less blocked but still stifled, to 3) ***compassion***, where *energy* begins to shift, to 4) ***forgiveness***, where *energy* flows freely. Let's look at them separately below:

> 1. **Revenge**—(Blocked Energy) First when one believes that they have been injured, he or she embraces fantasies of revenge, which is quite natural. From the perception and vibration of *victimization* comes the feeling that one's *worth* and *value* have been brought into question. As such, the "injured one" desperately tries to right the situation with thoughts of avenging oneself by getting revenge. Believing that one is advocating for oneself and being self-protective, one is ultimately *seeking relief,* unable to see what part he or she may have had in the *matter*.

> 2. **Detachment**—(Stifled Energy) Next one goes through a process of detachment and begins to slowly release fantasies of revenge, which is often facilitated by positive distractions. Here the expression that "Time heals all wounds" comes to bear on the *matter*, because after one calms down for a week or so, one generally begins to feel better. And as more time passes, one feels better still. By now, one has had time to think, often discussing it with others who helped disperse the toxic *energy* by uncovering the blind spots that were hidden (due to one's low *frequency*). At this point, one has replayed the incident in one's mind enough until one now is able to recognize that he or she may have actually had a part in the *matter*. Regardless if it were a big part or small, one now realizes that he or she originally minimized one's role, since one's hurt and anger stifled clarity at the time.

3. **Compassion**—(Energy Shifts) As a result of having taken time to review the *matter* from every vantage point possible, one begins to summon compassion for oneself and the other person and starts to reframe the *matter* from a broader perspective. Now, one truly begins to feel the *relief* he or she was originally seeking through revenge, but instead, here it comes through compassion and understanding. One can now recognize and know that one was not a victim, and was, instead, a participant involved in an occurrence where all parties were unaligned to some degree.

4. **Forgiving**—(Energy Flows) After having time to collect one's wits about the *matter*, finally one is ready and able to let the *matter* go. Even if one decides that the other person was still more out of alignment, he or she finally recognizes that one deserves the benefits and ongoing relief that fully releasing the toxic *energy* provides. Here, one benefits from knowing that very few people, when wounded, are able to forgive for just spiritual or altruistic purposes. So, it is here that one begins to contemplate "what's in it for them", since the first law of nature, again, is self preservation. Therefore, it is the personal and *vibrational* quantum leap in *energy* that is brought about through the *release of the matter* that tremendously facilitates one's ability to come back into alignment, fully forgive and feel totally free.

I suggest you adapt these stages to apply to yourself, whereas you change the word "revenge" with "self-reproach" since it is you that we are first focusing on forgiving. Then once you have forgiven yourself and see how freeing that feels, then you can try forgiving another. And the good news, here, is that you can forgive another person without ever having to tell him or her. You don't even have to ever interact with the person again, if you don't want. It's okay to walk away and stay away. It was one of your rights (Chapter Four) which we will get back to in a moment. But in the meantime, forgiveness is strictly a vibrational offering that we only need to clear for **your** heart.

You can start with the people that committed a smaller offense, and then try using it for the people that offered the more horrendous acts you experienced. It's fine to take it in stages as described above. Just know that they, like you, were more than likely thinking thoughts that they probably didn't know were *self-fulfilling prophecies* or the *law of attraction* in action, which started their negative acting out.

Therefore, when it comes to forgiveness, it really seems as if it ends up ultimately being no one's fault, due to the multigenerational conditioning of it all. Surely, it may be someone's responsibility. But fault and responsibility are not vibrationally synonymous. Nevertheless, it is certainly our responsibility to come into alignment and recognize the injurious *energy* we send out into the world, and take responsibility for our mis-creations.

I know it still feels better to most people to assign blame. We want it to be somebody's fault, since it's not nearly as satisfying to own the incident as a co-creative manifestation. But if we extract what was surmised from the speeches we did in the **mutant rage exercise,** we saw that the energetic laceration goes back so far that it was nearly impossible to pinpoint where to place the onus. This is because "this one said something or did something to that one, and that one did something to another one that said and did something to them over there, and they said and did something to your great grandfather's father who said or did something to your great aunt, who said or did something to your grandmother, who said and did something to your father, who may have said and done something to you." So these thoughts get passed down, get shared and become manifestations. And lo and behold, we are back to the effects of conditioning, memes and old linguistic programming.

So we *can* forgive, because now we understand *how* it happened, not that we accept the specifics of *what* happened. We know what happened occurred out of unaligned thoughts, but we can't change *life experience that has already been lived*. But what we can change is our perspective on how it was lived, and that can be transformative, empowering and bring tremendous relief because now we know *it wasn't personal, it was vibrational.*

The bottom line is, no one really meant to hurt you, and no one meant to desert you. They were trying to feel better themselves and didn't know *how* because they were holding onto the same kinds of chronic low vibrational thoughts that you were holding in similar ways. At the time, you two just happened to meet at that misaligned moment that was mutually unaligned.

The funny thing is the same person who was rude to you in the parking lot is the same person who 15 minutes later helped a senior citizen to cross the street. Charged with human decency at the core of one's DNA, that batterer who beat his girlfriend is the same advocate for children's rights; and as it turns out, he was battered as a child and watched his mother beat his father. The same friend who cursed you out last week is the same friend that consoled and "walked the floor with you" last year. That homophobic guy who was mean to the gay guy at the box office is the same volunteer at the homeless shelter around the corner. That same nurse who stole the narcotics from the hospital is the same one that wiped the urine off of your thighs that morning. That person whom you know as a complete jerk at work is the same person who took her aging mother in last week. So, we would be wise to not size one another up so swiftly; for surely we are all capable of manifesting the good, the bad, and the ugly.

Of course, there are souls that you have encountered that you may not want to keep engaging, even though you may have forgiven them directly or just within your heart. You may feel that you just don't want to invest any more time or expend the amount of *energy* it takes to align yourself to prepare to deal with them. And so, you may prefer to just release them from your life. This is perfectly okay, as stated above and in your *Spiritual Bill of Rights* from Chapter Four. You are free to walk away from anyone or anything that in *your perspective* threatens, drains, or impedes your ability to maintain your well-being. Even though you now understand that it is your thoughts about the person or situation—or his or her words that you are actually attaching your own meaning to—which is what causes you to prefer to release the person. And that's still okay, too. We never have to try to be further along in our individuation (psyche evolution) than we have yet achieved. So remember: *Let go, what goes*, and let it be.

Still, for those who remain a part of your life, it's about giving them the benefit of the doubt, which can be challenging—especially when it is a "loved one" who habitually seems to push your buttons or deplete your energy. To practice not being yanked from your well-being by the person, let's try doing some role plays with family or friends for the sheer purpose of seeing how you can elevate your mood. Try the clearing exercise below that can help you stand firm in the awareness that you are a well being despite what's going on with others.

EXERCISE: Remembering That I Am a Well Being

For instance, if your father usually offers words from a low vibrational frequency that irritates the heck out you, or usually causes you to go into a depressed or anxious state, then let's practice on him (or feel free to substitute him with someone else). But before we can practice on him, we have to maintain our own alignment with our mind, body, and spirit, so that we get to dominate the interaction. According to psychologist Dr. Thelma Moss' research on emotional states and aura color, done at the Neuropsychiatric Institute of UCLA, the intensity of one person's aura illustrated by color influences the emotional state of another person's aura. Therefore, the dominate aura gets to control the vibrational frequency of an interaction. If you are feeling good or at least feeling better than the object of your aggravation feels, which in this case would be your father, then your vibration can set the tone for the entire conversation. And it also means that your higher vibration can hold you in a place of well-being during the conversation. You may even lift him up, though that is not the goal. The goal is to keep your own mood up and not let it be altered by him. You do this in the following ways:

1. By building yourself up and recognizing that you and he have the same God source within; because starting from a place of equal footing is important so that you don't mistake your value and worth, or his. In one of Marianne Williamson's lectures about *The Course In Miracles*, she states, "We thank you holy spirit, for your opinion of us is higher than our opinion of ourselves." Her CD on *Self Esteem* is a wonderful resource for working on issues surrounding self worth. (See Resources.)

2. Write down your sacred intention with this person. Do you want to promote connection or disconnection? I'm assuming connection. And if so, then like you did in the previous chapter for yourself, come up with something you really value in your dealings with him. Then put yourself in his shoes. Empathy helps a lot. In fact, *compassion* is considered one of our divine powers, according to the book, *The Anatomy of Spirit* (1996), by Dr. Carolyn Myss. Since compassion is one of our divine powers to share, let's utilize it in this situation. But know that compassion and empathy are not the same as feeling sorrow for someone. That would mean that you are still out of alignment, if you feel sorry for others— because that means you are not employing what was just discussed in number one: Honoring the other person's value and worth as well as his capacity to tap into his own well-being, too. So just because he may not choose to embrace his well-being does not mean he is unable to. Most everyone, like you, can reach out for help, find a therapist, or pick up a self-help book free at the library. And don't let him say that he can't afford it, because there are plenty of free mental health agencies offering help out there. (See Resources.)

3. Practice in the mirror what I call **Reflection-Inspection-Direction**, where you will use your mirror reflection to inspect and direct your non-verbal communication, any time when what you plan to say to him usually ends up in an argument. The bathroom mirror or a large hand held mirror will do. Looking in the mirror lets you see the expression on your face, and whether or not you are scouring and appearing unpleasant. Then, once you see yourself looking mad, put a smile on your face to convey that you come in peace. Even when you have conversations over the phone, people are able to tell if you are smiling or frowning because, remember, vibes are invisible rays of energy that go right through that phone. So smile while you practice.
You may be thinking that what you have to say to him is not pleasant and so no smile is warranted. Well, if that is the case, then postpone the conversation until a smile is warranted. If you are really trying to live the life you came into the physical realm to live, know it is one of joyful co-creation with other souls, and if you are choosing to engage with your father, he is one of those souls. So peace and harmony is achievable for you, if you are willing to raise your own vibration to that level. If he is cranky and unpleasant during the conversation, you won't be yanked by it anymore, because if your vibration is higher he won't be able to penetrate you. Trust me, he will notice that. And he will respect it, even if he never admits that to you.

Everyone takes notice of a *still deer*, which is my metaphor for peace. So practice. There is always a better way to say everything, if you will just continue to try. Then, once you are ready for the real encounter over the phone, I suggest you still look in the mirror while you are having the conversation, paying attention to your vibrational countenance the entire time. Not his. Keep telling yourself,

"It is not my father's job to lift me up; it's my job to lift myself up." He owes you nothing. He—like you, like me—came into the physical realm with the desire to be happy and experience certain things. And he—like you and like me—has tried his best to do that, ever since he was born.

You will undoubtedly blow it sometimes in your new approach because of your old habituated pattern. Yet, in time this new way of being will become your "new normal." Therefore, when you blow it, just try to laugh it off and tell yourself, *"I look forward to practicing on him again soon."* Then tell yourself, *"I did better in the conversation today than I usually do. And I held on a bit longer before I blew a gasket. And next time I'll hold on even longer."* So please, no self-reproach, just compassion and self-love.

You **can** let it go now, *for you*, if you want to. You can begin raising your own vibration, so that you can begin creating the type of experiences you want more of in your life, like the ones you've begun to preserve. This is part of what it takes to remember that you *are* a well being. And as you begin to think thoughts that match what you desire NOW, you will feel the relief-inducing vibrational offering that the following empowering statements summon in the below exercise: *Forgiving Stream of Consciousness.*

EXERCISE: Forgiving Stream of Consciousness

Instructions: Repeat the following statements to yourself and out loud in your mirror.

I am worthy of forgiveness.

I am compassionate and generous enough to forgive.

I like the idea that it wasn't personal, it was vibrational.

I feel better about myself and no longer feel like a victim.

I really do want to forgive everybody for everything.

I see now that it wasn't me that they were after;
it was my vibrational resonance they latched on to.

I am excited to know that we live in a vibrational universe of
which I am a part.

I love knowing that I have the power to actually affect my own experience.

I really am an okay person and didn't do anything that
is beyond forgiveness.

I was just living life *unconsciously*, unaware of these universal laws and
conditioning.

I love understanding that freewill means that:
I am free to think about what I want or what I don't want.
I feel so empowered knowing that things really can be much better now.

I'm going to be more patient with myself as I integrate
this new information.

Rome wasn't built in a day, so little by little

I will improve my quality of life.

I already feel so much better.

It is so freeing to know that I can now go forth
unencumbered by yesterday.

Utilizing the above empowering *forgiveness stream of consciousness* can serve
you when the old thoughts come up. And they will. But as they do, just accept
that those past thoughts became habituated. But so will your new healthier ones,
over time. You were just thinking a certain way for what seems like forever and
those thoughts became ingrained and automatic. Yet, penetrating the old ways
of thinking definitely gets easier and easier with practice as does using tools that
keep you fortified. Therefore, while you continue the moment-by-moment work
of aligning your mind, body and spirit, please be patient with yourself during the
process because NO ONE is ever aligned 24/7. Not the preacher, not the teacher,
not the therapist, not the monk, not anyone. Still, you can and will be aligned
much more often than not, but it is unrealistic to expect to ***always*** be fully aligned.
The human aspect of our beingness accounts for this disparity since the physical
realm is full of diversity, which includes the *conditioning, memes* and *old linguistic
programming* that we have all been exposed to.

The Teachings of Abraham—Law of Allowing Workshops (Hicks, 2005), reminds
us that "We came into these physical bodies for the contrast." I love having that
emphasized, because what it underlines is that everything that does not appeal to
one person, somebody else may need and love. Therefore, that "disliked thing"
(whether illness or abuse or addiction, etc.) is a necessary part of someone else's
evolution or sacred contract, and it represents part of the variety of life we obviously
came forth to experience and observe.

So what we have to do to keep our *perception* of the *matter* "neutral" is to stay
conscious of the re-education process—that is, knowing how to continue to release
the automatic responses that interfered with yesterday; and not let them interfere
with our ability to be *fully present* in the "here and now" moment. We do not
want to be like non-thinking robots. A robot is defined as "a machine capable of
carrying out a complex series of actions automatically." A human being, however,
is defined as "an earthly being, man, woman, or child…distinguished from other

animals by superior mental development and power of articulate reasoning…."
That "reasoning" is what gives us the ability, unlike a robot, to be *fully present* in
the moment. It allows us to consciously be aware of our "*in the moment choice*" to
think independent spontaneous thoughts.

We can choose in that moment what is the best course of action or reaction *to
create*, in order to experience what we want to see manifest. And so, moment by
moment, we get to ask ourselves, "What do I want to create for myself and enjoy in
the *next moment*," since we are finally coming to understand that today's thoughts
become tomorrow's manifestations of *matter*.

To have the mental and emotional well-being that you want on a more sustained
basis means living consciously, not unconsciously. It means understanding that
tonight's flippant comment (manifestation), if interpreted or offered from a low
vibration, can be tomorrow's depression. So you are aiming to make a conscious
effort to be less affected by your memory banks that store *life that has already been
lived*. And I hope you are coming to understand that you don't have to think
thoughts just because you have tons of thoughts in your long-term memory banks
to think. Nor do you have to let stimuli in your environment trigger the stored
automatic thoughts. But rather, you must understand that the thoughts you think
can be more authentic representations of your *here and now*; and they can be used
solely to create the positive manifestations that will allow you to experience emotions that
keep you "feeling good" now. Surely this is the life you were meant to live.

EXERCISE: Final Clearing—The Post Letter

The final exercise in this subsection is the ***post-letter*** that was discussed in
the previous chapter. If you were able to forgive above, then this letter can now
be written as a ***final energy disbursement*** from your new broader perspective of
the *matter* not being "personal but vibrational." This letter can be written to the
God-source in the universe, describing how you view the situation (s) now in your
more aligned state of being (**See Appendix E for the outline of the post-letter**).
Then be sure to have it witnessed by your confidant or therapist. This is a true *rite of
passage* into fully acknowledging the soul-filled person that you are and coming to
understand all others as soul-filled, too. Congratulations on this major vibrational
leap from whence you came. Once the letter has been completed, seal it and place
it in the container marked *The Past* along with the other work you placed in your
sacred vault. **Pause here** and execute the tasks.

After those tasks are completed, you will be ready to move onto the next step. However, if you didn't refresh yourself with an *energy* treatment at the end of the last chapter, I strongly suggest you get one now, after having done so much release work. Of course, it is optional but highly recommended since you could undoubtedly benefit from an "energy" alignment, having peeled off so many layers of that pent up energetic onion. So use the other energy medicines available by getting a Reiki or Prana treatment. They will fortify your clearing work in the Sacretherapy® process so far. And as stated, both treatments share the same energy basis, with just different names and slightly different techniques and/or emphasis on breath-work. Check your local area for a certified practitioner of either energy form. Once you have re-energized your mind, body and spirit, you are ready to move on to the next step. Please understand moving on to the next step means that you have successfully cleared, forgiven, released, and restored and can, therefore, *skip* the next chapter and go straight to *Step Six* in Chapter Eight.

However, if for some unforeseen reason, you were unable to do the clearing and release work in this chapter and are still feeling extremely depressed with *suicidal* thoughts or considering suicide or have attempted, and/or are stuck because a loved one completed suicide, then please read the upcoming Chapter Seven titled: *Ending The Matter*; **otherwise, skip the next chapter** and move on to Chapter Eight.

7
ENDING THE MATTER

Suicidal Ideation, Suicide Attempts,
Suicide Manipulation, & Transitioning To Realign

Stepping Out

NOTE: Only read this chapter if you or someone close to you is CURRENTLY having suicidal thoughts, has attempted, may be using suicidal threats as manipulation, or completed suicide. Otherwise, PLEASE SKIP THIS CHAPTER and continue focusing on the *matter* of living in the physical realm, and go to Chapter Eight—*Step Six*.

Caveat: FOR THOSE CURRENTLY FEELING SUICIDAL:

If you are currently feeling suicidal, it is imperative that you take your feelings seriously and reach out for help. Please call the National Suicide Helpline at 800-273-TALK (8255) and someone will assist you in finding local help in the U.S.

> *"Sometimes, when we reach this point in our soul's progress…we are no longer satisfied to go on living the old life, without the knowledge of our oneness with God, the source of our being."*
>
> —Myrtle Fillmore

The quote above by Myrtle Fillmore (co-founder of Unity) is quite apropos when applied to the subject of depression with suicidal thoughts and behaviors, because so many are trying to feel the goodness and joy that they inherently know comes from our connection to the God-source of our being. The fact that so many are in pain when they don't feel that connection means that they know somewhere deep down inside that they should and could, if they could only reconnect. This, of course, is the cornerstone of the Sacretherapy® perspective, in that it lights a pathway for us to reconnect with the divinity and the well-being that was wired into our DNA when we came into this physical experience, as was described in the *stream of consciousness* in Chapter Two. As such, that comfort and divinity one seeks while depressed is sometimes mistakenly viewed as an ascension sought outside of oneself; and therefore, when thoughts of suicide come up, one mistakenly believes that reconnection with spirit—realignment—can only occur in the nonphysical realm.

In this case, one has lost the understanding that integration with the *energy* of God is not only in the heavens but also exists within us, here on earth. It is this very same *energy* that I have been describing throughout this book, and that Leadbeater (1903) taught is the prana (life force), attached to the oxygen molecules; for it is this *energy* that gives us our *breath of life* that we call God. As such, the ascension one seeks is always accessible by merely elevating one's vibration to the frequency where well-being exists, which is achieved by shifting one's thoughts. This, in turn, shifts one's *energy* to the frequency where the consciousness of God can be accessed.

Yet, many times one becomes fixated on the negative *matter* of one's physical journey and looks outside of oneself for relief. One is hoping and praying that something or someone outside of oneself will fill one's life with the peace of mind and joy one seeks. And in so doing, one becomes externally focused and develops what psychology calls an *"external locus of control."* But the relief one seeks is not outside of oneself. As such, the only thing that is broken is one's "perception of separation" between themselves and the source of their being. Thus, when one does not understand this premise or has not been taught about their "oneness with God," due to conditioning or memes and other life experiences, it may be difficult to believe that restoration is an inside job.

As a result, one can become weary of one's emotional **reactions** to what was described as the "flawed (misaligned) initiation" into the physical realm (see Chapters Two—Four) and become tired of going from pillar to post searching for relief. When this happens, one can mistakenly believe that the answer to one's question eludes him or her, and one often gives up, not recognizing that the desire to feel one's divinity is in actuality the call of the God-source within and is the enduring well-being one seeks. Yet, when one does not understand that the source of one's being is omnipresent—*on the inside and outside of them*—one can remain in a constant state of flux, anxious, and depressed.

That feeling of disconnection, along with despair and desperation about not having the joy-filled life one seeks, however, can vary tremendously. As such, for the remainder of this chapter I will describe this versatility by shedding light on a gamut of issues with regard to suicidal ideation, from the holistic perspective, such as: **1)** the different types of depression that accompany suicidal thoughts and behaviors; **2)** why using suicidal threats to control the behaviors of others is a very bad idea; **3)** the ability each soul has to tap into emotional self sufficiency; **4)** ways to redirect fantasies of taking loved ones along; **5)** how to relieve those that are trying to live their lives for another; **6)** what to do when realignment with wellness feels too hard; **7)** how one can summon the *energy* to realign with well-being here in the physical realm; **8)** how transitioning and returning to the *nonphysical* realm to realign may be viewed metaphysically; **9)** how to get immediate help as it relates to the paradox of split *energy*; **10)** how to dissolve the idea of a punishing God and eternal damnation as it relates to those who completed suicide; and **11)** how survivors can embrace acceptance and realign with their own well-being via *A Special Note to Survivors of Loved Ones who Transitioned* via suicide.

Four Types of Depression with Suicidality

While there are distinct differences amongst the four types, I want to note that there are also similarities within these reactions and the misaligned thoughts. The first commonality is that ***all four types are genuinely depressed*** within their individual degrees of misalignment (See Alignment Scale—Chapter Two) while seeking re-alignment. Each wants the emotional pain to stop; but each wants something or someone outside of himself or herself to stop it, due to having an external locus of control. Each, however, truly wants to experience the joy of living. But each misunderstands the universal principles surrounding the *law of creation* (See Pro-creation—Chapter Eight) and the *law of attraction/self-fulfilling prophecies* (See Chapters Four-Six), which determines how both negative and positive *matter* manifests in one's life. And as a result, each one is vibrating at the frequency of despair and powerlessness but *only* in the moments of depression. Let's now look at the differences:

A. Type One: Threatens Suicide to Control Others Behavior

B. Type Two: Has Suicidal Thoughts That Frighten Them,
                          But Don't Plan to Carry Them Out

C. Type Three: Attempted Suicide Before and May or May Not Contemplate It
                          In the Future

D. Type Four: Completed Suicide
                          (Also, See Note to Survivors at end of chapter.)

Type One: Threatens Suicide to Control Others Behaviors

Let me start by offering an important reminder here that all four types are sincerely and *truly* depressed. So Type One, like the others, is out of alignment and wants to feel better while desperately trying to figure out how to get his or her needs met. And, for the record, every human being is trying to get his or her needs met; so attempting to get these needs met in and of itself is a natural thing. But the issue is the use of *manipulation* that Type One will often employ to get what it thinks it needs. I chose to discuss this type first since this is the type I hear about and treat most often due to the impact it has on loved ones and the distress it causes the unaligned person. Type One really ***doesn't*** mean to manipulate others, but due to a lack of tools and skills to self soothe, this type inadvertently tries to control the behavior of other people in the process. Unfortunately, this type ends up testing people's loyalty and resolve. No one wants to feel manipulated. So manipulating people is really a very bad idea and the least effective strategy to get one's needs met, since it can't bring anyone into a feeling of sustained alignment.

Therefore, if this is you that I am describing, please take heed. Making the statement, "*If you don't do this or that, then I'll kill myself,*" to get someone to do what you prefer won't usually work, at least not for long. (It may be helpful to take a peek back at the aligning processes I offered in Chapter Three for depression, anxiety and also two personality reactions called **borderline personality** and **dependent personality** to help release manipulative and dependent tendencies.) Eventually, your loved one(s) will become tired trying to please you, because what is being asked for is more than what is humanly possible to give on a sustained basis.

They love you and they care, but no one can hold another up long enough without his or her own knees buckling in the process. The *energetic* life of another soul just carries too much weight; it's too heavy. This is why coming into alignment with your own mind, body and spirit is so very crucial. We must all be willing to become emotionally self-sufficient. It's just not anyone else's job to make you feel better. It's your own sacred task. And the good news is that you came into the physical realm to create your life the way *you* wanted to live it, and no one else knows how to do that for you, but you! So it is crucial to stop trying to make others responsible for the *matter* in your life. They don't know how.

Sometimes that dose of reality may seem unkind, unfair, and unacceptable. And as a result, due to the unaligned and manipulative tendencies indicative of Type One, such a person may start to think that he or she wants to commit suicide as a sort of final revenge, or proof, to show others that he or she ***really was hurting*** as much as he or she said one was, and was not merely being manipulative. And if this is you, please know that your loved ones already know your pain! Your loved ones truly want to help and have tried everything they can think of to help—it's just that no one can do more for you than you can do for yourself. Remember, it's an inside job. And if that makes you feel that they don't love you as much as you feel they should, then I'm truly sorry you feel that way, because more than likely, ***they do love you very much!*** They cry for your pain all the time, in my office and in therapy offices all around the world.

However, people are not naturally wired to put your wishes before their own. It's that proverb "first law of nature is *self preservation*" thing, coupled with the fact that everyone who came into this physical experience came for his own *self actualization*. According to psychologist Abraham Maslow's *Hierarchy of Needs,* "self preservation" is the very first tier and "self actualization" is the fourth tier and the goal we are all seeking (Maslow, *Motivation and Personality*, 1954). Therefore, I believe that your loved ones are simply trusting that you came forth for the same. The fact that you haven't yet come into alignment with your own *peace of mind* around a given issue or issues is okay; there is still time for you to acquire the tools and skills necessary to bring yourself into alignment. And the interesting thing is, once you are in alignment with your own well-being, you will then understand just how much your loved ones were rooting for you all along.

Well-being is available to everyone, as evidenced by the emphasis placed on the attainment of "well-being" by the World Health Organization, which uses the term "well-being" within its definition of health. The only hitch, however, is that *well-being* has to be **wanted**—not because your mother or grandma wants you to be happy, or your father, sibling, child, spouse, companion or friend wants it for you, but because you want it for yourself! You, on the other hand, are free to use these people as your initial inspiration for wanting it, since any catalyst will do, but ultimately it has to be because you want it. You just have to learn how to acquire patience and the *delay of gratification* necessary to see your desires manifest. It may also require a willingness to be accountable for the *matter* you created so far based on your decisions; and overcome any fear you may have of being responsible for yourself, whether that be emotionally, physically, financially or otherwise. Granted, it may be scary, but you *can learn* to shift your *energy* and get your needs met in healthier ways by reading the rest of this chapter which aims to offer additional insight and comfort which will assist you in learning how to ultimately live the life you want to live, which is thoroughly discussed in the next Chapter on Pro-creation. Then, in the chapter after learning to pro-create please pay close attention to the subsection: *Using Psychotherapy, Medication & Herbal Remedies in The* Sacretherapy® *Process* in Chapter Eight.

Type Two: Has Suicidal Thoughts That Frighten Them, But Don't Plan to Carry Them Out

Type Two people have suicidal thoughts but are pretty sure that they would never carry them out. But the thoughts still frighten them because they know these types of thoughts are not healthy. So they keep the thoughts under wraps and are often afraid to tell anyone. If they do get up the courage to tell, they only share these desperate feelings with maybe one other person or just a therapist, if they have one. Type Two people mistakenly see depression and suicidal thoughts as weakness and put undo pressure on themselves to hide the desperate feelings that come up. They don't interpret the *matter* as simply an indicator that they are out of alignment and are trying to figure out how to come into alignment in healthy ways. Type Two people mainly suffer because they focus all of their attention on *only* the negative *matter* that manifested. As a result, self-fulfilling prophecies begin to ensue, and before they know it, they can be in the midst of a full-blown depressive reaction, due to a marked misalignment with their mind, body and spirit. (See the Alignment Scale in Chapter Two.)

However, Type Two is quite resilient and always finds a way to keep going, thereby realigning with the desire to continue one's physical journey. Type Two is a master at using *distractions* to neutralize the *matter*. The distractions albeit that one employs may not always be positive, but one knows how to distract oneself from the *matter* long enough to shift one's *energy*. Although Type Two has difficulty sustaining the shift and can become frustrated with needing to constantly use distractions, in doing so, has been able to persevere through the depressed, agonizing moments, and bounce back, oftentimes with the help of psychotherapy. So, if this is you that I am describing, please read the rest of this chapter which aims to offer additional insight and comfort, then review Chapter Six on *How to Stay Clear of the Matter* and pay close attention to Chapter Eight on *Pro-creation—It's a Whole New Matter Now—* which focuses on creating the life you want to live. Also, if you don't have a therapist, please pay extra attention to the subsection: *Using Psychotherapy, Medication & Herbal Remedies in The* Sacretherapy® *Process* in Chapter Eight.

Type Three: Attempted Suicide Before and May or May Not Contemplate It Again In The Future

Type Three people have experienced at least one, excruciating moment when they were so depressed, agitated and drained with the inability to sustain their alignment that they wanted to give up and actually attempted suicide. Type Three people know all too well what it is like to be that desperate and irritated with the work involved in bringing themselves back into alignment. Type Three may have seen a therapist (or maybe a few) before the attempt and just got sick of talking about the *matter*. However, after the attempt, one may have gained a greater sense of value for his or her physical life and resumed therapy for additional help. And depending on the degree of help that one may have received at the time, Type Three may or may not ever contemplate suicide again, depending on whether they are Type Three-G or Type Three-F.

Type Three-G - is the larger percentage of Type Threes, and fortunately they usually never attempt suicide again. I call them Type Three–G (TTG)—"**G**" meaning ***grateful energy***. Having been to the brink before, TTGs value their second lease on life and are committed to using whatever *energy* and tools they may have acquired to assist them through the challenging *matter* of life. They are grateful to be alive and often become more optimistic intentionally viewing the glass as half full instead of half empty. If this is you that I am describing know that you have done a great job in selecting the right *frame* as discussed in the previous chapter on *reframing thoughts*. Please carry on with your resolve to recognize that life challenges are decision making opportunities to remold the *matter* and turn lemons into lemonade, as you are now beholden to finding the joy of living.

Type Three-F - is the other smaller percentage of Type Threes. I call them: TTFs – "**F**" meaning *fearful energy*—because they go forth after an attempt lacking confidence that they will be able to surmount the major *matter* of life victoriously since they were unable to self-soothe before. TTFs have a great deal of nervous *energy*, fear and anxiety as a result of their previous attempt or attempts. Therefore, TTFs are rather hypervigilant in their attempt to ward off any future stressors that may be perceived as insurmountable, regardless of how big or small that *matter*. As a result, TTFs intentionally make sure that one never forgets the negative *matter* that manifested in one's life, believing that if one doesn't remain vigilant, one may find oneself in the midst of a full-blown depressive reaction and severely misaligned. (See the Alignment Scale.) One often fears that he or she may accidently, impulsively attempt again, given an onslaught of negative thoughts.

What TTFs don't realize, however, is that the fear and intentional unwillingness to *let the matter* go is what is interfering with the well-being one seeks. TTFs don't realize that focusing on negative thoughts begets more negative thoughts. As such, the best thing one could do to prevent another severe depression is to think about what *one wants* to happen NOW, not, what happened in the past or what one *doesn't want* to happen in the future. Without this information or some other type of holistic intervention, a TTF could certainly be "at risk" for another attempt, due to one's lack of understanding universal principles surrounding the law of creation and self-fulfilling prophecies/law of attraction, which is covered more in the next chapter on Pro-creation.

In either case, whether one is a TTG or TTF, having experienced a suicide attempt is a serious *matter* and usually means that one has needed or could currently benefit from psychotherapy and medication to facilitate his or her ability to realign. (See *Using Psychotherapy, Medication & Herbal Treatments In the* Sacretherapy® *Process* in Chapter Eight.) But first, please read the rest of this chapter which aims to offer additional insight and comfort as you continue to acquire more tools.

Type Four – Completed Suicide

Suicide, from the metaphysical vantage point, reflects an extreme way of wanting to re-align with well-being. It is a manifestation of a desire for the emotional pain to cease after having exhausted all the ways the person could think of to get his or her needs met and change the *matter*. Type Four, therefore, was severely depressed, tired of being tired, exasperated, and mistakenly believed that his or her *matter* could not be remolded. Likewise, Type Four felt stuck and in a desperate, *unaligned* moment, or series of moments, believed that due to the longevity and intensity of one's pain that it was too great to endure; and therefore, (without the mental and emotional tools needed) decided to employ a permanent solution to a temporary *vibration*—seeing suicide as the only choice that would give the relief one sought.

There is much speculation as to why anyone would resort to this desperate action. Psychiatrists point to deficits in brain chemistry, but the research is still inconclusive. It's just pieces of a puzzle, because truth be told, researchers really don't completely know. What we do know, however, is that anyone who is *aligned*, mind, body and spirit, would ***not*** seriously consider suicide as an option. Therefore, the Type Four person unfortunately did not gain access to the empowering information (mental and emotional tools) he or she needed to ascend to the level of well-being that was available in the physical realm and/or felt what was required for realignment was just too doggone hard. (See *Note to Survivors of Loved Ones Who Transitioned to Realign*, at the end of this chapter.) Therefore, in honor of those who transitioned to realign and for the sake and well-being of all those experiencing any of the four types of suicidal behaviors I offer the below subsection: When Healing and Re-Alignment Feel Too Hard.

When Healing and Re-Alignment Feel Too Hard

The agony that comes from not *feeling good,* as we have seen, can cause suicidal ideation, attempts, desperate and manipulative pleas and, for a small minority, completed suicides. For many, regardless of what type of depressive reaction one has, the work involved in healing and realigning can sometimes seem too hard, and the degree of difficulty, in and of itself, can feel like an overwhelming *matter*.

However, despite one's resistance to the work involved in realigning, no one wants to really hurt him or herself or leave a legacy of having given up. But the pain of not having lived the life one truly wanted to live, often due to conditioning, memes, etc., can lead to thoughts of suicide if one believes that one does not possess the ego strength needed to act on one's liberties and exert his or her freedoms.

Most people, however, regardless if they have ever met the criteria of clinical depression or not, can relate to feeling extremely unhappy and having experienced desperate moments. I've certainly been there and experienced suicidal ideation before. (See *Healing The Healer*—Chapter 11). So, what's being described in this chapter is no different than what I've been describing throughout this book—when one is vibrating at a very low frequency, it's hard to believe that one can ever reach the higher frequency where good thoughts are available.

Therefore, the thread sewn through ***all four types*** of depression is a tendency to ***focus*** on the negative *matter*. In fact, the focusing of one's thoughts is the only thing that keeps activating more of what one hates to think about but one simply doesn't realize it at the time. This cannot be emphasized enough, because since "like attracts like," the bad thoughts will keep summoning more bad thoughts, just like good thoughts summon more good ones. Recall the example of positive and negative *energy* with the car battery from *Step One*, where I pointed out that *positive must be connected to positive* for the battery to jump. (See *What's the Matter*—Chapter Two.)

Everyone naturally wants to be happy. Individuals experiencing depressed *reactions* just haven't figured out how to make that happiness last. And it's the anxiety surrounding ***making it last*** that greatly reduces their ability to handle future disappointments. Lots of times, one thinks that every time he or she seems to be headed in the right direction, something happens that removes one from his or her sense of well-being. This sets up a *self-fulfilling prophecy* of expectation for things to go wrong, which in turn causes one to experience what most psychotherapists call *low frustration tolerance*, where almost any little thing has the potential of yanking one from his or her sense of well-being, if one allows it.

Thus, due to the self-fulfilling prophecy, *"the thought waves and their power of reproduction cause the law of attraction to match the vibration,"* according to William Atkinson—author of *Thought Vibration or the Law of Attraction in the Thought World* (1906). Therefore, the thing one expects to happen, happens, just like they were expecting, So when it happens, they get tired and weary and have thoughts about giving up, believing that they can't have the life they want. They remain totally unaware that the *self-fulfilling prophecy* or *law of attraction* is what's in play. This however, is premature thinking because one ***can*** learn how to remold the *matter* and get what one wants "if" one is willing to acquire a delay of gratification and reframe the tasks in doing the work, which is described in more detail in Chapter Eight: *Pro-creation—It's A Whole New Matter Now*—which focuses on creating the life you want to live.

Suicidal Ideation and Fantasies of Taking Loved Ones Along

If you are like most people, you may not even believe that I am about to discuss loved ones, in this regard; but I believe we need to, in order to help prevent it. Unfortunately, on rare occasions people who contemplate suicide also consider taking loved ones or someone else with them. It's because, oftentimes, if they have children, they mistakenly fear that the children will not be taken care of if they leave them behind. They also believe that if they do commit suicide, they will have ruined the lives of their family members. So many, out of guilt, mistakenly decide it is better to take their children with them than leave them and ruin their lives, too. But when they take the physical life of someone other than their children, their motivation for sacrificing another soul is often about revenge. Naturally, there are exceptions to this *matter*, but either way it is murder and the absolute worst choice! Yet, in that agonizing moment, it unfortunately feels rational to them, because of where they are mentally, which always determines where they are *vibrationally*. And that *vibrational frequency* determines what thoughts are available to them in the moment. Unfortunately, however, one forgets that it is just a "moment" that could change for the better in the next moment, since a thought is *energy that vibrates* and constantly changes positions moment by moment, as described in Chapter Two.

A "moment," then, in terms of time and space, is such a sacred thing. A single *moment* can be devastatingly painful at one point and wonderfully life-giving and fulfilling at the very next, as we discussed a little in the section on "extracting the good" in the previous chapter. Every single *moment* has the ability to be life-changing. Therefore, if you've been having these types of suicidal thoughts about yourself and homicidal thoughts about your loved ones or another person, ***please***, **get help**! And please know that survivors of family members that complete suicide do struggle but are *eventually* all right; so ***there is no need to ever consider ending another soul's physical journey.*** Your loved ones' lives are unfolding moment by moment, too; and therefore more life-giving and fulfilling moments await them, just as they await you. So please give that other soul the opportunity to come into alignment with its own well-being. I, along with many other therapists, have helped survivors through the *matter* of loss, year after year and they ultimately are okay. Granted, they will never forget how their loved one chose to exit the physical plane, but they will ultimately come to understand that it was their loved one's decision, and not their fault. And with that realization, they will *eventually* be able to go on.

That knowledge may not sit well with some people. Sometimes the idea of loved ones eventually being "okay" without us makes some people feel like they must be unloved or insignificant to their loved ones, which is ***far*** from the case. Still, the sentiment of some is: "I dare they be all right!" Yet, the reality is that life does and will go on. It has to, since as stated before "*the first law of nature is self preservation.*" As such, the *Teachings of Abraham—Art of Allowing Workshops* (Hicks, 2005) have reassured me that "no one came into the physical realm to fully focus on someone else's life, even if they are a parent, child or spouse." Apparently, we all came into the physical realm with our own divine intentions according to both Abraham-Hicks (2005) and William Atkinson (1906). Therefore, none of us can put someone else's life ahead of our own; that is, at least not for a sustained period of time. Obviously we were not meant to, which has been further fortified by Maslow's (1954) *self preservation* premise discussed earlier. As such, your loved ones will persevere. They have to. They should not believe that they are *totally* responsible for someone else's life experience. At best, at any given time, all we can hope to be for others is a temporary comfort, kindred spirit and guide.

Suicidal Ideation: Trying to Live One's Life for Another

To anyone seriously considering releasing your body temple, I want to relieve you of feeling any guilt, if it stems from an undue burden to live your life for others who may be telling *you* that they can't make it without you carrying them, as opposed to the reverse. Please don't let the pressure of trying to be there for someone else make you want to commit suicide. You, too, ***can*** free yourself of feeling responsible for their well-being and live your life for yourself! No *matter* how dogmatic and guilt-inducing their words and actions may be, you **can** be free. You did not come to please them. You came to please yourself! Furthermore, know that there are plenty of tools and skills on how to become a more assertive person and implement healthy boundaries. (See Chapter Eight: *Pro-creation—It's A Whole New Matter Now*—which focuses on creating the life you want to live; and Chapter Nine: *Entering The Sanctuary*.) The information in those chapters can assist you in understanding that the God-source within the universe is always ready, willing and able to help you bring yourself back into alignment, without shedding your body-temple. Then, go back through the steps and do all of the exercises, if you missed any or re-do them with a greater resolve or with the support of a psychotherapist. (See *Using Psychotherapy* in Chapter Nine.)

Remaining in the Physical Realm: Summoning the *Energy* to Realign

Now, I know you may be tired. I know you may be weary. I know you may want to give up. I know your body may feel as if it has given out. I know that sometimes you may think that it would just be better if you weren't here. I know you may be panicked with all kinds of thoughts and feel like sometimes your mind is going crazy, but it's **not**. That's *just* "brain" chemistry. Your mind is larger than your brain, because your brain is plugged into *universal mind,* which is the God-source of the universe and omnipresent, within you and around you. Brain chemistry, therefore, can be realigned (Recall Illustration E-3, from Chapter Two, below.)

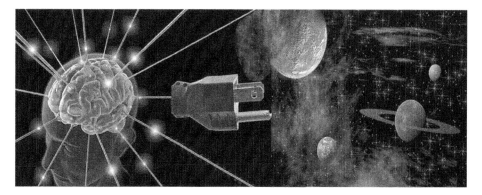

So the temporary inability to recognize and access universal mind is only due to your brain chemistry, which in the panicked moment is producing those pain mediating hormones, like cortisol, etc., and the release of those hormones is what's adding to your feeling overwhelmed and awful. (Sort of like getting a needle that hurts but the medicine it carries will ultimately help you to heal). Please know that those hormones were only triggered because of your low *vibrational* thoughts, and **you**

can begin to stop the release, right now, by summoning your natural healing endorphins by employing the following exercise that can help you to access higher-vibrational-better-feeling-thoughts.

Exercise: Summoning Healing Endorphins to Achieve a Sense of Well-being

Instructions: Please recall the relaxation exercises (Breathe the Breath of Life™ Relaxation Series) that I shared in Chapter Five—the guided audio version is available for ***free*** on my website listed in the Resources section in the back of the book. Please feel free to use one now! The exercise will summon serotonin, which in turn will trigger your natural healing endorphins in the brain, and can help you return to a feeling of well-being. Then, you can begin to slowly gain access to thoughts that feel better, as I explained in the last Chapter. (Also, see *Using Medication and Herbal Remedies in the* Sacretherapy® *Process* in Chapter Eight.)

The *matter* of coming back into alignment can be slow paced which is frustrating for everybody (recall the "sneeze" and "battery" examples from Chapter Two), but it's what many have discovered to be a "slow but sure" approach that works, if you are willing to do a little work to shift your *energy*. Hopefully, understanding that others have walked this path and succeeded will help you to know that you are not the only one that has wanted a new vantage point from which to begin again. Many people are searching for how to improve their quality of life. As such, you are obviously not the only one who has felt the pain and torment that low *frequency* emotions bring. But, believe it or not, you, too, can start right here and right now to reconnect and realign with your well-being. I know you have heard the wisdom of the "one day at a time" philosophy; but sometimes a day can still be too long, so just living "one moment at a time" and "one thought at a time" is much easier.

Also, before I go any further describing how you can summon the *energy* to realign and resume your sense of wellness, right here and right now, I want to ask you something: Did it ever occur to you that in the "nonphysical realm," you will not be able to manifest the ***physical*** things that you are already upset about not having yet achieved, here, in the physical realm? For, it is ***only*** *in the physical realm* that your soul can experience life *physically*. And according to most metaphysicians, *this is why your spirit came into the physical realm in the first place—wanting to experience the joy of physical manifestations. Therefore, if this physical dimension were not extremely valuable to our spirits, we wouldn't need to be physical.* In other words, there is something ***here***—in the physical realm—that the spirit cannot obtain ***there***—in the nonphysical realm. Therefore, from that perspective, returning to *nonphysical* could be viewed as wanting to go somewhere to reenergize, like a fabulous vacation, to refortify and rest up a little bit in order to *begin again*, all of which can be done right here in the physical world.

Returning to the Nonphysical Realm

In addition, to what was stated above about the physical realm, I'm not sure if you have ever really thought about what the "**nonphysical**" realm might *really* be like. Returning to the *nonphysical* realm is really just what it sounds like, **nonphysical**. Please don't misunderstand: I am sure it will offer us the most magnificent triumphant and glorious celestial exaltation of *energy* that we imagine the heavenly plane to be; where we are once again total subtle *energy* joining the light body of God and other nonphysical energies. I just want to point out that the joyful creation I imagine that will be experienced in that dimension will be likened to the sensation of astroplaning and be "telepathic" **only**, because it will be **nonphysical**, where the physical senses are null and void.

Thus, since you are already *physical*, enjoying your *physical senses*, re-energizing in the physical dimension will allow you to pick back up where you left off. Here, you can continue going about bringing your heart's **current physical desires** into manifestation, where you can experience them viscerally through your physical senses. For surely, this is the way you intended to experience those desires when you went through the steps of the creation process to become physical. You came forth into the physical realm with very specific intentions to experience life with physical senses. You obviously, cannot do that in the nonphysical realm, since there your physical senses are left behind. You will undoubtedly feel joyful relief in the nonphysical, but you won't have gotten to do or have that thing or things you wanted here. You will have to start all over in another body-temple to experience your desires physically.

Some believe that suicide is a way out. They say they want to stop living. But I say one really needs to think that reasoning out, because releasing the body temple does not end life! We simply go from dimension to dimension, so there is life and life, not life and death. You're either allowing your spirit to live in your "physical body" here, or your spirit is *living* as its "light body" there. The universe is just one humongous multi-dimensional body of energy. "All is one," therefore there really is no where to run.

I can only imagine those who transitioned through suicide finding the initial relief they sought, but realizing: "*Wow, you mean I really didn't have to do it this way to achieve the peace I sought? And, I really could have done it there by simply realizing that the God-source I have realigned with 'here' is the same one I had within me 'there' all along? So, all I had to do was to be willing to trust my own 'inner knowing' on a moment by moment basis to reestablish that conscious connection?*" I imagine they would probably laugh to themselves thinking something like, "*I wish I had stayed physical long enough to have known that, so that I could have experienced or achieved or gotten that blank,*" whatever "blank" was. And now they have to do the exact same thing they did here, to create what they want there, since even "there," everything begins with a thought. So they have to think the thought of becoming physical again, and wait until the thought manifests into a zygote and start all over (as described in the *Stream of Consciousness—the Matter of You*, in Chapter Two).

However, while thinking the thought to become physical again, I imagine it probably will be with an even stronger desire and commitment to enjoy every moment of their physical experience next time, with the added desire of getting to the exact moment that they left, and making sure that they remember that these uncomfortable moments CAN pass. As they remember to shift their *energy* moment by moment, they will recall that they are an *"energetic being vibrating,"* and *vibrations* are always changing positions (as described in Chapter two); so, too, will their emotions, and so will their circumstances.

So, if you are going to ultimately come to that type of clarity anyway of what it truly means to **begin again** as the *eternal spiritual being* that you are, then you can save yourself the trouble of pre-maturely leaving only to return again. You can "resurrect" new life **now** without waiting to reincarnate to come back to the physical realm. The spirit's journey of coming in and out of bodies was depicted beautifully in the movie *Defending Your Life* (1991), which illustrated that we have many lifetimes and can emerge beyond fear and painful moments.

Thus, we can start here in the physical realm with the broader understanding that *a new vantage point* is always within our mist, since the spirit we are seeking is not only *there* in the nonphysical, but it is also within us right here and right now. Here, we can decide to stand on a new platform of *inner knowing* that assures us that the universe is set up to support us and guide us home. The proverbial "home" is that "inner sanctuary" that is fully described in the chapter titled: *Entering the Sanctuary*, in *Step Seven*, where the comfort of well-being is always accessible to you. Thus, depression is just a *temporary vibration* that can be elevated to a new *frequency* that is attuned to the *well being* within. Many have discovered this truth and most are enriched by it! You, beloved, are not an exception to the rule. Well-being is achievable for everyone who earnestly seeks it. And "seeking it" is the key.

The Paradox of Split Energy—Wanting to Stay and Go

At this point, if you are still on the fence, experiencing ambivalence, I want you to understand that the *ambivalence* itself means that part of you has a desire to reconnect with your well-being. Your *energy* is split and your *vibration* is mixed, which is what ambivalence is, hence: split *energy*. Therefore, we can disentangle the mixed signal that you're sending out by working with the part of you that **wants** to feel and experience your well-being in the physical realm. In a way, you are already listening to that part; otherwise, you wouldn't be reading this book, even if someone else gave it to you and begged you to read it.

So please, continue to honor that part of you. It is equally as real as the other part. Therefore, the way to come back into alignment with the fullness of your being—mind, body and spirit—and have the life you prefer is to do the moment by moment work of learning how to **self-soothe** while you are here (in the physical realm), and go about creating the joy-filled life you are seeking, which is described in detail in the next chapter on **pro-creation.**

Now, if you just opened this book and jumped to this chapter—since this is where you are, and it called to you—then feel free to jump ahead and read my testimony in the last chapter of how I did it, since inspiration can also come from those who have emerged victoriously out of depression. Then start at the beginning of this book. Please do **all** the exercises and then see how you feel. And if Sacretherapy® is all that I believe it is cracked up to be, I don't think you will feel like *ending the matter,* once you're done. However, if you've already come through all the previous chapters, then after you read my testimony, go to the next chapter, *Pro-creation*—Chapter Eight, which will assist you in creating the life you want to live.

Now, if you didn't already take my suggestion at the beginning of this chapter to seek help, then here is a *divine idea* that can bring some immediate relief while you are progressing through the *steps*:

Exercise: Divine Idea—Don't Stall Make the Call

I call it a *divine idea* because at times like these, it seems that if help is going to come, it can only come from what many of us recognize as *divine intervention.* So, *Don't Stall. Make the Call*, regardless of which *type* of suicidal ideation you may be experiencing. If you would like some help and didn't write down the number when I offered it before, the **Suicide Prevention Hotline is: 800-273-8255** in the U.S. or **dial 211**, which is a national helpline. Counselors are available 24/7, and ready, willing and able to listen and guide you to what to do next.

If this book resonates with you, take it with you if you are referred to a therapist and see if the clinician will be willing to help you with this. If this approach is not something a particular therapist can embrace, please know there are many out there eager to embrace a holistic paradigm. And eventually there will be ***Certified Sacretherapy® Practitioners*** all around the world, listed on my website, certified directly by me. You will be able to check there to see if a certified practitioner is in your city yet. And, as a measure of quality control, **only** practitioners listed on my website are certified. If there is not one listed in your area yet, just share the book with any therapist you find. And be assured that many psychotherapists will be willing to support you through the book, even if they choose not to become certified. The important thing is that you get the help you need today! Right now! Please. Because *"right now"* is the moment that you have been waiting for; and *"right now"* is the impetus for change. *Right now* is filled with the urgency that lets you know that your well-being is calling you, trying to send the message that it's time to realign. So, *Don't Stall. Make the Call.* Good luck! You will be in my prayers.

A Note to Survivors of Loved Ones Who Transitioned to Realign

This is a special note for survivors of loved ones who transitioned to realign. I have had the honor and sacred experience of treating many people whose loved ones are now nonphysical. And as a result, I have noticed that many family members who have these types of experiences struggle to come to grips with two main issues:

1. The inability to release the idea that they may have been able to prevent their loved one from doing it.

2. And a deep concern about whether or not the loved one is with God.

Let me start by addressing the first issue and try to help you release some of your pain. I know many of you believe that you could or should have been able to intervene. There have been many clients who insist that if they had just gotten there a few minutes before they could have stopped the loved one's transition. I tell them, maybe, but you wouldn't have been able to stop him or her forever, because if someone (without the mental and emotional tools) is *truly intent* on releasing one's body temple, he or she oftentimes will try again. Others say, "But if I had only visited or called more often…" I tell them more visits and calls still wouldn't have stopped that act if one (without the mental and emotional tools) is intent on doing it. Others, still, say, "But if I had just lent them the money…" I tell them the money would never have been enough, because alignment cannot be purchased. Others proclaim, "If I had just forced him or her to get help or to have kept getting help…" I tell them that when people really and truly want help, they *find* a way to get it for themselves.

I explain that their loved one was just tired due to not having the mental and emotional tools, and/or didn't want any more earthly help. But then they say, "What if this, or what if that." And I still have to tell them, you still couldn't have stopped the act. No one could have, at the time, if again, the person (without the mental and emotional tools) was intent on doing it. I explain what I already shared in the section on Type Four and offer that the loved ones released their body temple, seeking relief, and sometimes trusting or at least hoping that their *subtle light* body would endure.

Therefore, survivors *everywhere*, please, hear me now: You couldn't stop them! And nor would it have been healthy or appropriate for you to have been given that kind of power over someone else's life. We all must honor each other's experience, even though it looks very different from the way any of us would have preferred anyone's transition from the physical realm to be. It was that person's life and physical experience to live, even though it included suicide. Granted, no one wants to hear this. It is difficult to hear and even more difficult to process.

It breaks all of our hearts and can make us feel so helpless. And it can be a devastatingly painful moment, I know. Many of us have had a relative to commit suicide. And even if you were not close, upon being notified about it, most people still cry their eyes out. We understand all too well the depth of that type of desperation. So when it is someone who really is close, like your child, parent, spouse, sibling or best friend, you can feel excruciating moments of emotional pain. Yet, it helps if you can accept that your loved one was just trying to realign with well-being, not knowing how to obtain it here; and then try to understand the limits of our responsibility to another by doing the following affirmation.

Exercise: Affirmation of Responsibility to Others

Instructions: Repeat this affirmation to yourself regularly:

My loved one(s) came forth with his or her own divine intentions, as did I. I did the best I could at the time to support and honor his or her physical journey. As such, I release responsibility for how another soul chooses to live the life one came forth to live. Therefore, I take solace in the fact that there is "life and life" and that my loved one lives on in peace, continuing to honor our sacred agreement. And so it is.

—

This brings us to the second issue of whether or not our loved ones succeeded in their quest to realign with the Creator of the universe and obtain the well-being they sought. This I believe was achieved. I trust that they are with that which we call God, and **NOT** somewhere being eternally punished. I believe this because I believe in a loving *unconditional* God. Therefore, there are *no* conditions that a soul must meet to realign with this loving Source.

Likewise, that obviously means that I don't believe in eternal damnation or a punishing God. This, of course, is my personal spiritual belief. And I am offering it to relieve those of you whom I recognize as having this concern about your loved ones who released their own bodies from the physical realm. Just know that your concern and fear is more than likely due to your *conditioning* that has caused you to believe in the wrath of God. But, please know that the vibration of "punishment" is no where near the frequency of God—for surely, the God I believe in knows all, understands all, created all, loves all, and welcomes all!

Therefore, their inability to find their alignment while they were physically focused did not interfere with their ability to realign in the nonphysical realm—for it is still a sacred interaction to transition from the physical to the nonphysical, since the soul experiences "life and life'" regardless of whether it is within or outside of a body temple.

Thus, let us honor these souls, for they teach us the precious value of mental and emotional well-being. They remind us how short our time is here in the physical realm and why it would behoove us to release any *matter* that ails us due to our own mis-creation. They also serve to inspire us to question and doubt religious dogma that tries to frighten us into believing that we serve a punishing God. And since I believe that there is only a loving unconditional God-source in the universe, I believe that this Source lovingly and compassionately received our loved ones.

Many of those who pierced the time space continuum made it a point to leave us signs; signs to let us know that they had, in fact, realigned. And, I think we can trust all of the little clues that our loved ones sent us that transcend the physics of heaven and earth. All the little things that clients have shared with me over the years that seemed out of the ordinary can be trusted as a sign. Things such as the butterfly that made sure it got your attention, or the penny that suddenly appeared on the night stand, or the missing jewelry that showed up from nowhere, or the rainbow that came without rain, or the voice that was clear and spoke to you, or the transparent silhouette you could have sworn you saw, or your loved one's favorite rocking chair that was moving. Or it could be the kiss you felt on your cheek, or the book that was opened for you to read a certain passage, or the medium that gave you a message, and other little incidents that go on and on. All of these, I believe, were communications from the other side that tell us that our loved ones are, in fact, all right and in the place of well-being they sought. And for this we thank the Creator!

So let **not** your heart be weary. Our heartbeat is one. We all come forth with sacred intentions to share and transport loving *energy* "to and from" the dimensions that are physical and nonphysical (God-Source).

> "Your loved one, like you, and like me, came as an aura of light, an energy, vibration, and tone, echoing the melody of life, eternally writing the lyrics to one song with many different beats. Be in harmony, and let your music play on…" (Kemp, One, 2007-2014).

Let us now, turn our attention to the *matter* of physical life in the next chapter, where we focus on creating new life through pro-creation.

8
PRO-CREATION: IT'S A WHOLE NEW MATTER NOW!

Step Six

"The mind is everything, what you think you become."
—Buddha

Procreation and pro-creation both bring forth new life. Both involve the creation process or universal laws of creation that impregnate manifestation. Yet, I'm not talking about the traditional **procreation** between *two souls* engaged in bringing forth another soul, but **pro-creation** meaning a *pro* versus a con, where *one soul* is engaged in bringing forth the positive aspects of new life.

The latter also focuses on the *pros* of life that has already been lived that can propel us toward creating the life we were meant to live. What stopped many from creating the lives they wanted before was an innocent acceptance of the conditioning, memes and old linguistic programming that were downloaded unbeknownst to them. So we could say that the detour from there to here was simply due to having been blindsided or misinformed. But now, you are a bit savvier. You know better. You now have new information, understand your divine rights, have sacred tools and strong anti-viruses to prevent any future unwanted download. Therefore, at this juncture there is nothing to stop you from thriving and creating the life you want to live, except yourself. You merely have to unequivocally trust your *inner knowing* and follow your own independent thought. It means summoning a little more courage. And just a spoonful will do nicely, in order to act with confidence versus placating the fearful whimperings of what pop psychology calls the "inner child" that we spoke of in Step Four. That is what world renowned psychiatrist Sigmund Freud called the "id" in his book *The Ego and the Id* (1923).

I mentioned before that some come into the therapeutic process with the intention of only using it to vent, usually about the horrors done to them that contributed to their mental and emotional reactions, or to confess an equally horrendous act they did. Sometimes, they hope that what was shared will be the one thing or things that will convince me that they are correct and unable to create the life they want. But fortunately, nothing ever has changed my belief that anything out of alignment can come back. And, although a positive ventilation outlet and confessional can do wonders for the soul, they are not enough to affect true change. The reason is those elements are facilitative but not in themselves transformative.

True change requires one to leave one's comfort zone and venture out with a willingness to experience the anxiety that often comes with risk, even when the risks are modest and backed by universal laws that say in fine print: *like attracts like.* That being the case, to get comfortable with taking risk, it may behoove you to familiarize yourself with *Maslow's Hierarchy of Needs,* from the book *Motivation and Personality* (1954). It's a hierarchy that has been highly debated but continues to be "required reading" for psychotherapists. I believe it reminds us that "the first law of nature is self preservation," which means we don't usually take risks that will cause us to be without food, clothing, shelter, or compromise our safety. That would **not** be an intelligent, calculated risk; it would be a reckless denial of one's most fundamental needs.

So when it is suggested that one take risks outside of one's *comfort* zone, it does not mean to be without *basic comforts;* but rather to be willing to stretch and expand one's beingness beyond fear of evolving, and daring to be one's best and most *self sufficient self.* Therefore, to become comfortable with taking these types of risks, it may require that one begin with releasing hold of one's loved ones if you are overly dependent. By this *step,* it is expected that you would no longer be attempting to utilize your loved ones as shields to protect yourself from experiencing the natural anxiety that comes from tapping into emotional self-sufficiency. Individuation is a rite of passage that every *soul-filled-being* must pass. Therefore, you must cease to beckon them; and untie their wings that hover. And as you free them, you are also freed. They can **care for you** but they can no longer **take care of you**, emotionally all the time. That's soul work. Yet, once again, I do not mean to imply that you must go it completely alone. No. We all need a support system. So it's always okay for loved ones to offer a helping hand but they should not be holding your hand 24/7. Thus, with support, we can overcome and accomplish just about anything. But there is a big difference between support and dependency.

Therefore, to assist you with creating new life, it would be wise to find yourself a likeminded support system. There are folks who model living *soulfully and wholeheartedly* who live all around you. They have the *matter* down. Gravitate to them. They may not be family and they may not be your friends. In fact, they may be strangers; but they are your soul-mates and therefore, they are kin. They fully understand the *pro-creation* process; for they have already birthed many dreams and are, therefore, able to impregnate within you a seed of hope and positive expectation. Find them and they will find you. As is said: "When the student is ready, the teacher appears." Honor them and I guarantee they will honor you. (See *How to Develop a Mastermind Support System* in this chapter).

As you go forward in the pro-creation process, go without the analogous birth control but with the assurance that what will be born out of you is your own courageous self-love that will be life altering, joyful and fulfilling. Pledge not to get sidetracked by the "unseen," since faith by definition, according to most religious doctrines, is "the evidence of those things **not seen** and the belief in those things hoped for." Plus, you have already more than likely come this far by faith. So today, that faith is just being *crystallized* as you understand that *if* a higher quality of life is truly what you seek, you must go to higher ground. Higher ground offers a new vantage point where you are able to shine a brighter light on the *matter* and see what you can see that will help you get from here to there. *There* is where you always meant to be. And *there* is where you are headed. With a support system in tow, *there* is finally within your reach.

You can now dare to "suppose" what it would be like to *really* have what you want. As you take a few moments right now to think about this, you will come to realize that what *you* want *matters*. Not what you think you can have, but *what you want*. Not what you are willing to settle for, but what you want. Not what you think you have the *energy* to amass, but what *you want*. Not what society said you shouldn't want; but what *you want*. Not what your family or friends want you to have, but what *you want*. Sometimes, answering the call of what you want can feel a bit strange, since you were in the habit of accidently creating what you didn't want. You did not understand the universal axiom that states that you are going to get what you think about, whether you are thinking about what you desire or what you don't desire. Based on the tenets of the law of attraction, this concept was beautifully dramatized in the hit documentary *The Secret* (2006).

And again, that *"law of attraction"* is based on the same premise as what we psychotherapists call a "self-fulfilling prophecy," which is magnetic, and therefore, kept us magnetized to attracting what we didn't desire but *only* because we kept focusing on what we didn't desire. Hence, a *self-fulfilling prophecy* can only bring something into manifestation because the *law of attraction* replicates our dominant thoughts, i.e. vibration. But now that we understand that, we recognize that the universal *law of attraction* must also work in the reverse. This means that if we begin making it a point to focus on what we *do* desire, then what we *desire* will also manifest. This, too, was demonstrated beautifully in the documentary, *The Secret* (2006). I strongly suggest you watch the video. I believe that although the book and audio version are nice, they don't bring these concepts to life the same as the video does, because it dramatizes these principles.

The movie, *What the Bleep Do We Know!* (2004), also dramatizes the point. However, as you watch these films, just keep in mind what I offered above about *Maslow's Hierarchy of Needs* as you become inspired to create the life you want to live—you create it alongside your fundamental needs remaining intact. I emphasize this because some people were so motivated by the films that they spontaneously quit their jobs to stay home and visualize all day, which they quickly learned was not in alignment with creation principles. Therefore, after the films, I recommend that you review more information about *self-fulfilling prophecies* aka *the law of attraction* by checking out the oldest book I could find on the subject: *Thought Vibration or the Law of Attraction in the Thought World* (1906), by William Atkinson. His book shows that these universal truths about the creation process have been around for more than 100 years and offers additional information on how to balance them. And as I stated in the Acknowledgements, I'm sure these laws were debated even before his time, since universal truths remain truths, but still his book does a great job. Then after you understand the historical basis of the law, read the most contemporary version of it, which is simply **outstanding** and has been taught for more than 25 years in the *Teachings of Abraham—Art of Allowing Law of Attraction* workshops that culminated into several books. One of them was *The Law of Attraction*, by Esther and Jerry Hicks (2006), the current leading authorities on the subject, worldwide.

With all that powerful fortifying information, in addition to this book, you can begin to **pro**-create—instead of **con**-creating—by "purposely" thinking about the good things that have happened and the good things you want to happen. You already have a pretty good head start, if you continue to utilize the good memories you chose to preserve in Chapter Six. You can use those wonderful preservatives from "life that has already been lived" as compost or *vibrational* fertilizer to help you grow your new *matter*. And by doing so, the "what ifs" that used to stop you can now be reframed into positive *vibrational* attractors, just as you saw in the last chapter. You don't have to let any mental or emotional reactions stop you from living the life *you* want to live.

In pro-creation, we create consciously and on purpose with clear intent, versus unconsciously with wobbly self regard and without passionate nurturance. We borrow from Marianne Williamson's take on *A Course in Miracles* and recognize that "the universe will take us seriously when we take ourselves seriously." It is of no consequence where you are or where you started; it only *matter*s where you are going and want to become. "We are here to be creators; we are here to infiltrate space with ideas and mansions of thought; we are here to make something of this life." (*What The Bleep Do We Know!* 2004.) Therefore, start thinking: what would you want "if" you really thought you could now create the life you truly desire?

To create means that you are a creator, just like the Creator of the universe, since you were made in that image and likeness. And every creator is an artist of sorts. And artists have studios where they like to create. The Creator of creators' studio just happens to be the entire universe. So in that spirit, we want to first create the right environment for you to *pro-create*. We want an environment that is spiritual, therapeutic, and inspiring. It is usually somewhat cozy and full of natural elements, with warm lighting by night and natural sunlight by day. I used to call these *therapeutic environs* when I first began prescribing them to my clients. Later, I began calling them *sacred spaces* since the area should invoke reverence that you can feel as soon as you enter the space. It can be a whole room or smaller area dedicated to honoring the fullness of your being. As long as there is enough space for your artist tools such as a chair, small table, books, journal, pens, lamp, candles, etc. it will be all right. It can be something straight out of *House and Garden* magazine or it can be simple, but it must call you home—to your internal home. For, here is where you sit down and spend quality time developing your *inner knowing*. Here is where you commune with God. And here is where you invoke the presence.

Here is where you begin to mold the *energy* into the *matter* you want to see manifest. Here is where you daydream and transport yourself into a virtual reality of what it's like to be the "well being" that you are. You are not just daydreaming for daydreaming sake, or just mining the imagination off in "*la-la land.*" La-La land elicits lazy pro-creation, where one doesn't feel like summoning up new energies or taking action, but prefers to just daydream. But we should view daydreaming with the understanding that all creation begins with a thought, and purposeful thought. Purposeful thought promotes right action and helps it take shape and form; hence, "thought form," so that it can come into manifestation, where the evidence of your time spent in the *thought world* is now brought into fruition and is tangible.

Your studio is where you practice, practice, practice; thinking and creating on purpose, being **free** to conjure up the quality of life that you were meant to live. Practice means giving regular and consistent time and *energy* to your desires, not haphazard creating, but taking yourself as seriously as you want the God of the universe to take you. It's like with any new life or *matter*, you must first plant a seed and water it regularly, knowing that if you don't, no new life with be forthcoming. However, you don't tend to it all day long since 'a watched pot never boils,' instead you balance your attention to it within the rest of your life tasks.

Just keep in mind that watering the seed is the most crucial aspect to giving life, for water represents nurturance. If we don't nurture our desires, whether they are ideas or relationships, they will wither and die. Much seems to be taken for granted in the life-giving process, but nurture is imperative. And nurture must be reciprocal. As you feed your desires, your desires feed you. Thus, say if one of your desires for your mental and emotional well-being is to have more fulfilling relationships, then by feeding your relationships, they in turn must feed you. If not, during the watering process, pluck out any thorns or weeds from your *life-giving garden* and fertilize the rest. Double check, however, to ensure that any of the unwanted elements didn't spring forth due to your own negligence, thinking that nurture was a one-way street.

Often times people with mental and emotional reactions become so accustomed to others checking on them and helping to prop them up that they fall into a pattern of *learned helplessness* as defined in Chapter four. As a result, they accidently forget that others are in need, too, of that same nurturance. One need not be in the midst of a reaction or experiencing unaligned thoughts to deserve nurture. We bring forth new life and sustain it by planting seed, watering, fertilizing, pulling weeds, watering and watering, eating of its fruit, watering, digesting wholeheartedly, watering, and planting more seed.

Yet, sometimes what goes awry for people with mental and emotional reactions is their belief that there is "only one seed of seeds" that can be planted to bring forth their sustenance and joy. This is not the case. I understand that a specific thing may be desired and would be pleasing in thy sight; however, rigid creating limits energy flow and new possibilities. Believing that there is only one way to be happy, or one way to serve the world, or one way to make your mark, or only one soul you can ever love, or only one soul who will ever love you, is the complete opposite of universal extravagance. In fact, it means one is *vibrating* at the level of universal poverty and lack, and for naught, since we came into the physical realm to experience an abundance of creations and creators.

I once treated a professional athlete (whose occupation has been changed to protect confidentiality) who could no longer play the sport due to an injury. The meaning she attached to having to give up the sport caused her to go into a major depression, which caused her to be severely misaligned. She believed her identity as a sports figure was the only thing she could or should do with her life. Yet, through the therapy process, it was clear that the reason she set out to play professional sports was so that she could afford to do something else that she once loved equally as much, many years earlier. And here it was, she could now afford to do this other thing, and had forgotten about it.

She hadn't kept up with her own expansion. Yet, once identified, the joy in her eyes returned and she felt invigorated. But it wasn't even the old idea that lifted her; it was the realization that there was "other life" that could be lived, "other joy" that could be summoned, that could lead to "other avenues" for fulfillment. As it turns out, she didn't even do the old thing, but the idea of the old thing led her to a new and better idea; and so she began planting new seeds, watering them, fertilizing, and her new desire became manifest.

Therefore, please know that since we all share the same creation process, you can do the same, whether it be a career, person, place or thing. Pro-creation honors the Chinese proverb that reminds us that everything can go away or die but "winter *always* turns into spring." Therefore, new life is on the horizon. Below are exercises to facilitate this life-giving work; exercises that will assist you in clarifying what the *matter* is that you would like to pro-create for yourself. They will help you to achieve what it is that you intuitively know will increase your quality of life, so that you are able to actualize what Oprah Winfrey calls "living your best life now!"

Sculpting Your Sacred Intention

The main material in this exercise will be *water*, since in order for our desires to manifest, they must be nurtured. Water is soft, flexible, and can also be solid when in the form of ice. Therefore, metaphorically we will create ***ice sculptures.*** That way, if you decide that you'd rather carve out something different from what your original idea is, nothing has to stay frozen; it can be melted and eventually evaporate. The same, of course, goes for your mental and emotional manifestations—no matter how long they have kept you feeling frozen in time and space, you have the power within you to let them melt away. Technically, you have already begun chipping away at the "block of ice" that will be used to sculpt your sacred intentions, ever since you started this book. The entire Sacretherapy® process has led you here. And now, having done all the previous exercises, you are ready to decide what you want to bring into manifestation, ***now***!

What's your dream? I'm sure you have imagined it at some point. So get out your sculpting knife and let's prepare to carve out the dream-life you want to live by "living as if" it's already the way you prefer it to be. The concept *"living as if"* was coined by psychologist Dr. William Miller in his book, *Living As If—How Positive Faith Can Change Your Life* (1985). That's how the highly successful do it, and that's how ordinary souls do it, too. The psychology of achievement says that it can't be some far off in the distance summoning, but a 'right now and right here' gut feeling that I am going to "blank" or can have "blank" and seeing yourself doing it or having it now. I already recommended other sources above, but again, the book *Creative Visualization* by Shakti Gawain (2002) can be helpful in imagining what you want to manifest. (See Resources.)

In the exercise below you are going to just brainstorm for a few minutes and come up with some ideas. It's not a test, so don't get bogged down with whether or not it's perfect. Just make sure it's what ***you*** want and feels good to imagine it. Therefore, in preparing to do the exercise, use your mind's eye to visualize what your current intention is for your life. Think of some of the ***pros*** you already uncovered throughout some of the previous processes. Ask yourself which of those would you like to create more of or begin to create for the very first time? It's the same process whether you are expanding or creating anew. And it doesn't appear to make a difference whether the *matter* is big or small. It takes the same amount of *energy* to create a million tree leaves as it does to create one. And so pick something that will convince you that it "came to pass" as a result of sculpting your sacred intention.

Exercise—Part A—Sculpting: The Block of Ice

Let's suppose that what you want is just a day of peace. Then let's imagine yourself doing what is peaceful to you, undisturbed. Maybe you see yourself lying at a beach with sunglasses and a cool beverage, counting the waves. Or, maybe your peace is just sitting in a bubble bath with no one at home and enjoying the quiet. Whatever it is, do it now in your mind. The book will wait. So go ahead and try it by following the *Instructions* below:

Instructions: Close your eyes and sit quietly in your chair. Visualize the beach or hot bubble bath. Then, add the other effects that make the visualization vivid, such as sunglasses, cool beverage, sand and waves. Or, bubbles, candles, soft music and aromatherapy. Then, see yourself at peace. Do this for only a couple of minutes. **STOP**.

Okay. Did you viscerally feel like you were at peace, in a relaxed state of mind or just chilling? If not, please do it again, and with a little more gusto next time. Remember, we feel what we think. Our passionate feelings correspond with the level of confidence we have about what we want to bring into manifestation. As the famous quote by New Thought advocate Napoleon Hill, author of *Think And Grow Rich* (1937), suggests, "Whatever the mind of a man can conceive *and believe,* it can achieve." That's truer than we ever imagined. And the part where it says "believe" is where the *passion* and *inspiration* comes in, which is demonstrated by your emotional ***enthusiasm***.

Enthusiasm, I believe, is the energetic basis from which inspiration is born. This was reinforced by Dr. Wayne Dyer, writer and producer of the inspiring movie, *The Shift* (2010). Dr. Dyer reminded us that the word "enthusiasm" came from two Greek words: *entheous*, meaning "the God within"—and *ism* or *ismos*, meaning "the act of." According to most dictionaries, the two terms mean "the act of acknowledging the God within." So remember that definition when you are about to *vibrationally* sculpt anything. Your *enthusiasm* about utilizing "the God within" *matter*s; for it is surely what inspires us to bring forth the *matter* we desire into manifestation. So follow the instruction below and try it again.

Instructions: Do the exercise again, but this time with *enthusiasm*, for only a couple of minutes. And feel the difference that passion and enthusiasm makes. It should really feel like you are there, almost a holographic experience.

Exercise—Part B: Sculpting—The Ice Pick

Once you have used your thoughts to visualize what it is that you want to sculpt, the second part is turning it into "thought form," which again, is a part of bringing it into form. And the only thing you need to do here is think about it more often and give it positive *energy*, which you do with your positive thoughts. You can even do creative things that help you think about it more often. I learned this at a metaphysical church where we did manifestation collages. Some people call them Manifestation Boards or Vision Boards or Creation Boards. But what you call it isn't important. What's important is that you do whatever it takes to keep you inspired about your new sculpture. It's just a focal point, symbolism, and a reminder. I've been doing them for the past two decades, but I used to do them only on *New Year's Day* each year and then put the boards in my filing cabinet; and I didn't take them out until the end of the year, to see what had manifest. Everything was always achieved. Yet, it wasn't until I saw *The Secret* (2006) that I began keeping the collages out in the open where I could see them on a daily basis; and sure enough things came into manifestation faster, with my giving them more attention and *energy*. And so, I would like for you to do a collage of what it is you want to manifest. Call it whatever you want. Now, we will gather what you need to complete this exercise.

Instructions: You can use magazines to find pictures that represent what it is you want or clip art from your computer or photos from an album. It doesn't have to be all pictures; it can be artifacts, crafts or words stapled to the board. It's just whatever you need to begin sculpting. These images are metaphorically the ***ice pick*** that will help you carve it out. Just keep chipping away at it a little every day. And a little everyday is enough to mold the *matter*. Please take time to do this project now:

Exercise—Part C—Sculpting: The Ice Freezer

Once the ice has begun to take shape and form, you must keep it in the freezer to prevent it from melting. This is where a support system comes in. This is where a few like-minded people come together to give more energy to that "sculpture of an idea." This is also known as a *synergy of compatible consciousness* and referred to as a *Mastermind*. Masterminds help you to keep your ice sculpture cool by believing in your vision. They can support you over the phone or in person. Many spiritual centers have Mastermind groups. You simply take turns focusing positively on each other's *matter* for a few minutes. You share exactly what you want each of them to place in their minds, and everyone either quietly thinks about it for no more than a few minutes or the vision can be shared as a guided imagery, where you narrate your vision. Then it's the next person's turn.

Some groups also like to brainstorm even more plausible ways the *matter* could manifest. That can also be fun and fortifying. Here you can use the support system that you were asked to begin creating earlier. Most of them will know all about the concept of *Masterminds*, and so ask if one or two of them would like to join you in giving your *matter* some extra *energy*. Do this especially anytime you notice that your sculpture seems to be melting. Take time now to think of at least three people who you believe would be supportive and fortify your *enthusiasm*. Be sure to let them know that they only need to be willing to spend five minutes a week with you via the phone or in person holding your intention.

Instructions: Get your journal out and write out the following:

Potential Mastermind Participants: Day_____Time _____

1. _____ Phone _____

2. _____ Phone _____

3. _____ Phone _____

Call them and proceed. If you don't know anyone who you think would be supportive of your idea yet, just develop your list as you meet the like-minded individuals I spoke of at the beginning of this exercise. You can also check to see what centers in your area may already be doing these exercises. And, you can also gain support online once you have completed all of the Sacretherapy® steps and are invited to participate in the free interactive Mastermind community I created, which I describe in Chapter 10. In the meantime, it is not recommended that your sculpture be shared with skeptics. Skeptics are like heat waves and will cause your masterpiece to melt by draining your *energy*. It's a waste of time trying to convince skeptics of anything. It is better to stick with like-minds to increase the *energy* flow.

Pro-creating Emotional versus Physical Manifestations

The creation process is the same whether what you want to manifest is something physical or emotional. Pro-creation, therefore, can be done in a million ways. Being creative with artistic things like writing a poem, a play, a song or a rap about the thing you are bringing into manifestation; or drawing, painting and literally sculpting it, can be quite rewarding. Just do whatever helps you to remain *enthusiastic* and give your desire more *energy*. This should be an uplifting experience and feel very easy. No *anxiety* should be induced from this because you have total control over how you want to do it. In fact, let's say that the *matter* for you really is "anxiety and panic" and you would just like to stop having panic attacks. The desire to stop having panic attacks would be an example of *pro-creating an emotional manifestation*. Let me show you what I mean by us trying the following example:

Exercise—Emotional Pro-Creating

Start by thinking of a fun or joyful area in your life that never triggers any panic. Make a short list of those things or borrow from the list you created in the last chapter of memories you are preserving. I told you they would come in handy. So pick one or two that you will purposely recall to replace thinking about the anxiety-provoking thing. Let's say that two of the things you picked were "eating popcorn" and "watching stand-up comedies" as the thoughts that make you feel good. Let's follow one of those thoughts by visualizing it with the popcorn fragrance and everything. After each sentence below, close your eyes and visualize it:

Instructions for Emotional Pro-creation Visualization:

> Visualize the bag of popcorn in your mind, and now see it in your hand. Put it on the stove or microwave; smell the butter, salt and corn; hear the popping; feel your mouth watering; grab a bowl; take the bag out of the microwave or off the stove; pour it in the bowl; put one piece in your mouth; sprinkle with more salt if needed; grab a beverage out the fridge; take both over to the couch or favorite chair; select the stand-up comedy you want to watch, put it in your DVD, push play; start digging in the popcorn; start smiling; start laughing.

Now, did you notice that during the visualization you actually moved your *energy* to a new vibration, one that is in alignment with the very well-being you seek? Seriously, in just those past few seconds, you were not fixated on your fear. You were only focused on the popcorn and then the comedy. And that is how you will continue to diffuse your thoughts away from the fear.

It really is just that simple. Granted it's easier said than done, when it comes to a full day of sustaining your emotional well-being. But it's much easier if you think of doing it "moment by moment" instead of one day at a time. If you begin to *live one moment at a time,* it becomes very doable. Next thing you know, you will have gotten through just about all of the moments of your day more peacefully. And don't forget to keep the list of good you preserved from the last chapter near, so that when something threatens to remove you from your peaceful *vibration*, you have your tools and know exactly what to do in the next moment to bring you back. This is one of the most empowering benefits of pro-creation, knowing that at ANY moment you can call up a positive memory, extract the life-giving *energy* from it, and change the *matter*.

The more you practice thinking about the things you prefer, versus what's bothering you, less and less of your attention will be on what you don't like. And, again, it doesn't *matter* that the *popcorn and comedy* example was not on the subject of the thing that was causing the anxiety. All that *matter*s is that you come into alignment with the vibrational resonance of what you are trying to achieve. Do this as often as you can and ride that wave (wavelength of a vibration) all the way to well-being. Then, you will be ready to "pair" the popcorn and comedy with the anxiety inducing stimuli as shown next:

We talked a little about "pairing" in Chapter Four when we discussed "associative learning." So let's pretend that the anxiety inducing stimuli for you was having the panic attack while driving. In this case, pop the popcorn before you leave the house and eat it on the way to your destination. Also, tape record a comedy and listen to it while driving. Now you have given yourself some alternative choices regarding which thing you want to focus on while driving. And driving, then, will eventually be associated (paired) with an enjoyable experience.

Remember, *The Teachings of Abraham—Law of Allowing* workshops (2006) reminds us that "the *direction* of our thought is *always* our choice, even when it doesn't seem like it." Psychotherapists agree, suggesting that you simply choose the focal point that feels better. We just aren't used to intentionally thinking this way, but that doesn't mean that we don't have the ability to think this way. We do. And you are no exception. Just remember that we are all products of the same *energy* source of the universe. And pretty soon, you will be living the life of the "well being" you came into the physical realm to be, unencumbered by yesterday's thoughts. Pro-creating like a pro!

Let's do another one, but this time let's *pro-create a physical manifestation* to show that both emotional and physical manifesting go through the same creative process, since everything that has ever been created began with a thought.

Exercise—Physical Pro-creating

Let's say that due to your mental or emotional reactions your finances got out of whack, or you were never financially self-sufficient, and so your economic situation is what's causing you distress. And now you want to be financially capable of taking care of yourself, or you have already been taking care of yourself but want to serve the world in a way that is less stressful economically. And let's say you've decided that the way you would like to now manifest money to take care of yourself is by making furniture, specifically creating upholstered chairs—like the one you may be sitting in now, which was also created out of someone's thought. Here's an example of how to pro-create a financial base making chairs:

Instructions for Physical Pro-creation Visualization

> Close your eyes after each sentence and visualize it: First come up with your chair "idea" (which of course is a thought), and then give it more thought by transferring the thought to paper as a sketch. Then start visualizing the fabric you want to cover it in; then see yourself shopping for the fabric, and then actually go see some fabrics and while you are in the store, close your eyes and picture the fabric again on your chair. Take some pictures of the fabrics. Ask for some swatches. Then go home and give it some more thought and figure out what type of springs you will use. Picture the color thread you'll use. See the thickness of the cushion you want and then see yourself squeezing it. Picture it being sewn together. See it on the front cover of a furniture magazine. See it in the furniture stores. See it in catalogs. See people at the counter buying it. See you at the bank making the deposits of the prosperity that has come as a result of your creation. Then marvel at how your actual chair begins to take shape and form. Then once it is completed, look at it, sit in it, and feel your appreciation for how all of it came out of the nonphysical realm of *thought* into the physical manifestation of *matter*.

Everything that has come into manifestation is created much like that. So whatever it is you want to manifest can follow those same steps, augmenting for your particular *matter*. That is basically the way to expedite the creation process, by purposely giving positive *energy* to what you are intending to manifest. Perhaps you didn't realize it, but it really is true that everything that has ever been created really came into manifestation similarly. And so, I want you to go shopping, not to shop but to take notice of other soul's physical creations. Thus, I want you to employ what I call project *Creation Observation*, which will be described next.

Exercise—Creation Observation

Pick a department store that has a large variety of products. Let's call the products what they are, *manifestations*. Going somewhere like Walmart or Target will do. Go into the parking lot and start there. *Observe* the parking lot. Notice the gravel, the parking lines, the lights and the sidewalk. Well, someone created each of those things the same way your chair was created. Before that stuff was there, the space was probably full of trees or just dirt. Now look at the building that houses the store. Someone created that the same way the chair was created, too. Now walk in. The doorway you just passed through was someone's creation. Imagine the thoughts of the first person who created doors. Now move in a little more and see the carts that carry the items. Someone created those carts just like you are creating your chair. Go ahead further in. Face the cash registers. Notice two things here. Someone created the paper that the cash was printed on, way before there was an idea for a cash register, which was also a thought first.

Now, moving right along, stop at every single creation (item) on aisle one of the store. Pick it up if it isn't too heavy or just look at it. Think about the creative process that whoever created it went through to bring it into manifestation, just like you will be doing with your chair. And don't overlook the Styrofoam and plastic and decorative boxes that were also created to package most of the creations. It's a lot. In fact, you will not be able to stop at all of the creations in the store, even if you spent the entire week there, because there are millions of creations there. Isn't it amazing that we haven't been looking at these items from the perspective of creations before? It's mind-bottling when you really think about it from this perspective, at least it was for me when a metaphysics minister suggested that the names of all stores should conjure the idea of *creation*. I can't recall the exact terminology used as she began joking around but it was something like: Creation Manifestation Stores and Warehouses, Exotic and Luxurious Creation Catalogs, Nonphysical to Physical Manifestation Clubs, etc.; and now with the internet having emerged since that time, you could easily add "dot com" to all of those just to be in vogue.

Viewing products as creations made me come up with the idea to visit stores from that vantage point, therefore, based on experience—you probably won't have time to check out all the creations in the entire store, so do just a couple aisles. Better yet, even before you go to the store, you can start by just going around your home and stopping at every single item there. Start by looking at the rug, hardwood floor or tile you are about to stand on. It was brought into manifestation the same way your chair comes into being. And so, go through your place and think about what the creator of the item must have been thinking to bring it into manifestation.

I hope you take time to do this. It can really be an eye opener to the creative process. Just think about that keep-sake box or drawer in your house that you have stored all of your *own creations* in, then take a sacred moment to acknowledge how you have already been doing this (pro-creating) throughout your entire life. Remember the picture that you drew. The stuffed animal you made. The Popsicle stick jewelry box, the necklace, the model car, the painting on the wall, curtains, pottery, the wine rack, etc, are *creations* you made that began with a thought. You brought all of these things into manifestation not even realizing you were bringing something from the nonphysical into the physical. So you already have tremendous experience with this. All you need to do now is expand your knowingness with regards to the creation process and practice how to intentionally pro-create the sacred desires that you presently hold. Just remember, what we discussed before: plant seed, water, fertilize, pluck weeds, water, and plant more seed. (**PAUSE** and do the Creation Observation exercise.)

***

Now, at this point, I could be wrong, but if you did the exercise, at least at home and have looked at some of your own creations, I think you may be smiling. If so, keep smiling because it only gets better from here. Therefore, regardless of whether it is the emotional pro-creating or the physical pro-creating examples above, you can see how pro-creation works. Naturally, there are tons of things you may want to experience or do to increase your quality of life. And the myriad ways available are as individual as each soul, since everyone is not trying to overcome anxiety or find ways to take care of their financial needs by creating chairs. One size does not fit all. But what is consistently uniform for everyone is the *pro-creation process,* since we create *money* the same way we create *peace of mind.*

Living the Life You Were Meant To Live

In the section on Creation Observation, you saw how *matter* is pro-created prior to coming into manifestation. Now we want to focus on the final creative part which is *"manifestation."* Once things become manifest, they are now a part of the physical world. But keep in mind, as the examples demonstrated, a manifestation can be physical, mental or emotional. So your new *chair* or *peace of mind* is a manifestation that will now be noticeable. Once that manifestation is in the physical realm, it becomes a form of stimuli for oneself and others. Your own personal reaction will undoubtedly be one of tremendous gratification and joy. And you certainly deserve to feel the joy of your own creations. Be sure you do. And look at all that you did to bring it from the nonphysical to the physical. It took some doing. So be proud.

Creation is an awesome thing. This is why when it comes to physical creations, people want to register their copyright or register their trademark. They are proud as a peacock that they did, in fact, create the creation. It holds part of their *energy.* It's their way of wanting to leave their mark, their legacy and their name; for this is one way they let it be known that their particular soul "came by here" or "through here" from the nonphysical to the physical on their way back to nonphysical. Yet, they inherently know that their creation is going to stimulate others' reactions and actions as it becomes a form of stimuli for other creations. And lo and behold, the creation process starts all over again.

Once anything becomes "physical," people are going to have thoughts about it, feelings about it, then react or take action with regard to it. Their reactions or actions, which are often offered by way of *words*, can affect you, positively or negatively, as the original creator of the manifestation, if you let it. Certain people can be very *sensitive* to what other people think—which is why it is so important to create the life you want to live, not the one you think others want for you. This way, regardless of the feedback you get about your creations, you can maintain your good feeling and pride in what you created. They don't have to like it. They don't have to agree with it. They have just observed it; and their interpretation of it only has to do with what they think, not what you think. If others think your creation is crazy, strange, stupid or weird, that doesn't make it so. It's just their point of view.

So go ahead and pro-create your heart out. The theologian: Matthew from the Bible put it this way, "Let your light shine so that others may see your good works" (*Matthew 5:16*). He seems to have picked up on the fact that historically, we have been *conditioned* to highlight our inadequacies versus spotlighting our wonderful gifts. And as such, spotlighting one's creations is often inaccurately considered being vain or not being humble. But Marianne Williamson, in her book *Return to Love* (1992), helps to demystify this mistaken premise with her famous passage: "Our deepest fear is not that we are inadequate; our deepest fear is that we are powerful beyond measure…when we allow our *light to shine*, we give others permission to do the same." Likewise, we have all come forth with this creative light and whether we choose to shine the light of our creations boastfully and brilliantly, or shyly and dimly, what we manifest in the world will still be seen by others. In fact, by the time our powerful creations have manifested, it is the witnessing of our creations by others that often indicates that we are at the end of the creation process for that particular creation.

However, many people mistake the comments **(words)** that were made about the creation as the beginning of the creation process; forgetting that all creation begins with a "thought" not the words expressing the thought. And that is the case whether the creation is a physical creation or an emotional creation. Nevertheless, the reason words are often mistaken as the beginning of the creation process is because people usually identify the spoken word as the stimulus that motivated them towards, or steered them away from, their creative spurt and/or sense of well-being. That is how comments (words) about physical creations (chairs) can easily become the impetus for an emotional creation (anxiety) since how one interprets the comments about their creation will produce thoughts that produce feelings. And this is where many people choose to back-down from *"letting their light shine for others to see their good works,"* because of the fear of **their own thoughts** about **other people's thoughts** triggering a negative emotional creation. The reason being, that they believe that someone else's words are what triggered their sad or anxious mood, (which is an emotional creation). But it really was **not the words** at all. **It was the *thoughts* one had, with regards to the *words* and the meaning**

one attached to those words. And so, here again, even though the creation was emotional, it still began with a thought, not the comments or words offered.

Recall what we discussed about old linguistic programming with regard to **what's in a word** in Chapter Four. So, we **don't want to confuse communication with creation.** Although our words will always be expressions of our thoughts, it is our *thoughts* that hold the power to "attach meaning" to what is communicated to us. This premise is true whether it is *words* or someone's *behaviors* that we are thinking about and then reacting to. The below section on *pro-creation versus communication* will clarify this premise further.

Pro-creation Versus Communication

In any communication, there is a **Sender**, a **Receiver** and a **Message** being transmitted between the two that is being sent and received. But the *verbal* message is not the only information the sender communicates. Most communication experts tell us that depending on the context 55 to 60 percent of all communication is nonverbal and another 30 to 38 percent is the *tone of voice* that accompanies the message. *Tone*, of course, is *sound*, which equals the *vibrations* you send out with your message. Therefore, from an *energy* point of view, **only 10 to 15 percent of what you communicate is actually being transmitted by your words.** As such, it's very important to be mindful about your nonverbal communication when conveying your thoughts. That's because **if** the nonverbal aspects of your sentiments are not in alignment with your words, then the true *energy basis* of your thoughts and tonality is what the recipient will undoubtedly be responding to—that being the larger part of what was communicated and, as we just learned, is not your words.

Nevertheless, having offered that caveat, it's important to also understand something equally important, which is that the full message being transmitted is still **not** what dictates the receiver's response. It is the **receiver's thoughts about the message** that gives it the meaning. So the energy you send with the message can **only influence** the way the receiver chooses to interpret the message. The onus, then, ultimately rests with the receiver on how the message is interpreted.

Let's see how communication works by following the below step-by-step progression and see how it further clarifies the distinction between communication versus creation:

A Creation Manifests Providing Stimuli and Triggers
> A Thought > Feeling > Action / Reaction

1. First there comes the **creation**, which triggers our attention, since the *matter* or manifestation acts as some sort of **stimuli** or antecedent (cause).

2. Then, we **think** about the *matter*/creation/stimuli, and we attach some type of meaning or interpretation to it.

3. Then we viscerally **feel** what we are thinking.

4. And lastly, we **act** or **react** based on what we were thinking and feeling about the *matter* that manifested, which is done with our **nonverbal communication** (*55-60 percent*), **tone** (*30-38 percent*), and lastly our **words** (*10-15 percent*) that are simply expressing our thoughts.

Therefore, the **power is always with the receiver** on how to react to the *words*, because it is the *receiver who interprets the words* based on the receiver's vibrational frequency in the particular moment in time. And so, when we say "Choose your words carefully," it means "Choose your thoughts carefully," since every word is simply an expression of thought that is also *vibrating* at its own *frequency*. You can catch a "vibe," so to speak, as discussed in Chapter Two. And how you respond to those words on Sunday morning may not be the way you would respond Sunday night, depending on your higher or lower *vibration* or mood.

Think about it. How many times have you or someone you know said something to the effect that went like this: "Sorry, I was in a funk when I said that; I didn't really mean it at all." They were basically stating the same thing that I am sharing here, that the *words, nonverbal communication, and tone* they offered when they communicated that sentiment were based on their lower or higher *vibration* that made the difference in their interpretation of the *matter*.

Therefore, it is crucial that you understand the difference between *creation and communication,* as you go forward creating the life you want to live; because when it comes to other people's reactions to your manifestations and your reaction to theirs, you have the power to *decide* how you are going to interpret them, even when their reaction is disappointing and unaligned. This is especially important now that you are aware that your reactions to their reactions are what will greatly affect the quality of your life, your mental and emotional health, and your relationships with others. Say, for instance, someone says he or she doesn't like your *chair*. You can interpret that as him or her being tasteless and/or jealous, or you can simply interpret it as he or she enjoys a different style of creation.

The same goes if the manifestation is your *improved mood* and someone says, "You seem overly confident now that you are no longer anxious." You can interpret it as that person being intimidated by your evolution, or you can interpret it as that person projecting the fact that she or he hasn't broken through his or her own mental or emotional reactions and is just misaligned in the moment. In both examples, you have a choice of how you will allow another person's reactions to your manifestations to affect you.

It's very similar to what you may have experienced when you first started to feel better, as we discussed in the previous chapter on the reactions of family and friends. If they "acted out" when you were beginning to change, then it is quite possible that they may certainly react as you begin to live the life you always wanted to live. Don't expect them to act negatively, since we often get what we expect, just know that you have the choice to interpret their reactions positively or negatively. If you have a negative reaction to their reaction, that may be an indicator that you, too, are out of alignment in the moment—but just in that moment. And so were they, in that single moment. Yet, you may be thinking, they must have a lot of moments, because they are always critical and negative to anybody's creations or especially yours. And that may seem true. As was stated in Chapter Two, there are *degrees of alignment*. However, it is **your** alignment that *matters* in the pro-creation process, not theirs. You are creating the life you want to live, not the life you want someone else to want "you" to live.

Therefore, learning how to reframe another's opinions about your *matter* is the goal here. In this way, you can continue to pro-create freely without worrying about how others will accept or reject your manifestations. Many of the disorders that I call *reactions*, listed in Chapter Two, were stimulated or exacerbated by other people's interpretations of the different ways that the *God-source* within each of us is uniquely flowing. Here is where you get to empower yourself by pre-determining "now" what you believe is the reason that anyone's *words* could affect you negatively. You get to decide, by simply taking a few extra minutes or days to think: first—if another person's action or reaction has anything to do with you and your creation, or second—if you attracted the negative response due to your own insecurity about your creation. Either way, if it was negative, it probably reflects a mutual moment of misalignment. And I continue to emphasize "moments" of misalignment; because no one is *misaligned* 24/7, just like no one is *aligned* 24/7.

One way to proceed if someone's reaction "really hurt" is to take time to gather your thoughts about what meaning you plan to attach to the reaction. In the case of "major hurts," take at least a week or two to ponder it; but if it is a "smaller slight," just sleep on it at least one night. Then, if you still feel the need to address it, you can try offering communication to clear the air. As psychotherapists, we say don't pretend to **not** see the elephant in the living room. It's okay to address it. But the goal of the communication should be clarity and healing. We have all been *hurt by words*, and we have all been *soothed by words*, too. Therefore, communication can be a viable option.

I must, however, offer the caveat that verbal communication may or may not clear up the *matter*, depending on where one or both are *vibrating* at the moment. Still, if the goal is a positive outcome, there's a greater chance for restoration by communicating. Yet, if communication is just to vent, I recommend you forego communicating and focus on adjusting your own *vibration*. Knowing in advance that if someone misunderstood your good intention, he or she was more than likely just misaligned at the moment, as was illustrated in the section on forgiveness in Chapter Six. Yet, due to the law of attraction, the interaction indicates that something within you was also a bit out of alignment.

If we remember that universal laws are always operating just under the surface of every communication, it can do a world of good in handling the reactions of others, when it comes to our prized creations. Plus, when outward communication is not an effective choice, dealing with the *matter* through "thought" and visualizing a peaceful understanding can be effective. Our words can facilitate clarity but are not mandatory to effectively communicate our intentions. In some cases, we are almost communicating telepathically at the level of pure consciousness. Here, another's spirit picks up our spirit's signal and works it out *vibrationally*. Dr. Catherine Ponder also talks about this to a degree when she discusses communicating with a soul's angel in her book, *The Dynamic Laws of Healing* (1972). (See Resources.)

In any case, the point is to understand that the *words* conveyed to express reactions to creations are usually what people think has caused them to feel good or distressed. Someone says something that pulls you away from your well-being, and another word gets you back. And though you feel better, nothing else changed at all; only a *word* was spoken. I try to show this to my clients. They may come in feeling terrible and end up feeling better in less than 60 minutes. I point out to them that nothing changed in their outer circumstances to elicit the peace they achieved *other than my words, nonverbal communication and tone* that helped to stimulate their thoughts into a more positive flow or direction. Think about that. How many times have you called someone when you were upset, hoping they would say something that would make you feel better? And they did. Nothing changed other than your *thoughts* about the situation. When your thoughts changed about the situation, your mood, which is set at a *vibrational frequency*, also improved. This, in turn, causes a shift in *energy* as you to begin creating a new type of *matter* (emotional or physical) and that always manifest into something more pleasing.

By now, from having read the previous chapters, more often than not you will be able to choose to skip the step of calling someone in a distressing moment, if you remember that they *only* nudge or stimulate you to change *your own thought*. You are capable now of changing it yourself, or will be soon, with the tools you have gathered so far, including the pro-creation process as just described. It just means getting into the new habit of taking time to **self**-soothe.

Psychotherapy, Medication, & Herbal Treatments in the Sacretherapy® Process

At this point in the Sacretherapy® process, if you are still finding it extremely difficult to self-soothe or cannot self-soothe at all, despite having done **all** of the exercises, then it's probably clear that we are not just dealing with "a dark night of the soul." This is a phrase used in spiritual circles to describe the transformation that the soul goes through when remembering who one really is. Throughout this book we have described this as *realigning with the fullness of your being*, and it is also described in detail by psychotherapist and former monk Thomas Moore in his book, *Dark Nights of the Soul*, (2004). Thus, when there is a persistent impediment interfering with moving on and reconnecting with the authentic self, we must look elsewhere for clues that may solve the psychic puzzle.

We spoke earlier about using whatever tools we need to align with our wellness. This may need to include getting professional help from a psychotherapist, if you don't have one. And also, as stated in Chapter One, include medication or herbal remedies, if you are not already using them. However, I believe the assistance of a psychotherapist should be used first. Oftentimes, more assistance with cognitive restructuring (developing healthier thought patterns)—to release the distress or trauma and/or reframe misaligned thoughts, conditioning, memes, and old linguistic programming—from the Sacretherapy® point of view is all that needs to be tweaked in order to completely realign. As such, medication should only be added **after** it is evident that working with a psychotherapist is not enough help to penetrate the *matter*. Here is where best practices suggest that both counseling and medication be used (from the Sacretherapy® perspective, the medication could also be herbal compounds depending on the degree of the stressor). However, if you are already doing those things and are still unable to realign, you may be in need of an adjustment in medications or your herbal compounds and/or a new therapist for a second opinion. And if it's the latter, preferably you will see a psychotherapist who understands the mind, body, spirit connection.

Unfortunately, however, some people with certain spiritual convictions refuse to obtain professional help when it comes to their mental health, believing that only prayer and faith in God is all they should ever need. They are not seeing the vastness of God and how the Creator uses "people" to bring into **creation** holy interventions that can help us to realign with the very well-being God represents. Spiritual or religious fanaticism is an extreme form of rigidity, which is severely misaligned (see Alignment Scale in Chapter Two and *religious addiction* in the list of reactions in Chapter Three.)

Please don't misunderstand the Sacretherapy® process. As I stated in the Introduction, this book was never about abandoning the interventions within mental and emotional healthcare, but instead about fortifying them. Thus, any positive "pro" within the pro-creation process that can be utilized should be utilized; otherwise, you must ask yourself, "Am I truly doing everything I can to become emotionally self-sufficient" in order to get back to the *well being* you became physical to be. If not, please do.

Once cognitive re-structuring (healthier thinking patterns) and brain chemistry are realigned, you are free to tap into spirit more easily and can begin to self-soothe more often. Still, you may question, "How am I self-soothing or doing it myself if I end up using medication or herbal remedies?" Well, that's like saying how do people with broken legs really move around if they are using canes, crutches or wheelchairs? They use the *creations* that another soul made available to them and enjoy remaining mobile. We all pro-create as co-creators having been stimulated or facilitated by the *creations* of others, as described earlier in this chapter.

Either way, if you have gotten to this juncture in the Sacretherapy® process and are still having trouble pro-creating, this is the time for soulful contemplation and active demonstration of your willingness and desire to realign. This means that whether you decide you need: I. *Professional Help*; II. *Medication*; and/or: III. *Herbal Remedies* for managing lighter stressors; all tools have their place in holistic healing. Let's discuss each one separately in greater detail below.

I. Professional Counseling—The details of your life are sacred and now, with Sacretherapy®, healing can be, too. However, as stated above, some people with spiritual convictions hesitate to get professional help, sometimes fearing that their faith will be minimized; but mostly, it's due to conditioning, memes, etc. Yet, these people would not likely depend only on their faith or on calling their pastor if they broke their legs. Surely, due to the pain of the broken leg, they would not hesitate to go to the doctor or hospital and seek treatment for the broken leg. Yet, they fail to see the validity of that same rationale when it comes to getting professional treatment for their other "broken parts or broken hearts," i.e., mental and emotional reactions. But in the case of the leg, they would naturally seek and use all healing methods available: the primary doctor, surgeon, anesthesiologist, nurse, pharmacist, and then call the pastor for prayer. This same logic should be just as natural for mental and emotional health. We all should be willing to do whatever it takes to bring ourselves back into alignment with mind, body and spirit.

The Sacretherapy® Process has already underlined the crucial importance of adding one's spiritual aspect to the healing of mental and emotional reactions. But understand that the "spirit" is being honored and *added to, **not** replacing,* the other equally important aspects of the treatment plan. Therefore, you may benefit from a professional psychotherapist and at the same time have your pastor continue to pray and direct you along whatever your specific religious path is that will also facilitate healing. This would complement the holistic healing approach, which is a multi-disciplinary approach honoring the mind, body and spirit. Also, know that a psychotherapist, especially a holistic clinician or Certified Sacretherapy® practitioner, will honor your path and actively utilize "spirit" within the treatment plan. So, if you are having any difficulty *pro-creating* the life you were meant to live, please know that professional counseling and support with the Sacretherapy® *Process*, which of course includes psychotherapy, could be divinely beneficial to you.

II. Medication: Psychotropics—Many people fear psychotropic medication, which is designed to **realign** brain chemistry, one's mood, and/or behavior. The operative word in the previous sentence that is most important to understand with regard to medication is "realign," for surely, had conditioning, memes, etc., not gotten one out of alignment, one would not need medication to realign. But due to conditioning, memes, trauma, etc., many get so far out of alignment that brain chemistry becomes altered and affects one's ability to pro-create and realign. Interestingly, fear of psychotropic drugs appears to be tied to concerns of a diminished quality of life and that the medication will overtake one's ability to be in control of one's mind, actions, or behavior. But one does not realize that it was the conditioning, memes, etc., that already control one's mind, actions and behavior. Therefore, if one truly prefers the freedom to act on one's own accord, then, the medication may be the answer; because it is charged with the divine intention of bringing people back into alignment, so that they are once again free to choose their own quality of life. So with that caveat, let me further assuage any fears about medication.

When medication is working properly it should assist people in feeling more, not less, like themselves. It should assist the multifaceted neurotransmitters in the brain in releasing the natural healing endorphins that give us the sense of well-being. Thereby, it should make people feel more in control of their mind and body temple, allowing them to feel more *energy* (*spirit*) and allow for the proper perspective of the *matter*. That's all the medication is intended to do. When it does *not* do that, and any side effects are *not* relieved within a few weeks, then it is either the wrong dosage, wrong medication or needs a supplemental medication to assist in the promotion of the divine intention previously described.

A few medications, however, due to their potency, have enduring side effects that are usually experienced as mild or at least manageable. And, in that case, recognize that if there is an increased sense of well-being, despite the side effects, then it is worth being *aligned* more often than not. In either case, the side effects should be likened to stitches, a cast, crutches or cane, as is the case with a broken leg; and as such, hobbling around for a short period of time should be expected, until the "leg" resets.

The brain goes through the same sort of adjustment as the leg in that the introduction of the psychotropic meds to the brain is an adjustment to one's brain chemistry; but the brain will gladly accommodate the medication since our neuro-cellular intelligence knows exactly what has been introduced into the body temple. One may experience some slight fatigue, sleepiness, dry mouth, and other temporary discomfort for a few weeks while the brain adapts. But in four to six weeks, the optimum therapeutic value of the medication should be realized. If not, one may have to try different medications before the right match is found for one's unique chemistry.

So, just like each cast has to be molded for each unique leg, every soul came forth with its own unique body temple and therefore, what works for one brain may not be the correct treatment for another. Some of you may have already tried a medication or two that didn't serve you, but please know there are many available that may. However, if you have already tried *several* and you feel nothing seems to work, that may be an indicator that the misalignment may not be related to brain chemistry but has more to do with a reaction within your *personality*, which got out of alignment due to conditioning, memes, etc. If that's the case, professional counseling, as described earlier in this section, is what's needed to help you realign. (See *Misaligned Thoughts and Aligning Processes* for the eleven Personality Reactions: *antisocial, avoidant, borderline, dependent, histrionic, narcissistic, paranoid, passive-aggressive, obsessive-compulsive, schizoid and schizotypal* in Chapter Three.)

In any case, when it comes to medication, it may be relieving to know that most medications will only need to be taken temporarily, until one comes back into alignment with the fullness of one's being. For some, that could be months and for others it could be years, depending on how far out of alignment one strayed. However, the temporary timeframe in and of itself is not all that's important, but just knowing that anything that has gone out of alignment can come back—with the assistance of others' creations—can be viewed as holy.

Statistics from the CDC show that in the United States today, one in five people with mental and emotional reactions use some form of psychotropic medication. So people are using this type of relief, but I recommend that it be used with the holistic balanced multidisciplinary approach just described, where spirit is honored within the treatment plan. Please do not suffer unnecessarily due to misinformation regarding the utility of different forms of relief. You deserve to freely pro-create and live the life you want to live.

Cyndi Dale states in her book, *The Subtle Body—An Encyclopedia of Your Energetic Anatomy* (2009), that "all medicine is energetic anyway." And as I said in the *Introduction*, a pill and psychotherapy alone may not be enough to **sustain** the well-being you seek; but they can be very powerful allies in assisting you to align with the fullness of your being, mind, body and spirit, (when and if necessary), as can herbal remedies. (See below.)

III. Herbal Remedies—Many people prefer what is considered the natural path, believing that trees and plants that come forth from Mother Earth with medicinal intentions are of greatest value to one's body temple. This is often also due to an understanding of the circle of life, where one acknowledges that one day the body will be absorbed into the earth, while one's spirit ascends back to the nonphysical realm. Natural herbal medications, therefore, honor the circle of life and as such are often preferred, as a result of this reverence and perceived compatibility, which echoes the "all is one" paradigm.

The National Center for Complementary and Alternative Medicine (NCCAM), a division of the United States National Institutes of Health (NIH), is the agency that researches the utility of alternative medicine. This agency is one of several research institutes that substantiate how herbal remedies are finally beginning to be respected as a viable option and will hopefully stop being minimized by the traditional medical model. Although, based on a compilation of studies and articles on the World Health Organization website and the U.S. National Library of Medicine Division of NIH website, I noted that herbal remedies and alternative medicine, in general, are a much more accepted form of relief in world populations outside of the United States. Western medication has surely been introduced and integrated into other countries and cultures, but in most cases it coexists harmoniously as simply another alternative form of relief alongside the natural path. As such, we would be wise to honor the medicinal properties of natural herbal remedies, which are also known as botanical medications. My own experience with using herbal remedies is also a motivating factor in offering this section. (See *Healing the Healer*—Chapter Eleven.)

It is important to note, however, that herbal treatments should be treated as a *medication* and used carefully and not dismissed as *folk treatments or old wives tales.* In my coursework on Herbal Medications, I learned that many people assume that since herbal remedies are natural, they don't have negative side effects like the ones found in psychotropic medications made with synthetic compounds. But, I was enlightened by the knowledge that some herbal medications have side effects, too. Yet, despite the potential for side effects, herbal remedies are generally considered less toxic to the body temple, primarily due to the lower potency, and can be very beneficial to one's well-being, if taken properly.

Unfortunately, according to The National Center for Complementary and Alternative Medicine (NCCAM), a 2004 literature review by Robinson and McGrail, supported by a 2010 Survey by the Drug and Therapeutics Bulletin (DTB), revealed that *most primary care physicians (PCP) are not educated about herbal medications and are unable to advise adequately on herbal options. This, unfortunately, has caused people seeking this information to not mention it to their PCP or mental health professional, expecting the herb to be unknown or unappreciated.* But, there are naturopathic physicians and alternative practitioners who can advise you on the safe usage of these herbs for mental and emotional reactions, and prevent any adverse interaction between the herbs themselves and/or negative interactions the herb could cause with one's other mainstream conventional drug regimen.

Having cautioned that guidance from a naturopathic doctor or alternative practitioner is best, I also note that many herbal remedies are available over the counter at drug stores, natural vitamin and herbal centers, and through online pharmacies without a prescription. This is because **herbal remedies are not**

usually as strong or potent as conventional medications, and, therefore, appear to be helpful with *only mild to moderate* forms of distress. Therefore, stressors that are *marked to severe* may need to be treated with traditional psychotropics, especially if suicidal ideation or desire to inflict pain and injure oneself or another is being experienced.

At least, that has been my clinical observation, although there are always exceptions to any rule. For instance, at one point within the medical field we saw how *sometimes* the prescription of *sugar pills* as they relate to the placebo effect were effective in *some* patients during clinical trials, which ultimately demonstrates that it is *not always* necessarily the strength of dosage but, rather, how one's faith in a pill or herb, combined with the power of *thought*, can help to realign the *matter*.

It would be interesting to see the research on what additional medicinal benefits would occur if stronger doses of herbal remedies were prescribed. In either case, research in this area is ongoing. Nevertheless, keeping those caveats in mind, you may want to discuss the following list of herbs with a naturopathic doctor, since I am *not prescribing* but merely *describing* for you the most popular compounds for mental and emotional wellness strictly for your convenience:

- **St. John's Wort** is currently used as the number one prescribed drug for mild to moderate depression in Germany.

- **Valerian Root** is for anxiety and insomnia. It has been mentioned on nationally syndicated television talk shows.

- **Passion Flower** is for depression and mild anxiety.

- **Kava** is for anxiety, insomnia and stress.

- **Gaba** is for anxiety and insomnia.

- **Schisandra** is for depression and anxiety.

- **Sam-E (S-adenosyl-Methionine)** is for depression and mood.

- **Gingko** is for memory.

- **Black Cohosh** is for hormone replacement.

- **Hops Flower** is for the promotion of sleep and insomnia.

- **Camomile Tea** is for anxiety and other ailments.

- **Nerve Control** is a combination of several herbs for nervous system support by Nature's Sunshine.

And there are many others. Also, it is worth noting that any time a natural compound is being used as the number one choice for an entire country as is the case with number one above, or is being shared on nationally syndicated television shows, as in the case with number two above, the implications, efficacy and potential of herbal remedies is gaining respect.

But again, **any decision to incorporate herbal remedies should be discussed with one of the trained professionals** I described previously within this section. Overall, with regard to psychotherapy, psychotropics and herbal remedies, I believe that whether you choose to add any of them or a mixture, all that matters is that you find healthy ways that "support" your ability to ***self-soothe*** as you come back into alignment. I say "support" because according to neuroscience, the natural healing endorphins in our brains that give us a sense of well-being are already ***10 to 48*** times stronger than morphine depending on the type of endorphin. That's strong! And according to other sources the strength of the endorphins is even stronger. Thus, at best, the only thing we can do is support our endorphins in their divine intent to soothe us.

According to most dictionaries, the word "soothe" means to bring comfort, composure or relief. Most health practices, traditional, alternative and holistic, aspire to offer this. Yet, often, this same soothing and relief is only associated with heaven, nirvana, or some other word used to describe the nonphysical realm where it is hoped and expected that sustained comfort will be found. If you recall, in the *stream of consciousness* in Chapter Two, I described a version of our incarnation from the nonphysical into the physical, with an assurance that our *spirit* remains with us when we become physical. As such, any "ascension" back to this soothing place can also be obtained by simply seeking this higher knowing within, which is equivalent to the level of *spirit*. I fully described this in Chapter Seven for those considering transitioning in an attempt to realign with the God-source already within. But again, here, our brain chemistry must be aligned to reach this place. Then, to be soothed by spirit is to feel the wonderful relief that alignment with one's mind, body and spirit brings. Our ability to realign with spirit, moment by moment, is what pro-creation is all about. So be assured that most creations **approved by the FDA** that are intended to be used for medicinal purposes ***are holy*** and vibrating at the resonance of well-being. Therefore, when you recognize the value of these interventions and use them with that sacred intention, they can be beneficial in your alignment processes.

Once aligned, you will really start to value your ability to pro-create and self-soothe 'before and after' your *matter* manifests. Then you will notice that not only do you have a 'studio space' in your home where you can go to pro-create and be soothed, but that you have also entered into an *inner sanctuary*. This is a sanctuary that you can interact with wherever you go, which is described in detail in the next chapter, *Step Seven*.

9
ENTERING THE SANCTUARY

Step Seven

"Knock and the door shall open."

—Jesus

Here, we crawl up into the lap of the divine. Snug, we finally honor the invocation that we are capable of consoling and ministering to ourselves, most of the time. We understand that to be seated in the inner pulpit means that we share a sacred lineage; trusting, knowing, and finally believing that the only thing that *matters* is that we remain cognizant that at the core of our threefold beingness is spirit.

Here, we find an inner sanctuary with holy water, stained glass, and candlelit corridors that shine a gleaming light on all our *matter*. Here, there is always a pew with your name on it because wherever you are, *spirit is* with you. It was never meant to be contained in a brick and mortar place; rather, it is a psycho-spiritual space. Here, we accept with greater conviction that we came forth as *well beings* that merely got distracted on our way, due to the insufficient initiation, and totally forgot that we were so majestic.

And now, we go forth with this broader awareness recognizing that we have mighty influence over the quality of our physical experience. Thus, as fellow soul travelers we now come to understand that we are co-creators with the God-source of the universe and are beholden and empowered by this truth.

Having pro-created in the last chapter what you want to experience ***now***, you have more than likely been inspired into right action. And now since you have *entered the sanctuary,* you are ready for the additional sacred processes that will refine and expand your spiritual awareness of how to maintain your re-awakened *inner knowing.* This "knowingness" was always within you; you simply used this book to tap back into it by your willingness to discover: *What Was the Matter* to *Reframing the Matter.* You realized that you weren't sick, you were sacred, after having discovered possibilities of: *How the Matter Manifested* from nonphysical to physical; to what caused the *flawed (misaligned) initiation;* to that unspoken "rite of passage" of what were always your *God-given human and spiritual rights.* You moved from getting to *The Heart of the Matter* and having your *sacred rage* witnessed and validated; from *blaming to reframing* your journey; to learning how to *Stay Clear of the Matter* by fully clearing and releasing it. You discovered how to *extract the good;* and that you deserved to reap the benefits of *forgiving and being forgiven;* to learning how to *let go what goes;* to understanding that one need not transition to begin again. You learned how to come into a psychological place where you could finally begin to *Sculpt Your Sacred Intentions* and allow yourself to *pro-create the life you were meant to live.* It sounds like you have truly been engaged in the wonders and glory of *Sacretherapy®.* I honor your journey thus far!

The Akashic Universal Altar Call

The doors to the sanctuary are now open, even if there only be one; for this is truly what it feels like to be a *well being* and stand on holy ground. You may now remove all of the contents from your symbolic vault that we labeled "The Past" and place them into one large envelope. And seal it. Sealing the larger envelope now will be a symbolic gesture to allow all of your life experience up to this moment to be absorbed into the *Akashic Records.* The Akashic Records are likened to a cosmic library within the universe that is said to contain all knowledge of all human experience. (*Akashic Records* is a term popularized by the Theosophy Society but originates from Ancient Eastern philosophies.) Once you have sealed your envelope, release it! You may bury it or burn it, sending it back into the nonphysical realm from which it was created. A small informal ritual of some form may be done with just you and the Creator. This can be something as simple as reciting the following words or using sentiments of your own as shown below.

Exercise: Universal Altar Call –
Allowing Past to Be Absorbed Into Akashic Records

Instructions: Once you have selected a spot to bury or burn the contents from your sacred vault, place them before you and recite the following statements facing east – where things begin, with your arms lifted up to thee:

Here within these contents, rests *life* that has already been lived;

life experiences that I once allowed to distract from my quality of life;

pieces of matter that came into being with the focusing of thought;

thoughts from which I now withdraw my attention.

And so, I release **The Past** and focus my attention on the precious present **now.**

As I go forward with the fullness of my being: mind, body, and spirit,

I recognize that I am a "well being" at my core,

made of energy, matter and vibration.

And as a threefold being, I recognize that I am a co-creator with the Creator.
Having been blessed with **sacred** tools,

I bask in the awareness and assurance that my wellness is always accessible when I seek The Sanctuary within.

Blessed be.

Remaining Conscious of Your Inner Knowing – *Divine Sight*

As you go forth embracing the fullness of your being and all that you have become and want to amass, there is always room for thanksgiving – a precept for expansion. So let us make time here to rejoice at having reacquainted ourselves with the nonphysical aspects of our being, appreciating our conscious decision to move beyond yesterday's conditioning of one-dimensional thinking, at the physical material level. Here, we remain conscious, of our *inner knowing* recognizing that "what was true in the morning is no longer true in the afternoon of our lives," as taught by world renowned psychoanalyst Carl Jung, quoted in *The Shift* (Dyer, 2009). Here, we sip on the afternoon tea of life and allow it to awaken us to a place where we are able to expand our *sights* to the multidimensional layers of the universe and interconnectedness of all *matter* at the level of energy. Expanding our *sights* is symbolic in and of itself, given that most people aren't aware that when they *see anything*, they are first *seeing* it "upside down," and that it is the visual cortex that turns the object around. As such, our physical eyes are much more comparable to a lens on a camera, since it is **not** the eyes that see.

With that having been said, in order to see into the nonphysical, we recognize that we do not look with our physical eyes but rather through what most encyclopedias state the Indians first termed as the *third eye,* meaning *the eye of knowledge,* which they also refer to as: *"the teacher inside* or *sixth sense",* where we look through the bifocals of *inner knowing.* For, the *inner sanctuary* taps into a kind of peripheral vision where all of our sensory perception is honored. And likewise, the *sanctuary* is all about *perception* and what it means to perceive. Therefore, here we will sharpen your ability to perceive the fullness of who you are beyond your usual perceptive lenses, employing what I like to term as *divine sight.*

Divine sight uses all five senses *plus* the sixth sense, recognizing that there is obviously more to process than what meets the eye. "It is one of the commonest of our mistakes to consider that the limit of our power to perceive is also the limit of all that there is to perceive," said Charles Leadbeater, author of *Man Visible & Invisible: Examples of Different Types of Man As Seen By A Trained Clairvoyant (1903)*. (See Resources.) And what there is to perceive is the psycho-spiritual state of consciousness that is achievable for those willing to open themselves to it – as many of you have just begun to do throughout this book, as you came forth with your mental and emotional *reactions* (or what the DSM and most medical references called *disorders*) and laid them at the altar of the *sanctuary*.

Yet, those "emotional concepts are time-space dimensions of reality and do not explain other realities... [seeing as,] most people do not know how to be *divine* and human at the same time," according to Valarie Hunt, Ed.D., author of *Infinite Mind – Science of the Human Vibrations of Consciousness* (1996), whose book discusses her groundbreaking research at UCLA on the human energy field. I strongly recommend this book for anyone seriously interested in understanding more about subtle energy. (See Resources.)

However, decades before Hunt's work there was another pioneering book titled: *The Human Atmosphere (1920)*, written by Walter J. Kilner, M.A., M.B. Ch.B., M.R.C.P. His book was accredited as the ***first book of its kind in scientific history*** that described the "aura," which was and is this same *subtle energy* we have been discussing throughout this book. As such, we have come full circle now, extracting from *Step One* what we learned about: matter, energy and vibration. The energy field that was illustrated in that chapter, which is shown in the illustrations below, is the subtle energy dimension of divinity that embodies *divine sight.*

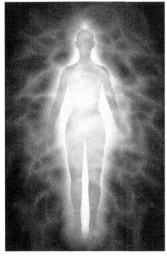

Illustration E-2

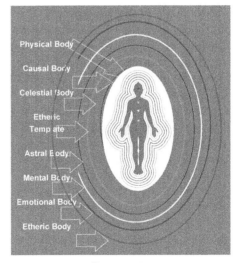

Illustration E-5

As you look closely at the illustrations, you will see that they depict the auric layers of the energy field that Kilner (1920) stated extends beyond the body. This auric layer was also confirmed to exist through the research of co-authors Dr. Lawrence Bendit, a psychiatrist, and his wife, Pheobe Bendit, a clairvoyant. They stated in their book, *The Etheric Body of Man – The Bridge of Consciousness* (1989), that "the vital aura is, in effect, the bridge mechanism between the objective physical world and the individual within." (See Resources.) As such, the aura is simply a synonymous term for the same energy field used in metaphysics and parapsychology that describes a field of subtle or luminous radiation surrounding all living organisms. This can be seen by instruments, as stated in Chapter Two, or by *clairvoyance,* a French term meaning "clear seeing." Here, however, it is also being described as an extension of the spiritual aspect many call the *soul or atman,* or what I refer to as *the inner sanctuary* or *inner knowing.*

However, depending on one's belief system, conditioning, and memes, there are naturally those whose thoughts are vibrating at a frequency that will not allow them to embrace the spiritual realm as truth. These people are known as skeptics. Because this energy field is not readily seen by most humans, it is easy for many people – skeptics and some professed believers, alike – to minimize or dismiss it. But, the spiritual subtle realm has been demonstrated to truly exist, and co-exist, with us here in the physical dimension as we travel through space and time. Dr. Hunt's research on subtle energy at UCLA, helped to clarify for me that conventional scientific methods of research are based on the *Euclidian geometry* system (Hunt, 1996); and therefore, this system is not capable of deciphering the sophistication and mathematical equations of subtle energy. Hunt's research (along with the Bendits', and Kilner's) demonstrates that just because some people can't see auras or a machine can't accurately decipher the subtle energy, doesn't mean it isn't there.

At the same time, however, according to some clairvoyants, everyone could see auras if they were willing to learn how to develop this skill. The details of how to see one's aura are beyond the scope of this particular book, since, from a *Sacretherapy®* standpoint, we are connected to it and served by it even without seeing the aura. Just knowing it is there is enough. As noted in the *stream of consciousness* creation story of nonphysical to physical in Chapter Two, some people came forth intending to focus on that which appears to be predominately *physical,* while others preferred to be more cognizant of their duality to pierce both dimensions. Nevertheless, there are books and resources available for those interested in further developing their sixth sense. (See Resources.) Still, even though most cannot see their subtle energy/spirit, most do not deny *feeling* its presence. Some call it goose bumps, some call it chills, others call it an anointing; but regardless of what it is called, it is undeniable that something is *vibrating* within that informs our *inner knowing.*

Therefore, since most can feel the presence of spirit, let's describe its frequency by acknowledging that the spirit within the *inner sanctuary* is mostly felt when one *vibrates* at the resonance of gratitude, compassion, appreciation and love –

Agape love, that is, for ourselves and fellow soul travelers. Understand now that the spirit-filled *sanctuary of inner knowing* is **not** just reserved for saints and sages; rather, it is a psycho-spiritual consciousness made of **energy** that all mankind possesses. Likewise, we use our pulsating *energy* to facilitate these higher *vibrations* that fortify our mental and emotional health; and we release the old programming as we stop pretending that the nonphysical realm can be discarded as mythological folklore, or only embraced by the most desperate and naïve amongst us. Instead, as we step into our energetic maturity and wherewithal, we embrace this sacred *matter* with our God-given grace and wisdom, knowing that all of us who came into the physical realm can mold the *energy* in whatever way we desire it to appear —given the knowledge.

That *knowledge* is the same *eye of knowledge* that allowed you to sculpt your sacred intention, in the last chapter, that helped you clarify your vision of what it is that you want to *manifest,* now. You do this with the understanding that for something to *manifest,* it must be created to *appear* a certain way. Therefore, having done **all** the exercises so far, your new found *quality of life* and what's to come should now *appear* to look pretty good from the standpoint of *divine sight.* And if this is the case, by all means, please prepare to cross over; for this is your "*Initiation Ceremony,*" having righted the "flawed (misaligned) initiation" of yesteryear.

The Initiation Ceremony – Revamped

Crossing over through the initiation process means that you can now see the previous *matter* for what it truly was: *matter* that you created out of misalignment, as a result of universal laws; or *matter* that was created out of a divine intention all along. Crossing over means that you truly recognize the sacred intent of your being. Crossing over means you have proven to yourself that you can pro-create the *matter* the way you want. Crossing over also means you have seen the new *matter* manifest or are seeing it begin to manifest in tangible ways. Crossing over means, then, that you go forth in your threefold beingness now understanding through *divine sight* who you are, and that all other souls are interconnected with you as *energy* beings in this universal and spiritual quest to happily evolve and unfold. What an achievement! Just look at the heights you have reached in consciousness in just a book length of time. For surely, you have come through this *rite of passage* victoriously! Even if at times it felt like an uphill climb, you still reached this mountaintop. So by all means, please now consider yourselves ***properly initiated!*** You may now step up to the platform and obtain your free *Sacretherapy®* certificate, details of which are described in the next chapter. Congratulations!

Orientation: Standing On the Mountaintop - Recalling the Valley

As the newly initiated, we welcome you and would like to take this time to orient you to the higher *frequency* of consciousness you have achieved. We also want to familiarize you with the new *matter* that is forthcoming, recognizing, as is often said that "at the top of one mountain is the bottom of another" where we begin again. The mountains are a standard analogy used by "metaphysicians everywhere" to depict higher consciousness which is why spiritual retreats are often held there. It helps people to see the *matter* from a much broader perspective and appreciate the growth from whence they came.

We recognize that it couldn't have been easy, having climbed the analogous mountain and gotten to the top. So by all means: *Welcome to Orientation* and congratulations, again, for evolving to these greater heights of consciousness.

I imagine that many of you made the journey with what may now *appear* as only minor difficulties. And others of you may have arrived having overcame major obstacles. Either way, you stand on the mountaintop with your sensory perception in tact. Way to go! All who have journeyed to the top of the mountain, like you have, undoubtedly acquire a more expansive perspective of life's *matter* that will serve them and all of mankind. Therefore, you can be proud of your ascent. I noted "all of mankind" because there is a "we-ness" to having arrived; a collective consciousness assisted each and every one of us on our journey. As a result, you made it. You own it. You earned it. It's yours; it's ours!

Now, when it comes to sharing our newly amassed perspective with those still in the valley, we needn't use the lofty metaphysical jargon and unfamiliar words. They haven't yet taken the same steps you took to climb the vibrational Mount Everest; therefore, they don't share the same mountaintop viewpoint. This is very important for you to recognize as you view the valley from the top of the mountain; for you are literally up in the clouds and everything looks really tiny from there.

I know this personally, because I go to the mountains a lot to commune with the God-source within me. It is truly holy ground and, trust me, things look really, really different up there. Your senses have to adjust, your ears pop, more oxygen is needed; and if you stand anywhere near a cliff, it can feel like you are suspended in air. Everything is heightened and the valley *appears* quite small. Your old problematic *matter* will undoubtedly look like the energy-based-atoms that they were made from, up there. And from that vantage point your family and friends' *matter* may also seem like molecules. But your perception of their problems is quite different from theirs.

Therefore, we want to remain cognizant that *perception* is relative and that your broader perspective of others' problems does not outweigh theirs or make them dismissive. That would be an unaligned and shortsighted interpretation *you created*. For they, like you and like all of us, were not properly initiated into their physical experience; and they need love and compassion for having their own *reactions* to the same conditioning, memes and old linguistic programming that you have begun to let go. Some of their *reactions*—or what most medical references call disorders—are the same ones you may have been diagnosed with that were listed in Chapter Three with regards to "What's the Matter?" So please don't become impatient with others, wondering "what's the *matter* with them." You now have a pretty good idea what the *matter* is. Therefore, when sharing your broader, expanded knowingness, be selective of the *words* you offer to communicate your aligned perspective; and keep it simple, but reverent.

Reverence and simplicity are embodied within the lifestyle of mountaineers – for they immediately cut to the chase. Energetically, mountaineers are as old as the trees they sit under – embodying mother-wit. *They protect the forest while the forest trees protect us.* Mountain trees, like mountaineers, are, therefore, like guardians, watching and extending their branches out towards us, allowing us to climb up and see the majestic view from their perspective. The perspective of mountain trees is always vast, diverse, generous and life-giving. Some trees are so old, with roots so deep, that they reach down through the earth, fade into the Bermuda triangle and come out on the other side. They feed us, shelter us, protect us, shade us, heal us, and breathe us. They are the single most vital life force next to the sun for living organisms. They are alive and well and share that well-being with us. They have weathered many storms triumphantly and still stand tall, all while *temporarily* lending their strength to weaker branches – for even trees understand the divinity of self-sufficiency and **inter**dependence.

So this is why we come to the mountains – not to just marvel at the peaks and valleys but to understand the native tongue. Mountains speak the language of metamorphism and transformation. Born out of volcanic explosions, mountains have learned how to settle themselves and settle the earth. In order for a mountain to be formed, its foundation (earth plates) has to erupt. And so mountains take great pride in their majesty but are gracious with their knowledge. Mountaineers are the same; many bush doctors have roots in the mountains. They have discovered mountains to hold an enchanted pharmacy, full of life-giving resources for the mind, body and spirit.

Our goal here, then, is to blend in with the mountaineers and learn the lingo. They are very welcoming but can spot a soul that *does not bring forth fruit* by reading one's *energy*. So act like you belong! Wave to the locals and be sure to say hello. They appreciate kinship, unaware of any separation. What's mine is yours and what's yours is mine in "God-land" – which is my nick-name for mountains. Those who enter are assumed to be aligned *more often* than their counterparts in the valley. Valley consciousness doesn't take well to the oxygen up here. As such, mountaineers claim "air rights," refusing to allow anyone to obstruct the view or disturb the peaceful *energy*. So by all means, please feel free to unpack and make yourself at home. When you head out at night (into the dark aspects of life) mountaineers caution that you avoid "skunk burrows," which are among the *lowest vibrational points* in the valley; plus as they say, *"It stanks (not stinks) like the dickens."* So better for you to aim for higher ground, where the birds lay their nests—the *highe*st vibrational vantage point in the mountains "right up dere next to God."

You see, the mountaineers understand that the *energy, vibration and matter* that are alive in mother-nature are the same *subtle energy* we call God. As such, manifesting *"matter"* to the mountaineers simply means appreciating life for life-sake, turning over the earth, planting a seed, watering it, adding a little fertilizer, watching it grow and enjoying its fruits. This wisdom, which I shared a little in the last chapter on "pro-creation," dictates why we would do well to take heed of their simplistic, yet reverent knowing.

Go forth, therefore, and embrace both the mountaineers and valley dwellers with the duality that comes from your experience and growth. Your experience in the valley will serve you and those who come behind you. Your ascension from the valley will remind you to continually consult the *inner sanctuary* for the balance needed to interact with the rest of the world. For, surely, through the widened eyes of *"divine sight"* the world may begin to look different, too, whether it be the local news or an internet blog, or tennis with the girls or golf with the guys. It may all seem a bit different now. That's a good thing. Although it may appear as if you no longer have as much to contribute to the dialogue anymore, since it may all begin to seem so one-dimensional, but don't worry, you still do! The world is looking for souls that shed new light on the *matter*. And you, dear one, have been given sacred tools and a compass to find the extraordinary in the ordinary superficiality of life.

Likewise, the *inner sanctuary* ordains you to offer a broader perspective to others, at the frequency of light. It isn't always easy to notice the divine light in others, but it is there—diminished but not extinguished. If you look close enough, you will see small flickers of red embers emanating from their campsites. The embers will produce just enough heat to keep them warm, but the fire is not bright enough to guide them through the dark. That's where you come in, offering lighter fluid and coal to boost their flame. And before you know it, they will begin to seem like full-fledged mountaineers—telling stories, roasting marshmallows, offering you a beverage, causing you to almost forget who got this party started. And this is as it should be—for the divinity in others is always waiting to be ignited; all it ever needed was a little kindling and air. Next thing you know they'll want to go zip-lining. Of course it doesn't always go as smoothly. The vibrational imbalance sometimes between valley visitors and mountaineers can be extremely uncomfortable, cold and dark. But, if you're going to try to strike a "match" *vibrationally* to boost their flame, it is best that your own *inner* campfire be hot and crackling.

A Balancing Act – Finding the Middle Way

As a mountaineer you will inevitably try hiking and climbing. Exploring the landscape of life is built into your DNA. However, balancing the mountain and the valley can be challenging at times, given the steepness of the cliffs. The terrain has very few smooth passages; instead, it is rocky and has lots of erosion. So it can be tricky depending on the altitude or depth. But every mountain climber knows that to keep your footing, a *vibrational* harness, axes and hooks are mandatory; for it is the correct gear that will allow you to realign quickly, as you embrace stumbles and falls in consciousness. The harness will support you while you dangle, and the axes will help lift and elevate you back to higher ground. Readjusting your compass will also facilitate your balance and prevent you from getting "lost in the clouds," which are pretty thick, as you elevate higher into the spirit world. The harness will keep you steady while applying the hooks to bring you back down to earth. Balancing your gear is important, too, to make sure that you aren't carrying too much or too little. Remembering to simplify and lighten your load will help you keep your balance more often. Then when the occasional *matter* of life takes you out of balance, you are equipped to find *the middle way*. "**The middle way**" is a term used in Buddhist traditions that means "a path that integrates a spiritual life without going to extremes." It has been embraced by the metaphysical western culture as a synonym for achieving balance. It's been known by other familiar expressions such as "the middle of the road," "midway," "finding one's center, and "grounding oneself." But regardless of the phrase, it requires that all of the *senses* be used to balance and align with spirit. See the exercise below.

Exercise: Coming to Your Senses Embracing the Aura – A Glimpse of the Soul

We find balance when we release our "non*sense*" and come to our senses. We understand that we find "the middle way" usually somewhere between the valley and the mountain peak. So let's use our imagination and picture yourself in your cabin right there in the middle. Once there, sit on the porch, choose a glider and rock a while. In fact, you can do this "literally" on your own porch, as well. Employ, the relaxation technique, *Breathe the Breath of Life*™ that we went over in Chapter Five; and then begin to contemplate "balance" using your *six* senses: sight, hearing, touch, taste, smell, and your *inner knowing* (sixth sense). Follow the instructions below.

Instructions:

1. *See* only the *matter* at hand. (Determine "what's the matter".) And use foresight to anticipate what the *thought* that I'm thinking *in this moment* may be creating right now? Meaning, if I go right, this may happen; if I go left, that may happen; if I go forward, this may happen; if I do nothing, this may happen, etc. (Recall *Step One* in Chapter Two.)

2. *Hear* the vibrational resonance of the frequencies in your immediate space, taking time to listen and home in on the symbolic meaning that offers a more aligned, non-rigid, alternative point of view. Ask yourself, "What higher frequency might this *matter* be trying to show me or call me to, in sacred terms?" (Recall *Step Two,* Chapter Three.)

3. *Feel* what you are thinking. This means that if you feel bad or sad, you must be *thinking* a bad or sad or *automatic thought*. Ask yourself: "Is this an *automatic* thought coming from my old programming, conditioning or memes?" Then, reframe the thought and decide how you would prefer to feel, and then think the thought that matches that preferred feeling. (Recall *Step Three* in Chapter Four and *Step Five - Reframing Part II & III* in Chapter Six.)

4. Then *sniff* it out. Pledging to use your God-given *sense* to check it *all* out for yourself by digging into the *matter*, even if that means spending lots of time and money researching it, speaking to experts on the subject, or an attorney, if needed, to figure it out. Then grab a pen and paper to decide what needs to be done by thoroughly weighing the *pros* and *cons*.

5. Once you've made a decision, get a *taste* for what is now needed to sustain that level of competency and feeling of wellness. Employ your aligning processes and affirmations that affirm your good; and as you continue to nourish the *matter* from a sacred perspective, remember that one's alignment with well-being is a moment by moment endeavor. (Recall *Step Four,* Chapter Five.)

6. Now, before you act, based on all the information you gathered above from embracing your five senses, confirm it all by running it through your sixth sense: *inner knowing,* which is felt in your gut. Ask yourself if *"something"* is telling you to do it, or is *"something"* telling you **not** to do it? That *"something"* is your *inner knowing,* which offers you *self-validation*. Remember to trust it, in order to maintain your elevated vibration of well-being. (Recall *Step Five,* Chapter Six.)

7. Now, **be still** with your decision on how to handle the *matter*. No need for second guessing. You've done the work and penetrated the *energy* basis of the *matter*. Hence: *be still and know!*

8. Now, it's time to eat some grub. ***Nourishing the body-temple*** fortifies the *energy* needed to pro-create the new *matter*. Begin sculpting your sacred intention, using all the divine tools you have been given so far. (Recall *Step Six,* Chapter Eight.)

9. Then, **sleep on it** for the night. Once you wake up, just stay still and take a few moments to become aware of the *energy* field that is surrounding your physical body. You may not be able to see it, but you may feel it. (Recall *Step Seven,* Chapter Eight.)

10. If you want to feel your subtle body, just take your dominate hand and prepare to feel the energy emanating from you by following the next few steps.

11. Put your hand a quarter of an inch to a half inch from your skin, and feel the warmth of the energy. You can remain stretched out in the bed or sit up to do this.

12. Slowly scroll over your arms, chest, belly, and any other part that is comfortable to reach. Take slow breaths, counting one-one thousand, two-one thousand, three-one thousand, etc. Do this for as long as you feel like doing it. Feel the heat. If you don't feel enough heat, just quickly rub your hands together like you are washing them with soap, and then scroll over the areas again. The friction will heat up the molecules. Then the molecules in your hands will sense the molecules in your subtle body. You will then feel the warmth.

   Note: What you were just feeling and sensing was the *subtle matter* dimension of your body temple, which is composed of light energy and has been said to extend up to three feet from the body. I've only been able to see about 18 inches, but there are many others who see the entire width and depth. Your hands, then, were in your energy field; and what you were actually feeling was that body heat which, metaphysically speaking, is the energy that links us to universal intelligence, to the Creator, from which *inner knowing* comes.

   As stated above, for those who can see it, this is the dimension that we call the aura, which is what I call a glimpse of the soul. What you felt, then, was the eternal part of you that goes back to that which we call God as *pure energy* when we transition and release the body temple (which we have been conditioned to call "life and death," but from the metaphysical paradigm is viewed as "life and life"). Indulge the energetic warmth of your own sacred subtle body; for it is there to comfort you.

13. Now, while you are aware of your auric energy, embrace the *"thought world"* of this dimension, and once again, imagine the *matter* the way that you have

decided that you want it to be, in order to remain balanced and aligned. Remember, at this point, it makes no difference what the subject was that originally got you out of balance (before you slept on it); the only thing that's important to remain in balance is that you visualize it the way you want it to manifest now!

14. Then, finally, once you have captured the *matter* the way you prefer it to be, having pinpointed "the middle way," offer sheer appreciation and gratitude by thanking the God-source within you, (which is also omnipresent) for assisting you in consciously realigning with your threefold being: mind, body and spirit. For surely, balance is restored when we embrace the fullness of our being and remember to come to our **senses**. All six!

Looking Through the Window of the Divine – The Aligned Psyche

We all tend to marvel at the gorgeous and breathtaking architecture within cathedrals, chapels and sanctuaries. Therefore, as your friends and loved ones begin to take notice of how different you are, recognize that what they are witnessing is the beautiful transformation of an *aligned psyche*. As such, feel free to *simply* share. This time, their curiosity is not inspired by fear of losing you or envy, but rather a true desire to figure out if what you're doing may help them to penetrate the *matter* in their own lives. So employ agape love and compassion.

Please also feel free to give them a copy of this book. Tell them how it gave you a broader perspective in ways that can only be described as sacred. Tell them that you have come to understand that you are more than just your body. And then patiently let them go through these same steps at their own pace. Not yours. For, in your excitement to bring them along and have them understand where you have been coming from, your intensity can sometimes feel intrusive. Let them be. If they choose not to read it, that's perfectly fine. They were just inquiring, but they must ultimately listen to their own *inner knowing,* as well. Just trust that they are evolving and seeking what all of us have sought, which is realignment with our own well-being. Don't worry, they will either embrace it or move on to another path that is equally sacred for them.

Remember, *opposites attract* only at the level of personality, but at the level of spiritual vibration, *like attracts like*. In other words, you mainly connect with people on the same vibe. So, whether or not they choose to accept this particular path of alignment has nothing to do with their ability to evolve – for all paths ultimately lead to God. Therefore, any rigid preference on your part for them to join you on the same path can now be released; for the divine is a diverse and multi-faceted *energy*. As such, their chosen path needn't have anything to do with your ability to maintain the non-resistant vibe of a mountaineer, looking through the window of the divine.

Granted, it may feel a little lonely sometimes, not having your family or friends understand your new found alignment. This is why I suggested that you **not** describe yourself in metaphysical terms, since words can be used as labels that separate our common goals rather than connect them. Yet, be encouraged *"as more of us awaken to this [metaphysical] mystery,"* as predicted in the blockbuster hit movie: *The Celestine Prophecies* (2005). *The movie* predicted a completely different new worldview *"redefining the universe as energetic and sacred."* Any time fiction movies that espouse the "all is one" universal principal become blockbuster hits – including *Avatar* (2009) and *Cloud Atlas* (2012) – you can go forth assured that many people are seeking this type of an awakening, just like you. In fact, more than likely they frequently retreat to the mountains, like you, too. So take time to fellowship with your neighbors since emotional self-sufficiency embraces *inter-*dependence, which, again, means knowing when to stand on one's own but also when to seek support. Of course, no one expects you to knock on his or her door every week or every month, but sharing a cup of hot chocolate here and there can warm the spirit.

Looking through the window of the divine, therefore, means remaining free –free of other people's validation; free of conditioning; free of the memes; and free to embrace words and linguistics that set your spirit free. Being free means that no outwardly circumstance can deny you the right to choose freedom. Freedom brings peace. And peace of mind, we now know, is mandatory to maintain mental and emotional wellness.

It's a job, though, but an inside job that mandates you to work within the *sanctuary,* utilizing your divine sight. You get no time off; but the work is fulfilling, for it simply requires you to honor your free-will and make whatever changes you deem necessary as you continue to bring yourself into alignment with your heart's true desires. To prevent burn-out the EAP office will pay for you to sit down on *the therapy couch of the God-source within* to rejuvenate the *matter.* And as you do that, your perception of the architecture within your *inner sanctuary* will change and be restored with you.

In fact, new windows have already been ordered – the stencil pattern was fading causing the *inner light* to look dim. Upgrades, then, are always being done somewhere within the sanctuary, evidenced by contractor plastic here and there. We therefore, carefully remove our shoes on the way in and out wanting to avoid any unnecessary slips or falls in consciousness.

We then take time to flick holy water with humility and boldness. But mostly, we bow with gratitude – gratitude that emerges from "a wish" that came true. For, gratitude is really a soft and silent prayer – a prayer that asks for nothing but to be at peace with one's mind, one's emotions, and to feel good in one's skin! It is, likewise, a prayer of tranquility with total appreciation for having arrived, for having survived, for having thrived, and for just being alive. It's a tempered gratefulness that is quite personal yet honors *all that there is* in ways that are universal; and honors our understanding that molding the *matter* is the only *matter* that matters. So it's a thought-filled prayer. Knowing that *thought* is the true energy basis of our existence and portal to everlasting life, we finally optimize this sacred exaltation, trumpeting the wellness discovered in the urgency of "now." Governing ourselves accordingly, we gratefully submit to the divinity inherent within this invitation.

So, here in the *sanctuary,* we pray. We pray with sincerity the prayer of humility as we offer our thanks. We thank the Creator of the universe for revealing to us how to cooperate with this all powerful spirit of restoration that belongs to us by divine right. We trust that within us is this higher consciousness, this God source, this source energy, which shows us the way to sanity, fused with our humanity, which fortifies our allegiance to mental and emotional well-being. So, we pray. Searching for words that convey our sentiments accurately, we pray. Trusting our faith in our faiths, we pray. Seeking confirmation that we are not alone in our quest, we pray. Using affirmations that affirm our resolve, we pray. Knowing and believing our words are transmitted and received with the vibrational resonance we intended, we pray. Thanking Thee, as we continue to acquire the vocabulary that is most representative of our energetic offering, we pray. And so it is. Amen.

10
AFTER-CARE: STAYING ALIGNED!

Step Eight

"You are indeed being given the choice of how much faith and involvement you place in your ascension from here...."

The Ascended Masters

Having been lifted up out of the depths of fragmented beingness to the heights of integrated holism, we recognize our need for continued nudges that allow our *inner knowing* to be a forever comfort and guide. For this, we embrace *aftercare* as a final step in the Sacretherapy® process, understanding that this step is more than just a step; it's a lifestyle. Therefore, here you'll practice how to quickly gain access to what you have learned throughout all the previous steps; since no one is aligned 24/7, but we can recall what steps are needed to maintain our alignment the majority of the time. Aftercare, therefore, is about the future and how to safeguard the new *matter* that you will be constantly molding, in addition to preserving the feeling of alignment you have achieved and come to value. As such, due to the insidious nature of conditioning, memes and old linguistic programming, we want to be proactive.

Naturally, there are literally millions of divination systems to tap into that can assist you in maintaining your inner knowing. You already have been given some great ones that you can continue to use as things come up. Continuing to do the aligning process three times a day for as long as you need to is one. Living consciously and regularly asking yourself the questions in Chapter Three should keep you from being manipulated by the conditioning and memes, and help you to begin using NLP positively as it was intended. The letter writing technique is certainly another positive ventilation outlet as is the technique of forgiveness and communicating with *reflection-inspection-direction* in the mirror.

The sacred rage and mutant rage letters, as well as the speeches that describe how you prefer things to be, will always be powerful sources of connection back to spirit if anything else gets pent up. And the *balancing act* exercise almost always jolts you back to center. Just keep the harness, axe and hooks nearby. But if you are living consciously, you should be able to disperse any of that kind of *energy* way before it festers. Also, if the ancient Chinese meridian system sparked your interest via *tapping,* keep visiting those founders' websites and tap. But if it didn't resonate with you, just keep doing the traditional cognitive portion and positively *reframe* your thoughts as a part of your soulful lifestyle.

The bottom line is to use whatever inspiration you can find that resonates with you and is capable of bringing you back into alignment. Many people get their spiritual inspiration weekly, just on Sundays, and let it go the rest of the week. Our spirit, as you have come to realize, is not compartmentalized like that. It, therefore, needs regular nourishment. This does not mean attending church more often during the week or running oneself ragged doing more spiritual activities. It simply means being at peace, going into the silence, right there within the *inner sanctuary,* more often. Just like we feed the body temple every day, it's good to also nourish the spirit on a daily basis, too, without fear of becoming a spiritual fanatic, like we talked about with regard to "balance" in Chapter Nine.

Yet, the sensation many describe as "goose bumps" or "chills" or an "anointing" when experiencing the divine can certainly be hypnotic. It feels wonderful and alerts us that we are vibrating in the zone of spirit. Rarely, do I have a day without this taking place. I feel it when I do my morning and evening ritual of prayer, meditation, and Tai Chi. I also feel it often when I am doing therapy with clients or lecturing. But regardless of where I am or what I'm doing when the anointing happens, I see it as pure communication from the God-source within me, telling me that I am embracing or interpreting the *matter* correctly.

Feeling the anointing, however, is certainly not the only way to feel one's connection with the Creator. So just do *you*! We are each unique individualized expressions of this God-source, and so it is logical that what makes one feel connected would not necessarily be the case for another.

Thus, all you have to do in order to experience these soul-felt moments more often is to make it a point to practice living your life more soulfully. Again, this is not a call for you to run out and join a place of worship, unless you are inspired to do such; for this is not about religion at all, just strictly about spirit. In fact, you can live soulfully and never even leave your house, since your body temple is the housing. Many of the below suggestions can be done right in your own home. Alignment, then, is never somewhere *outside of you*; it will always be an inside job. However, gathering with other like-minded souls can certainly be inspirational, but is not mandatory for spiritual evolution.

Having offered that, I have found that there are some specific sensory stimuli that facilitate aligning with *spirit*. If you recall from the Introduction, the original meaning of psychology (in addition to studying the mind) was "the study of the soul (spirit)" which during that time was studied in order to help people to align with it.

Thus, here, we reinstate that broader, original, and sacred intent. Whereas, I offer **Twelve Sacred Tools** of a spiritual nature to facilitate your ongoing alignment; as well as **The Soulful Living Exchange.** I will describe each one; however, when you contemplate incorporating these sacred suggestions remember that "aftercare" is a continuous life long journey. Thus, what may resonate with you this year might not the next, because your spirit is always changing and growing and may call you to some other soulful expression. That is the way it should be, especially since more than likely only a few of the ideas will resonate with your spirit. Some of them are much easier to integrate than others.

Learning how to incorporate just one or two of the offerings into your daily or weekly physical experience could be challenging and require a bit of an adjustment. Therefore, I suggest that you only *add one at a time* to prevent from overwhelming yourself. Keep in mind that there are only so many hours in a day. So remember to maintain your **balance**, since you will still be doing some of the other processes from the previous chapters in addition to any of the *Twelve Sacred Tools,* below:

Twelve Sacred Practices – For Staying Aligned With Spirit

1. Going into the Silence is another way of saying *"entering the sanctuary"* where we embrace that *still soft voice* within, described by many names whether it be spirit, soul, or the God-source within. Here you take time to just *be, no do.* Learning to *"be still and know"* by pulling away from the hustle and bustle all the stimuli in your environment for just a little while can be a sacred *ma* It offers you some "me time" and solitude. It can be done at home in your *creation studio* or in the bathtub; at a lake, pond or any water stream r the backyard or the park; or just anywhere there is peace and quiet. It to practice one hour a day if possible, or for as long as you can, but a least, a few times a week.

2. Prayer is the most popular divination system used worldwide. supplication where you are asking and thanking the God-sor universe for guidance on how to experience your optimum we for others' well-being is also widely practiced because it is a send them positive *energy*. Also, beginning the day with a and ending it the same has immeasurable benefits for fort

3. Meditation is about going within. It is often said community that "if prayer is where you talk to God listen." You listen for that still soft voice from the your focus is also on your breathing mechanism of consciousness. For it is our breathing mechanism that is said to carry with it the *prana or life force* that is attached to the oxygen molecules, according to clairvoyant Charles Leadbeater. Our breath is what many believe ties us to our spirit, which is why it ceases when the body temple is shed. This sacred breath is also emphasized in many forms of relaxation that coincide with meditation. (Check my website for *Breathe the Breath of Life™ Relaxation/Meditation* CDs.)

4. Tai Chi is one of my favorite aligning exercises because you can actually feel the chi (life force) flowing through the body temple. It is the most beautiful exaltation of spirit I have ever experienced next to music. There are a variety of Tai Chi styles, but what is consistent among each is the divine execution of deliberate slow movements and artistic disciplined postures that allow the life force (chi) to circulate and fortify the inherent wellness within. Thus, as a therapeutic modality and/or physical exercise it triggers the release of the natural healing endorphins in the brain. This offers a sense of mental and emotional well-being. There are also numerous benefits to doing Tai Chi with regard to physical reactions as well. Some insurance companies offer reimbursements for ʳercise programs including Tai chi.

ʲʳinal desire for learning it was to teach it to clients who were overcoming
physical trauma, to get them back into harmony with their body
and spirit. You needn't be an expert to practice Tai Chi. I am
nd adapted the names of the movements to fit the way the
ʳgh me; and since my version deviates from the traditional,
ʳ up with a name that clarified that difference. I added
ʳences to what I call: SpiritNme™-Tai-Chi. (Check your
ʳoogle for Tai Chi centers in your area and feel free to
tNme-Tai Chi™.)

ʳmended since it also offers energy benefits. There are
and what is consistent among each is also the divine
stimulate and support the mind, body and spirit.
ʳphasis on the breath-work through meditation,
ʳnd movements. Thus, as a therapeutic modality
n also trigger the release of the natural healing
6. ʳa sense of mental and emotional well-being. It
how medical field as a viable stress reducer. Some
ʳe for yoga as an exercise program. (Check
ʳ Yoga centers in your area.)

ʳf the strongest testaments of spirit and
that we have as human energies. Just

interfacing with nature, without harming it, can help one realign quicker than using many man-made divination systems. Invoking spirit can be done fairly simply by communing with Mother Nature, whether it be contemplating a sunset, watching the sun rise, paying attention to a lady bug, rubbing a leaf across your skin, hugging a tree, stomping in a wading pond, feeding the geese, bird watching, swimming in a lake, visiting a nature center, gazing at the stars, playing with fire flies, digging your hands into Mother Earth, planting a garden, etc. There are many ways to capture the oneness of the energy that connects us with nature.

7. Reiki / Prana Healing is a form of *energy medicine* that allows the practitioner to act as a vessel receiving universal energy, which is sent to areas within your body temple where energy is blocked. The practitioner may or may not touch the body temple and works in the auric area while you remain fully clothed. The chakras are often focal points, but I feel it is also good to scan the entire body temple. Thus, whenever you do a lot of release work or if your mental or emotional reactions cause you to feel fatigue, pain, stiffness, along with many other symptoms, Reiki or Prana healing can be very beneficial. (See Resources.)

8. Music Therapy and Sound Healing are pure vibration; and "OHM," is said to be the musical tone in the universe, and often hummed during relaxation and meditation. As vibrational beings, hearing is the last sense humans (with hearing) lose before they transition. As such, music can trigger well-being in ways that are energetically profound, as some of you may have discovered if you took me up on the option to listen to soft background music while reading this book and going through the Sacretherapy® process. Music researchers, in fact, have demonstrated that music therapy is associated with a decrease in depression, improved mood, and reduction of anxiety. This is partially because singing and listening to music increase serotonin in the brain. Sound healing offers the equivalent medicinal benefits via tones that attune to the higher frequencies of the universe.

However, *sound healing* is often done with sonic instruments such as gongs, crystal bowls – aka singing bowls, chimes, and drums which are wonderful remedies via psycho-acoustics. Dr. Masaru Emoto is one of the most famous alternative medicine researchers in the area of sound healing. He demonstrated the impact that certain frequencies, tones, music and words have on altering *matter* through his water and ice experiments. His research has far reaching implications of what certain sounds, words and thoughts can have on our body temple being 70 percent water. (Emoto, Masaru, Messages From Water, 1989.)

Thus, sound and music can soothe the emotions and evoke the "spirit" in our everyday lives, whether we are simply listening, humming, whistling, or singing and our tapping feet, etc. However, sad music and low vibrational sounds should be avoided if one is depressed, unless using it to purposely purge and release – as used sometimes in psychotherapy and psychodrama (below). Even then, it should be used in very small doses, since sadness triggers pain and pain, as you learned in Chapter Six, triggers the pain mediating hormones that cause temporary discomfort. This demonstrates the tremendous impact music and sound have on the psyche. They contribute to one's feeling of wellness and summon the alignment one seeks with the mind, body and spirit.

To learn more about music therapy and sound healing, contact the American Music Therapy Association; or the Center for Neuro-Acoustic Research. (See Resources.)

9. *Dancing* is an excellent way to move *energy* and rejoice in spirit. When music inspires us to tap our feet, it is for many people the impetus for ***dancing;*** but unfortunately, dancing for the sake of dancing or partying hardy is often underutilized by people who consider themselves spiritual, or they go out of town to get away from their church in order to "let loose." They mistakenly believe enjoying the body temple by shaking the upper torso and hips is not proper, which by now I hope you understand is a meme. Dancing is a form of holy jubilation, too, whether within a church celebrating spirit or a secular setting celebrating the joy and fun of dancing with spirit, since wherever we are, our God-source is within us, too!

Our body temple houses a vast range of energy (aka *kundalini*) that flows through the *sacral* to the *crown chakra*. It is, therefore, also to be enjoyed as we acknowledge that every part of the body temple is holy, and embrace the fact that our hips, chest or breast bring much joy and warmth to ourselves and other souls. (For more on Kundalini and Chakras, see Resources.) The television show: *Dancing With the Stars* is an example of people showing the world the true inspiration that can be evoked from the beauty and sensuality associated with moving one's bosom, hips and limbs to the wondrous sounds of music. As such, feel free to enjoy releasing and gathering the *energy in motion* that comes from dancing, without fear of ridicule from onlookers.

Judgmental onlookers are simply those whose conditioning has caused them to squelch their own experience and unfortunately many grow into old *crones and drones* who despite their age did not acquire wisdom. And therefore, they are often critical, fussy, overbearing, and prey on the young or the young at heart for their carefree spirits. They resent the fact that they themselves never had the courage to fully let loose; or worse, they may be hypocrites that once danced their tails off (publicly or privately) and possibly were shamed by a generation of "old crows" before them, and are now projecting their own limitations, attempting to de-sanctify the joyful exuberance of organic fun.

10. *Psychodrama* is a form of treatment that can help you to release toxic energy and gain deeper insight into your own processes with the use of dramatization and role playing. Here, people act out their thought processes; and it is where most find that the true villain they "thought" was preventing their joy was the antagonist within. The term *psychodrama* was coined by sociologist Dr. Jacob Moreno in the 1920s. He believed in the power of the *"here and now,"* where one can discover new solutions and learn new roles in what I describe as "the off-stage drama of real life." Psychodrama has been used to heal multiple issues past, present and future. However, I now only use it for dramatizing how you desire your life to be *now* or in the future, **as opposed to** replaying how it was; because I no longer want to unintentionally assist others in their unconscious mis-creation. Remember *"energy flows where attention goes."* Therefore, used as prescribed, psychodrama can be a powerful way to help release pent up energy and to practice molding *new matter* the way you would prefer it. (See Resources.)

11. *Retreats* offer a withdrawal away from stress and an ascent into a spiritual refuge where one gathers oneself, reclaiming the authentic self, communing with that which is sacred. Cabins and spa resorts in natural environments with a variety of influences from Mother Earth seem to be the best external sanctuaries for retreats. Retreats include going into the silence, but the duration of silence usually depends upon whether the retreat is a weekend or a week, etc. Finding time for spiritual retreats may seem like a luxury due to time constraints, so they tend to coincide nicely with taking advantage of holidays, since the etymology of "holi–days" comes from the old English word "hāligdaeg" – *hālig* (holy) and *daeg* (day) meaning "holy days" which in ancient times were strictly set aside for these types of religious and spiritual occasions and later extended to secular tributes. (See Resources as well as check search engines online for retreats, also visit the website for Sacretherapy® *Mountain Retreats* where abbreviated versions of the ***Eight Steps*** are offered with most time spent in *the sanctuary* and *pro-creating.)*

12. *Inspiration* is a form of "awe" and reverence for life that can come from some of the most unexpected places. Thus, anything that taps into the joy of living would be considered inspiring. This would include humor, since comic relief serves us in ways that I can only describe as sacred. There is nothing better than a jolly ole' belly laugh that reminds us that life is supposed to feel good and be fun. Hobbies are another form of inspiration – at least the ones that trigger a deeper connection with spirit, like interacting with nature. An additional daily source of inspiration can be found in service to others – even small acts of kindness; reading inspirational books and listening to positive self-help tapes and/or CDs that tell you how wonderful you are and how pleasing you are to the Creator. And what's great about auditory inspiration is that it can be done in your car while driving, exercising or doing household chores. Also, please keep in mind that anything that makes you feel guilt or sadness is *not* inspiration. Inspiration *always* feels good and gives you energy. (See Resources.)

The Soulful Living Exchange – An Online Community of Soul-Filled Living

Here you are invited to attend optional online biweekly booster sessions that I call *The Soulful Living Exchange,* created specifically to support the *aftercare* of those who have completed the first seven steps within the Sacretherapy® treatment plan. These are *free* 45-minute aftercare sessions done (2nd & 4th Monday evenings) via the internet with me and other likeminded souls who have reached this level. The exchange is about pro-creating the life you want to live. There is *no* sharing, *no* venting and *no* processing of the *old matter,* just pure positive energy. It's designed to support your desire to live a soul-filled existence, which can be enhanced with the support of others, but again is *not* necessary. Therefore, the exchange was only created to enjoy the benefits of shared consciousness and to help you remain cognizant of your connection to your spirit by being consistently rejuvenated.

Allow me to describe how it works:

I commence the session by leading the group with one of my *Breathe-the-Breath-Of-Life™ Relaxation/Meditations.* Attendees verbalize *energy* requests for the Mastermind, and quantum time is spent on each request. The Mastermind, as described previously, is simply a group of likeminded souls who believe in and hold each other's desires in their mind for a designated period of time to intensify the energy surrounding the specific creation that is attempting to come into manifestation. If time permits, depending on the number of participants, we *go into the silence* with only soft vibrational music in the background. The purpose of going into the silence in the presence of others is twofold: *contemplation and pro-creation. Contemplation* reminds us that we are spiritual beings having a physical experience and that communication does not have to be verbal. By now you understand that our words carry *energy* and are merely an expression of our thoughts. The *pro-creation* aspect of going into the silence reminds us that the pro-creation process occurs at the *level of thought* and is being fortified by the added subtle energy of the Mastermind.

Next, I lead a silent abbreviated Reiki scan where participants mimic my movements on their own body temple to feel their auric extension. Then we do an abbreviated segment of my version of Tai Chi, which I call Spirit*N*me-Tai Chi™, to re-align with the life force within the body temple and shift any stagnated energy. (**Note**: *My version of SpiritNme-Tai Chi™ is not a substitute for any of the authentic versions, for I am a forever student/amateur. My abbreviated version simply offers a* *glimpse into Tai Chi's energetic possibilities*.) Next, the mastermind comes to a close with attendees being encouraged to give voice to the appreciation they have for the fullness of their being. This is done while breaking bread together (even though we are in cyberspace), eating something raw from mother-nature (celery, carrots, apples, etc.), honoring the eternity of the circle of life, and remembering that we are co-creators who came forth to live in concert with one another while we exchange soulful living ideas.

To honor confidentiality, those interested in participating in *The Soulful Living Exchange* only need share their first names if they have a Mastermind request. If so, you would state your name and request, as shown below, using the two examples borrowed from Chapter Eight on Pro-creation, *Step Six,* with regards to: 1) pro-creating one's *emotional* self sufficiency and, 2) pro-creating one's *financial* self sufficiency with chairs.

1. **Example One:** "This is Soul-Filled _____ from New York. My Mastermind request is to continue to become ***emotionally self-sufficient.***" The group will join you in a collective consciousness and spend one and a half to two minutes sending energy to your request, depending on the number of attendees that evening.

2. **Example Two:** The next attendee makes a request, beginning with the same greeting: "This is Soul-Filled _____ from Canada. My Mastermind request is to become financially self-sufficient ***creating chairs.***"

The Mastermind is then concluded with a group mantra/affirmation and the session is over. (For more information check the website listed under Resources.)

The Sacretherapy® Certificate

Anyone who has taken ***all*** of the steps in this book, whether or not you decide to join *The Soulful Living Exchange,* will be sent the sacred Sacretherapy® *Certificate* mentioned in Chapter Nine, for having evolved to this level of mastery in the alignment process. Naturally, the certificate is totally ***optional***. However, if you would like one, all you have to do to receive it is send me your personal testimony on how the Sacretherapy® steps helped you align yourself with the fullness of your being. **Please limit it to two short paragraphs maximum (300 words).** If you send more than that, unfortunately due to time constraints, only the first two paragraphs or 300 words will be read. You may just sign your testimony with your first and last initial, and city and state, to protect your confidentiality. The certificate will be emailed back to you for you to print out in private. That way, you can print it out and add your own name without ever having given us your full name or address.

In any case, please trust your own *inner knowing* on all of this. I truly have no preference for how you do your aftercare. I simply stand behind my work and want anyone embracing Sacretherapy® to enjoy the potential *lifetime* benefits of it. So do only what makes *sense* to you, for as you have learned, sanity is restored when we come to our senses. All six!

Finally, having come through all of the steps, I will now share with you in the next chapter my personal testimony of coming into alignment with what I ultimately coined Sacretherapy®. Before you proceed, I want to take a moment to thank each and every soul who has taken this journey with me. It has truly been a pleasure being a vessel of divine healing light!

11
HEALING THE HEALER – HOW I DID IT!

Stepping On!

"Physician, heal thyself."

Hebrew Proverb

I t's been said that teachers are always teaching that which they need to learn the most. Thus, with that caveat, I want to teach from the clarity and appreciation of my own example. Plus, sharing my journey may help you to know that I have walked my talk and have the personal authority beyond professional training to offer all of the previous chapters of healing balm to others. My intention here is not to place emphasis on what took me away from my sense of well-being, but rather describe what brought me back. Therefore, I will focus on my search for help, getting help, and what help was ultimately enduring and saved my life.

There must be a way to share my journey without reactivating thoughts of the sad parts of life that's already been lived. I want so much to tell you how I came into alignment without taking you or me out of vibrational harmony to hear it. However, I realize that even sharing a quick synopsis may cause both of us to experience some uncomfortable emotion; but since it will be brief and ends in a higher vibration of well-being I think we can go in and out of it and quickly realign.

My journey, in important ways, is no different than yours when put in terms of having experienced negative and positive emotion. I could actually wrap the whole story up by stating, in general terms, that some things happened that I would have preferred not to have happen. These things pulled me away from my sense of well-being for a long time, and I didn't know that I was *allowing* them to pull me away. And the more I focused on those sad things, the more bad things seemed to happen, as is always the case with self-fulfilling prophecies. I could also restate my past more specifically, which I'm about to do, and still say the same thing, although instead of saying it succinctly, it will take several pages to sum it up, even with me editing out the specific details.

Let me begin by briefly describing my family of origin, because it was my *perception* of my family that was the impetus of my greatest pain. I was born to what traditional society would describe as an alcoholic father and an emotionally ill mother. My mother emotionally abused me most of my life until she transitioned. From her I learned that "people who are hurting" hurt others. My father, whom I adored, loved me and was the most functional parent between the two despite his alcoholism until he transitioned. From him I learned that "hurting people" can hurt themselves. The two of them in their pain attracted each other and had four children. From my siblings, I learned several lessons just by watching them. I learned that psychological labels can marginalize who we are, and that when we don't adapt or conform to what society has determined is normative, we are apt to have strong "reactions" in an attempt to realign. This, in turn, sets us free to create our own reality. I also learned from observation that going into an altered state of intoxication for relief was not empowering or sustaining. I further learned that religion could be as unhealthy and mind-altering as any other dependence, when used as an escape and/or controlling force versus an empowering source to tap into well-being.

I was the youngest child and, over time, watched each of my family members move further and further away from their mental and emotional well-being, but not without my own pain and dis-ease. I was a sensitive soul and saw light around others but was told to never say that out loud again, if I didn't want people to think I was crazy. That admonishment frightened me to death. I had no idea that others couldn't see the light. It made me think something must have been wrong with me. So I kept quiet and just ignored it.

I was later diagnosed with anxiety at age 12 due to chronic dizziness and fainting. I was referred to counseling, and there I was told that the anxiety was a result of being raised in a chaotic household and having been molested prior to kindergarten by a friend of the family who lived in our basement. Then on my 13th birthday, another adult who was a cousin by marriage also molested me. This time, however, I was able to get away with less touching. And this time I told. As a result, for what seemed like revenge, he would show up from time to time along my way to a summer camp and stalk me. I began to have panic attacks and flashbacks of the ongoing incidents by the first abuser, along with the one incident by the other. This made me wonder if all older men were abusers. Unfortunately, while in college, I would learn that young men could abuse you, too, when I was date raped and then robbed the same year at gunpoint by two teens. I began to feel like a magnet for trauma but couldn't understand what I was doing to attract this. I knew nothing about self-fulfilling prophecies or universal laws of attraction at that time.

So I became fearful and began obsessing about all the bad things that happened to me and to my family. I had graduated from college (undergrad) and had been working for a while by then; but these thoughts caused me to become severely depressed, with repeated fantasies of driving my car over a bridge. I ended up being hospitalized for three weeks, diagnosed with major depression. I was in my early 20s at the time, and the team of doctors stated that the depression was due to my family of origin's dynamics and the unresolved sexual traumas. After being released from the hospital, I was in and out of therapy looking for the answer to my most pressing question: Why did these things happen to me and my family and would I ever be completely all right.

I tried to move on, and got married at 25, but I had tremendous problems having sex without flashbacks. I continued to get dizzy, and sometimes I would faint. I sought help again and found help. It helped, but the help didn't last. Then, after we had our son, I became paranoid that someone might abuse my child. While in the mist of trying to be the best parent I could be, my own father transitioned (died) in the middle of the night. I was awakened by his voice that said, "I'm okay, sweetie." I sat up in the bed and said, "Daddy is that you?" He repeated his statement that he was okay. I couldn't see him, but his voice was clear and coming from the end of my bed. Minutes later the phone rang; it was my sister saying my father had died. I said, "I know." But Daddy's visit wasn't believed. Then a few minutes later, while awakening my 3-year-old son, the first thing he said was, "Grandpa isn't sick anymore." I said, "How do you know?" He said, "He told me." That was confirmation and turned out to be the biggest validation in my life that the nonphysical realm was real. It meant the auras I had been seeing were real and nothing to fear. I had been given a big chunk of proof that there truly was no life and death, but life and life. Still, it didn't have the impact that it later came to have, because at the time, I wanted Daddy here and mistakenly believed that I could not go on without him.

This sent me into an extended bereavement. I knew to look for help, but this time it took antidepressants plus therapy. I had refused medication years earlier while in the hospital. But this time, I had a child and husband who needed me, so I surrendered. I couldn't afford to fall apart. And although I was initially afraid of the medication, it did take the edge off. I got better for a longer period of time, but that sense of well-being still didn't last.

Panic attacks and dizziness returned after I discovered that a loved one had also been sexually abused. It shook me in ways both expected and unexpected. It confirmed, once again, that "hurting people" hurt others; but it also showed me that we could still really love people who hurt us and hurt the people who love us, too. It caused me to contemplate what it would take to soothe both the one abused and the abuser – I mean abusers everywhere, whether the abuse was sexual, physical or emotional. It was this experience where I began to gain a deeper level of compassion and desire to forgive everyone.

Then my mother transitioned. The news of her passing initially brought relief, as I realized she couldn't hurt me anymore; but, eventually came great sorrow and the understanding that she was just a wounded mother. I didn't get a chance to tell her that I had forgiven her. As a result, the simultaneous events of her passing and the abuse of my loved one sent me back into therapy. I was given a higher dosage of the medication, plus a sleeping pill, to get through that; but there was only a minimal sense of well-being and even that didn't last.

At that point, I was completely frustrated and ready to give up. I didn't want to try another therapist. I was tired of repeating my life story over and over again. Just bringing it all back up would make me feel depressed for days and sometimes even weeks. They all kept asking the same questions, convinced that my yesterdays were responsible for the present day distress. And that just didn't make complete sense to me. To keep being told it was my childhood and family of origin stuff that was interfering with my *here and now* was both irritating and perplexing. Dad and Mom were no longer physical, so as far as I was concerned, it was time to stop pointing at them. I understood healing could be like an onion, but it wasn't an abyss. The fact of the *matter,* as I would come to learn, was that it wasn't what happened in my past that was interfering with my well-being, but rather the awful tendency to place my thoughts and attention *on the past* is what was interfering with my sense of well-being at the time. And that was a big difference. So I temporarily gave up on psychotherapy, hoping that the meds alone would be enough. But that idea was moot because with each change in the meds or increase I felt more and more spacey and disconnected from myself. So I quickly realized that medication alone was not enough.

But I was also angry with myself for even needing medication and even angrier at the medication for not working the way I was told it could. So I sought out a natural pathologist and he put me on some natural herbs. They worked very well as long as the pressure wasn't too great; but when the "stuff hit the fan," the natural herbs just were not strong enough to mediate that type of pain. But when there was no major crisis in sight, the herbal remedies served me pretty well.

I liked that I had gotten to a point where I was functioning without medication, yet, all was still not well within. But the idea of returning to therapy was not appealing since I was not content with the explanations traditional psychotherapy had offered. Nevertheless, I desperately wanted to find the answer. There had to be a way to have better control over my thoughts. So I kept searching, and decided to go to graduate school in mental health, thinking, "What better way to get to the bottom of this than by becoming a therapist myself?" Yet, graduate school was quite anxiety-provoking. I fainted at school once and was dizzy half the time, especially the first year when I had to Baker Act (hospitalize) a loved one.

Learning about my stuff and my family of origin's stuff was tremendously painful. Oftentimes, I had to sit on the ground between walking to classes to not faint. At that point, unaware of any other options, I reluctantly got back into therapy. Looking back, it is truly amazing that I didn't just give up. I did, however, take one semester off to process all that I was learning but then went back to finish graduate school.

Fortunately, graduate school did provide me with some answers, although there were many I didn't like. Yet, overall graduate school was very validating of what I had intuited about my family, as a child. And this knowledge gave me the courage to finally extricate myself from that and move away from my dysfunctional family of origin. Surely, I could no longer plead with them to get their own help, and I didn't want to Baker Act a loved one again. So releasing them was the most humane, restrained thing I could do, even though that choice caused me to go into a major depressive episode – one that I did not think that I would survive, but I did. It was strictly about self preservation; but the overwhelming guilt of wanting to save myself was literally debilitating. I had to accept that they could get help if they wanted it for themselves. Therapy had clarified that no one could be an unyielding source of support for others. And from there my mental and emotional health improved tremendously. It was at that point that I realized that *nothing* bad had happened *"directly to me"* in 10 years; and that it was mostly my focus on other people's problems that I was allowing to pull me away from my own sense of well-being. With that epiphany, I truly began reconnecting with my own wellness.

Still, when I laid their burdens down, I had to deal with how I kept activating thoughts about the past sexual traumas that infiltrated my marriage, fully recognizing that none of the past needed to have power over my *now*. So that needed to be released. And since I knew the extent to which traditional psychotherapy could lend itself, I went looking for a different type of help that was non-traditional. I recognized, however, that there was still value in psychotherapy, especially when it finally focused on the "here and now." Graduate school was confirming that, but still something wasn't allowing the benefits of it to be sustaining.

Something was missing, at least for me, because psychotherapy and pills had not been enough. They eventually helped in the short run, enabling me to even think about the long run. But in the long-long run, they *didn't make the difference* that would make a *sustaining difference* in advancing my quality of life to the degree that I was seeking. They had kept me from ever needing to return to a hospital, and they kept me calmer, but calmness is not the same as peace. As such, there was no sense of total well-being, and so there was no real joy. There had to be more. I was tired of being told that I was already a success story for having survived. I was tired of being told that I should just be grateful and content with having thrived. But this couldn't be as good as it gets. I wanted more. Good enough was not good enough! I wanted my peace and I wanted my joy! Then life would be good enough. So, it needed to be figured out. There was obviously a missing link and I was determined to find it. And I did.

In a piercing moment of contemplation, I recalled that a psychic once told me that *I was a healer by divine right,* and she didn't even know that at the time I was in school becoming a psychotherapist. But activating that memory caused me to home in on the word "divine," which made me think of spirituality and healing with *spirit,* as opposed to any specific *religion,* since by that time I had already embraced six different religious paths searching for relief. Once I began adding spirituality to the mix, which I later learned was termed "holistic healing," clarity came. I was able to release the anxiety and began coming into alignment with the fullness of my being.

I began reading books on other paths to spirituality, metaphysics and universal principles, one of which was titled, *Lessons In Truth,* by Emily Cady. Cady stated: "I could not even desire something that was positive unless God wanted it for me, too." And that said to me that I couldn't want the *peace of mind* that I had been seeking without God wanting it for me, too. Then while on vacation in Jamaica, a minister there gave me the book, *The Dynamic Laws of Healing* by Catherine Ponder, and her book validated that I was on the right path. I read the book and did a few of the suggested processes, such as affirmations, and learned about what she termed as "chemicalization," which described that when you truly begin to come back into alignment, a literal chemical reaction occurs that breaks things loose. It can look like a crisis but is not. Her suggestions started working and so I began being attracted to other information like it.

I started spending hours in metaphysical bookstores and regular stores in the alternative healing and self-help sections. I found a music audiotape by Louise Hay and Joshua Leeds at the Unity Bookstore with a song on it titled: *I Love and Accept Myself Exactly As I Am.* (See Resources.) It was my first introduction to her work. I would cry my eyes out to her tape, for it was truly purging me and I was allowing it. The tape was like *music therapy* to me; and since I am also a vocalist, it penetrated me in ways I was not expecting. It was the absolute most vivid turning point in my healing. It was the day that I realized that I had found what I was searching for: ***something that fed my soul.*** This happened during my final year of graduate school to become a therapist, and it made me question what I was doing. I wondered for a brief second if I was becoming a part of an establishment that had not completely been enough for me. And could I prescribe it in good conscience? The thought took my breath away. It passed, but was never to be forgotten. It's what compelled me to keep looking into alternative healing.

I then purchased Hay's book, *You Can Heal Your Body* (1984), which had a list of physical problems and their probable causes. I located fainting and hypoglycemia and began doing those affirmations along with the ones from Ponder's book. I also continued to use the natural herbs given to me by the herbalist. I was truly impressed by the effectiveness of both of the alternative remedies. There was so much more to it than just old wives tales and positive thinking. Therefore, I felt it was worth mentioning to one of my professors, since at the time I was still in school becoming a psychotherapist. Unfortunately, I was told that those affirmations and natural stuff "was a bunch of nonsense," and not to suggest it to my clients but instead inform them of what was considered *real* relief, which was only psychotropic meds and traditional therapy.

Still, I insisted that the alternative stuff had helped me. I admitted that I agreed that the herbs weren't strong enough to combat major stress like suicidal ideation, which is why I totally respected and understood the validity of medication. But, for the other stressors, the metaphysical philosophies, affirmations and herbal remedies seemed to work quite well.

Unfortunately, my advocacy for when the utility of alternative methodologies could possibly be effective fell on deaf ears and was not acknowledged. What I was told is that if I wanted to get into that type of work, I should have gone into pastoral counseling, not mental health. I walked away thinking, "Do I really have to choose? Why couldn't there be both?" It wasn't like I was suggesting that spirituality was the only necessary piece. Of course, it wasn't. But it *was* a crucial piece. Plus, I wondered what was so intimidating about spirituality, holistic healing, and metaphysics, anyway?

Nevertheless, once I graduated, I heeded the professor's caution and kept the two worlds apart, at least *professionally,* during my first 10 years of being a psychotherapist. But by my 11th year of being a psychotherapist I could no longer ignore that many of my clients were also seeking holistic healing which included spirit. And *personally,* I fully recognized that embracing the holistic and metaphysical principles was certainly what I needed.

Lo and behold, there was the missing link. It was the "spirit" being left out of the equation in all of the therapy treatment that I had sought. In fact, I couldn't recall any of my therapists ever asking me about my spiritual life. The closest I got to any discussion of that was when I brought it up during grief counseling about my parents, and it focused more on the stages of grief and readjusting to life without the loved one. But when I mentioned hearing my father's voice after he transitioned and asked if the therapist believed me, she said that she believed that I believed it. Needless to say, I didn't feel comfortable adding that I saw auras, recognizing that she didn't seem to be versed in *extra sensory perception,* which, in all fairness, is only vaguely covered in traditional schools of psychology.

In any case, after recognizing that it was the *spirit* that had been left out of the treatment plan, it seemed really weird to be right back at the place that I had started my search! I mean, I had already searched for spiritual relief going from church to church and path to path since childhood! But I could not find it there. The music moved me; but stripped of the emotion music can evoke, I was distracted by how punitive most of it was; how this wonderful God that I believe we are all apart of was being made out to be vindictive, petty and small. That's when it really hit me that religion was **not** synonymous with spirituality. So, no wonder being told that all I needed to do was go to church or read the Bible, didn't work. The religious focus was more on describing the daunting list of what I couldn't or shouldn't do in order to get my spirit *back to heaven* (the nonphysical realm), and not on how to co-create joyfully and freely with the loving God-source *within me, here and now,* in the physical realm.

Filled with this greater insight and distinction between religion and spirituality, I would ignore anything in the Bible that spoke of God as a punitive source. I didn't want to get pulled away from my natural well-being again reading that. So I searched for the *good parts* in religion and ended up having to release the rest. At the same time, I recognized that every scripture written in the Bible or any religious doctrine was written with the "intention" to assist mankind in our connection to the source of the universe, even if that *intention* was not realized. I also understood that since each of us is at a different place in our quest, that one path couldn't possibly resonate with everyone. So what seemed totally "off base" to me might actually have spoken to someone else. Therefore, I empathized with that *intention*, recognizing also that all paths are attempting to honor God. Having said that, I also noticed while in graduate school that the *Diagnostic and Statistical Manual of Mental Disorders (DSM)* had a category for "religious and spiritual problems" and I immediately thought, "Well, no wonder! Of course there would be issues."

In light of all of that, the only way to maintain my well-being was to create a little sanctuary of my own making that I could go to, because it was hard to find many churches that weren't selling "fear" and spewing *hell and damnation*. All of which was stated under the guise of it being labeled the "disciplinary actions" of a heavenly father's tough love – for not following a set of memes. When in actuality what it really felt like was *fear based thoughts* conjured from the consciousness of conditioning. At least that's how I viewed the parts that didn't resonate with me.

Thus, in my search for spirituality versus any specific religion, I discovered there was a blending of eastern and western thought that the early Christian ancients and other paths tried to communicate. There were only subtle nuances in terminology found throughout all the writings from Theosophy to Unity, to other Esoteric traditions, including Taoism to Buddhism. I was moved to embrace a diversity of paths, understanding the "all is one" paradigm.

Then I read the modern works of Father Leo Booth's book, *When God Becomes A Drug* (1991), about religious addiction, and heard psychotherapist John Bradshaw's take on "religious mystification" in his audio CD titled: *Creating Love* (1992), and read Neal Donald Walsch's *Conversations With God* (1995) where he agrees that God is not a punitive source. I was overwhelmed with joy. Next, I fell absolutely in love with Marianne Williamson's many lectures on *A Course in Miracles,* which she says "is not a religion, but a psychology based on love rather than fear," which, of course, echoes these same sentiments.

Unfortunately, however, during my youth I had not heard of any of these scholars or their teachings about an unconditional God. I was instead tormented by the idea of a "man-God" in the sky that would judge and punish me for not honoring an abusive mother, for questioning the Bible, and for breaking many of the Ten Commandments. And the whole idea of the "get out of hell, free card" by repenting and "not doing it again" was not comforting. I knew I would keep going off the churches' prescribed beaten path, since at the time I would continue to recognize that my mother was abusive; so "*honoring thy mother*" did not resonate with me.

I was also pretty sure I would keep breaking a few other Commandments too; and I would surely keep questioning the Bible and other religious dogma that portrayed God as punitive. Therefore, based on religious dogma, I was either doomed to live a vicious cycle of doing what was supposedly wrong to feeling guilty, to repenting, to doing what was wrong again, to feeling guiltier for doing it again, and repenting again, to doing it again, and so forth.

The good news, however, was that, thanks to trusting my own *inner knowing* and finally finding a path that embraced an unconditional God, the above authors, and being open to a variety of spiritual philosophies, I would learn that the Creator was an invisible spirit, a loving energy, and not some man in the sky staring down at me, disappointed. That brought me tremendous relief. And with this expanded knowledge, I had a wonderful conversation with a non-traditional Christian minister back in 1989, and we discussed "conditioning" as it related to the passage in the Bible that warns of *false prophets* and how people often conclude that anything non-traditional should be feared. We agreed that she and other non-traditionalists were just like me and you: individualized expressions of God. That meant that if we all have God within us, there are no false prophets but only the variety of levels of understanding about, who and what God is to us. So fear of different paths was put to rest; it turned out to be a meme used to keep people inside the box, as were all of the absurd earthly analogies of how God supposedly punishes, like parents punish their children. That simply said to me that someone got it twisted and was now making God in man's image, instead of the reverse.

Amazingly, despite all of my tormented days and nights about a punishing God, coupled with all that I had been through, somewhere deep down inside I knew that this loving source we call God had brought me through all of that, and did **not** put me through any of that as some punishment or test. What happened to me was vibrationally based (as described in the previous chapters). Being frightened and controlled by the whole *eternal damnation* thing no longer resonated with me. I decided that the term "hell" was *not a physical place* that one is relegated to but is rather *a psychological space* experienced when one is out of alignment with one's mind, body and spirit. A psychological space, then, as it relates to "hell" is merely a thought – a vibration, that is tuned to the frequency of despair, and *burns* you up inside, but only in the heat of the *fiery* passing moment; and any fear of eternity in that *damned* place can be eradicated in the very next moment of clarity and redemption, which is conveyed to us by our mind and body reconnecting with spirit and expressed as relief.

As I began to understand the difference between spirituality and the man-made religions, I wrote my own morning and evening prayer, along with using the *Lord's Prayer,* since it didn't fully convey all of my personal sentiments. I needed to cultivate my own personal relationship with God, not the one I was told to have. I needed to go into the silence. I needed to embrace something good that was already *inside of me*, not get something bad *out of me*. And there inside of me was the peace I had been seeking; peace that could only be described as *sacred*. It was a peace that was cultivated by doing many of the processes I shared with you in this book. And it was a peace that has fortified me for the majority of the past two decades, minus one year where I spiraled way out of alignment due to total marital disconnection, which to my delight and surprise was restored and brought back into alignment.

From there, my peace came rushing back, stronger, by homing in on my thought processes, which were validated tremendously after I watched the documentary *The Secret* (2006). I had already been taught about the *law of attraction* and *law of creation* during my universal truth classes, and of course my psychological training also taught me about this from the perspective of *self-fulfilling prophecies.* But all of what I had previously learned was suddenly crystallized. I guess as they say "a picture is worth a thousand words," and so seeing the dramatization of these principles was extremely fortifying. It made me recall having been introduced to the *Teachings of Abraham* (Hicks, 2004) a year or so earlier, which was all about the *law of attraction* and had been around 20 years before *The Secret* (2006). I decided to take another look, and purchased Abraham's introductory cd—*An Introduction to The Teachings of Abraham* (1988-2006) and tracks 7-18 sang in my heart, validating all of the ancient writings about an unconditional Source in the universe, and all I could think was, "Wow, I was surely right to have trusted my own *inner knowing!*"

Plus, *The Teachings of Abraham—Law of Allowing Workshops* (Hicks, 2005) also finally provided a logical answer to one of the questions I had for some time with regards to the Bible, which was the scripture in Genesis 1:26 that says, "God said, let *us* make man in *our* own image." I wanted to understand who the "us" was referring to, since "us" means more than one, especially since man was here way before the Bible existed. I figured the statement couldn't be based on the Trinity – seeing as the word "Trinity" is not even in the Bible (it means the Godhead), but also because the Old Testament was written before Jesus was born. And Jesus is quoted in *John 16:7* as saying that the "Comforter," which was the *holy spirit (aka holy ghost)* would be coming *after* his transition; and so neither of those *latter two aspects* based on the concept of the Trinity, (i.e., Godhead) were even around when God first created man. So, when I heard *The Teachings of Abraham CD,* an answer to that question was finally satisfactory, that the "us" aspect of the Creator was a *collective consciousness* consisting of pure positive energy, that I was *already a part of* and would someday transition back to.

Then I was flabbergasted to further discover that more than a half a century earlier, William Atkinson wrote, *Thought Vibration or the Law of Attraction in the Thought World* (1906), which described the exact same unconditional Source and Law of Attraction that Abraham talks about. It was shocking to discover that this empowering information had been available my *entire life-time!* From that point, I was determined to do ongoing research of *spirituality* for myself! Further research became my way of honoring my previous struggles but also the struggles of my clients and people everywhere who were having mental and emotional reactions coupled with and/or due to their own religious and spiritual conflicts.

This ultimately led me to expand my education beyond traditional mental health and pursue non-traditional knowledge available through a doctorate in metaphysical theology, where I titled my dissertation: *"In Search of God,"* which, due to many requests, may be expanded into a book with the same name. So, it is my ongoing research, coupled with all the other works I have acquired, which continue to be extremely reinforcing of the philosophies that formulated my spiritual beliefs. I almost became *very sad* to learn that most of this *freeing information* about spirituality had been around since antiquity without many people knowing it. Most of it was not readily available, having been "underground" due to the conditioning of the times. But still, it made me wonder about how much suffering I could possibly have foregone, had it not been for the conditioning and memes; and had I simply researched it all ***for myself*** much sooner.

Nevertheless, I quickly self-soothed, realizing that it was my constant *seeking spirit* to understand *spirit* that continually attracted me to all of the information I had been gathering for decades; and so, my life had been unfolding incrementally, as it should. For surely, had I not gone through all of the challenges, I would not have become a psychotherapist. I would have continued to pursue my first career choice and become a singer. But I obviously came into the physical realm, like you, able to discover that there are many probable paths that lead to fulfillment. For me, one of them was to offer you this healing sutra. Now, all of the pain I experienced, and any mistaken interpretations I may have made about it, no longer *matter;* because like you, and like all of us, I am so much more than my mistakes! And according to many metaphysicians there are no mistakes. It's merely life that's been lived. And I am pleased with its relics. Therefore, I choose to preserve only that which amplifies within me the exhilaration of my "now moment" where I get to embark upon the creation of new and sacred *matter.*

Plus, I must say that from this higher vibrational vantage point, when looking back *now*, I can see that more years of my life than not have actually been pretty good. The last two decades, especially, have fortified me in ***sustaining*** an even higher level of peace and a true desire to live *my truth* – a personal truth that's felt like a *reawakening*. It's coinciding with what has been called a planetary awakening, commanding to be articulated and shared with all of you who are seeking this type of *liberation*, as souls unfolding, trying to understand, too, your connection with the Source of the universe that many of us call God. It is what has ultimately culminated into Sacretherapy®.

Therefore, I truly honor my journey. It has caused me to tap into all that I am, and all that I've become and am becoming still. So as I journey on, tweaking my alignment moment by moment, like you, constantly discovering the best in me, which is the spirit within, I pray that you and every soul on the planet honors and appreciates your journey, too! Be well. And be free!

Blessed Be!

Dr. Kemp at the Arc de Triomphe, meaning "Triumph" (Paris, France).
Thanking GOD!

APPENDICES

APPENDIX A

Psycho-Spiritual Biographical Questionnaire™ - Full Version (PSBQ)
Copyright© 2007-2014 Amelia B. Kemp, Ph.D., LMHC

(**NOTE**: The following questions are *adapted* from questions I usually ask clients in a clinical setting. Therefore, if any of the questions in this form make you feel uncomfortable in any way please <u>do not complete the form.</u> Instead, you may need to answer these questions in the presence of a psychotherapist in what may feel to you like a safe environment. However, if you choose to proceed, feel free to skip any questions that feel uncomfortable or use the alternative version of this form, which is the Radical **PSBQ-R** (Appendix B), since that form does not deal with any of your past history and begins with the "here and now.")

Instructions: The PSBQ is designed to allow you to summarize your journey in this physical life experience, so far. The questions are mostly "yes or no" responses along with some short answers. The purpose of the "yes or no" is so that you don't attempt to process your answers at this juncture. Processing your experiences will be done systematically throughout the remaining steps in the Sacretherapy® process. Therefore, the PSBQ is simply allowing you to give yourself an overview of the matter. Please answer the following questions as succinctly or elaborately as you want and allow yourself at least an hour to complete. Some questions in the spiritual section you may never have asked of yourself before, seeing as the nonphysical/spiritual aspects of life often go without query. And so, please go with your gut on those questions, since they only serve to offer you a broad inventory of possible spiritual experiences that you may have encountered in your physical experience. Also, remember, this form is for your eyes only (unless sharing with a psychotherapist or other Certified Sacretherapy® Practitioner), so feel free to be as candid as possible. Once you have completed the form, don't forget to seal it in an envelope marked "The Past" and store it in a place you deem private and sacred. Place answers on separate sheet.

Soul's Advent into the Physical Realm

First name your soul uses: _____ Date of PSBQ _____
Name of the maternal soul (mother) for your advent into the physical: _____
Name of the paternal soul (father) for your advent into the physical: _____
DOB _____Date of conception: (Count back 9 months or less): _____Age ____

How much sacred time have you had in this physical life experience? Note: Sacred time is divisible by quantum moments/seconds (the smallest physical quantity that can exist, i.e., one hour = 3,600 seconds, one day = 1,440 seconds and one year = 525,600 seconds). How many moments (seconds) have you been creating your life? (Multiply your age x 525,600)_____

How many moments do you estimate have been experiences/manifestations that were **not** pleasing? _____

Subtract the unpleasant moments from the total moments of your physical life. (Put total here.)_____

Please check the appropriate box or share the requested information:

Married___ How long ___; Divorced ____ How long ___; Previous marriages? Yes __ No __ How many ____

Single ____; Separated ___How long___; Widowed___ How long ____ ; Cohabitating ____ How long ___

Do you live with: Yourself ___ Spouse ___ Lover ___ Parent ___ Children ___ Friend ___ Other___

What part of your *being* do you feel is *most often* out of alignment? Mind __ Body __ Spirit ___All areas ____

What's The Matter? (Share what is bothering you here.)

_____

_____
_____
_____
_____

SACRETHERAPY® CONNECTIONS & AGREEMENTS

This section will review the quality of your relationships with other souls:

If you are a parent, how many souls have you assisted in coming into the physical realm?_____
Briefly rate your co-creative sacred connections with each of them or check n/a if not applicable:

1. _____N/A___Close____Just okay ____Poor ___Totally Disengaged ____Transitioned ____
2. _____N/A___Close____Just okay ____Poor ___Totally Disengaged ____Transitioned ____
3. _____N/A___Close____Just okay ____Poor ___Totally Disengaged ____Transitioned ____
4. _____N/A___Close____Just okay ____Poor ___Totally Disengaged ____Transitioned ____
5. _____N/A___Close____Just okay ____Poor ___Totally Disengaged ____Transitioned ____
(If more, please use an additional sheet.)

Psycho-Spiritual Biographical Questionnaire™ - Full Version (PSBQ) Page 3 of 7

What other soul-filled beings outside of your parents and/or children hold a major role as part of your support system, assisting you through this physical experience? (Your spouse, partner, friends, etc.; top three is sufficient; five is the maximum you would need to list.) List their first names, role and impact on your life?

	Name	Role	Time invested embracing their presence and the impact they have on you:
1.	_____	_____	_____
2.	_____	_____	_____
3.	_____	_____	_____
4.	_____	_____	_____
5.	_____	_____	_____

MENTAL & EMOTIONAL HISTORY

Have you ever been diagnosed with a mental or emotional reaction? Yes __ No __
What is or was the diagnosis (es):_____
Did the matter bothering you now or during any part of your life involve any trauma?
Yes __ No __
a) Were you physically abused as a child? No___ Yes__ When _____By whom____
b) Have you physically abused or been physically abused by a spouse or partner?
    No __ Yes __ When_____
c) Sexually abused as child or adult? No__ Yes __ When _____By whom_____
d) Ever Emotionally/Verbally Abused? No__Yes__When_____By whom____
Did you report the abuse? N/A____Yes__ No__ To police___To parent___
    To teacher___Other_____
Have you had therapy before? Yes ____ No____ How long? A few sessions___
    Few months___ Year___ Years___
For above reasons: Yes___ No___ If no, what was it for? _____
Did it help? Yes__ No __ A little __ For a while __ ___
What did you learn? _____
Ever had suicidal thoughts? No___ Yes___ When was the last time?_____
Ever attempted? Yes___ No___
How many attempts? _____ Last one _____What did you do? _____
Ever cut, hit or hurt yourself without trying to commit suicide? No___ yes___
    How often? _____
What did you do? _____ When? _____
Why?_____
Any hospitalizations for a mental or emotional reaction? Yes___ No____
How many? _____
Are you currently taking any medication for the issue? Yes____ N ____
Were you ever prescribed medication that you refused to take? Yes ____ No ____
Why was it prescribed? _____

Psycho-Spiritual Biographical Questionnaire™ - Full Version (PSBQ) Page 4 of 7

Why didn't you use it? _____

Any history of substance abuse/dependence? Yes__ No __ If so, what: Alcohol __
    Pot__ Coke__ Other_____

If so, age started_____Age stopped _____Ongoing_____
    Check here if only experimented in the past_____

Any DUI? N/A___ No__ Yes___ When? _____
    Ever had rehab? Yes____ No ___When?_____

Any treatment programs: N/A __ Alcohol Anonymous __ Narcotics Anonymous _____
    In-patient __ Other _____

Current use? No__ Yes__ Rarely____ Socially____ Describe:_____

Ever incarcerated? Yes __ No__ Currently ___ Multiple times _____
    Only as a teen (before age 20) _____

Why?_____

Any family members diagnosed with mental/emotional issues/alcohol/drugs? Yes___
    No___ Don't know___

Who? Mother __ Father ____ Sibling (s) _____ Maternal side of family ___
    Paternal side of family _____

If yes, does family's history cause you to fear that you may attract the same? Yes__No__
    A little____ I have__

Highest education? Left school__ HS or equivalent__ Some college __ Bachelor's__
    Master's__ Doctorate__

Has your level of education allowed you to do what you want in the world? Yes__No__
    Somewhat __

Do you have any learning differences? Yes __ No __ If so, do you feel okay about the
    differences? Yes __ No __

Do you currently feel inhibited by your perceived ability to create and manifest what
    you want? Yes __ No __

SPIRITUAL INQUIRY

Do you believe the premise that you are a spiritual being having a physical experience?
    Yes __ No __

Do you believe in a Higher Power? Yes__ No__Undecided___

What do you call your higher power: God__ Creator__ Allah__ Universal Mind __
    Source Energy __ Other ____

Are any religious/spiritual issues causing you guilt, shame, anger or confusion at this time?
    Yes __ No __ NA___

If so, what? _____

Do you see your higher power as a loving source or punishing force? Loving ____
    Punishing ___ Both___ NA___

Do you believe that your higher power is everywhere present (omnipresent)? Yes__No __

Do you believe that your higher power is always with you? Yes__ No__

If so, do you believe that your higher power is inside you? Yes__ No__

Do you call the spiritual part of you your spirit or soul? Yes __ No __

If so, how do you nurture your spirit? _____

How do you communicate with your higher power? _____

Psycho-Spiritual Biographical Questionnaire™ - Full Version (PSBQ) Page 5 of 7

How does your higher power communicate with you? _____

Do you declare any specific path/religion? Yes__No__

Do you feel you are on the right path? Yes __ No __ Unsure __

What souls on the planet (living or transitioned) have influenced your spiritual beliefs?
_____

Have you come up with any of your own spiritual beliefs? Yes___ No ___

If not, do you feel that the thoughts linked to the God-source in others are more valid
   than the thoughts linked to the God-source in you? Yes ___ No ___
   Never thought about it ___

Have you wondered why you are here in the world? Yes__ No __

Do you pray? Yes ___ No___ If so, what happens? _____

Do you meditate? Yes ___ No ___ If so, what happens? _____

When you are sad or distressed in any way, how does your spiritual belief/faith help you
   to self-soothe? _____

Do you consider the breath you inhale in and out as sacred and divine?
   Yes __No__Never thought about it ___

Do you intentionally take deep breaths to honor the life force it gives you?
   Yes__ No__ Never thought about it__

Since your breath leaves the body temple when you transition, do you think that it is
   attached to your spirit? Yes __ No__ Never thought about it___

If you identify yourself as a believer, what do you think your spirit came into your
   physical body to experience? _____

What have you created or manifested so far in relation to that purpose or desire?_____

What has been your most pleasing creation yet? _____

What service (vocation) do you offer the world?_____

Do you believe the world is a mostly safe or mostly dangerous place?
   Mostly safe ____ Mostly dangerous ____

Do you believe that there is mostly good or mostly bad in the world?
   Mostly good ___ Mostly bad ___

How good are you about picking up others' vibes (vibrations)?
   Good ___ Not very good ___

Can you feel energy? Yes __ No __

Have you ever felt someone was near you without seeing the person first? Yes __ No __

Do you believe in a "sixth sense"? Yes ___ No ___

If so, do you believe it's attached to your spirit? Yes ___ No ___

Can you see your own aura? Yes __ No __

Can you see the auras of others? Yes __ No __

Have you ever experienced déjà vu? Yes __No __ Not sure __

Ever had any prophetic dreams or known something was going to happen before it
   happened? Yes ___ No _____

If so, would you describe that "knowing" as intuition or clairvoyance? Yes__ No__

Do you consider yourself psychic? Yes __ No __ Why? _____

Do you ever hear music or pleasing sounds (clairaudience) that others don't hear?
   Yes __ No __

Psycho-Spiritual Biographical Questionnaire™Full Version (PSBQ) Page 6 of 7

When you are awake, do you ever see things that other people can't see, or hear voices that others can't hear? Yes__ No__ Maybe ___

Have you ever seen or been visited by any loved ones that have already transitioned (died)? Yes__ No__ Possibly__ Not sure, but once or twice I could have sworn ____

If so, did the experience scare you? Yes __ No __ A little __
OR did it comfort you? Yes __ No __

When something deeply meaningful touches you emotionally what sensation do you feel: Goose bumps? __Chills?____Anointing?____Something comes over me?____ Tearfulness?____

Does soft music, art, dance, a natural landscape or waterscape, awaken anything within you? Yes __ No __

What do you consider sacred in your life? _____

Do you believe in *soul* mates? Yes __ No __ Don't know __

Do you believe in angels? Yes __ No __

If so, has anyone ever appeared in your life that you felt was an angel? Yes__No__N/A __

Do you believe in spirit guides, mediums or channels? Yes __No __

Have you ever had an outer body experience (astroplaning)? Yes__ No__

If yes, did it add confirmation to your spiritual beliefs or change them in any way? Yes__No __

Ever had a near death experience? Yes ____ No___

If yes, did anything spiritual happen? Yes __ No __ N/A __

If so, what happened? _____

Have you had a spiritual healing? Yes __ No ____ What happened?_____

Have you ever experienced a miracle? Yes __No__What happened? _____

Do you think that when your body ends, that it's the end of you?
Yes__No__ Don't know_

Do you believe in past lives or reincarnation? Yes __ No __

Where do you think you will go when you shed your body temple?
Heaven__Hell__ No where __Don't know___Never thought about it __

What do you hope will happen when you shed your body temple? _____
_____

BODY TEMPLE

Do you have any physical manifestations that are troubling your body temple now?
Yes __ No __

If so, what part (s) of your body temple troubles you? _____

If it's possible that we choose our body temple, why do you think you may have chosen your particular one?_____

Are you pleased with your body temple? Yes ___No___If not, why not? _____

What do you do to exercise the body temple? _____

What foods and beverages do you feed your body temple? Healthy foods___
Junk foods___Mixture ____

How's your appetite? Normal ____ Poor____ Over-eating_____
Binge and purge ____ Binge only _____

Do you believe in or practice fasting? Yes __ No__

Do you believe in or practice breatharianism? Yes __ No __

Psycho-Spiritual Biographical Questionnaire™ - Full Version (PSBQ) Page 7 of 7

Do you rest the body temple on purpose without being sleepy? Yes__No__

Do you have trouble sleeping? Yes__No__How many hours do you sleep
   on the average? _____

If you have trouble sleeping, check if it is trouble: Falling to sleep____Staying asleep ____
   Both ____

Rate your energy level: Too high ____ High __ Moderate__Low__Extremely Low __

Have you been neglecting your body temple? Yes _No __Somewhat __

If so, how? _____

Do you treat your body temple to massages and sensual pleasures? Yes __ No __

Do you allow your body temple to be sexually gratified? Yes ___ No ___
   Sometimes___ Not often ___

Are you experiencing any sexual issue that interferes with your sexual gratification?
   Yes__ No__

Do you view sex as a sacred act? Yes__ No__

Do you see your coming into the physical realm through the act of sexual union as
   divine? Yes__ No__

Do you think that sexual desire and sexual gratification is only for procreation? Yes __ No __

Were you taught that sexual desire and sexual expression were bad? Yes __ No __

Do you think that souls who come forth and never marry should never experience
   sexual union? Yes __ No __

Would you marry someone you don't really love or don't know well -
   just to have sex? Yes __ No __ I did __

What souls on the planet (living or transitioned) have influenced your sexual beliefs?
   _____

Do you feel free to have your own opinions about this subject and others?
   Yes __ No __ Not this subject __

Does your spirit feel completely free in your body temple?
   Yes __ No __ Not really __ Somewhat __

If not, when do you feel most free?   N/A __   _____

What would it take to feel freer? N/A __   _____

OUTLOOK & SACRETHERAPY® GOALS:
                    (Use additional paper if needed)

This physical life experience would be great if _____

So far, my physical journey has been mostly_____

And the future looks _____

So far, the best thing about me is _____

So far, I'm really talented at _____

If I could, I would go for my dream of manifesting _____

The thing that's stopping me is _____

If I could, my relationships with other souls would be _____

My biggest fear is/and the reason I fear it is because_____

I'm hoping Sacretherapy® will help me to _____

APPENDIX B

Psycho-Spiritual Biographical Questionnaire™ - Radical Version (PSBQ-R)

Copyright© 2007-2014 Amelia B. Kemp, Ph.D., LMHC

(**NOTE:** The PSBQ-R is adapted from the full version of the PSBQ for those individuals interested in starting the Sacretherapy® process in the "here and now" without reviewing the past. Therefore, 99 percent of the mental and emotional historical questions have been removed from this version.

Instructions: The PSBQ-R is designed to be a skeletal summary of your current here and now physical life experience. It should take less than 45 minutes to complete. The questions are mostly "yes or no" responses along with some short answers. The purpose of the "yes or no" is so that you don't attempt to process your answers at this juncture. Processing your experiences will be done systematically throughout the remaining steps in the Sacretherapy® process. Therefore, the PSBQ-R is simply allowing you to offer whatever you believe is currently interfering with the matter. As such, please answer the following questions as succinctly as possible. Some questions in the spiritual section may never have been asked of you before, seeing as the nonphysical spiritual aspects of life often go without query. Please go with your gut on those questions, since they only serve to offer you a broad inventory of possible spiritual experiences that you may have encountered in your physical experience. Remember, this form is for your eyes only (unless sharing with a psychotherapist); so once you have completed the form, don't forget to seal it in an envelope marked "the past" and store it in a place you deem private and sacred. Place answers on separate sheet

Soul's Advent into the Physical Realm

First name your soul uses: _____ Date of PSBQ-R _____
Name of the maternal soul (mother) for your advent into the physical: _____
Name of the paternal soul (father) for your advent into the physical: _____
DOB _____Date of conception: (Count back 9 months or less): _____Age ____

How much sacred time have you had in this physical life experience? Note: Sacred time is divisible by quantum moments/seconds (the smallest physical quantity that can exist, i.e., one hour = 3,600 seconds, one day = 1,440 seconds and one year = 525,600 seconds). How many moments (seconds) have you been creating your life? (Multiply your age x 525,600)_____
How many moments do you estimate have been experiences/manifestations that were ***not*** pleasing? _____
Subtract the unpleasant moments from the total moments of your physical life. (Put total here.)_____

Psycho-Spiritual Biographical Questionnaire™ - Full Version (PSBQ-R) Page 2 of 6

Please check the appropriate box or share the requested information:
Married___ How long ___; Divorced ___ How long ___; Previous marriages?
   Yes __ No __ How many ____
Single ____; Separated ___How long___;   Widowed___ How long ____ ;
   Cohabiting ____ How long ___
Do you live with: Yourself ___ Spouse ___ Lover ___ Parent ___ Children ___
Friend ___ Other___
What part of your *being* do you feel is *most often* out of alignment? Mind __ Body __
   Spirit ___All areas __

What's The Matter? (Share what's **currently** bothering you here.)
_____
_____
_____
_____
_____
_____

SACRETHERAPY® CONNECTIONS & AGREEMENTS
This section will review the **current** quality of your relationships with other souls:

If you are a parent, how many souls have you assisted in coming into the physical realm?_____
Briefly rate your **current** co-creative *sacred connection* with each of them or check n/a if
not applicable:

1. _____N/A___Close_____Just okay ____Poor ___Totally Disengaged ____Transitioned ____
2. _____N/A___Close_____Just okay ____Poor ___Totally Disengaged ____Transitioned ____
3. _____N/A___Close_____Just okay ____Poor ___Totally Disengaged ____Transitioned ____
4. _____N/A___Close_____Just okay ____Poor ___Totally Disengaged ____Transitioned ____
5. _____N/A___Close_____Just okay ____Poor ___Totally Disengaged ____Transitioned ____
                    (If more, please use an additional sheet.)

What other soul-filled beings outside of your parents and/or children hold a major role
as part of your support system, assisting you through this physical experience? (Your
spouse, partner, friends, etc.; top three is sufficient; five is the maximum you would need
to list.) List their first names, role and impact on your life?

	Name	Role	Time invested embracing their presence and the impact they have on you:
1.	_____	_____	_____
2.	_____	_____	_____
3.	_____	_____	_____
4.	_____	_____	_____
5.	_____	_____	_____

Psycho-Spiritual Biographical Questionnaire™ - Full Version (PSBQ-R) Page 3 of 6

MENTAL & EMOTIONAL HISTORY

Are you **currently** diagnosed with a mental or emotional reaction? Yes __ No __
What is the diagnosis(es)? _____
Are you **currently** abusing or dependent on any substance? Yes_____No_____
    If so, age started _____
Which substance(s)? Alcohol __ Marijuana__ Cocaine__ Other_____
Are you **currently** dealing with the consequences of a DUI? N/A___No___Yes___
Are you **currently** in rehab? Yes __ No __ Alcoholics Anonymous ___
    Narcotics Anonymous ___ In-patient ___ Other ___
Are you **currently** incarcerated? Yes__ No__ First offense? Yes __ No __
Why incarcerated? _____
Highest education completed: Left School__ High School__ Associate __ Bachelor's__
    Master's__ Doctorate___
Any current learning differences: Yes __ No __ Do you **currently** feel okay
    about the differences? Yes __No _
Does your **current** level of education allow you to do what you want in the world?
    Yes __ No __
Do you **currently** feel inhibited by your perceived ability to create and manifest what
    you want? Yes __ No __

SPIRITUAL INQUIRY

Do you believe the premise that you are a spiritual being having a physical experience?
    Yes __ No __
Do you believe in a Higher Power? Yes__ No__Undecided___
What do you call your higher power: God__ Creator__ Allah__ Universal Mind __
    Source Energy __ Other ___
Are any religious/spiritual issues causing you guilt, shame, anger or confusion at this time?
    Yes __ No __ NA___
If so, what? _____
Do you see your higher power as a loving source or punishing force? Loving ___
    Punishing ___ Both___ NA___
Do you believe that your higher power is everywhere present (omnipresent)? Yes__No __
Do you believe that your higher power is always with you? Yes__ No__
If so, do you believe that your higher power is inside you? Yes__ No__
Do you call the spiritual part of you your spirit or soul? Yes __ No __
If so, how do you nurture your spirit? _____
How do you communicate with your higher power? _____
How does your higher power communicate with you? _____
Do you declare any specific path/religion? Yes__No__
Do you feel you are on the right path? Yes __ No __ Unsure __
What souls on the planet (living or transitioned) have influenced your spiritual beliefs?
_____

Psycho-Spiritual Biographical Questionnaire™ - Full Version (PSBQ-R) Page 4 of 6

Have you come up with any of your own spiritual beliefs? Yes____ No ____
If not, do you feel that the thoughts linked to the God-source in others are more valid
    than the thoughts linked to the God-source in you? Yes ____ No ____
    Never thought about it ____
Have you wondered why you are here in the world? Yes__ No __
Do you pray? Yes ____ No____   If so, what happens? _____
Do you meditate? Yes ____ No ____ If so, what happens? _____
When you are sad or distressed in any way, how does your spiritual belief/faith help you
    to self-soothe? _____
Do you consider the breath you inhale in and out as sacred and divine?
    Yes __No__Never thought about it ____
Do you intentionally take deep breaths to honor the life force it gives you?
    Yes__ No__ Never thought about it__
Since your breath leaves the body temple when you transition, do you think that it is
    attached to your spirit? Yes __ No__   Never thought about it___
If you identify yourself as a believer, what do you think your spirit came into your
    physical body to experience? _____
What have you created or manifested so far in relation to that purpose or desire?_____
What has been your most pleasing creation yet? _____
What service (vocation) do you offer the world?_____
Do you believe the world is a mostly safe or mostly dangerous place?
    Mostly safe ____ Mostly dangerous ____
Do you believe that there is mostly good or mostly bad in the world?
    Mostly good ____ Mostly bad ____
How good are you about picking up others' vibes (vibrations)?
    Good ____ Not very good ____
Can you feel energy? Yes __ No __
Have you ever felt someone was near you without seeing the person first? Yes __ No __
Do you believe in a "sixth sense"? Yes ____ No ____
If so, do you believe it's attached to your spirit? Yes ____ No ___
Can you see your own aura? Yes __ No __
Can you see the auras of others? Yes __ No __
Have you ever experienced déjà vu? Yes __No __ Not sure __
Ever had any prophetic dreams or known something was going to happen before it
    happened? Yes ____ No _____
If so, would you describe that "knowing" as intuition or clairvoyance? Yes__ No__
Do you consider yourself psychic? Yes __ No __ Why? _____
Do you ever hear music or pleasing sounds (clairaudience) that others don't hear?
    Yes __ No __
When you are awake, do you ever see things that other people can't see, or hear voices
that others can't hear?
    Yes__ No__ Maybe ____
Have you ever seen or been visited by any loved ones that have already transitioned
(died)? Yes__ No__ Possibly__ Not sure, but once or twice I could have sworn…. ____

If so, did the experience scare you? Yes __ No __   A little __ OR did it comfort you?
    Yes __ No __

When something deeply meaningful touches you emotionally what sensation do you feel:
    Goose bumps?__Chills?___Anointing?__Something comes over me?___Tearfulness?__

Does soft music, art, dance, a natural landscape or waterscape, awaken anything within
    you? Yes __ No __

What do you consider sacred in your life? _____

Do you believe in soul mates? Yes __ No __ Don't know __

Do you believe in angels? Yes __ No __

If so, has anyone ever appeared in your life that you felt was an angel? Yes__No__N/A __

Do you believe in spirit guides, mediums or channels? Yes __ No __

Have you ever had an outer body experience (astroplaning)? Yes__ No__

If yes, did it add confirmation to your spiritual beliefs or change them in
    any way? Yes __ No __

Ever had a near death experience? Yes ___ No___ If yes, did anything spiritual
    happen? Yes __ No __ N/A __

If so, what happened? _____

Have you had a spiritual healing? Yes __ No ___ What happened? _____

Have you ever experienced a miracle? Yes __ No __ What happened? _____

Do you think that when your body ends, that it's the end of you? Yes__No__Don't know__

Do you believe in past lives or reincarnation? Yes __ No __

Where do you think you will go when you shed your body temple?
    Heaven__Hell__No where __ Don't know__ Never thought about it __

What do you hope will happen when you shed your body temple? _____
_____

BODY TEMPLE

Do you have any physical manifestations that are troubling your body temple now?
    Yes __ No __

If so, what part (s) of your body temple troubles you? _____

If it's possible that we choose our body temple, why do you think you may have chosen
    your particular one?_____

Are you pleased with your body temple? Yes ___No___If not, why not? _____

What do you do to exercise the body temple? _____

What foods and beverages do you feed your body temple? Healthy foods___
    Junk foods___Mixture _____

How's your appetite? Normal _____ Poor_____ Over-eating_____
    Binge and purge _____ Binge only _____

Do you believe in or practice fasting? Yes __ No__

Do you believe in or practice breatharianism? Yes __ No __

Are you dieting? Yes __No __Feel good about your weight? Yes __ No __

Do you enjoy taking your divine time to cleanse and/or soak your body temple? Yes __No__

Do you rest the body temple on purpose without being sleepy? Yes__No__

Psycho-Spiritual Biographical Questionnaire™ - Full Version (PSBQ-R) Page 6 of 6

Do you have trouble sleeping? Yes__No__How many hours do you sleep
  on the average? _____
If you have trouble sleeping, check if it is trouble: Falling to sleep___Staying asleep ___
  Both ___
Rate your energy level: Too high ___ High __ Moderate__Low__Extremely Low __
Have you been neglecting your body temple? Yes _No __Somewhat __
  If so, how? _____

Do you treat your body temple to massages and sensual pleasures? Yes __ No __
Do you allow your body temple to be sexually gratified? Yes ___ No ___
  Sometimes___ Not often ___
Are you experiencing any sexual issue that interferes with your sexual gratification?
  Yes__ No__
Do you view sex as a sacred act? Yes__ No__
Do you see your coming into the physical realm through the act of sexual union as
  divine? Yes__ No__
Do you think that sexual desire and sexual gratification is only for procreation? Yes __ No __
Were you taught that sexual desire and sexual expression were bad? Yes __ No __
Do you think that souls who come forth and never marry should never experience
  sexual union? Yes __ No __
Would you marry someone you don't really love or don't know well -
  just to have sex? Yes __ No __ I did __
What souls on the planet (living or transitioned) have influenced your sexual beliefs?
  _____
Do you feel free to have your own opinions about this subject and others?
  Yes __ No __ Not this subject __
Does your spirit feel completely free in your body temple?
  Yes __ No __ Not really __ Somewhat __
If not, when do you feel most free?   N/A __   _____
What would it take to feel freer? N/A __   _____

OUTLOOK & SACRETHERAPY® GOALS:
(Use additional paper if needed)

This physical life experience would be great if _____
So far, my physical journey has been mostly_____
And the future looks _____
So far, the best thing about me is _____
So far, I'm really talented at _____
If I could, I would go for my dream of manifesting _____
The thing that's stopping me is _____
If I could, my relationships with other souls would be _____
My biggest fear is/and the reason I fear it is because_____
I'm hoping Sacretherapy® will help me to _____

APPENDIX C

Energy Field Form

Amelia Kemp - Certified Reiki Practitioner©2013

Instructions:
Highlight Areas
With Energy
Blockages

Indicate Location:
R = Right
L = Left

Client Name:_____

Date of Scan/TX_____

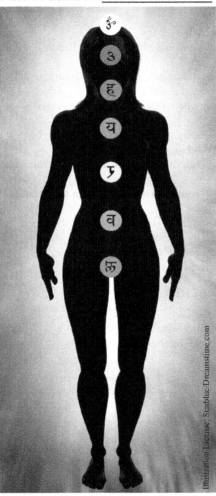

Crown Chakra
Brow Chakra
Throat Chakra

Heart
Chakra

Solar Plexus
Chakra

Sacral Chakra
Spinal/Root
Chakra

NOTES

_____
_____
_____
_____
_____

Head
Eyes
Ear/Nose
Throat/Neck
Back
Shoulders
Arms/Hands
Chest/Breast
Heart
Stomach
Intestines

Genitalia/Hips
Thighs
Legs

Knees
Joints
Ankles
Feet
Toes

Illustration License: Starblue/Dreamstime.com

APPENDIX D

Pre-Letter Template
*(Complete with **Sacred Rage** exercise in Step Four—Chapter Five)*

Instructions: Here you share your **perception** of exactly what happened and why you felt it was wrong. Using this outline for each paragraph may help you, but it is only a suggestion. The purpose of the outline is to structure your outpouring in a way that will be more in alignment with clearing and articulating your perspective versus "just venting," since venting just vents and doesn't transform. So please proceed, trusting that the toxic *energy* you are about to release will be another step towards healing and assisting you with coming back into alignment.

NOTE: Once completed, remember to have your letter witnessed. Then seal it in your envelope marked "The Past."

PARAGRAPH ONE—Share your "**perception**" of the *matter.*

Definition: Perception is the understanding one gathers through one's subjective sensory awareness of what one observes, experiences, or takes in.

Example: "When 'such and such' occurred, I perceived that I was being violated or abandoned."
(In the example, you are speaking from your own perception, which takes into account that you acknowledge that another's perception could, in fact, be different.)

PARAGRAPH TWO—Share your "**feelings**" about the *matter.*

Definition: Feelings are generally considered an emotional state or disposition.

Example: *"Therefore, I felt hurt and angry."*
(In the example, you are sharing emotions that describe "your feelings." At the same time, you are acknowledging the fact that these are feelings "you felt" versus saying that someone "made you feel" a certain way.)

PARAGRAPH THREE—Share the "**meaning**" you attached to the *matter.*

Definition: The meaning is the thoughts you have about what you perceived (in paragraph one) and where you attach your interpretation of the *matter* or conclusion as it relates to what someone's words or actions meant to you.

Example: *"What I assumed was meant by what was said or done was that I was not worthy of being loved and respected."*
(In the example, you are clearly acknowledging that you are the one that attached your own meaning to other people's words and/or behavior, and that their intent could be different.)

PARAGRAPH FOUR—Share what your **"preferences"** were at the time.

Definition: *Preferences* are what you want or wish had happened at the time. Sometimes, preferences are mistaken as a "have to" or mandatory, when in fact they are just what you would have preferred. So it's okay to express what you felt you needed at the time, understanding that it was simply what you would have preferred.

Example: *"What I would have preferred was to have been offered softer and kinder words of praise and affection.* (In the example, you are sharing what you wanted or needed, and at the same time you are acknowledging the fact that it was your particular preference and that you had a right to have wanted something different.)

APPENDIX E

Post-Letter Template
(Complete with the final Clearing exercise in Step Five—Chapter Six)

Instructions: Here you write a new letter about the *matter*. This one, however, is only to your Higher Power, which is the God-source within the universe. Here you share what you have learned from your broader perspective and higher vibration. This letter articulates your new insight, compassion, and ability to forgive any and all co-creators, including yourself, for the *matter* that manifested.

NOTE: Once completed, remember to have your letter witnessed. Then seal it in your container marked "The Past."

PARAGRAPH ONE—Share your "new perception" of the *matter*.

Remember: Perception is the understanding one gathers through one's subjective sensory awareness of what one observes, experiences, or takes in.

Example: "After having given the *matter* more thought and acquired a broader perspective, I now sense that what happened had more to do with…."

PARAGRAPH TWO—Share your "new feelings" about the *matter*.

Remember: Feelings are generally considered an emotional state or disposition.

Example: "Therefore, I now feel much better knowing that I am as good as I originally thought I was, and so…."

PARAGRAPH THREE—Offer your "new and broader interpretation" of the *matter*.

Remember: The meaning is the thoughts you have about what you perceived (in paragraph one) and where you attach your interpretation of the *matter* or conclusion as it relates to what another's words or actions now mean to you.

Example: "I now understand that my worth and value comes from within and…."

PARAGRAPH FOUR—Share what you "now prefer."

Remember: Preferences in this context are what you want or wish will happen. Sometimes, preferences are mistaken as a "have to" or mandatory, when in fact they are just what you prefer happens.

Example: "What I now desire is for me to remain cognizant of my own ability to self-soothe…."

GLOSSARY OF METAPHYSICAL TERMS

NOTE: The following definitions of terms are based on the author's metaphysical training and understanding of how the terms relate specifically to Sacretherapy®. Therefore, for a more comprehensive understanding of any specific term, it is recommended that books or encyclopedias in the field of metaphysics be obtained.

Akashic Records—A universal library that is said to contain all knowledge, i.e., thoughts, words and deeds, similar to the ancient Book of Life. Term was popularized by the Theosophy Society in the early 1900s but was borrowed from ancient Esoteric and Hindu philosophies.

Alignment—A preferred balance between mind, body and spirit, where one has greatest access to the highest vibrational frequencies of well-being.

Biofeedback—A brain imaging device that shows the biological impact of thoughts and feelings on the body temple; used with the goal of understanding one's ability to affect physiological changes at the level of thought in conjunction with relaxation exercises.

Chakras—Portals or vortices within the body temple that send and receive prana or life force between the subtle body and physical body. The number of chakras can generally range from seven to twelve depending on the cultural model.

Divine Intention—is an intention that the soul comes into the physical realm with and, therefore, the *matter* is a manifestation that has been divinely molded the way it is. A soul may chose to live part or all of its physical experience in this way for its own expansion.

Divine Sight—The ultimate use of the five senses along with awareness and use of the sixth sense, which is one's *inner knowing* or divine mind.

Energy—The core of every particle in the universe including one's body temple is subtle *energy*, which is an amount of heat, light, radiation or power being released or absorbed as life force or vital essence. Thus, the *energy* basis of anything is its divine essence or life force.

Energy Medicine—Interventions that work in concert with one's divine essence or life force, clearing *energy* blockages that interfere with one's vitality, electro-magnetic power and overall well-being; also referred to as vibrational healing. (See Reiki or Prana Healing.)

Herbal Remedies—A botanical offering or mixture of natural compounds from which the medicinal properties have been extracted and used to promote one's natural well-being.

Law of Attraction—A universal law that states that dominant attention to a *matter* will bring it into manifestation. In other words "like attracts like." If you give a great deal of attention to something, "what you think about, you will bring about" becomes a self-fulfilling prophecy.

Matter—A substance that is solid, liquid or gas depending on the density of the *energy* and frequency. *Solid matter* vibrates much slower than *subtle matter,* which vibrates much faster. The faster the *energy* within the *matter*, the lighter it becomes; and the lighter it becomes, the more difficult it is to see. One's thoughts are also a form of *matter*—a gas, if you will, which is light and subtle (invisible). This is why thoughts are also called *subtle matter* or *subtle energy.*

Meme—A unit of thought (belief) that is transferred into one's mind often without conscious awareness or one's intention.

Metaphysics—A traditional branch of philosophy with three focuses: *ontology, universal science* and ***natural theology.*** The latter is the focus of Sacretherapy®— which is concerned with explaining the fundamental nature of being and the world at the level of quantum physics (beyond the physical), at the level of divine energy and consciousness.

Metaphysician—A philosopher concerned with explaining the nature of beingness at the level of energy and subtle *matter* from a *natural theology* (study of God or the divine) perspective; where quantum physics and consciousness are examined at the level of thought, which is the nucleus of the creation process. Metaphysicians look into the energy basis of one's mental health and well-being is at the level of thought, where one ultimately creates one's health or dis-ease.

Misaligned Thought—is a thought that is not in sync or is incongruent with the fullness of your being, which includes your mind, body and spirit. Therefore, the *matter* manifested this way due to an unconscious and unintentional clash or inconsistency between the three.

Naturopathic Doctors and Practitioners—Healing professionals who encompass an understanding of the delicate balance between mind, body and spirit. They offer natural and holistic remedies extracted from mother earth and/or the divine that honor the natural creative and regenerative process of life at the level of energy, prana or chi (qi).

Prana—One's life force or vital energy; also called qi, chi or wind.

Prana Healing—Aka Pranic healing, which is a form of energy medicine that focuses on one's breath of life (where prana enters). It is co-creative in that the practitioner becomes a vessel using his or her own subtle body to invoke the sum total of all energy in the universe and transfer the divine energy to the etheric layer of another's subtle body. The aim is to fortify the vital energy and clear energy blockages that have manifested in the other's body temple (chakras) as stress or dis-ease. (See Reiki and Energy Medicine.)

Quantum Medicine—uses quantum physics to research how the human body is controlled and regulated by the human *energy* system in order to treat and prevent dis-ease.

Quantum Physics—Deals with discrete, indivisible units of energy called "quanta," the smallest increment of matter (atoms) that can be subdivided. This overlaps metaphysics in that metaphysics also views the world beyond the physical and focuses on the matter/energy basis of all existence.

Reiki—A form of energy medicine that is sometimes referred to as "the laying on of hands." However, the hands of the practitioner don't usually touch the body temple and instead work within the subtle layer or lightly touch the body. Like Prana healing, Reiki is also co-creative in that the practitioner becomes a vessel using his or her own subtle body to invoke and transfer the divine energy of the God-source to the etheric layer of another's subtle body. The aim is to fortify the vital energy of the other and clear energy blockages that have manifested in the other's body temple (chakras) as stress or dis-ease. (See Prana Healing and Energy Medicine.)

Reaction versus Disorder—A **reaction** according to most dictionaries is "a response to some stimuli, situation or treatment." The operative word, then, is "response" in that it is a reaction to something. This suggests that the matter may be a temporary manifestation and/or can be neutralized and realigned with the right antidote. On the other hand, a **disorder** is said to be a derangement or abnormality of function, "a morbid physical or mental state," which suggests that the manifestation did not manifest correctly. This interpretation is not in agreement with universal principals surrounding the law of creation.

Sacretherapy®—A holistic therapeutic modality created to treat mental and emotional issues; it includes psychotherapy or counseling. Yet, *Sacretherapy* is more comprehensive in that it involves a sacred process of aligning one's mind, body and spirit. The goal is to allow the whole or holiness of one's being to inform and clarify the soul's sacred intention that it is divinely unfolding in this physical experience.

Self-Fulfilling Prophecy—An expectation based on a strong or inherent belief or thought that causes itself to become true. This is due to the "law of attraction" that matches one's dominant thoughts to what manifests in the physical world.

Subtle Body—The core energy or life force of a living organism at the quantum physics level that transcends the body temple and can be seen as light or an aura with instruments or clairvoyance. It is often referred to as the spiritual faculty, light body, subtle matter, energy field, energy body, soul, spirit or atman that interacts with the physical body and nonphysical dimensions.

Subtle Emotional Body—The portion of the "subtle light body" that interacts with the "subtle mental body" so that when one thinks a thought, emotions are triggered to offer a positive or negative feeling as a form of guidance from spirit. The emotional guidance according to esoteric traditions, metaphysicians and channels is said to be offered to indicate the degree of one's alignment with the subtle mental body, the body temple, and the divine.

Subtle Mental Body—The portion of the subtle light body that is the source of consciousness and subconscious beingness within the collective psyche, which is connected to universal mind and corresponds with the mental processes within one's physical brain.

Symbolic Meaning –The ability to see what a diagnosis symbolizes at a deeper level, beyond just the description of symptoms, as it relates to Sacretherapy®. It incorporates the use of intuition, which is in the spiritual realm of the nonphysical. It asks us to discern what we intuitively extract from the *matter*.

Tai Chi—There are a variety of Tai Chi styles, but what is consistent among each is the divine execution of deliberate slow movements and artistic disciplined postures that allow the life force (chi) within one's body temple to circulate and fortify the inherent wellness within. Thus, as a therapeutic modality and/or physical exercise it triggers the release of the natural healing endorphins in the brain. This offers a sense of mental and emotional well-being.

Vibration—A particle (neuron or photon) that continues to move its position—it is *energy* or *matter* in motion, It can often be viscerally felt as a vibe (meaning vibration), although what is actually being felt is the energy or matter that is vibrating at a certain frequency. The fact that the *matter* is constantly in motion and changing positions illustrates that the energy or *matter* that manifests in anyone's life is not static or permanent and, therefore, can be changed or elevated to a higher frequency.

Yoga—There is a variety of yoga styles; but what is consistent among each is the divine integration of practices that stimulate and support the mind, body and spirit with emphasis on the breath of life through meditation, body postures and movements. Thus, as a therapeutic modality and/or physical exercise, yoga triggers the release of the natural healing endorphins in the brain. This offers a sense of mental and emotional well-being.

HOLISTIC AND ALTERNATIVE HEALING RESOURCES

**(The following 8 Pages of Resources Are For Your Healing and Aligning Pleasure.
See Traditional Mental Health Resources following the Holistic Sources)**

A Certified Sacretherapy® Practitioner Locator
United States and Worldwide Listings
P.O. Box 13964, Tallahassee, FL 32317
Website: Sacretherapy.com
or DrAmeliaKemp.com

A Therapist Referral Service
(Some holistic practitioners listed)
Psychology Today Magazine Referral Website
(Listings throughout United States and Canada)
PH: (212) 260 7210
Website: therapists.psychologytoday.com

American Holistic Health Association
Referral Listing of Holistic Healers
Website: www.ahha.org/ahhasearch.asp

National Center for Complementary and Alternative Medicine
(NCCAM)
31 Center Drive, MSC 2182
Building 31, Room 2B-11, Bethesda, MD 20892-2182
PH: 301-496-4000
Website: www.nccam.nih.gov

HOLISTIC AND SPIRITUALLY EMPOWERING
Movies & Videos
(Outside the box)

The Secret (DVD)
Website: www.thesecrettv.com

The Shift (Movie)
Website: www.drwaynedyer.com

What the Bleep Do We Know (DVD)
Website: www.whatthebleep.com

You Can Heal Your Life (DVD)
Website: www.healyourlife.com

The Celestine Prophecies (Movie)
Website: www.celestineprophecies.com

Out On a Limb (Movie)
Website: www.shirleymaclaine.com

Defending Your Life (Movie)
Website: www.amazon.com

Avatar (Movie)
Website: www.avatar.com

Cloud Atlas (Movie)
Website: www.amazon.com

The Spiritual Cinema Circle
(Movies/DVDs)
Website: www.spiritualcinemacircle.com

(For Holistic and Alternative Books, See Bibliography)

RELAXATION AND MEDITATION
Modalities / CDs / Audiotapes

Breathe the Breath of Life™ Relaxation and Meditation CD
by Amelia Kemp, Ph.D., LMHC
Website: DrAmeliaKemp.com

Getting into the Vortex® Guided Meditation CD
Teachings of Abraham by Esther & Jerry Hicks
Website: abraham-hicks.com

Songs of Affirmation — I Love and Accept Myself Meditations
by Louise Hay and Joshua Leeds
Website: hayhouse.com

Meditations and Celebrations
by John Bradshaw and Stephen Halpren
Website: www.johnbradshaw.com

The Center for Mindfulness
University of Massachusetts (Worldwide Practitioner Locator)
Website: http://w3.umassmed.edu/MBSR/public/SearchMember.aspx

───────── ✿ ─────────

ENERGY MEDICINE – YOGA – TAI CHI – TAPPING – AURA
(Also Check Local Listings)

International Association of Reiki Professionals
Website: www.iarp.org (Find a Reiki practitioner)

Reiki Healing Institute (Do It Yourself Workbook)
Website: http://reikihealinginstitute.org/book.html

International Listing of Prana Healers
Global Pranic Healing Institute for Inner Studies
Website: globalpranichealing.com

American Tai Chi and Qigong Association
Website: www.americantaichi.org

International Tai Chi Association
5 Side Road Mono, Ontario L9W 6L2, Canada
Website: www.taoist.org 248305

American Yoga Association
Website: americanyogaassociation.org

International Yoga Association
343 Soquel Ave Ste 201
Santa Cruz, CA 95062
Website: www.internationalassociation.com

Kundalini Global Associations
Website: http://www.ikyta.org/global-associations

Tapping by Dr. Roger Callahan (Original Founder)
Thought Field Therapy
Website: rogercallahan.com

Tapping by Roger Craig
Emotional Freedom Technique
Website: emofree.com

Aura Reading For Beginners by Richard Webster
Website: http://www.richardwebster.co.nz

How To See and Read the Aura by Ted Andrews
Website: http://www.amazon.com

MUSIC THERAPY AND SOUND HEALING

American Music Therapy Association
(Offers listing of music therapists)
Colesville Road, Suite 1000 Silver Spring MD 20910
PH: 301.589.3300 8455
Website: www.musictherapy.org

The Sound Healing Network
(Offers an international directory of sound healers)
Website: www.soundhealingnetwork.org

Center for Neuroacoustic Research
Website: www.neuroacoustic.com

World Drumming Association
Website: http://worlddrummingassociation.yolasite.com/

New Earth Records
Background Music – *Devotion* from the CD: *Beyond*
(Used throughout the writing of Sacretherapy®)Website:
www.newearthrecords.com

Songs and Poetic Exaltation
Sung by Author, Dr. Amelia Kemp
(Music Therapy)
Website: www.DrAmeliaKemp.com or www.Sacretherapy.com

———— ✣ ————

WORKSHOPS, LECTURE SERIES and CLASSES
(Holistic Healing)

Art of Allowing Workshops
The Teachings of Abraham with Esther Hicks
Website: www.Abraham-Hicks.com

Caroline Myss Education Institute Online Classes
Website: www.myss.com

Hay House You Can Heal Your Life Workshops
With Louise Hay and authors of Hay House
Website: www.hayhouse.com

Inner Visions Spiritual Development Workshops
With Iyanla Vanzant
Website: www.innervisionsworldwide.com

A Course in Miracles Lectures and Online Classes
with Marianne Williamson
Website: www.marianne.com

From Psychotherapy to Sacretherapy® Lecture Series/Workshops
With Amelia Kemp, Ph.D., LMHC
(10 City International Book & Lecture Tour)
Website: www.DrAmeliaKemp.com or www.Sacretherapy.com

Sounds True Annual Workshops and Festival
Website: www.soundstrue.com

Oprah's Life Class (Oprah Winfrey Network TV)
Website: www.oprah.com

Certified Sacretherapy® Providers Trainings
(CEU available for Mental Health professionals and Clergy)
Website: www.DrAmeliaKemp.com or www.Sacretherapy.com

The Soulful Living Exchange (Online Mastermind Network)
Join Dr. Kemp twice a month for direct support.
Website: www.DrAmeliaKemp.com or www.Sacretherapy.com

RETREATS
(Holistic Healing)

Deepak Chopra Center for Well-being
2013 Costa Del Mar Road, Carlsbad, CA 92009
PH: (888) 736-6895
Website: www.chopra.com

The Hippocrates Health Institute
1443 Palmdale Court, West Palm Beach, FL 33411
PH: 561-471-5867
Website: www.hippocratesinst.org

Omega Institute for Holistic Studies
150 Lake Drive, Rhinebeck, NY 12572
PH: (877) 944-2002
Website: www.Eomega.org

Optimum Health Institute
6970 Central Avenue, Lemon Grove, CA 91945
PH: (800) 993-4325
Website: www.optimumhealth.org

Women's SpiritNme™ Annual Mountain & Sacretherapy® Retreats
Mind-Body-SpiritNme Counseling Center & Retreats
Killearn Court, Building A, Tallahassee, FL 32309
PH: (850) 297-0500 3841
Website: www.DrAmeliaKemp.com

TRADITIONAL MENTAL HEALTH RESOURCES

Alcoholics Anonymous (National Headquarters
P.O. Box 459, New York, NY 10163
PH: (212) 870-3400
Website: www.aa.org

Al-Anon/Alateen Family Support Group (Headquarters)
1600 Corporate Landing Parkway, Virginia Beach, VA
PH: (888) 425-2666
Website: www.al-anon.alateen.org

First Call for Help(Hotline and Referral Resource Nationwide)
Sponsored by The United Way
PH: Dial 211 (In most US cities)
Website: www.211.org

National Alliance on Mental Illness (NAMI)
2107 Wilson Boulevard. Ste. 300 Arlington, VA 22201
PH: (800) 950-6264
Website: www.nami.org

National Domestic Violence Hotline
PO Box 161810, Austin, Texas 78716
PH: (800) 799-SAFE (7233)
Website: www.thehotline.org

National Institute of Mental Health (NIMH)
6001 Executive Blvd., Bethesda, MD 20892
PH: (866) 615-6464
Website: www.nimh.gov

Narcotics Anonymous (National Headquarters)
P.O. Box 9999, Van Nuys, CA 91409
PH: (818) 773-9999
Website: www.na.org

National Sexual Assault Hotline (Rape/Abuse/Incest)
1220 L Street NW, Suite 505, Washington, DC 20005
PH: (800) 656-HOPE (4673)
Website: www.rainn.org

National SUICIDE Prevention Lifeline
Funded by SAMHSA – Administered by MHA of New York
PH: (800) 273-TALK (8255)
Website: suicidepreventionlifeline.org

OTHER WORKS & RESOURCES BY THE AUTHOR

Amelia Kemp, Ph.D., LMHC - Official Websites:
www.DrAmeliaKemp.com or www.Sacretherapy.com

Certified Sacretherapy® Practitioner Trainings
(For Mental Health Professionals and Clergy)
Visit Website

The Soulful Living Exchange (Aftercare)
Bi-weekly Online Mastermind Support with Dr. Kemp
Pre-requisite: Must have completed first seven Sacretherapy Steps
Visit Website

From Psychotherapy to Sacretherapy® Radio Show (Weekly)
blogtalkradio.com/DrAmeliaKemp
Visit Website for schedule

Encore podcasts from the weekly on-air show (Daily)
From Psychotherapy to Sacretherapy® with Dr. Amelia Kemp
Visit Website

Sacretherapy® Mountain Retreats
Visit Website

Breathe the Breath of Life Relaxation and Meditation™ CDs
Visit Website

Sacretherapy® Newsletter (Free)
Visit Website

Songs and Poetic Exaltation – Sung by Author (Music Therapy)
Visit Website

Sacretherapy® Spiritual Bill of Rights Scroll (Free)
Visit Website

Follow Dr. Kemp on
Facebook, Twitter, LinkedIn, Blog at Word Press, Youtube

BIBLIOGRAPHY

American Psychiatric Association, *Diagnostic and Statistical Manual of Mental Disorders – Edition 5,* American Psychiatric Publishers, Washington, D.C., 2013.

APA Monitor, Volume 43, No. 6, Smith, Brendan L., *"Inappropriate Prescribing,"* American Psychological Association, Washington, D.C., June 2012.

Arntz, William, Chasse, Betsy, Hoffman, Matthew, *What the Bleep Do We Know,* Lord of the Wind Films, Twentieth Century Fox, Beverly Hills, CA 2004.

Asante, Molefi K., *The Egyptian Philosophers, African American Images*, Chicago, 2000.

Asante, Molefi K. and Ama Mazama, (eds.) Egypt, *Greece, and the American Academy,* AA Images, Chicago, 2002.

Atkinson, William, *Thought Vibrations or The Law of Attraction in the Thought World,* Kessinger Publishing, Whitefish, Montana, 1906.

Bandler, Richard and Grinder, John, *Neuro-linguistic Programming and Transformation of Meaning, Real People Press*, Moab, Utah, 1982.

Bendit, Lawrence and Pheobe, *The Etheric Body of Man—The Bridge of Consciousness,* The Theosophical Publishing House, Wheaton, Illinois, 1977.

Booth, Leo, *When God Becomes a Drug,* Jeremy P. Tarcher, Inc., New York, 1991.

Bradshaw, John, *Creating Love*, Random House, New York, 1992.

Brodie, Richard, *Virus of the Mind, The New Science of the Meme*, Hay House, Carlsbad, CA, 1996.

Brooks, Albert, *Defending Your Life*, Geffen Pictures, Burbank, CA, 1991.

Burns, David, *Feeling Good,* Penguin Group, New York, 1981.

Byrne, Rhonda, *The Secret DVD*, TS Production LLC, Stockholm, Sweden, 2005.

Cady, Emily, *Lessons in Truth*, Unity Church, Unity Village, Missouri, 1896.

Callahan, Roger, *Tapping the Healer Within: Using Thought-Field Therapy to Instantly Conquer Your Fears, Anxieties, and Emotional Distress*, McGraw Hill, New York, 2002.

Cameron, James, Avatar, Twentieth Century Fox, Beverly Hills, CA, 2009.

Daishonin, Nichiren, *The Writings of Nichiren Daishonin ("Winter Always Turns to Spring")*, Soka Gakkai International, Santa Monica, CA, Reprinted in USA, 1975.

Dale, Cyndi, *The Subtle Body-An Encyclopedia of Your Energetic Anatomy,* Sounds True, Inc., 2009.

Dawkins, Richard, *The Selfish Gene,* Oxford University Press, New York, 1976.

Dyer, Wayne, *The Shift*, Hay House, Carlsbad, CA, 2009.

Einstein, Albert and Infeld, Leopold, *The Evolution of Physics: The Growth of Ideas from the Early Concepts to Relativity and Quanta,* Volume 14, Issue 54, Cambridge University Press, 1938.

Einstein, Albert, *"Does the Inertia of a Body Depend Upon Its Energy Content?",* Annalen der Physik 18 (13): 639–641, 1905.

Ellis, Albert, *Rational Emotive Behavior Therapy: It Works for Me—It Can Work for You,* Prometheus Books, New York, 2004.

Estes, Clarissa Pinkola, *Women Who Run With the Wolves,* Ballantine Books, New York, 1992.

Ferguson, Don, *The Lion King,* Walt Disney, Burbank, CA, 1994.

Freud, Sigmund, *The Ego and the Id,* W. W. Norton & Company, New York, 1923.

Gabran, Kahil, *The Prophet,* Alfred A. Knopf, New York, 1923.

Gibson, Barbara, *The Complete Guide to Understanding and Using NLP,* Atlantic Publishing Group, Inc., Ocala, FL, 2011.

Glasser, William, *Reality Therapy,* Harper Collins, New York, 1975.

Gawain, Shakti, *Creative Visualization,* Bantam Books, New York, 1978.

Hay, Louise and Leeds, Joshua*, Songs of Affirmation* Audiotape, Hay House, Carlsbad, CA, 1986.

Hay, Louise, *You Can Heal Your Body,* Hay House, Carlsbad, CA, 1976.

Hay, Louise, *You Can Heal Your Life,* Hay House, Carlsbad, CA, 1984.

Hicks, Esther and Jerry, *Ask and It Is Given (Teachings of Abraham),* Hay House, Carlsbad, California, 2004.

Hicks, Esther and Jerry, *The Law of Attraction (Teachings of Abraham),* Hay House, Carlsbad, California, 2006.

Hill, Napoleon, *Think and Grow Rich* (Originally Published in 1937), Aventine Press, Chula Vista, CA, 2004.

Holy Bible, *Genesis 1:26, Matthew 5:12, Matthew 7:7, Luke 4:23, and Exodus 20:1-17,* African Heritage Edition, The James C. Winston Publishing Company, Nashville, TN, 1993.

Hunt, Valerie, *Infinite Mind—Science of Human Vibrations of Consciousness,* Malibu Publishing Company, Malibu, CA, 1996.

Hunt, Valerie, *The Human Energy Field and Health,* Malibu Publishing Company, Malibu, CA, 1997.

Leadbeater, Charles, *Man Visible and Invisible: Examples of Different Types of Man as Seen by Means of Trained Clairvoyance,* (Published 1903), Reprinted by General Books, Memphis TN, 2010.

Maslow, Abraham, *Motivation and Personality,* Harper and Row, New York, 1954.

Merton, Robert, *The Self-fulfilling Prophecy, The Antioch Review,* Vol. 8, No. 2, Yellow Springs, Ohio, 1948.

Mitchell, David, *Cloud Atlas,* ARD Degeto Films and A Company Productions, Frankfurt, Germany, 2012.

Moore, Thomas, *"Dark Nights of the Soul—A Guide to Finding Your Way Through Life's Ordeals*, Penguin Books, New York, 2005.

Moreno, Jacob, *Who Shall Survive? Foundations of Sociometry, Group Psychotherapy and Sociodrama,* Beacon House, New York, 1934, 1977.

Moss, Thelma, *The Body Electric,* Jeremy P. Tarcher Inc., New York, 1979.

Myss, Carolyn, *The Anatomy of Spirit,* Random House, New York, 1996.

Myss, Carolyn, *Sacred Contracts Awakening Your Divine Potential*, Three Rivers Press, New York, 2003.

Panchadasi, Swami, *The Human Aura: Astral Colors and Thought Forms,* Advanced Thought Publishing Company, Chicago, Illinois, 1918.

Pavlov, Ivan, *Conditioned Reflexes*, International Publisher Co., Inc., New York, 1928.

Ponder, Catherine, *The Dynamic Laws of Healing,* Devorss & Company, Marina Del Ray, California, 1985.

Redfield, James, *The Celestine Prophecy*, Celestine Films/Sony Pictures, Hollywood, CA, 2005.

Seigal, Bernie, *Love, Medicine, & Miracles*, Harper-Collins, New York, 1991.

Shak-Dagsay, Dechen; Regula Curti, and Pit Loew, Devotion CD on the Soundtrack: *Beyond*, New Earth Records, Inc., Santa Fe, Mexico, 2010.

Skinner, B. F., *Science and Human Behavior,* Free Press, New York, 1965.

Smith, Brendan L., *"Inappropriate Prescribing,"* APA Monitor, Volume 43, No. 6, June 2012.

Steiner, Rudolph, *The Fifth Gospel: From the Akashic Record* (1913, 1914), Republished by Spiritual Science Library, Ann Arbor, MI, 1995.

Teilhard de Chardin, Pierre, *The Phenomenon of Man*, (1st Published 1955) Harper Perennial, New York, 2008.

Tolle, Eckhart, *The Power of Now – A Guide to Spiritual Enlightenment*, Namaste Publishing, Vancouver, Canada, 1997.

Troward, Thomas, *Edinburg Lectures on Mental Science* (1904), Republished by Kessinger Publishing, Whitefish, Montana, 1999.

United States Congress, *The U.S. Constitution,* Congress, Philadelphia, PA, 1787.

Vanzant, Iyanla, *One Day My Soul Just Opened Up,* Simon & Schuster, New York, 1998.

Vanzant, Iyanla, Oprah Winfrey Show, Harpo Productions, Chicago, Illinois, 1998.

Virtue, Doreen, *Archangels and Ascended Masters*, Hay House, Carlsbad, CA, 2004.

Waitley, Dennis, *The Psychology of Winning*, Penguin Group, New York, 1986.

Walsh, Neal Donald, *Conversations with God*, G.P. Putnam, New York, 1996.

Webster, Noah and G.C. *Merriam Co., Merriam–Webster Dictionary*, G.C. Merriam Co., Springfield, Massachusetts, 2003.

Williamson, Marianne, *Being In Light*, Hay House, Carlsbad, CA, 2003.

Williamson, Marianne, *A Return to Love, Reflections on the Principles of "A Course in Miracles,"* Harper Paperbacks, New York, 1996.

Winfrey, Oprah, *The Oprah Winfrey Show,* Harpo Productions, Chicago, IL, 2002.

World Health Organization, *International Classification of Diseases* (ICD-10), WHO, Geneva, Switzerland, 2010.

WEBSITES

American Drumming Association–
http://worlddrummingassociation.yolasite.com/, May 2013

American Holistic Health Association–www.ahha.org August 2013

American Music Therapy Association–www.amta.org, August 2012

Ascended Masters–http://www.iamuniversity.org/shop/categories/Ascended-Master-
Training-Courses/, August 2012

Association for Neuro-Linguistic Programming–http://www.anlp.org/,
August 2011

And International Association for Linguistic Programming–
http://www.ia-nlp.org/, August 2011

Center for Acoustic Research–www.neuroacoustic.com, Dec. 2012

Center for Disease Control (CDC)–www.cdc.gov/mentalhealth/basics/mental-illness.
htm, May 2012

Craig, Gary, Emotional Freedom Technique (EFT)–
garythinks.com, October 2012

Drug and Therapeutic Bulletin, Survey on Herbal Medicines (2010) http://dtb.bmj.com/
site/about/DTB_survey_on_herbal_medicines.pdf, March 2012

Ortner, Nick, The Tapping Solution–
http://www.thetappingsolution.com/, October 2012

Imhotep Biography–
http://www.notablebiographies.com/Ho-Jo/Imhotep.html, December 2012

Egyptian and Greek Philosophers–http://history.howstuffworks.com/history-vs-myth/
greek-philosophers-african-tribes1.htm, Dec. 2012

Encyclopedia Online–http://www.britannica.com/search?query=depression, May 2013

Hicks, Esther & Jerry, *An Introduction to The Teachings of Abraham*,
www.abraham-hicks.com, June 2006

Mental Health Dictionary–
http://www.stars21.com/health/mental_health_dictionary.html, May 2012

Mental Help.Net–http://www.mentalhelp.net/, April 2012

Merriam-Webster Dictionary Online–
http://www.merriam-webster.com/, May 2012

National Institute for Mental Health (Topics)–
www.nimh.nih.gov/health/topics/, June 2012

National Center for Complementary and Alternative Medicine; Robinson A, McGrail
MR. Disclosure of CAM Use to Medical Practitioners: A Review of Qualitative and
Quantitative Studies (2004) http://www.ncbi.nlm.nih.gov/pubmed/15561518, March 2012

Prana Healing–http://pranichealing.sg/about-us/about-pranic-healing/,
April 2012; http://www.pranichealingusa.com/, April 2012

Reiki International Center–
     http://reiki.org/FAQ/HowDoesReikiWork.html, April 2012
Sound Healing/Dr. Emoto/Water–
     http://www.masaru-emoto.net/english/emoto.html, Dec. 2012
The Free Dictionary–
     http://www.thefreedictionary.com/mental+health, July 2012
The Sound Healing Network–
     http://www.soundhealingnetwork.org/, December 2012
U.S. National Library of Medicine Division of NIH–
     http://vsearch.nlm.nih.gov/vivisimo/cgi-bin/query-
     meta?query=cam&v%3Aproject=nlm-main-website, March 2013
Webster, Richard–Aura Viewing For Beginners
     http://www.richardwebster.co.nz, December 2012
Web MD–www.webmd.com, May 2012
World Congress of Quantum Medicine–
     http://iquim.org/wcqm-world-congress-quantum-medicine/June 2013
World Health Organization (WHO)–Mental Health Topics–
     http://www.who.int/topics/mental_health/en/, June 2012
World Health Organization (WHO)–Complimentary and Alternative Health Topics–
     http://www.who.int/mediacentre/news/releases/release38/en/, May 2012
World Health Organization (WHO)–International Classification of Disease–http://
     www.who.int/classifications/icd/en/, May 2012

ILLUSTRATIONS

INDEX

CPSIA information can be obtained at www.ICGtesting.com
Printed in the USA
LVOW03s2308061015

457260LV00002B/2/P